ECOLOGY AND ECONOMY IN
NEOLITHIC EASTERN EUROPE

NEW APPROACHES IN ARCHAEOLOGY
General Editor: Colin Renfrew
Professor of Archaeology in the University of Southampton

The Spatial Organisation of Culture
Ian Hodder (editor)
Early Postglacial Settlement in Northern Europe
Paul Mellars (editor)

*Ecology and Economy in
Neolithic Eastern Europe*

PAUL M. DOLUKHANOV

Duckworth

*First published in 1979 by
Gerald Duckworth & Co. Ltd,
The Old Piano Factory
43 Gloucester Crescent, London NW1*

© *1979 by P.M. Dolukhanov*

*All rights reserved. No part of this publication may be reproduced,
stored in a retrieval system, or transmitted, in any form or by
any means, electronic, mechanical, photocopying, recording
or otherwise, without the prior permission of the copyright owner.*

ISBN 0 7156 1237 9

British Library Cataloguing in Publication Data

Dolukhanov, Paul M
    Ecology and economy in neolithic Eastern Europe.
    1. Neolithic period – Europe, Eastern
    I. Title
    947   GN776.22.E/

ISBN 0-7156-1237-9

---

*Photoset by
Specialised Offset Services Limited, Liverpool
Printed in Great Britain by
Page Bros (Norwich) Ltd, Norwich*

To the memory of my
father, Professor Marc
Pavlovič Dolukhanov

Contents

Preface	ix
Chapter 1. Prehistoric Man and His Environment	1
Chapter 2. The Near East	37
Chapter 3. South-Eastern Europe	59
Chapter 4. The South Russian Plain	81
Chapter 5. The West Russian Plain	113
Chapter 6. Conclusions	187
Index	203

Preface

The project which forms the basis of this book was initiated at the suggestion of the late Professor S.I. Rudenko in 1960, the year I graduated from the Geographical Department of Leningrad State University and joined the Research Institute of Archaeology in Leningrad. For the next few years I concentrated on the coastal area of the Baltic Sea, a study which resulted in my history of the Baltic.[1] In subsequent years field studies were carried out in the inner territories of the Baltic Republics, Byelorussia, the Ukraine and Moldavia (Fig. 1). With a small team of colleagues, including a pollen analyst, an archaeologist and several university students of geomorphology and soil science, I carried out geomorphological, palaeopedological and geochronological investigations on the most important Mesolithic and Neolithic sites in these areas. Many samples collected by our team were analysed in the radiocarbon laboratory of the Institute of Archaeology in Leningrad.

The era considered spans an important shift in the environmental setting – the end of the Last Glaciation about 10,000 years ago. This phenomenon affected the various natural zones of the earth in different ways: the environmental changes in turn influenced the prehistoric communities of the Old World, and triggered off economic and social processes which led to the emergence of complex civilizations in Asia and Europe. One of the main tasks of this study is to try to reconstruct these processes through palaeogeographical and archaeological evidence, in order to evaluate the role of environmental and social factors in the development of civilization.

It is hoped also that through the study of prehistoric society and its interaction with its environment, over a long span of time (between 20,000 and 4,000 years before the present) and over a vast territory (the Near East, south-east Europe, and the southern and western parts of the Russian plain), some light may be thrown on the present-day problem of man's relationship to his environment. This is a question of immense importance in the life of human societies. Global pollution and the mismanagement of natural resources are at present subjects of increasing international cooperation under the auspices of the United Nations. The Act adopted by the USSR Supreme Soviet in 1972 states: 'The achievements of the scientific and technical revolution in the framework of the socialist planned economy make possible the rational management of natural resources and the neutralization of the hazards to the environment presented by the waste products of industrial activity.'[2] Scientific consideration of the problem at present concentrates on the following points: the impact of the environment on the material and spiritual life of human society; the sufficiency of world resources to meet the needs of an increasing population; and the effects of industrial activity on the environment.[3] But science can also make a contribution by analysing the origins of the problem, and it is this direction that this book hopes to explore. As Marx and Engels wrote in 1845: 'Men can be distinguished from animals by conscience, by religion or anything else you like. They themselves begin to distinguish themselves from animals as soon as they begin to *produce* their means of subsistence, a step which is conditioned by their physical organization. By producing their means of subsistence men are indirectly producing their actual material life.'[4]

I am deeply grateful to all the people and institutions who have contributed to the completion of the project: Dr Levkovskaya, V. Timofeyev, Mrs E.N. Romanova, Dr A.A. Sementsov, Miss N.S. Malanova and Y.S. Svežentsev; Dr N.N. Gurina (Institute of Archaeology, Leningrad); Dr A.M. Miklyayev (the State Hermitage, Leningrad); Dr I.A. Loze and Dr F.A. Zagorskis (Institute of History, Riga); Dr L.V. Vankina (Latvian State Museum, Riga); Dr R.K. Rimantiene (Institute of History, Vilnius); Dr M.M. Ciernyavski (Institute of History, Minsk); Dr D. Ya. Telegin, Dr V.N. Danilenko, Dr S.S. Bierezanska (Institute of Archaeology, Kiev); Dr N.A. Ketraru and Dr V.I. Markievič (Institute of History and Ethnography, Kishinev).

I wish to express my gratitude to Professor A.C. Renfrew, at whose instigation this book was written, and who throughout has gently supervised its progress. My thanks are due to Miss Emma Fisher of Duckworth for revising the text and preparing it for publication.

P.M.D. 1976

NOTES

[1] P.M. Dolukhanov, *Istoriya Baltiki*, Moscow, 1969.
[2] *Pravda*, 21 September, 1972.
[3] I.P. Gerasimov, *Čelovyek, obščestvo i okružayuščaya sryeda*, Moscow, 1973, p.33.
[4] K. Marx, F. Engels, *Die deutsche Ideologie* (Works, 3), Berlin, 1968, p. 19.

TRANSLITERATION

The following transliteration of Russian, Ukrainian and Bulgarian letters is adopted in the present book:

Cyrillic letter	Latin letter
А а	A a
Б б	B b
В в	V v
Г г	G g
Д д	D d
Е е	Ye ye
Ж ж	Ž ž
З з	Z z
И и	I i
К к	K k
Л л	L l
М м	M m
Н н	N n
О о	O o
П п	P p
Р р	R r
С с	S s
Т т	T t
У у	U u
Ф ф	F f
Х х	Kh kh
Ц ц	C c
Ч ч	Č č
Ш ш	Š š
Щ щ	Šč šč
Ъ, ъ	,
Ы ы	Y y
Э э	E e
Ю ю	Yu yu
Я я	Ya ya

Abbreviations

P.P.S. – *Proceedings of the Prehistoric Society*, Cambridge
S.A. – *Sovetskaya Arkheologiya (Soviet Archaeology)*, Moscow

Chapter 1

PREHISTORIC MAN AND HIS ENVIRONMENT

Archaeology, palaeogeography, prehistory

What is the aim of archaeology? Why do archaeologists dig their sites and write their books? These questions are often asked by archaeologists and laymen in various countries of the world. To define its subject is one of the most important tasks of any science. In the words of a Soviet archaeologist, Y.N. Zakharuk, 'archaeology may be regarded as an independent historical science studying the past of human societies and based upon material records'. Dr Zakharuk writes further: 'The subject matter of archaeology consists primarily of archaeological records ... but also of human society, whose activity produces the materials that make up those records.'[1] The distinction between 'archaeological records' and 'human society' is of fundamental importance. Recognition of the distinction is characteristic of the present stage of the evolution of archaeology: it has indeed led some archaeologists to divide archaeology into two disciplines, archaeology proper and prehistory.

The American archaeologist Irving Rouse wrote:

Archaeologists search for remains: excavate, restore, display and categorize them; and publish reports about them ... Archaeology thus is a topical discipline, like the history of technology and the history of art. It is limited ... to the material traits of mankind that have survived in the ground ... The aims of archaeology are to recover remains and learn their nature. To accomplish the latter it breaks the remains down into categories and studies the relationships among them. Hence, its approach is analytic.

Prehistory takes the results of archaeological analysis and combines them with the results obtained in other analytical disciplines, such as linguistics, in order to reconstruct a picture of conditions and events during prehistoric times. Hence, its approach is synthetic rather than analytic.[2]

According to this definition, the main purpose of archaeology is excavation and the classification of the remains recovered. To carry out this analysis correctly archaeologists now use a system of concepts. These concepts may be summarized as follows:

Attribute: a logically irreducible feature of a man-made artifact;
Artifact: an object modified by a set of human-imposed attributes;
Type: a homogeneous population of artifacts;
Assemblage: an associated set of contemporary artifact-types;
Culture: a set of artifact-types which consistently recurs together in assemblages within a limited geographic area.[3]

Hence, in a purely formal way, territorial units such as assemblages and cultures may be regarded as areas within which finite sets of attributes consistently recur. A culture is a territorial unit singled out on the basis of the recurrence of all the types and assemblages identified in contemporary sites. A culture in this sense is a 'polythetic' operational unit. On the other hand it is also possible to distinguish 'subcultures' on the basis of the recurrence of particular sets of artifact-types (or assemblages). These would be 'monothetic' operational units. The addition of a third dimension (time) makes it possible to follow up the temporal evolution of the artifact-types of subcultures and of cultures.

It is vitally important to recognize that the concepts cited above are the operational units of archaeological analysis. They may not have (and in most cases do not have) a direct relation to definite patterns of human activity. The reconstruction of human activity (of social, economic and cultural patterns) is the task of a higher level of investigation, namely prehistory.

It is interesting to note that the science of palaeogeography meets almost the same set of problems. Palaeogeography is a synthetic discipline. Its main task consists in reconstructing features of the landscapes of past epochs which cannot be directly measured at the present time. Palaeogeographers draw their conclusions on the basis of the data provided by analytical disciplines: palaeobotany, palaeozoology, soil science, geomorphology, isotope chemistry and so forth. The analytical data obtained from a single profile may be presented as variables changing in time. The correlation of similar data obtained from a number of profiles within a large territory enables the analysts to follow up the evolution of variables in time and in space. Here, too, operational units may be distinguished within which finite sets of attributes consistently occur (pollen analytical zones, faunal complexes, etc). If the complex of data is dealt with some 'polythetic units' may be singled out (e.g. landscape zones).

The problems encountered by archaeology, prehistory and palaeogeography are common to the process of human knowledge as a whole. Philosophers[4] distinguish two levels of human knowledge: empirical and theoretical. The objective of empirical knowledge is often referred to us as a 'categorical synthesis'. At this stage a scientist tries to distinguish relationships within the object of study. The main purpose of empirical study consists of bringing directly observable data into certain categories, certain operational units. Concepts used in archaeological analysis (attribute, artifact, type, assemblage, culture) may be regarded as such empirical categories. The accumulation of empirical data then makes it necessary to rise to a higher level of knowledge, to the level of theoretical generalization. This implies a holistic approach, and a search for the inner essence of objects, for their fundamental regularities. For archaeology this theoretical objective is prehistory, the reconstruction of past societies, their social and economic structure, and the dialectic evolution of them. For palaeogeography it is the reconstruction of fundamental regularities governing the evolution of the Earth's surface.

One of the most powerful instruments for the reconstruction of the inner essence of complex objects is model-building. In the words of the British geographers P. Haggett and R.J. Chorley, 'a model is a simplified structuring of reality which presents supposedly significant features or relationships in a generalized form'.[5] They have outlined some fundamental features of models. Models are selective: they may be viewed as selective approximations which, by the elimination of incidental detail, allow some fundamental aspects of the real world to appear in a generalized form. Models are structured: selected significant aspects of the 'web of realities' are exploited in terms of their connections. Models are suggestive: a successful model contains suggestions for its own extension and generalization. Models differ from reality: they may be approximations or analogies. Models can be static, concentrating on constant structural features, or dynamic, concentrating on processes and functions through a period of time.

There are many difficulties in building models based only upon archaeological data. It has been noted that archaeological evidence is an incomplete record of man's activity or, to quote a well-known archaeologist, 'archaeological evidence is inevident'.[6] One of the central theoretical problems in the construction of reliable dynamic models consists in producing an adequate explanation; in social, cultural and economic terms, for observable changes in archaeological artifact-types and assemblages. Summarizing recent studies of prehistory (and some older studies), the following possible explanations of 'cultural change' may be cited: (1) adaptation to environmental changes; (2) migration of human groups; (3) diffusion of economic, technical and cultural information through trade, copying, etc.; (4) social evolution; and (5) cultural evolution.[7] Reliable dynamic models must include the possibility of realizing all these potentialities.

A model of prehistoric society must include units connected with the material basis of society, its production of material goods – in other words, its economic structure. The model must also include units connected with the superstructure, with the society's spiritual world. In both cases it is necessary to break down the polythetic archaeological culture; reliable prehistoric models may be built only on the basis of monothetic sub-cultures, on sets of artifact types connected with material production, spiritual life and so on. But because of the inadequacy of archaeological evidence it is practically impossible to build social models on archaeological data alone.

It is somewhat easier to build dynamic models in palaeogeography than in prehistory, first because of the many different kinds of analytical data at its disposal. These have considerably increased in recent years with the use of isotopic methods. Secondly, the building of models in palaeogeography is greatly facilitated by the widespread use of actualistic methods: the explanation of observable data by mechanisms established in present-day landscapes. Thus, the observed regularities in the distribution of fossil pollen and spores can be convincingly explained in terms of biogeography and meteorology. The correlation of geomorphological, palaeontological, pedological and isotopic data makes it possible to build comprehensive models covering the 'landscape sphere' of the earth as a whole.

One of the characteristic features of modern science is the ever-increasing use of formalized methods of investigation. The use of formalized language makes it possible to correlate data produced by the different branches of science and to form large-scale models or paradigms – interrelated networks of general concepts. This work represents an attempt to build a large-scale model including prehistoric human society and its natural environment.

The geographical sphere

One of the most useful achievements of Soviet geography is the elaboration of the concept of the geographical sphere (biosphere or landscape sphere) as a holistic material system. According to Professor A.A. Grigoriev,[8] the planet earth may be divided into a number of spheres. These are the gaseous sphere, the hydrosphere, the lithosphere, the mantle and the core. Grigoriev defines the geographical sphere of the earth's surface as an independent unit, different from the other spheres by nature of its chemical content and of the energy-transfer processes occurring in it. It embraces the lower levels of the atmosphere, the surface itself and the upper layer of the lithosphere. 'All spheres forming the geographical sphere of the earth are in a state of mutual penetration and interaction. They are inseparable ... No element can be changed without affecting all the others.'

The basis of the integrity of the geographical sphere is the inflow and the transfer of solar energy. Solar radiation plays a decisive role in the energetics of the geographical sphere, and climatic factors are thus of great importance in the structuring of all geographical processes.

The transfer of solar energy in the geographical sphere of the earth is characterized by two basic equations. These are: radiation balance (absorbed solar radiation minus effective long-wave radiation flux) and heat balance (the difference in energy flux between an area of the earth's surface and outer space).[9]

There are two fundamental laws relating to the structure of the geographical sphere: the law of continuity, and the law of zonality of the earth's surface. According to the second law, the division of the continents into natural zones is primarily due to the differences in values of radiation and heat balances.[10]

Vegetational cover

Solar energy, reaching the earth's surface, is absorbed by green plants. This absorption is the initial stage of energy transfer in the biosphere. Solar energy converted by photosynthesis provides energy for all the components of the biosphere. In this sense vegetation may be regarded both as an energy input and an energy accumulator in the biosphere.[11]

The processes occurring in vegetational cover are primarily dependent upon the quantity of solar radiation reaching the earths surface. Thermal conditions, as expressed in the heat balance, are important here. Investigations[12] have shown that so-called residual radiation directly affects plants. This residual radiation is the total solar radiation received by the earth, minus reflected short-wave radiation, and minus effective radiation from the surface. The residual radiation (B) is spent in heating the surrounding air (L) and in evaporation (V). Table 1 shows the distribution of these components in different natural zones of the USSR.

Table 1

Natural zones	Components of heat balance in cal/cm^2 per annum			Per cent	
	B	L	V	L/B	V/B
Taiga	29	7	22	24	76
Broad-leaved forests	37	10	27	27	73
Steppe-forests	39	11	28	28	72
Steppes	40	17	23	43	57
Dry steppes and semi-deserts	43	32	11	74	26

Wet and dry conditions may be expressed by a coefficient in testing the ratio of vegetation to the heat spent in the evaporation of precipitation. This is coefficient (A), by which four zones may be distinguished:

1. Exceedingly wet. Arctic deserts, tundra, forest-tundra, alpine meadows. Coefficient A: less than 0.45.
2. Wet. Forests. Coefficient A: 0.55-1.00.
3. Moderately wet. Forest-steppes, steppes. Coefficient A: 1.00-3.00.
4. Dry. Deserts. Coefficient A: more than 3.00.

It has been calculated that every plant has its favourite conditions of wetness or dryness. The following are the values of coefficient A for the favourite conditions of several European trees: oak, 1.09; maple, 1.0; lime, 0.88; spruce, 0.73.

The amount of solar energy stored in plants (by means of photo- and chemo-synthesis) is usually expressed in primary productivity. The net primary productivity of a plant community is the rate of storage of organic matter (not used by heterotrophs) during a year (usually during the growing season). Table 2 shows the values of the primary productivity of plants in different natural zones.[13]

Table 2

Natural zones	Primary productivity of terrestrial plants in kg./km.^{2} annually
Tundra	120,000
Taiga	300,000
Mixed coniferous/broad-leaved forests	500,000
Steppe-forests and broad-leaved forests	560,000
Dry steppes	50,000
Semi-deserts	40,000

The high productivity of steppe-forests and broad-leaved forests, and of mixed coniferous/broad-leaved forests, is remarkable.

The animal world

Animals cannot absorb solar energy directly. They get the energy they need by eating plants or other animals. The transfer of energy in the biosphere through eating and being eaten is usually referred to as a food chain. At each transfer of energy a large proportion (80-90%) is lost.[14]

According to modern ecology[15] there are two main types of food chain. The first type, the grazing food chain, starts from a green plant base, goes on to 'grazing herbivores' (organisms eating living plants) and then to carnivores (animal eaters). The second type, the detritus food chain, starts from dead organic matter, proceeds to microorganisms, and then to detritus-eating organisms and their predators.

The food chains are not isolated in the biosphere. Inter-locking food chains form what the ecologists refer to as the food-web.

In natural communities, organisms whose food is obtained by the same number of steps are said to belong to a trophic level. So in the case of the first type of food chain, green plants occupy the first trophic level, plant eaters are at the second trophic level (or at the primary consumer level), carnivores which eat herbivores occupy the third level or the secondary consumer level, and secondary carnivores or carnivores eating carnivores are at the fourth level (or at the tertiary consumer level). Man occupies a position at the top of the food chain.

The amount of solar energy reaching the surface of the earth directly affects processes occurring in the animal world, and this includes the functioning of food chains and food-webs. It has been experimentally proved[16] that the temperature of animal bodies depends upon the heat balance.

Two approaches are used to determine numerically the energy in the biosphere. The first measures the biomass or the amount of energy accumulated at a trophic level. The biomass may be expressed in a number of species by live weight or in caloric units per unit area. The second measures the productivity of the biomass. This is the rate of storage of organic matter in the biomass during a measured period. Table 3 shows the biomass of plants and animals in different natural zones of the USSR.[17]

Table 3

Natural zones	Plants, dry weight kg./km.^{2}	Animals, live weight kg./km.^{2}
Tundra	300,000	126
Taiga	13,000,000	224
Mixed coniferous/broad-leaved forests	22,000,000	552
Steppe-forests and broad-leaved forests	26,000,000	1292
Dry steppes	50,000	606
Semi-deserts	7,000	365

The absorption and transfer of solar energy carried out in the food chains make it possible to calculate the maximum biomass and the maximum productivity in various natural zones, based upon the data of heat and radiation balances. It is also possible to calculate the population density of various animal species. These highly interesting calculations are based on the assumption[18] that there are both upper and lower limits to the species' population size. The size of population of any species depends upon birth and mortality rates, which characterize the intrinsic rate of natural increase in the population. If the environment is unlimited the population expands rapidly. The population growth curve takes a J-form (in mathematical terms an

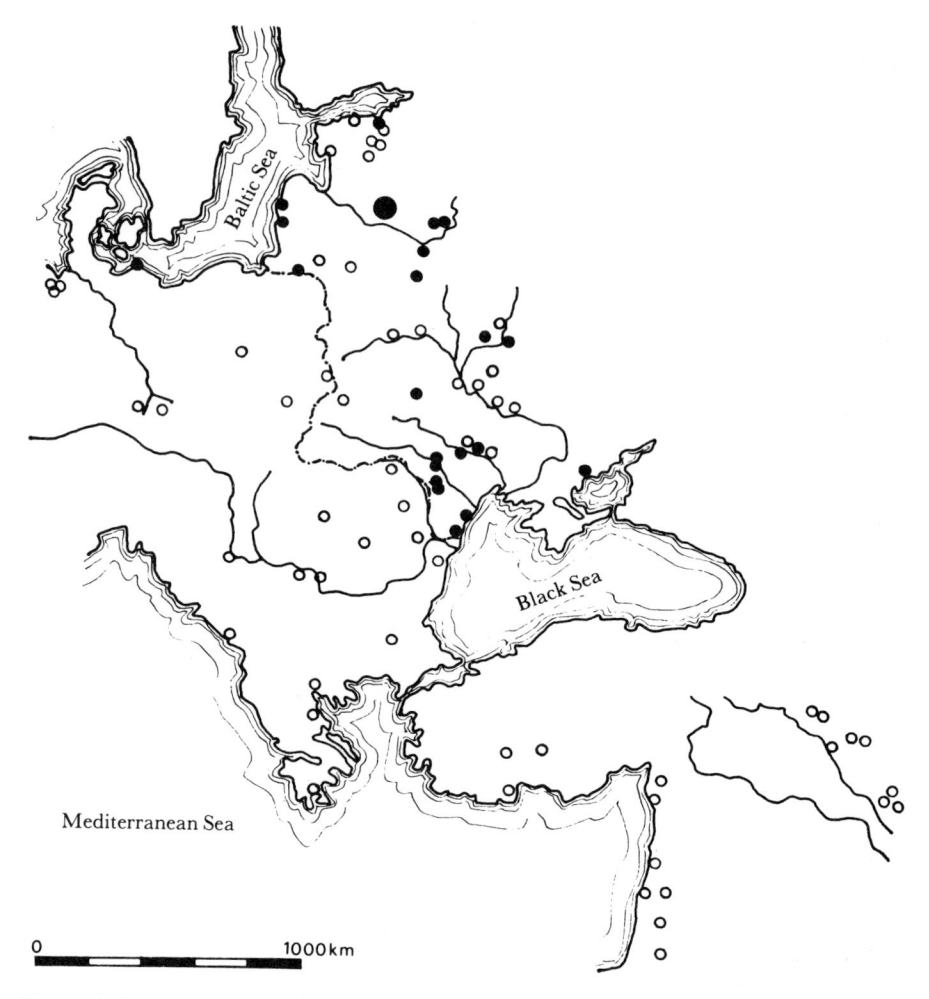

Figure 1 Investigated sites. Black dots = sites investigated by the author; large black dot = group of sites; white dots = sites investigated by archaeologists quoted in the text

exponential curve). In fact an unlimited environment never exists: there are always some limiting factors – space, food, other organisms. In reality the population growth curve is S-shaped (Fig. 2). At first the population increases slowly then more rapidly, but soon slows down gradually until a level of near equilibrium is reached. In mathematical terms this form of population growth may be represented by a 'logistic model'. The upper limit of the curve ('an upper asymptote') is called a carrying capacity.

One of the important factors limiting population density in the animal world is the existence of the third trophic levels (carnivores eating herbivores, or the secondary consumer level; and carnivores

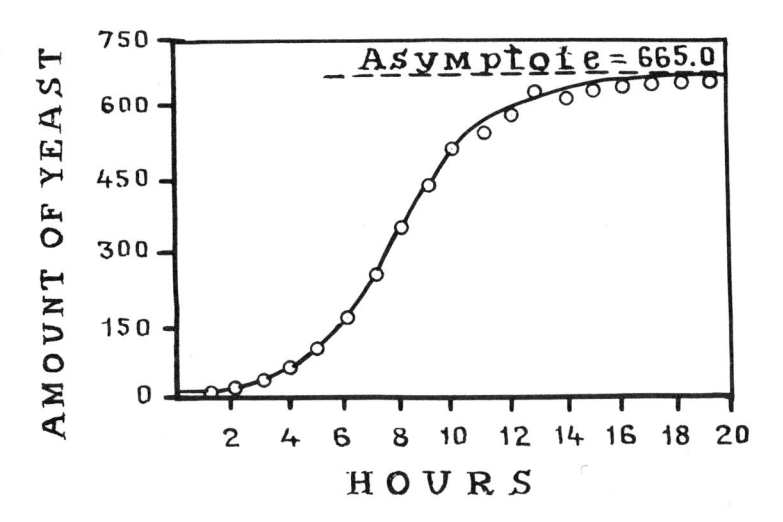

Figure 2 An example of intrinsic rate of population growth: the growth of yeast in a culture (after Odum, 1971; Note 1.14)

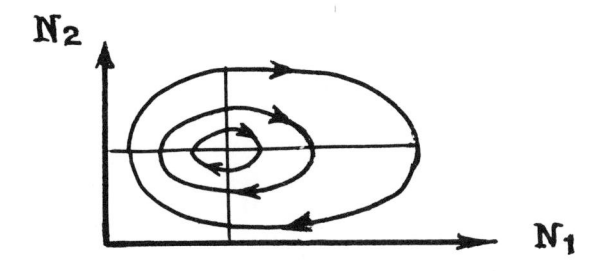

Figure 3 Trajectory of 'predator/prey biocenosis' (after Odum, 1971; Note 1.14)

eating carnivores, the tertiary consumer level). Both experimental observations and theoretical calculations[19] prove that there are stable relations between the numbers of predators and the numbers of prey (Fig. 3). The ratio of predators to prey reaches a stable level regardless of the initial numbers of each group.

Geosystems and ecosystems

One of the remarkable achievements of modern science is the elaboration and application of General Systems Theory, stemming from the works of Ross Ashby, von Bertalanffy and others. A system, according to this theory, is 'an intercommunicating network of attributes or entities forming a complex whole'.[20] In some cases the entities or elements forming the system cooperate with each other in such a way that a change or transformation in one may produce a corresponding transformation in another. In this case there is a functional loop feeding back information from the recipient to the stimulator. Such a connection constitutes a 'feedback loop' or simply 'a feedback'.

As Ross Ashby wrote, 'what is important is that complex systems, richly cross-connected internally, have complex behaviours and that these behaviours can be goal-seeking in complex patterns'.[21] The system tends to be in a state of stability or equilibrium. The search for equilibrium is one of the most important properties of the system, frequently arising from positive and negative feedback loops.

One of the most important aspects of the systemic approach is the search for system-formed connections inside a complex object. The concept of the geographical sphere is thus a highly suitable object for the application of the systemic approach. Soviet geographers[22] now regard the geographical sphere as not only a complex aggregation but a complex dynamic system consisting of a number of subsystems. Nowadays they generally use the term 'geosystem' in place of geographical sphere.

According to von Bertalanffy's classification, geosystems are regarded as 'open systems'. Their basis is the absorption and transfer of solar energy. Geosystems are regarded as self-regulating information systems; transfer of mass and of energy is a transfer of information. There are both positive and negative feedbacks. The geosystem tends to achieve a state of dynamic equilibrium and oscillates about the point of equilibrium.

Both in geography and in ecology the notion of the ecosystem has proved to be highly useful. The term was proposed in 1935 by Tansley,[23] the plant ecologist. According to the original definition the ecosystem includes the biome ('the whole complex of organisms, both animals and plants, naturally living together as a social unit') and its habitat. According to a more modern definition,[24] 'living organisms and their non-living environment are inseparably interrelated and interact upon each other. Any unit that includes all the organisms ('the community') in a given area, interacting with the physical environment so that a flow of energy leads to clearly defined trophic structure, biotic diversity and material cycles (i.e. exchange of materials between living and non-living parts) within the system, is an ecological system or ecosystem'. Enumerating the properties of the ecosystem, the British geographer D.R. Stoddart[25] wrote: 'First, it is monistic – it brings together environment, man, plant and animal worlds within a single framework; secondly, ecosystems are structured in a more or less orderly, rational and comprehensive way; thirdly, ecosystems function – they involve continuous through-put of matter and energy; fourthly, the ecosystem is a type of general system and possesses the attributes of general systems. In general system terms, the ecosystem is an open system tending towards a steady state under the laws of open-system thermodynamics.'

A systemic approach towards the study of natural complexes greatly facilitates the building of dynamic models, displaying the most important connections which determine the historical evolution of landscapes. A systemic approach also facilitates the quantitive modelling of natural processes.

Territorial division

There are three main approaches to distinguishing regional units. First, there are attempts to divide the earth into regions on the basis of single features. Plant geographers divide the earth into geobotanical zones; zoogeographers try to establish faunal regions; climatologists distinguish climatic regions; geomorphologists focus their attention on dividing the earth into geomorphological units.

The second approach is characterized by a division of the earth's surface into synthetic regions. This approach has been particularly successfully developed in Soviet geography. Following this approach[26] the earth may be divided into geocomplexes, each of which is characterized by a certain degree of internal uniformity. In more recent years the natural geocomplexes have often been treated as regional geosystems. Thirdly, Soviet geography has developed a system of hierarchical zonal divisions. Divisions of the highest rank are referred to as geographical belts. They are defined on the basis of marked differences in radiation and heat balances. The second most important units are geographical zones. They correspond to definite values of hydrothermal coefficients and roughly coincide with the most important geobotanical and soil zones. There is a hierarchy of regional units of ever decreasing magnitude: region, province, district, etc. There are in addition the so-called azonal regional units which are distinguished on the basis of relief features. Complex units are distinguished on the basis of the correlation of 'zonal' and 'azonal' territorial units.

Natural resources

We now return to the problem of the interaction between man and his environment. In 1845 Marx and Engels wrote that 'the first historical act of living human beings was the production of the necessary means of life. Therefore the first attested fact is the social organization of human beings and their socially conditioned relationships to the rest of nature.'[27]

The most important aspect of the problem of man-environment interaction is energy. Human society is fully dependent on the continuous inflow of concentrated solar radiation. The vital aspect of this energy inflow is the production of food.

Food production, guaranteeing a stable input of solar radiation, is subject to constant evolution. In this book we consider two levels of this evolution. The first level corresponds to so-called 'food appropriation'. The food needed for maintaining life is secured through hunting, fishing and food-gathering. The second level corresponds to 'food production'. The main sources of energy inflow are agriculture and stock-breeding. At this level the structure of the exchange of energy between society and environment is much more complicated. The transformation from the first level to the second was a very important step in the evolution of mankind.

The understanding of the interaction between human society and its environment is much facilitated by the notion of 'productive forces' developed in historical materialism. In Marxism 'productive forces' mean working tools and the human beings who use them. The energy input is provided by the interaction of the productive forces of human society with the environment. It is important to note that in securing the necessary inflow of energy men do not use all the components of the geographical sphere but only a small part of them. The range of the elements of the environment used by human society changes with the evolution of the productive forces. The notion of 'natural resources' developed in economic geography is very useful in this respect. Economic geographers[28] understand by natural resources 'natural matter and natural energy that may be involved in the process of production at a given level of social evolution' or 'objects and forces of nature that may be used by human society for the satisfaction of its demands at a given level of development of productive forces'.

Economic patterns

Socially patterned labour is the basis of the existence of any human society, as Marx and Engels have written.[29] The totality of the socially productive relationships governing and regulating the exchange of matter and energy between society and environment forms the economy or the economic pattern of society. If human society is treated as a complex system with subsystems, the economy or subsistence pattern may be viewed as a feeding component of the social system.

It has been shown in modern economic studies that the economic pattern functions in accordance with the optimizer or satisficer strategy concepts elaborated in game theory.[30] Roughly speaking the optimizer strategies try to get the best possible results under given conditions. Satisficer strategies are satisfactory and safe without being optimal. It has been noted that most human decisions are concerned with the discovery and the use of satisfactory alternatives; only in exceptional cases are they concerned with optimal alternatives. One of the most commonly used 'satisficer strategies' is known as the 'minimax' strategy. This strategy aims at maximizing the minimum outcome or at minimizing the maximum risk.

In our case, this principle of game theory may be interpreted in this way. The social system tends to choose a strategy in the quest for food that aims at maximizing the minimum energy input in the form of food and minimizing the maximum risk connected with the food quest. The choice between optimal or satisfactory strategy largely depends upon the information concerning the object, in our case natural resources.

Like biological systems, economic systems may be regarded as adaptive. Their 'behaviour' is largely dependent upon the structure of the environment. Change in the environment stimulates an immediate response in the economic pattern. A new strategy is chosen to guarantee the maximum input of energy with the minimum risk.

Natural economic zones

As noted earlier, zonality is one of the main features of the earth's surface. The zonality of the attributes of geo- or ecosystems provides for a zonality of natural resources. Human economies functioning in accordance with the principle of optimizer or satisficer strategies tend to exploit different resources in different natural zones. These considerations form the basis of the territorial division of the earth into natural and economic zones.

In Soviet economic geography the notion of the territorial productive complex is widely used. This territorial unit reflects the territorial division of socially patterned labour. Another term often used in Soviet economic geography is the 'natural region', that is a territory which possesses a more or less uniform range of natural resources.

Dealing with prehistoric societies, it seems to me convenient to use the term 'natural economic zone'. By this term we mean a territory possessing a more or less uniform range of natural resources at a certain level of evolution of the productive forces.

It should be noted that the idea of a 'natural economic zone' is not a new one either in archaeology or in ethnology. The Soviet ethnographers M. Levin and N. Cheboksarov[31] use the term 'economic-cultural type'. By this term they mean the concrete economic and cultural complex that emerged in different ethnic groups having similar levels of economic development and living in similar environmental conditions. There are also some similarities between 'natural economic zones' and the 'techno-complexes' proposed by the British archaeologist David Clarke.[32] However the terms 'economic-cultural type' and 'techno-complex' seem to me to be too loose. 'Natural economic zones' may be distinguished as the basis of certain attributes in accordance with the principles used in modern economic geography.

Population

Historical materialism treats human population or labour resources as the most important element of productive forces. The study of population plays a prominent role in historic and economic research. Demography is the particular social science which deals especially with the problems of human population. It deals with all trends in population evolution: fertility, mortality, marriages, divorces, age and sex distribution ('pyramids'), occupation distribution and so on. The study of population dynamics is particularly important: that is, the study of displacement and migrations, as well as of the influence exercised on demographic processes by social, economic and technological factors.

The concept of carrying capacity developed in demography is of vital interest to the present study. We have already mentioned this term when discussing animal ecology. In relation to demography, the carrying capacity is understood as the upper level of human population that may exist within a natural economic region at a certain level of the evolution of productive forces.

Culture

The notion of culture is of fundamental importance in archaeological and anthropological studies. But what is culture? It is very difficult to give a clear definition since different scholars hold conflicting views on the subject. In Soviet ethnography culture in a broader sense is usually regarded as 'that which is created by human beings as a result of their physical and mental work for the purpose of the satisfaction of their various material and spiritual demands'.

In recent years there has been a tendency to treat culture in terms of General Systems Theory. Of particular interest here is the work of David Clarke.[33] According to him, 'culture is the communication system of acquired beliefs which increasingly supplements instinctive behaviour in man'. He regards a cultural system as 'an organized structure integrating, amongst others, social, religious, psychological, linguistic, economic and material culture subsystems'. These subsystems are 'the equilibrium networks within any particular cultural system, coupled one with another and with the external environmental system'.

According to Clarke, cultural systems are information systems. He separates two categories in the transmission of information in the cultural system: 'adaptive' and discriminatory response to the environment, and the internally generated variety which corresponds to internal invention or innovation. The distinction between 'adaptive' responses to environmental changes and internally generated inventions or innovations seems to be highly significant. 'Adaptive' aspects in culture are stressed by many anthropologists. This aspect is emphasized in an extreme fashion by the American anthropologist Leslie White,[34] who considers culture as 'man's extra-somatic means of adaptation'; while the British archaeologist Colin Renfrew[35] stresses the importance of inner factors in cultural evolution. He defines culture as 'a constantly recurring assemblage of artifacts (including non-material ones, such as language and projective systems)'. The cultural system includes subsystems: the subsistence subsystem; the social subsystem; the projective or symbolic subsystem; the trade and communication subsystem. The process of cultural development is seen by Renfrew as being a result of 'the multiplier effect' and of interaction between subsystems.

Soviet ethnography traditionally regards culture as consisting of two categories: material culture and spiritual culture. In his most recent book the leading Soviet ethnographer Y.V. Bromley[36] includes working tools, weapons, means of transport, dwellings, food, domesticated animals and plants and so on in the category of material culture. Spiritual culture, according to him, is information stored in the collective memory of men: knowledge, customs, traditions, religious beliefs, legal norms, various forms of art and folklore. Another category distinguished by ethnographers is made up of material manifestations of spiritual creation: various objects of art, decoration of pottery, clothes, tattoos, make-up, perfumes and so on.

The structural heterogeneity of culture is a very important point which should not be overlooked. As a criterion for distinguishing different categories of culture, their relation to the production of material goods can be used. Production of the means of life is a condition of all forms of social life, and socially patterned labour is a source of all kinds of human culture; but different elements of culture reveal different relationships with the process of material production, the economic basis of human society.

The elements of material culture, such as working tools, weapons, means of transport, dwellings, food, domesticated animals and plants, reveal a direct contact with the economic basis and the subsistence pattern of a society. On the other hand, elements of spiritual culture, knowledge, customs, traditions, religious beliefs, arts and so on, reveal close relationships not with the economic basis but with the 'superstructure' of the society. This is also true of material manifestations of spiritual creation, such as art objects, decoration of pottery and clothes, architecture and so on. It was noted long ago that the elements of the superstructure possess a relative autonomy with regard to the economic basis of society. This is especially true of the elements of spiritual culture and their material manifestations. They are not directly involved in the process of the production of material goods, and they only indirectly reflect changes occurring in the economic pattern.

One of the most important features of culture is its continuity, the transmission of traditions. This feature is particularly characteristic of the elements of spiritual culture. Thus, in the complex of elements included in the notion of culture, it is possible to distinguish elements directly connected with the economic pattern, which are directly involved in the production of material goods and thus reveal 'adaptive' properties, from elements which are more or less independent of the economic structure, which reveal properties of continuity and the transmission of traditions. The elements of spiritual culture may be regarded as accumulators of knowledge, religious beliefs, ethics and aesthetic views, and together with their material manifestations they are regarded here as forming a 'cultural subsystem' of the social system. Functionally a cultural subsystem may be seen as a 'memory component' of the social system.

It is of interest to compare the notion of 'culture' in a broad sense with that important operational unit of archaeology, the archaeological culture. Let us quote David Clarke once more.[37] Like many other modern archaeologists, he believes that 'every attribute is equivalent to a fossilized action, every artifact is a modified sequence of actions and activities, and whole assemblages are tantamount to whole patterns of behaviour'. These equations are shown in Table 4.

Table 4

Action	Anthropology	Archaeology
An action	An attribute	An attribute
A cluster of actions	An activity	An artifact
Repeated clusters of actions	Behaviour	Assemblage of artifacts

In archaeology there is a constant tendency to treat operational and polythetic archaeological units in terms of concrete ethnic units: 'ethnocultural area', 'group', 'tribe' and so on. Ethnographers stress the fact that there seldom (if at all) exist direct correlations between polythetic archaeological cultures and ethnic groups. Examples are cited[38] where there are marked differences in the material culture of a single people (this is particularly the case with large nations spread over different natural zones) and, on the contrary, when similar traits of material culture were found in ethnically different nations.

In my opinion the main difficulty is that polythetic archaeological cultures, being formed of artifact-types, represent the 'fossilized' evidence of too many types of human behaviour which often cannot be compared one with another. The only way out, I suggest, is to compare groups of archaeological material which are truly comparable, using monothetic units. It is always possible to distinguish in an archaeological assemblage a group of artifact-types which we can connect (with an admissible degree of probability) with productive activity. In this group may be included working tools, weapons, means of communication, houses, production areas and so on. On the other hand, another group of artifact-types may be associated with 'spiritual culture' with the same degree of probability. In this group may be included works of art, decoration on pottery and on tools, shrines, elements of architecture and so on. I suggest that it is possible to build reliable prehistoric models only by working with uniform distributions of monothetic units (i.e. with subcultures). On this basis the following territorial units may be distinguished. Areas of uniform distribution of artifact-types of the first group (connected with the production of material goods and thus revealing correlations with parameters of the environment) are referred to as 'natural economic zones'. Areas of uniform distribution of the second group of artifact-types (elements of spiritual culture connected with the societal superstructure) are referred to as 'cultural zones'.

Reconstruction of past geosystems

As we have seen, nearly all the processes which have occurred in the geographical sphere of the earth are based on absorption and transfer of solar energy. That is why past climatic characteristics are an essential part of all palaeogeographical reconstructions. Climatic characteristics of past epochs cannot be measured directly, but are reconstructed on the basis of data provided by several analytical methods. These methods may be divided into three groups.

(a) Physical and chemical methods: analysis of fossil shells, deep sea cores and ice cores by means of isotopic measurements.

(b) Geologic and geomorphologic methods: study of land forms and study of sediments by pedological, lithological and other means.

(c) Palaeontological methods: investigations of deposits by palaeobotanic analysis (the study of plant remains, of fossil pollen and spores) and by palaeozoological means (the study of mammals, molluscan faunas and so on).

On the basis of these data dynamic palaeoclimatic models are built.

Among the physical and chemical methods particular importance is attached to the measurements of oxygen-isotope composition (O^{18}/O^{16}) in calcium carbonate samples.[39] As has been found empirically, the O^{18}/O^{16} ratio depends on the temperature of the water where the calcium carbonates were deposited. Fossil shells, deep sea cores and some cave sediments of the Quaternary age have been measured by these methods. In recent years oxygen-isotope composition measurements have been made in samples secured by deep cores drilled through ice sheets in Greenland and in the Antarctic.[40] As a result, continuous and detailed palaeotemperature curves covering the last 100,000 years have been plotted.

Most geologists agree that two tendencies characterized the evolution of the geographical sphere during the Quaternary: rhythmic and evolutionary. There are many reasons to believe that rhythms of different orders are reflected in the development of the earth's surface during the Quaternary period. The rhythms of the highest order corresponded to glacial and interglacial phases. There were also rhythms of lower order. Analysis of the ice-core palaeotemperature curve reveals climatic oscillations with periods of approximately 2,400, 400, 180 and 78 years.

Many Quaternary geologists use astronomical theories to provide an explanatory model for the observed changes occurring on the earth's surface during the Quaternary period. The most widely disseminated theories explain rhythmic changes in the Pleistocene climate by perturbation in the earth's orbit. A Yugoslav astronomer, Milankovitch, assumed that glaciations corresponded to periods during which the high northern latitudes received a minimum of summer solar radiation. Such minima arose when the tilt of the earth's axis was least (period: c. 41,000 years), and when the summer solstice occurred while the earth was in aphelion (period: c. 21,000 years). In more recent years astronomers in various countries have corrected Milankovitch's calculations.

But there are serious objections to the direct use of astronomical calculations for explaining the Pleistocene climatic changes. One of the most serious is that perturbations in the earth's orbit have always occurred, while the glaciations took place only during comparatively short-lived periods in the history of the Earth. It is possible, however, that the 'glaciation machine' was triggered only when temperature reached a critical point. It should be remembered that a progressive lowering of mean temperatures has been recorded for the Late Tertiary.

The rhythmic fluctuations of climate during the Quaternary were superimposed upon the linear evolution of the geographical sphere. The Soviet geographers K.K. Markov and A.A. Veličko[42] have described this linear evolution as a tendency to progressive cooling. It has been noted that during the Quaternary each cold phase was colder than the preceding one and every following warm phase was likewise cooler than the preceding one.

The linear evolution during the Quaternary is most clearly expressed in the development of the biosphere. The evolution of vegetational cover reflects the general tendency towards progressive cooling. The study of Pleistocene floras carried out by the Soviet palaeobotanist V.P. Gričuk[43] shows that the number of thermophilous plants in the vegetational cover of the Russian Plain was constantly decreasing from the Lower to the Upper Pleistocene. At the same time the number of arctic and boreal plants was increasing. A typical 'glacial' or 'periglacial' flora which consisted of both steppic and arctic plants was formed only during the second (and coldest) stage of the Last Glaciation.

The same tendency is visible in the evolution of the animal world. The formation of the so-called mammoth complex, which included large herd animals such as the mammoth, musk ox and woolly rhinoceros, occurred only during the second half of the Upper Pleistocene, about 35,000 to 30,000 years ago.

Analysis of palaeogeographical records led A.A. Veličko[44] to the conclusion that about 35,000 to 30,000 years ago a major change in the geographical sphere took place which is seen in extreme cooling and extreme aridity of the climate. The conclusions reached by him regarding the structural changes occurring in the geographical zonality of the earth's surface during the ice ages are of considerable interest. During the glaciation, according to Veličko, in medium and high latitudes there was a single, widespread and not greatly differentiated natural zone. Veličko labels this phenomenon 'hyperzonality'. During the warm interglacial epochs the geographical zones reappeared in medium and high latitudes.

The development of the geographical sphere in the Holocene was determined by the same factors as in the Pleistocene, the superimposition of rhythmic fluctuations on linear evolution.[45] The linear evolution of the geographical sphere was marked by two world-wide climatic changes. The first was the passage from the Pleistocene to the Holocene or from the later glacial to the post-glacial epoch, which occurred 10,500 to 10,200 years ago. This important change is marked by the disintegration of the ice-sheet, and by the increasing warmth and humidity of the climate. At this time there occurred the disintegration of the hyperzonal periglacial zone and the formation of steppic, forest and tundra zones. The extinction of the mammoth complex took place at the same time: not less than ten species of large Pleistocene mammals became extinct and many others changed their areas of distribution. At the same time animals trophically connected with forests (elk, deer, wild pig, beaver, etc.) enlarged their areas of distribution.

Another important palaeogeographical change took place about 5,000-4,500 years ago. This was a general cooling of the climate and the decrease of the broad-leaved forests throughout the temperate zone of the world.

The establishment of fluctuations in the sea-level is of particular importance for Quaternary research. During the maximum ice-sheet advance of the Last Glaciation, that occurred some 20,000-18,000 years ago, according to reliable evidence, the ocean level stood at 120-

125 metres below the present level. The transgression that then followed is known as 'the Holocene transgression'. By 'normal' geological standards it was a rapid transgression: during 20,000 years the sea level rose more than 100 metres. There is some disagreement among geologists about the behaviour of the sea level during the last 8,000 years. According to the most widely held opinion[46] the sea level has been slowly and continuously rising and reached its present level only recently. According to another opinion, held by a number of scientists,[47] the sea level reached its present position some 6,000 years ago and has fluctuated above and below it since that time (Fig. 4). In my own view, supported by investigations arried out in the basin of the Baltic Sea, the second opinion is nearer to reality.

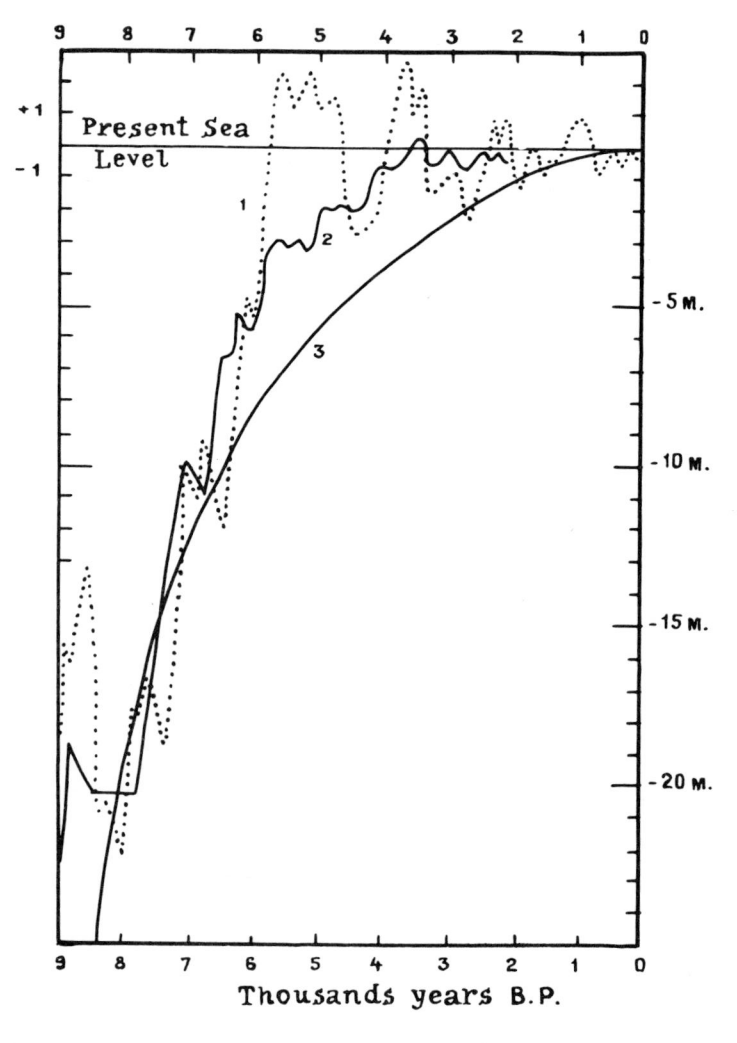

Figure 4 Eustatic rise of the sea-level (1 – after Fairbridge, 1961; Note 1.47; 2 – after Mörner, 1971; Note 1.47; 3 – after Sheppard, 1963; Note 1.46)

Investigations carried out in the western part of the Baltic Sea have made it possible to establish that the levels of the lakes of the inland territory fluctuated in accordance with the fluctuations of the sea level. The periodicity of these fluctuations was of the order of 1,000 years. In all probability these fluctuations reflect rhythms of short periodicity in the evolution of the geographical sphere.

Working tools

The socially patterned production of material goods is a distinctive feature of any human society. One of the most important categories of historical materialism is the mode of production: it is dependent on productive forces which include the means of production and the human beings who bring them into action. By manufacturing tools men enter into relationships with nature and with objects of labour with a view to producing material goods.

The reconstruction of working tools and their function is thus a very important aspect of prehistoric analysis. This process of inference is carried out by an archaeologist in a somewhat arbitrary manner: theoretically it is based upon the assumption that all artifacts are 'fossilized' evidence of human behaviour. But to determine how any particular type of artifact relates to a particular type of human behaviour is a major problem for explanatory archaeology. In practice, ethnographical evidence is used in most cases: the functions of implements are determined on the basis of the use of similar tools by modern primitive communities.

A valuable contribution to resolving the problem was made by Professor S.A. Semenov of the USSR, who developed a method of microscopic study of prehistoric tools. Semenov[48] gives the following list of the basic actions performed by ancient man: (1) shaping wood by whittling and chopping with a knife, axe, adze and chisel; (2) digging with a stick, mattock, scoop etc.; (3) dismembering the carcasses of animals and cutting meat with a knife; (4) treating skins with side- and end-scrapers and burnishers; (5) perforation of skins and furs for sewing with stone and bone awls; (6) boring wood, bone and stone with drills of various kinds; (7) dressing stone with striker stones and retouchers of stone and bone; (8) working bone with a burin; (9) grinding and polishing stone with various abrasive agents; (10) sawing stone with saws; (11) pounding, crushing and trituration of grain, colouring matter and so on by means of pestles, mortars, plaques, querns; (12) reaping with stone sickles, and so forth.

A peculiarity of the tools used by ancient man is the fact that most of them were used in several different ways. This is particularly the case with so-called sickles, pestles, mortars, plaques and querns. A precise definition of the functions of ancient tools is not always possible as a result of studying traces of wear.

Difficulties in the interpretation of implements and of their assemblages led to two conflicting approaches in modern archaeology connected with the interpretation of the differences observed in the chipped stone assemblages of Palaeolithic sites. The first approach tends to explain these differences in terms of the existence of different cultural traditions proper to different ethnic groups.[49] The second approach, advocated especially by the American archaeologist L. Binford and his followers,[50] is based on the assumption that 'ethnicity may not have always been a component of the cultural environment of man'. The differences observed in the artifact assemblage may be due to 'differences in the character and distribution of stimuli presented differentially to varying segments of a culturally homogenous population'.

I support the views held by Binford and his supporters in relation to the group of artifacts referred to as 'working tools'. Working tools are objects by means of which men enter into interaction with the elements of the environment (more precisely, with natural resources) with a view to producing the goods necessary for life (food, in the first place). Economic activity aimed at producing the necessary food was carried out in accordance with optimizer or satisficer strategies. Working tools, an important element of productive forces, must be sufficiently adapted to the parameters of the environment to secure a constant inflow of energy into a social group.

This does not exclude the existence of stylistic, or cultural, variations in the working tool assemblage. The aim of further investigation is to determine the degree of these cultural variations.

The reconstruction of demographic structures

Human population is the most important element in the productive forces of society. Therefore the evaluation of the demographic structure of past societies is a very important factor in prehistoric research. As noted earlier, a full demographic analysis must include the quantitative characteristics of population density and of its main trends – age and sex distribution and so on. The study of population dynamics (displacements, migrations) is also of vital importance for the reconstruction of prehistoric processes.

The estimation of prehistoric population in absolute figures is an extremely difficult problem which is still unresolved. We can only trace some approaches towards its solution. It has been shown that at the simple level of a generalized hunting and fishing economy the population density may be primarily determined by environmental factors. The theoretical considerations behind this assertion are simple enough. It will be recalled that a human hunting and fishing community can be regarded as occupying the highest trophic level in the food-chain. One of the possible approaches to the determination of the optimal size of a hunting group is to make calculations of the predator/prey type. Another way is to determine a maximum hunting and fishing population, assuming that this population must be in a stable equilibrium with the carrying capacity of a landscape unit. The data concerning the biomass contained in different natural zones may be used as a basis. It follows from ethnographical data that modern hunting communities consume from 500 to 1,000 kg. of biomass (750 kg. on the average) annually. Assuming that no more than 10% of the total animal biomass could be used for food, and using figures relating to the biomass distribution, we get the following tentative figures of maximum density:[51]

Table 5

Natural zones	Population density	
	km.^{2} per person	persons per 100 km.^{2}
Tundra	51	1.9
Taiga	32	3
Mixed coniferous/broad-leaved forests	14	7.4
Forest-steppes and mixed oak forests	5.8	17.3
Dry steppes	12	8

These figures may be used only as a first approximation: they by no means reflect the actual population densities of hunting and fishing communities. Ethnographic evidence shows that hunting provided no more than 30% of the total intake. The rest was provided mainly by food collecting. In the forested areas fishing was also a very important source of food.

It is interesting to compare our figures with the evaluation of prehistoric population densities made by other scholars. The Soviet archaeologist S.N. Bibikov[52] has suggested that the population density in the Crimea during the Mousterian period was one person per 40-60 square km., and in the Upper Palaeolithic period, one person per 100 sq.km. The American anthropologists Braidwood and Reed[53] expressed the opinion that the Near Eastern population in the Upper Palaeolithic period was three persons per 100 sq.km. and in the Mesolithic, 12.5 persons per 100 sq.km. J. Birdsell[54] reported that population densities of the Australian aborigines vary from one to two persons per square mile to one person per 100 square miles. It was noted that in Australia the mean annual rainfall is the most important environmental determinant of the native population density. Birdsell suggested that in the Upper Palaeolithic it required on the average 10 square miles to support a single person.

It has been proved that the population size of hunting and fishing groups stabilized at a particular optimal level largely determined by

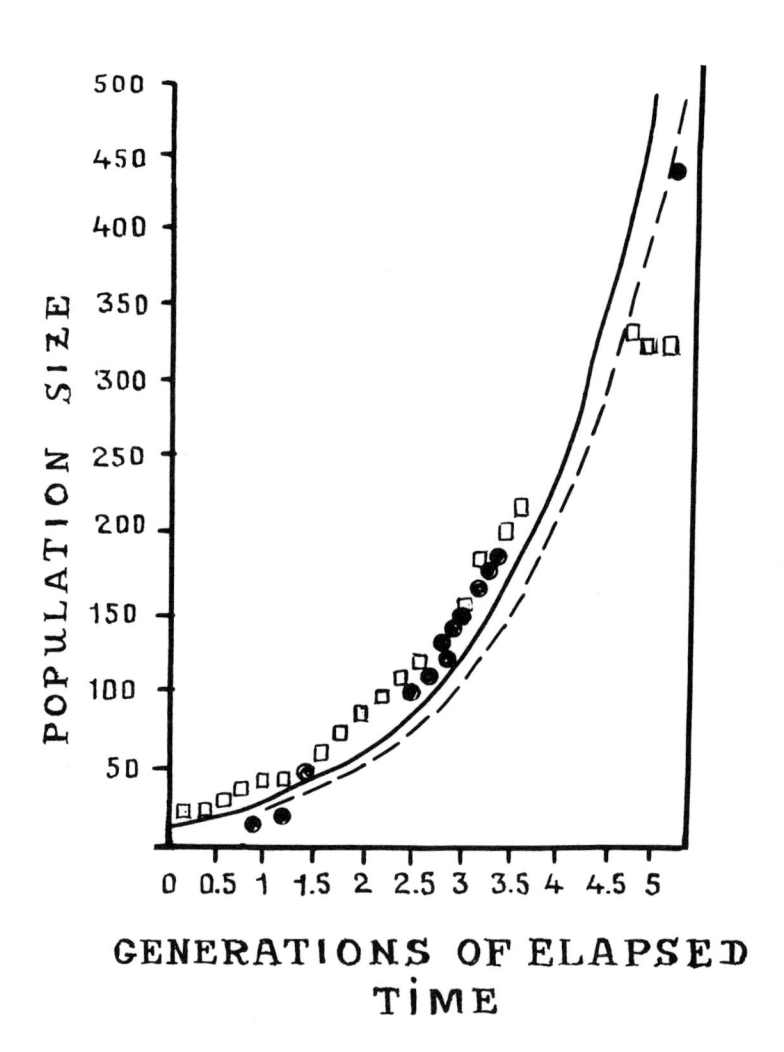

Figure 5 Intrinsic rate of population increase for Pitcairn (□) and Bass Strait (●) islanders (after Birdsell, 1957; Note 1.54)

the carrying capacities of natural areas. The native hunters had several means of restricting the size of their population. These means included primitive birth-control and infanticide. Russian statistical data support this evidence.[55] The size of the communities of hunting people of north Siberia did not change through to eighteenth and nineteenth centuries A.D.

The introduction of a new economic pattern, which included stable food production, agriculture and stock-breeding, led to a marked change in demographic structure and in population dynamics. Ethnographic evidence suggests[56] that simple horticultural populations follow an intrinsic rate of increase in which the population doubles in each generation. This rapid increase continues until the population's food resources exert marked pressure. The intrinsic rate of increase thus described was recorded in two Pacific islands populated in the eighteenth century, Pitcairn and Bass Strait (Fig. 5). As the population density nears its relative carrying capacity (which may range from 30 to 97% of the absolute carrying capacity) a hiving off of a part of the surplus population becomes unavoidable. The population growth curve takes a logistic form typical of population processes.

The population density of the agricultural Neolithic communities of the Near East was estimated by Braidwood and Reed to be some 25 persons per square mile. The population of some agglomerations reached a considerable size. The population of Çatal Hüyük was some 8,000 persons, that of aceramic Jericho A some 2,000 to 3,000.

The population of European Neolithic sites was much smaller. Colin Renfrew[57] has estimated the mean population of a Neolithic site in Greece to be 100 persons. On the basis of excavations of the Middle Neolithic site of Bylany in East Bohemia, which had a stable food-producing economy, B. Soudsky and I. Pavlů[58] have concluded that in each phase the site contained an average number of 24 families, which corresponds to about 50 adults and 100 children.

On the basis of a number of known Neolithic sites in Greece, Renfrew has calculated tentative figures for the Neolithic population in various regions of Greece. Two factors were estimated: the proportion of the original settlements represented in sites now accessible, for which a factor of $\frac{1}{4}$ is suggested; and the proportion of total sites which were occupied at the same time, for which the figure of $\frac{3}{4}$ was proposed. The figures arrived at by Renfrew are shown in Table 6.

Table 6

Region	Population density (persons per sq. km.)
Crete	1.53
Cyclades	1.20
Messenia	1.77
Euboia	1.35 (2.34)
Central Macedonia	0.84

The reconstruction of prehistoric economies

The study of past economy is an essential part of all prehistoric reconstructions. The economic pattern is a feeding component of the social system; it is by means of economic activities that the energy flow enters the social organism. Serious studies of prehistoric economies date from the publication in 1952 of a book by the leading British prehistorian, Grahame Clark, devoted to the economy of prehistoric Europe.[59] Since that time the number of studies on prehistoric economies has steadily increased. Now there is a tendency to regard prehistoric economy as a branch of general economics.

The Soviet archaeologist V.M. Masson[60] distinguishes four main forms of economic activity by ancient man: (1) production of food; (2) production of tools; (3) production of buildings; (4) manufacture of pottery. In the present section we deal only with the first heading.

How can this vital branch of prehistoric economy be reconstructed? Four important methods may be named.

1. Palaeozoological evidence: osteological identification of animal remains, study of their morphology, determination of sex and age relations, and so on. Recognition of animal domestication, often beset by many difficulties, is of particular importance.
2. Palaeobotanic evidence: botanical identification of plant remains is most important. The remains may be discovered in the cultural layers or stored in pottery vessels, or there may be impressions of plants on pottery. Palaeobotanists can now identify both grains and ears of cultivated cereals. Very useful information is provided by the modern distribution of wild cereals (research initiated by the Soviet biologist N.I. Vavilov) and by the analytical work of plant geneticists. Palaeobotany may provide indirect evidence of agricultural activity. Pollen analyses show very clearly the forest clearance that usually preceded agriculture and the appearance of weeds that accompanied crops.
3. Settlement pattern: the mode of settlement is an important feature which was determined in many ways by the prevailing subsistence pattern.[61] In recent years British archaeologists have used 'site-catchment analysis' for evaluation of the economic potentialities of the territory around settlements.[62] These analyses are based upon the assumption that a territory exploited from a site lies within certain limits (5 and 10 km. from the settlement). Based on this assumption a preliminary assessment of the productive potential of a site is made by measuring the percentage of territory within the catchment area occupied by arable land, rough grazing, marsh, and so on.
4. Determination of the functions of ancient tools is an important

source of information about the prehistoric subsistence pattern. Microscopic analysis of work traces, undertaken in the USSR by Professor Semenov, is of a great assistance in this respect. But due to the many uses to which tools were put, this method taken alone may lead to erroneous conclusions. Determination of the functions of implements may be successfully used for the reconstruction of prehistoric economies only in combination with palaeozoological, palaeobotanical and geomorphological evidence.

All the forms of economic activity of prehistoric communities looked at in the present study clearly fall into two main groups: economies based upon appropriation of food (hunting, fishing and food gathering), and economies based upon production of food (agriculture and stock-breeding). Food-appropriating economies may be divided, in their turn, into those based upon specialized hunting (the greater part of the meat food being provided by the hunting of a single species of animal) and unspecialized hunting. The latter form of economy may be further subdivided into subtypes depending upon the patterns of hunting, fishing and food gathering. The food-producing economy may be divided into groups in relation to the prevalence of either agriculture or stock-breeding in the subsistence pattern. Agricultural economies can be divided into those based upon either dry or irrigated farming; another kind of subdivision may be carried out on the basis of agricultural structure (the dominant position of particular cereals in farming) and on the basis of stock-breeding structures (the dominant position of particular domestic animals in the herd). A mixed economy should also be distinguished as a particular type. This can be either a food-producing economy with elements of food appropriation, or vice versa.

In all cases, as we have seen, the dominant economic pattern corresponds to the principle of optimizer or satisficer strategies. Prehistoric communities chose those strategies which guaranteed the optimal input of energy with the minimum risk in a given environmental setting.

The reconstruction of cultural subsystems

The reconstruction of the cultural subsystem is a very important aspect of the reconstruction of past societies. As noted above, the concept of a 'cultural subsystem' includes elements of 'spiritual culture' (knowledge, customs, traditions, religious beliefs, art and so on) and their material manifestations. To single out those artifacts related to the sphere of spiritual culture from the archaeological assemblage is a difficult task. Tentatively, I include in this group such artifacts as the decoration of pottery and of tools, art objects, and architecture.

As suggested earlier, the elements of spiritual culture are related to the superstructure of society and as such reveal a relative independence from the economic basis. This characteristic of spiritual culture is noticeable in archaeological evidence. Some elements included in the category of 'cultural subsystem' reveal a correlation with the economic pattern, while others do not. Anthropomorphic and zoomorphic clay figurines are clearly associated with a food-producing economy, and painted pottery is associated with the same economic pattern; some ornamental patterns of painted pottery are convincingly interpreted in terms of the mythology of ancient farmers.[63] At the same time, there are groups of pottery decorations which are surprisingly constant in time and space and which reveal no connection with the economic pattern of the social groups in the area where the pottery was produced. This is the case with the so-called monochrome pottery which spread throughout the Near East and Europe during the Neolithic period.

Classification is one of the most important tasks of modern science. Several sophisticated classifications of pottery have been put forward in recent years. In the present work a very simple method was used. I took into consideration two attributes: elements of ornamentation and ornamental patterns. The territories characterized by more or less uniform manifestations of these attributes are regarded as 'cultural zones'. It is probable that the cultural zones thus distinguished contain some ethnic elements, but the direct correlation of cultural zones with ethnic units seems improbable. As we shall see later, cultural zones almost never coincide with 'natural economic zones'.

Absolute chronology

In order to trace the evolution of prehistoric population and of natural environment, it is useful to have an absolute hard time scale. This was provided for the first time by the carbon 14 method, invented by the American physicist Willard F. Libby. Measurement of the content of the heavy carbon isotope in organic samples (wood, charcoal, shells, peat, bone) enables the age of the samples to be calculated with a certain degree of accuracy. During the past few decades, radiocarbon dating has been widely accepted, and has led to the reassessment of established chronological schemes in both archaeology and Quaternary geology. Although geologists had at their disposal some methods for the determination of absolute age (for example the counting and comparison of varves and calculations based on astronomic theory), all archaeological dates before 3,000 B.C. (when Egyptian written chronology began) were guesswork before C14 dating was introduced. With it, archaeologists and geologists have had a chance to work out an absolute chronology based on a method independent of their own techniques. During the 1950s, '60s and early

'70s thousands of geological and archaeological samples were radiocarbon dated, and serious attempts were made to compile chronological schemes based upon C14 dates.

In recent years the radiocarbon method has been found to contain some errors. First it was discovered that the value of the half-life of C14 (upon which the calculation of age is based), originally determined by Libby as 5570 ± 30 years, was not quite correct. The value of 5730 ± 40 indicated by Professor H. Godwin is nearer the truth. This is not a serious error; to obtain new figures it is only necessary to multiply the old ages by 1.03.

More difficulties arose from the recently discovered discrepancy between radiocarbon dates and the 'true ages' of many samples. These 'true ages' were determined by methods of absolute dating independent of the radiocarbon method. A Californian tree, the bristlecone pine (*Pinus aristata*), well known for its extremely long life, proved to be a great help in correcting the radiocarbon method of dating. By linking up ring sequences obtained from these trees, American dendrochronologists succeeded in building up a continuous tree-ring chronology going back nearly 8,200 years.[64] A series of samples of known true age, determined by precise ring counts, were submitted to a radiocarbon laboratory. As a result a picture of discrepancies has been obtained. These are summed up in Table 7.[65]

Table 7

Time period represented by radiocarbon dates	Average deviation of C14 dates (+ = younger; − = older)
A.D. 1525 − 1879	+50
A.D. 975 − 1525	0
25 B.C. − A.D. 975	−50
225 B.C. − 26 B.C.	0
675 B.C. − 226 B.C.	+50
1125 B.C. − 676 B.C.	+100
1325 B.C. − 1126 B.C.	+150
1750 B.C. − 1326 B.C.	+200
1900 B.C. − 1751 B.C.	+300
2050 B.C. − 1900 B.C.	+400
2225 B.C. − 2051 B.C.	+500
2650 B.C. − 2226 B.C.	+550
2850 B.C. − 2651 B.C.	+650
3700 B.C. − 2951 B.C.	+700
4366 B.C. − 4060 B.C.	+750

Thus it has been proved that the radiocarbon dates are too recent compared with the 'true ages'. These observations have been supported by other evidence: the radiocarbon dates of historically dated Egyptian objects in the period between 3,000 and 2,000 B.C. are too recent to the same extent as are the bristlecone pine dates.[66] The

Suess curve, called after the American physicist who constructed it, reflects the changes in the C14 content, which are probably due to the changes in the strength of the earth's magnetic field. On the basis of the data provided by the bristlecone pine datings, corrections (tree-ring calibrations) are being introduced into radiocarbon dates, and new chronological schemes based upon calibrated dates have been suggested by several archaeologists.[67]

It has been proved that the principle of simultaneity postulated by Libby, according to which the level of C14 at a given time is uniform all over the world, is valid. This means that even if the radiocarbon dates are too recent compared with the true ages, the mutual relationship between the dates remains unchanged. As a result, uncalibrated dates may be used for chronological purposes, though it should be kept in mind that the dates they show are not absolute but relative ages. They are not calendar dates, but give age in 'relative radiocarbon time units'. This is the system used in this book. The units are based upon the old ('Libby') value of the C14 half-life. No tree-ring calibrations are used. Dates are given as 'before the present' (B.P.). To convert these dates into A.D./B.C., it should be remembered that 0 B.P. corresponds to A.D. 1950.

Eco-social and socio-cultural systems

After this review of basic aims, methods and concepts, we may return to the problem set out in the first paragraphs of this chapter: the building of a complex model comprising both prehistoric society and its natural environment. This complex system must include two interconnected systems – the ecological system and the social system.

Let us recall once more some of the general properties of systems. In the simplest form a system consists of two black boxes (units whose function may be evaluated without specifying the internal contents) and a controlled quantity connected by output and input circuits or signals (Fig. 6). Control depends on feedback, which occurs when output, or part of it, feeds back as input. Feedback may be positive (deviation-accelerating) or negative (deviation-counteracting). The system tends towards a state of dynamic equilibrium. The state of equilibrium in relation to biological systems is usually termed homeostasis (from the Greek words *homoios* – same, *stasis* – standing).

In accordance with the accepted classification of systems, both ecological and social systems should be considered as open systems. The functioning of these systems largely depends upon the inflow and transmission of solar energy.

Let us start with the ecological system. This system must include at least three components. The first component is climate, by means of which an inflow of solar energy is introduced into the whole system. The next two components are represented by plants and animals. In

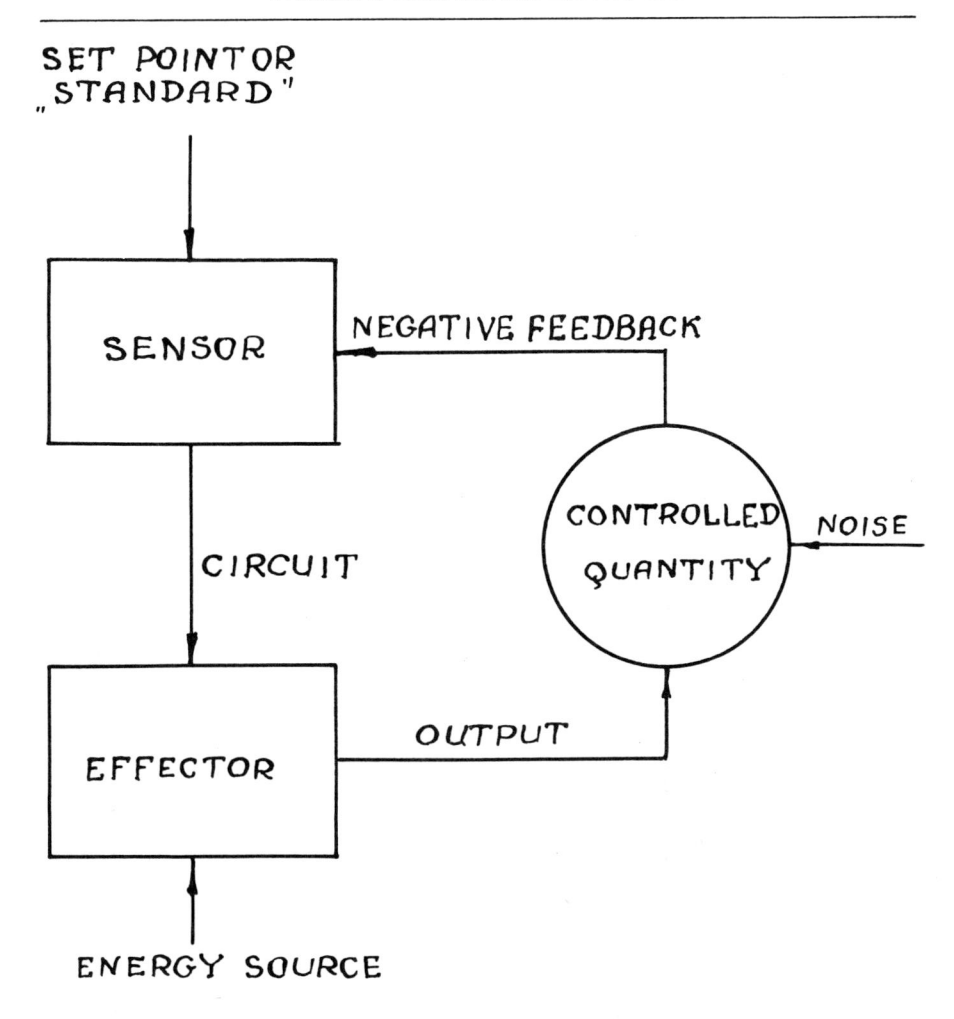

Figure 6 Model of a cybernetic system (after Odum 1971; Note 1.14)

real ecosystems the components are usually disposed in accordance with the energy flow, or in accordance with the food chain. Energy flow is greatly reduced at each trophic level by the dispersal of a part of the energy in unutilizable heat (in accordance with the second law of thermodynamics). There is a network of positive and negative feedbacks in the ecosystem which regulate its state of inner stability (or homeostasis). These feedbacks regulate the quantity of biomass present in the different trophic levels (producers, plant eaters, animal eaters) and thus stabilize the energy flow in the system.

The social system must include the economic pattern as its most important block or component. This is a feeding component of the social system, by means of which the energy flow is introduced into this system. The economy component is connected by both positive

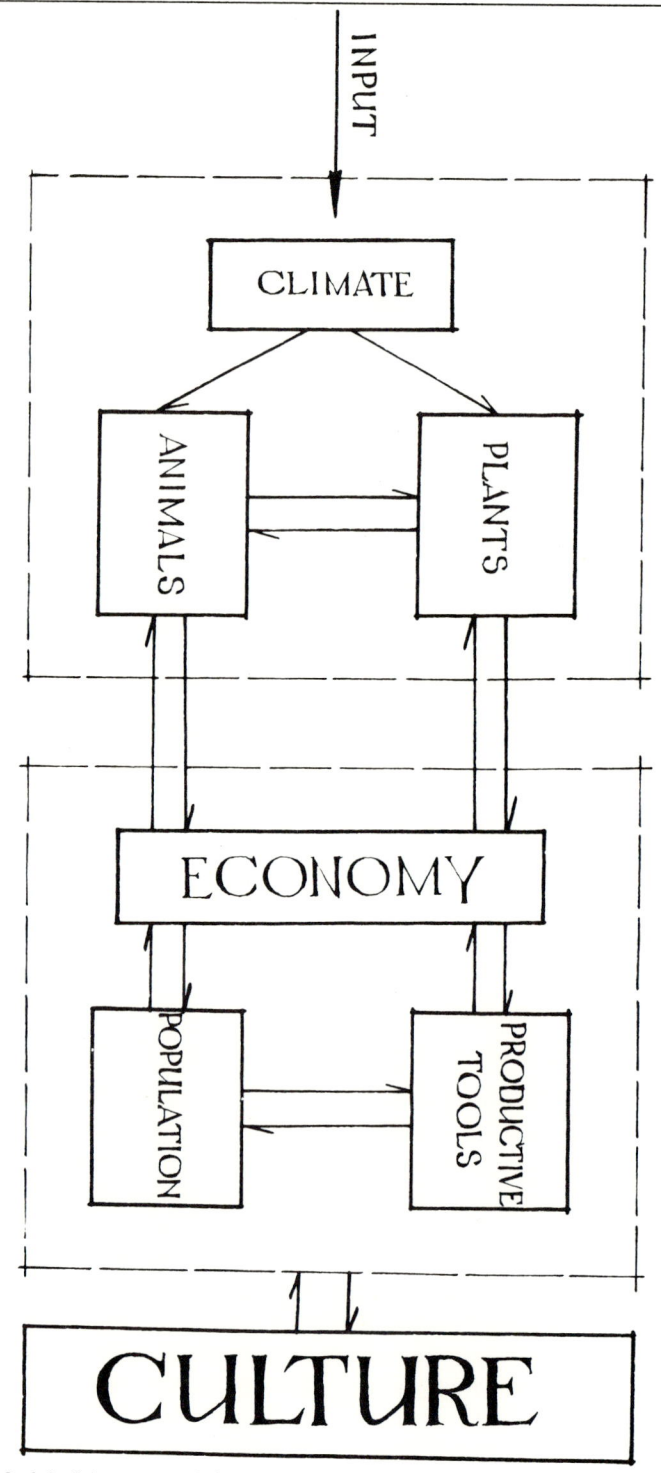

Figure 7 Model of the eco-social system

and negative feedbacks with the plant and animal components of the ecosystem.

The social system must include two more components: population and productive tools. Both these units correspond to the category of productive forces in terms of historical materialism. The population and productive tools components are interrelated and related to the economy component by positive and negative feedbacks. Population increase leads to changes in the economic pattern, which necessarily mean changes in working tools. Changes in the economy lead to new increases in the population, and so on.

One more important unit, which should be shown in the model, is culture. There are two possible ways of treating the phenomenon of culture in systemic terms. Culture is the final product of the eco-social system, that is, its output. On the other hand, it is a memory component of the whole system, an accumulator of knowledge, traditions, art and beliefs. No major changes in the economy or in tool production are possible until the volume of information in the memory component has reached a certain level. The major changes in the economic pattern, and consequently in the population structure and in productive tools, occurred at about 10,000 B.P., triggered off by the major changes that occurred at about the same time in the ecological system and which affected the energy flow from the eco- to the social-system. Comparable changes in the ecosystem occurred several times during the Quaternary epoch, but they did not lead to drastic changes in the social system. The plausible explanation is that at that time the volume of information in the memory component was not high enough.

Eco- and social-systems together form a complex eco-social system. The social system and the cultural subsystem together form a socio-cultural system (Fig. 7). In the next chapters we shall try to analyse our chosen case study and see how these systems functioned in the Near East and in eastern Europe between 20,000 and 4,000 B.P.

NOTES

[1] Yu.N.Zakharuk, 'Leninskoye teoretičeskoye naslyediye i arkheologičeskaya nauka', in B.A. Rybakov (ed.), Leninskiye idei v izučenii pyervobytnogo obščestva, rabovladyeniya i feodalizma, Moscow, 1970, pp. 7-9.

[2] I. Rouse, *Introduction to prehistory: A systematic approach,* New York, 1972, pp. 6-11.

[3] D.L. Clarke, *Analytical Archaeology*, London, 1968, p. 188. It should be noted that the hierarchical model of archaeological operational units cited here is not the only one possible, nor necessarily the best.

[4] N.K. Vakhtomin, *Genezis naučnogo znaniya*, Moscow, 1972.

[5] P. Haggett, R.J. Chorley, 'Models, paradigms and the new geography', *in* P. Haggett, R.J. Chorley (eds.), *Models in geography*, London, 1967, pp. 22-6.

[6] F. Hole, 'Questions of theory in the explanation of culture change in prehistory',

in C. Renfrew (ed.), *The Explanation of Culture Change: Models in prehistory*, London, 1973, pp. 22-3. The last expression belongs to S. Piggott who, in turn, quotes Rhys Carpenter.

[7] See C. Renfrew (ed.), op.cit. (Note 6), 1973, in particular, Section One, pp. 3-104.

[8] A.A. Grigor'yev, *Tipy geografičeskoi sredy*, Moscow, 1970, pp. 11-70.

[9] M.I. Budyko, *Klimat i žizn'*, Leningrad, 1971.

[10] A.A. Grigor'yev, M.I. Budyko, 'O periodičeskom zakonye geografičeskoi zonal'nosti', *Doklady AN SSSR*, 110, I, 1956.

[11] G.F. Khil'mi, *Osnovy fiziki biosfery*, Leningrad, 1966.

[12] M.P. Rusin, L.A. Flit, *Solnce i khleb*, Leningrad, 1971.

[13] Ye.M.Lavrenko, V.N. Andreyev, V.L. Leont'yev, 'Profil' produktivnosti nazyemnoi časti prirodnogo rastitel'nogo prokrova SSR ot tundr k pustynyam', *Botaničeskii Žurnal*, 49, 3, 1955.

[14] E.P. Odum, *The fundamentals of ecology* (3rd edn.), Philadelphia, 1971, p.63.

[15] Odum, op. cit. (Note 14), 1971, pp. 63-77.

[16] Budyko, op cit. (Note 9), 1971, pp. 365.

[17] K.S. Khodaševa, 'O geografičeskikh osobyennostyakh struktury nasyelyeniya nazemnykh životnykh, *in* Yu. A. Isakov (ed.) *Zonal'nyye osobyennosty nasyelyeniya nazemnykh životnykh*, Moscow, 1966, pp. 7-38.

[18] Odum, op. cit. (Note 14), 1971, pp. 162-233.

[19] N.T.J. Bailey, *The mathematical approach to biology and medicine*, London, 1967.

[20] The principles of the General Systems Theory are outlined on the basis of W. Ross Ashby, *An introduction to cybernetics*, London, 1956.

[21] Ross Ashby, op. cit. (Note 20), p. 54.

[22] V.S. Preobraženskiy, *Besedy o sovremennoy fizičeskoy geografii*, Moscow, 1972.

[23] The original determination was made in A.G. Tansley, 'The use and abuse of vegetational concepts and terms', *Ecology 16*, 1935, pp. 284-307; see also A.G. Tansley, *Introduction to plant ecology*, London, 1946.

[24] Odum, op. cit. (Note 14), 1971, p.8.

[25] D.R. Stoddart, 'Organism and ecosystem as geographical model', *in* P. Haggett and R.J. Chorley (eds.), *Models in geography*, 1967, pp. 524-28.

[26] V.I. Prokayev, *Osnovy metodiki fiziko-geografičeskogo raionirovaniya*, Leningrad, 1967.

[27] K. Marx and E. Engels, *Die deutsche Ideologie*. (Works, 3), Berlin, 1968, p. 19.

[28] A.A. Minc, *Ekonomičeskaya ocenka prirodnykh resursov*, Moscow, 1972.

[29] K. Marx and F. Engels, *Die deutsche Ideologie* (Works, 3), Berlin, 1968, p. 19.

[30] H.A. Simon, *Models of man*, New York, 1957, pp. 195-200.

[31] H.G. Levin, N.N. Čeboksarov, 'Khozyaistvenno-kul'turnyye tipy i istoriko-etnografičeskiye oblasti', *Sovyetskaya Etnografiya*, 4, 1955; see also N.N. Čeboksarov, *Rasy, narody, kul'tury*, Moscow, 1971, pp. 164-228.

[32] D. Clarke, op. cit. (Note 3), pp. 321-57.

[33] D. Clarke, op. cit. (Note 3), pp. 83-130.

[34] L. White, 'The concept of culture', *American Anthropologist*, 31, 1959, pp. 227-51.

[35] C. Renfrew, *The emergence of civilisation*, London, 1972.

[36] Yu. V. Bromley, *Etnos i etnografiya*, Moscow, 1973.

[37] D. Clarke, op. cit. (Note 3), p.8.

[38] A.A. Šennikov, 'O ponyatii "etnografičeskiy kompleks"', *Doklady otdelenii geografičeskogo obščestva SSSR, Etnografiya*, 3, Leningrad, 1967.

[39] C. Emiliani, 'Ancient palaeotemperatures', *Scientific American*, 199, 1958, pp. 54-63.

[40] W. Dansgaard, S.J. Johnsen, H.B. Clausen, C.C. Langway Jr., 'Ice cores and palaeoclimatology', *Nobel Symposium 12*, Stockholm, 1970, pp. 337-51.

[41] M. Milankovitch, *Théorie mathématique des phénomènes thermiques produits par la radiation solaire*, Zagreb, 1920. Recent calculations made in the Soviet Union: Š.G. Šaraf, N.A. Budnikova, 'Kolyebaniya solnyečnogo oblučeniya Zyemli, vyzvannyye vyekovymi izmyenyeniyami elementov zyemnoi orbity', *Doklady AN SSSR*, 182, 2,

1968, pp. 291-93. See also A.S. Monin, *Vrašceniye Zyemli i klimat*, Leningrad, 1972.

[42] K.K. Markov, A.A. Velicko, *Cetvyerticnyi period, Cast' III*, Moscow, 1967.

[43] V.P. Gricuk, *Osnovnyye certy istorii rastitel'nosti Russkoi ravniny v cetvyerticnom periode* (*Sovryemyennyye problemy geografii*), Moscow, 1964.

[44] A.A. Velicko, *Prirodnyi process v pleistocene*, Moscow, 1973.

[45] N.A. Khotinsky, *Paleogeograficeskiye itogi korrelacii etapov razvitiya rastitel'nosti Evrazii v golocenye*, Moscow, 1972.

[46] F.P. Sheppard, 'Thirty-five thousand years of sea-level', *Essays in marine geology in honor of K.O. Emery*, University of Southern California Press, Los Angeles, 1963, pp. 1-10.

[47] R.W. Fairbridge, 'Eustatic changes in sea level', in R.W. Fairbridge (ed.) *Physics and Chemistry of the Earth*, 4, New York, 1961; N.-A. Mörner, 'The holocene eustatic sea level problem,' *Geologie en Mijnbouw*, 50, 5, 1971, pp. 699-702.

[48] S.A. Semenov, *Prehistoric technology*, Moscow-Leningrad, 1957. (English translation by M.W. Thomson, London, 1964).

[49] F. Bordes, 'On the chronology and contemporaneity of different palaeolithic cultures in France', *in* C. Renfrew (ed.), op. cit. (Note 6), 1973, pp. 217-26.

[50] L. Binford, 'Interassemblage variability – the Mousterian and the functional argument', in C. Renfrew (ed.), op. cit. (Note 6), 1973, pp. 227-54.

[51] The figure of 10% may be an overestimation. Zubrow assumes that 5% consumption of the total biomass is an arbitrary but reasonable estimate. H.T. Odum suggests that 0.5% or less of the total biomass enters the human being as food. See R.W. Casteel, 'Two static maximum population density models for hunter-gatherers: a first approximation', *World Archaeology*, 4, 1, 1972, pp. 19-39.

[52] S.N. Bibikov, 'Density of population and hunting grounds in the Crimea in the palaeolithic times', *VIIIe Congrès international des sciences pré- et protohistoriques, Rapports de la délégation des archéologues soviétiques*, Moscow, 1971.

[53] R.L. Braidwood, C.A. Reed, 'The achievements and early consequences of food production: A consideration of the archaeological and natural-historical evidence', *Cold Spring Harbor Symposia on Quantitative Biology*, 1957.

[54] J.B. Birdsell, 'Some population problems involving the Pleistocene Man', *Cold Spring Harbor Symposia on Quantitative Biology*, 1957; Birdsell, 'On population structure in generalized hunting and collecting populations', *Evolution*, 12, 1958, pp. 189-205; Birdsell, '*An introduction to the new physical anthropology*', Chicago, 1972.

[55] S.K. Patkanov, *O priroste inorodceskogo nasyeleniya Sibiri*, St. Petersburg, 1909.

[56] J.B. Birdsell, op. cit. (Note 54), 1957, 1958.

[57] C. Renfrew, op. cit. (Note 35), 1972, p.253.

[58] B. Soudsky, I. Pavlu, 'The Linear Pottery culture settlement problems of Central Europe', *in* P.J. Ucko, R. Tringham and G.W. Dimbleby (eds.), *Man, Settlement and Urbanism*, London, 1972, pp. 317-28.

[59] J.G.D. Clark, *Prehistoric Europe – The economic basis*, London, 1952.

[60] V.M. Masson, *Posyelyeniye Dzeytun*, Materialy i isslyedovaniya po arkheologii SSSR, 180, Moscow-Leningrad, 1971.

[61] B.W. Blouet, 'Factors influencing the evolution of settlement patterns', *in* P.J. Ucko et al. (eds.), op. cit. (Note 58), 1972, pp. 3-15.

[62] M.R. Jarman, C. Vita-Finzi, E.S. Higgs, 'Site catchment analysis in archaeology', *in* P.J. Ucko et al. (eds.) op. cit. (Note 58), 1972, pp. 61-6.

[63] An attempt to interpret the semantics in the ornamentation of the Tripolye pottery by B.A. Rybakov, 'Kosmologiya i mifologiya zyemlyedyel'cev eneolita', *S.A.*, 1, 1965, pp. 22-47 and *S.A.*, 2, 1965, pp. 13-33.

[64] H.E. Suess, 'The three causes of the secular carbon-14 fluctuations, their amplitudes and constants', *Nobel Symposium 12*, Stockholm, 1970, pp. 595-605.

[65] E.K. Ralph, 'Carbon-14 dating', *in* H.N. Michael, E.K. Ralph (eds.), *Dating techniques for the archaeologist*, MIT Press, 1971, p.28.

[66] T. Säve-Söderberg, I.U. Olsson, 'C-14 dating and Egyptian chronology', *Nobel Symposium 12*, Stockholm, 1970.

[67] E. Neustupny, 'Absolute chronology of the neolithic and aeneolithic periods in central and south-eastern Europe', Part I, *Slovenska archeologia*, 16(1), 1968, pp. 19-60, and Part II, *Archeologicke rozhledy* 21(6), 1969, pp. 783-810; C. Renfrew, 'Carbon-14 and the prehistory of Europe', *Scientific American*, 225, 4, 1971, pp. 63-72.

Chapter 2

THE NEAR EAST

Iran and Iraq

Geologically Iran and Iraq form part of a gigantic folded belt of so-called Alpine geosyncline stretching from the Mediterranean Sea up to the Indonesian archipelago. In the structural sense the area under investigation is logically divided into two clear units: the folded zone and the foreland. The folded zone, the Iranian Zagros, is built as a series of regularly patterned symmetrical folds in marine deposits, mostly in limestone.

The highest peaks of the Turkish and Kurdish mountain reach 4,000 m. above sea level. In the high mountains important rivers have their sources – the Greater and the Little Zab, the Diyala, and the Tigris, which rush towards the lower zones as rapid mountain streams.

The high piedmont of the Zagros mountains lies at elevations of 400 to 1,000 m. above sea level. The area is known as 'the hilly flanks of the fertile crescent'. It comprises foothills, folds, and intermontane valleys between the ridges. The streams and rivers drain the intermontane valleys, breaking through low ridges at structurally weak points. The area lying between 250 and 400 m. above sea level may be called the lower piedmont. It consists of low rolling hills cut by the valleys of the Tigris and its tributaries.

Mesopotamia may be regarded as an area of foreland trough belonging to the Alpine geosyncline system. This trough is filled with deposits of the Tertiary and Quaternary periods, mostly of continental origin. Traditionally Mesopotamia is subdivided into two regions; the southern low valley where vast areas are taken up by land forms connected with fluviatile deposits (lagoons, marshes, braided channels and ox-bow lakes); and the upper valley where forms connected with erosion predominate.

The distribution of rainfall in the Near East is largely dependent upon the disposition of the main land features in relation to the rain-bearing winds. The south-east-facing slopes of the Zagros mountains now experience comparatively heavy rainfall of over 800 mm.

annually. The low piedmonts and lowlands are among the dryest regions of the world. Rain falls only during the winter and the mean annual rainfall level is between 25 and 500 mm.

The slopes of the Zagros mountains are covered with rich steppeland vegetation containing some trees, the deciduous Persian oak being the most common. The vegetation of the lowlands is a desert steppe, poor in overall plant cover. Fringes of palm trees, reeds and equatic plants stretch along the water-ways.

The history of the vegetation of this area gives rise to much speculation. For a long time the data provided by analysis of the pollen and trace elements in the Shanidar cave deposits were the only source of information. Using this record R. Solecki[2] has suggested that in Mousterian times, 50,000-30,000 B.P., dry steppes prevailed in the upper Zagros area. According to Solecki, conditions between 30,000 and 25,000 B.P. were cold and humid. Between 26,000 and 15,000 the climate was so harsh that the area was unfit for human habitation.

The situation was somewhat clarified by new evidence resulting from the pollen analysis of deposits in Lake Zeribar in western Iran. According to the Dutch pollen analyst W. van Zeist[3], the vegetation between 22,500 and 14,000 B.P. in the area lying at an elevation of about 1,300 m. was similar to the present-day vegetation of the plateau steppe of north-western Iran. The climate was cooler and dryer than that of today. Palaeobotanical records suggest important changes in the environmental conditions between 14,000 and 10,000 B.P. Annual temperatures and rainfall levels have been steadily increasing. Shortly before 10,000 B.P. the first trees made their appearance in the area. The vegetation cover between 10,000 and 6,000 B.P. had the appearance of an oak-pistachio steppe forest. About 6,000 years ago real oak forests appeared in the Zagros mountains. Using the palaeobotanical evidence van Zeist suggested that, between 22,500 and 10,000 B.P., treeless steppes covered the Mesopotamian lowlands as well as the Zagros piedmont, the forests being restricted to a very few areas in the mountains. Between 14,000 and 6,000 the vegetation of the piedmont area gradually took on the aspect of forest-steppes, the rainfall level still being lower than that of today. The natural vegetation of the region reached present-day conditions only about 6,000 years ago.

A vitally important factor in the economic and cultural evolution of the region during prehistoric times is that the Near Eastern mountains are the natural habitat of the wild ancestors of at least three species of early domestic cereals. The Soviet botanist N.I. Vavilov[4] discovered in the early 1930s that the area is one of the most important centres of distribution of wild cereals. New investigations[5] have clarified the picture. It was established that the distribution centre of the wild ancestor of einkorn wheat, the so-called *Triticum boeoticum*, lies in the fertile crescent belt of northern Iraq and in adjacent territories of Turkey and Syria. In these areas wild einkorn is part of oak-forest steppes or steppe-like vegetation. A wild ancestor of cultivated barley, *Hordeum spontanaeum*, is native to nearly the same area, the summer-dry belt of oak-forest steppes north and west of the Syrian desert and in the Euphrates basin. In natural conditions wild barley prefers warmer and dryer habitats and it is very rarely met with at elevations above 1,500 m.

Present-day evidence leads us to suggest that the Zagros mountains and in particular their higher piedmont belt were comparatively densely populated in Upper Palaeolithic times, between 40,000 and 10,000 B.P. Human settlements were situated almost exclusively in caves cut mostly in the limestone and overlooking deep valleys, the pathways of migrating game herds. It now seems that the economy of the Upper Palaeolithic dwellers was primarily based on the specialized hunting of migratory herd animals. This economic consideration in all probability dictated the choice of dwelling sites. The Upper Palaeolithic hunting economy was efficient and the population density in the areas suitable for such specialized hunting was relatively high. The hunting pattern of the Upper Palaeolithic dwellers in the area may be seen from the list of animal bones found in the deposits in Shanidar Cave in northern Iraq (Fig. 8). Only two animal species make up the bulk of game killed in Palaeolithic times;

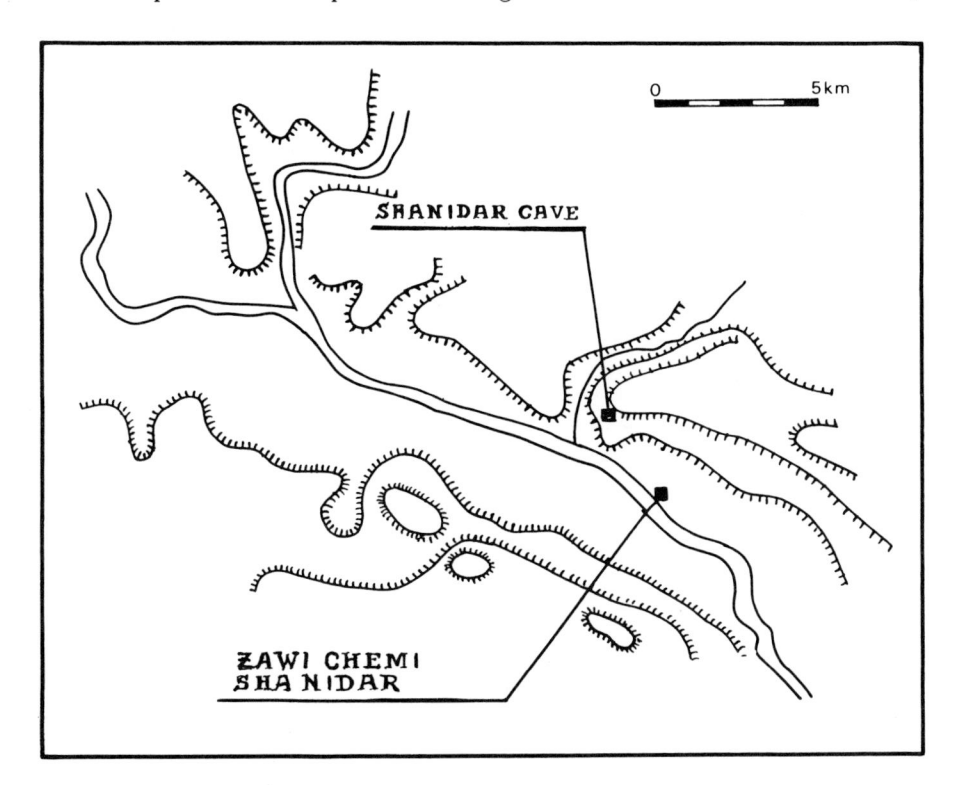

Figure 8 Greater Zab river valley (after Solecki, 1963; Note 2.2)

the bezoar or wild goat of the Near East and the small short-horned wild ox.

The stone tools used by the Palaeolithic dwellers of the Zagros mountains are regarded by anthropologists as belonging to a particular kind of Upper Palaeolithic industry, the Baradostian.[6] These tools are mostly made of long thin stone blades. A high proportion of burins, scrapers, notched blades and different points is typical of this industry.

About 14,000 B.P. it appears that changes took place in the economy and culture of the prehistoric inhabitants of the Zagros mountains. These changes are reflected primarily in the stone tools left behind by the hunters of those times. Large quantities of small implements with geometric forms appear: trapezes, triangles, small burins, small blades with retouched edges. Anthropologists have named this industry 'Zarzian', after Zarzi Cave where it was first established.[7] It is still difficult for anthropologists to find out for exactly what purpose this or that tool was used in prehistoric times. But it seems to be accepted that small tools were mounted compositely in special shafts, forming long projectile points.

The settlement pattern of Zarzian dwellers was no different from that of their Baradostian predecessors: they inhabited the same caves or other caves in similar situations. Even their subsistence pattern did not undergo any particular change: the hunting of wild goats and wild oxen procured the greater part of the food they needed. Some minor changes in the subsistence pattern are, however, noticeable: an increase in the exploitation of water resources, especially fishing and the collection of edible molluscs and crabs. It seems logical to link these changes in the economy with the environmental changes which took place in the same area.

The most remarkable changes in the evolution of the economic pattern in the Zagros mountains are recorded in the sites dated 11,000-10,000 B.P. As we recall, major changes in environmental conditions took place at approximately this time. These changes manifested themselves in the appearance of the first traces of artificial food production – stock-breeding and plant domestication. So far the oldest site in the Near East where this phenomenon has been documented is one of the uppermost layers of Shanidar Cave, and the nearby open-air site of Zawi Chemi Shanidar,[8] where some indications of the selective breeding of goats have been found. D. Perkins,[9] the zoologist, came to this conclusion on the basis of changes in the morphology of horn cores (they show medial flattening, an indication of domestication) and on the basis of the age composition (a high percentage of immature animals). In the early stages artificial food production provided only a small proportion of the food needed for survival. The general subsistence pattern had not changed much compared with Zarzian times. But the invention of a highly reliable source of food was of crucial importance for the further development of mankind.

The levels with the earliest traces of food-production in Shanidar Cave and in the Zawi Chemi Shanidar dwelling sites are radiocarbon-dated to 11,000-10,000 B.P. It is noteworthy that this time span coincides with marked changes in the environment, as shown by palaeobotanical records. From this time on, the prevailing type of human settlement in the area is the open-air dwelling site.

The next stage in the evolution of human settlements in the area is connected with the appearance of villages in the lower hilly belt of the Zagros piedmont. One of the most important sites to be excavated in this zone is Qal'at Jarmo.[10] The village site, covering an area of about 3.2 acres (1.3 hectares), is situated on the edge of a deep wadi crossing the Chemchemal plain. The economy of the village site had a well-defined mixed character. Grains of emmer wheat, einkorn wheat and two-row barley have been found. Morphologically the grains are close to the wild forms. Apart from these, the prehistoric inhabitants of Jarmo used field peas, lentils and blue vetchling for food. Pistachios and acorns were also eaten.[11]

Only one domesticated animal was known to the Jarmo dwellers – the goat. Most meat was provided through hunting pigs, sheep, gazelles and wild cattle. The collecting of edible snails was also important. The Jarmo villagers lived in houses built of clay, each consisting of several small rooms, 1.5 to 2 m. in length. The radiocarbon dates obtained so far from the aceramic layers of Jarmo cover a considerable span of time, from 11,500 to 6,000 B.P.

A very interesting data relating to Early Holocene economic patterns have been obtained through investigations of the Khuzistan plain of south-western Iran by American expeditions.[12] The lowland area (100-300 m.), now covered with steppe-like vegetation, has been continuously inhabited since 9,500 B.P. According to K.V. Flannery, the subsistence pattern in the earliest phase had five main aspects: (1) dry cultivation of cereals; (2) collecting of small wild legume seeds; (3) collecting of seeds of wild grasses; (4) herding of domestic goats and sheep; (5) hunting of wild ungulates. Fishing, hunting of water fowl, and collection of mussels, nuts and fruits were also an important source of food supply. Flannery emphasizes that at that time hunting and wild plant collecting were the major subsistence strategies. Hole and Flannery estimate the population density of the area before the introduction of irrigation as 1-2 persons per sq.km.

The Levant

Structurally the Levant[13] forms part of a gigantic north-east African platform. Its dominant feature is the presence of the Archaean basement. The basement underlies a series of horizontal or slightly disturbed sediments deposited during the continually repeated marine transgressions of the Mesozoic and Cenozoic ages. The Near

East is partly included in the East African rift system, an enormous pattern of fault-scarps that crosses the earth's surface. Parallel faults delimit the Red Sea trough and stretch northward forming the gulf of Suez, the gulf of Aqaba, the Dead Sea fault, the Jordan valley, the Beqaa and the plain of Antioch. The following natural zones can be singled out within the Levant area: (1) coastal plain; (2) high altitude plateau; (3) rift valley; (4) folded mountains.

The repeated fluctuations of the coastline occurring during the Quaternary were an important factor in the palaeogeographical evolution of the Levant area.[14] At the maximum stage of the Last Glaciation, c. 20,000 B.P., the sea-level seems to have dropped by about 90 m. and the coastal zone to have extended seawards up to 5 km. During the postglacial Flandrian transgression, 7,000-4,000 B.P. the sea-level rose by 2 to 4 m. Recent investigations[15] show that important fluctuations in the level of the inner lakes occurred during the Late Quaternary. It has been established that the level of the Dead Sea, now 397 m. below sea-level, rose to 180 m. below sea level between 70,000 and 10,000 B.P. (the so-called Lisan stage). At the time a considerable part of the Jordan valley was incorporated into a lacustrine basin which included both the present Dead Sea and the Sea of Galilee. The level of this lake seems to have fallen abruptly about 10,000 B.P.

Minor changes in the lake level took place during the Holocene. There was a rise in the water level between 10,000 and 6,500 B.P., followed by a regression between 6,500 and 5,500 B.P. This was succeeded by a rise in the water level between 5,500 and 4,500 years ago. A considerable regression of the lakes within the rift valley seems to have taken place between 4,500 and 3,000 B.P. From 3,000 up to 1,500 B.P. the level of the Dead Sea was higher than at present; this is supported by Biblical records.

The present rainfall in the Levant area follows the so-called Mediterranean rhythm of summer drought and winter rains. As throughout the Middle East, most of the precipitation is limited to west-facing mountain slopes. Only the coastal areas of the Levant receive more than 700 mm. of rainfall. The rest of the Arabian and Syrian plateau gets less than 250 mm.

The western part of the coastal plain is now covered with vegetation of the Mediterranean type. This vegetation includes walnut and poplar trees, olive and fruit trees, shrubs and herbs, many of them evergreen. Mediterranean vegetation includes the so-called maquis plant complex: densely set evergreen oaks, myrtles and broom with thick undergrowth of thorn bushes and shrubs. Evergreen oaks grow on low hill slopes up to 1,000 m. above sea level, usually in association with the Mediterranean pine. At higher levels grow cedars, maples, junipers, firs, valonia oaks and Aleppo pines. Still higher there used to be isolated groves of the famous cedars of Lebanon, now almost completely extinct.

The inner part of the Syrian plateau is covered with the steppe vegetation which forms the western flank of the huge Irano-Turanian botanical province of central Asia. On the lower slopes of the mountains a park-like vegetation is found which includes scattered carob, juniper, terebinth and bushes of Christ thorn. True steppes are covered with different species of seasonally-restricted grasses. The rest of the territory is taken up by semi-desert and desert vegetation. This vegetation consists mostly of plants highly adapted to dry and saline conditions, camel thorn, shrubs of the pea family and tamarisks.

Detailed reconstruction of the past vegetation of the area is not yet possible as the records available are too meagre. Palaeobotanists suggest[16] that during the maximum stage of the Last Glaciation the forest-like vegetation was restricted to the coastland of the Mediterranean. Pollen-analytical data recently collected from borings in the northern part of the Jordan valley show that during the Last Glaciation some oak forests existed along the slopes of the valley. In the drier periods these forests showed savannah-like vegetation. During the Holocene the forests grew thinner and the vegetation gradually took on its modern aspect.

The Levant forms part of the Near Eastern centre which was the origin of domesticated cereals. Botanists[17] have now pinpointed the original habitat of wild emmer wheat as the upper Jordan valley, the slopes of eastern Galilee and Gilead facing the Sea of Galilee, the basaltic plateaux of Golan and Hauran and the eastern slopes of Mount Hermon. Wild barley is found in nearly the same area.

The territory of the Levant was densely populated in Upper Palaeolithic times. Human settlements, mostly caves, were concentrated chiefly in the elevated areas, the uplands of Galilee and Judaea and in the Lebanon and Anti-Lebanon ranges. It has been noted that in most cases these settlements overlook river valleys or wadis. In all probability the sites controlled the principal migratory pathways of animal herds. Faunal analysis of the bone remains proves that the Upper Palaeolithic economy was based on specialized hunting of migratory game. The Upper Palaeolithic dwellers of Mount Carmel mostly hunted gazelles;[18] fallow deer was the principal prey of the inhabitants of Ksar'Akil (Lebanon);[19] and hunting of wild horses provided the bulk of food for the Upper Palaeolithic tribesmen in the Judean desert.[20]

The stone tools used by the Upper Palaeolithic people of the area are made mostly of blades, and the high percentage of different points is remarkable. The manufacture of microlithic stone tools began here earlier than in other parts of the Old World. Microlithic tools are especially typical of the so-called Natufian industry[21] which spread in the Levant between approximately 12,000 and 10,000 B.P. The subsistence pattern of the Natufian dwellers is not yet completely clear. It is probable that it was not essentially different from that of the Upper Palaeolithic people. Gazelle bones predominate in the

Natufian layers of the Mount Carmel caves. Food collecting and fishing played an important part in the subsistence pattern of the Natufian sites.

Some anthropologists have suggested that incipient forms of agriculture were practised by the Natufian dwellers. This suggestion seemed to be supported by the fact that in Natufian tool assemblages blades with a special gloss are always found, usually interpreted as sickles. Querns and mortars, pounders and pestles have also been found. But recently 'site catchment analysis' of the Natufian sites of Palestine has given a different result.[22] Assessments were made of the productive potentials of the site territories (the percentages of arable land, rough grazing, marsh, etc.) within the catchment area, at a distance of 5 to 10 km. from the settlement. This showed that there was a very low proportion of potential arable land within the catchment area of the Natufian sites (Fig. 9), which suggests that agriculture did not play any noticeable part in the subsistence pattern of the Natufian sites.

In many cases the settlement pattern of the Natufian sites was the same as that of the Upper Palaeolithic sites. Natufian layers have often been met with above the Upper Palaeolithic ones in the same caves. But the settlement area of the Natufian sites was considerably wider. Open-air sites appeared in the coastal plain and in the rift valley. The latter is particularly important. Human settlement in the rift valley was possible only after the fall in the level of the Dead Sea, which occurred, as we may remember, some 10,000 years ago. Once settled in the rift valley the Natufian people had access to the wild cereals growing within the catchment areas of their sites. It is possible that there, in conditions of the growing scarcity of food resources, the Natufians began systematically to use cereals for food. It is equally possible that it was in the rift valley that artificial cultivation of cereals began. The proportion of potentially arable land was much higher in the rift valley than anywhere else in Palestine (Fig. 10).

The Jordan valley became one of the principal centres in the evolution of farming communities in the Near East. One of the outstanding examples of this evolution is represented by the settlements of Jericho in the Jordan valley.[23] A late Natufian village had existed at the site with flimsy huts or shelters, and about 10,000 B.P. a new town occupying no less than 10 acres was built on the same site. It seems certain that the economy of the Neolithic settlement was primarily based on the cultivation of wheat and barley. There is still no proof of the domestication of animals. The bulk of meat was probably provided by hunting gazelles.

The city of Jericho consisted of round houses built of mud bricks on stone foundations. Most of the houses consisted of a single room 4 to 5 m. in diameter. At a later stage the town was fortified with a rock-cut ditch, a stone wall and a tower which still stands to a height of 8.15 m. Radiocarbon dates of the Pre-Pottery Neolithic A layers in

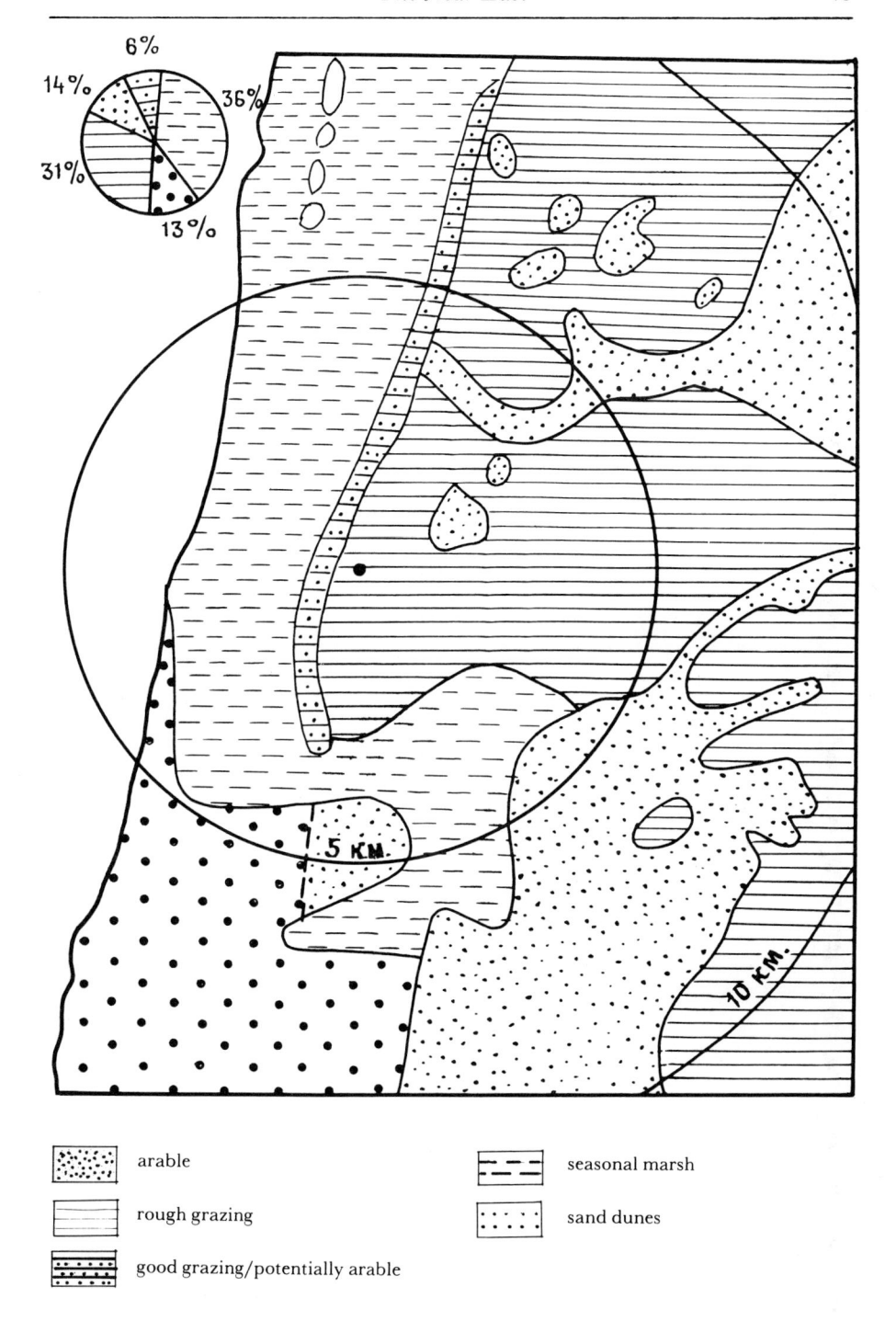

Figure 9 Site catchment of Wadi El-Mughara caves (after Vita-Finzi & Higgs, 1970; Note 2.22)

arable   rough grazing

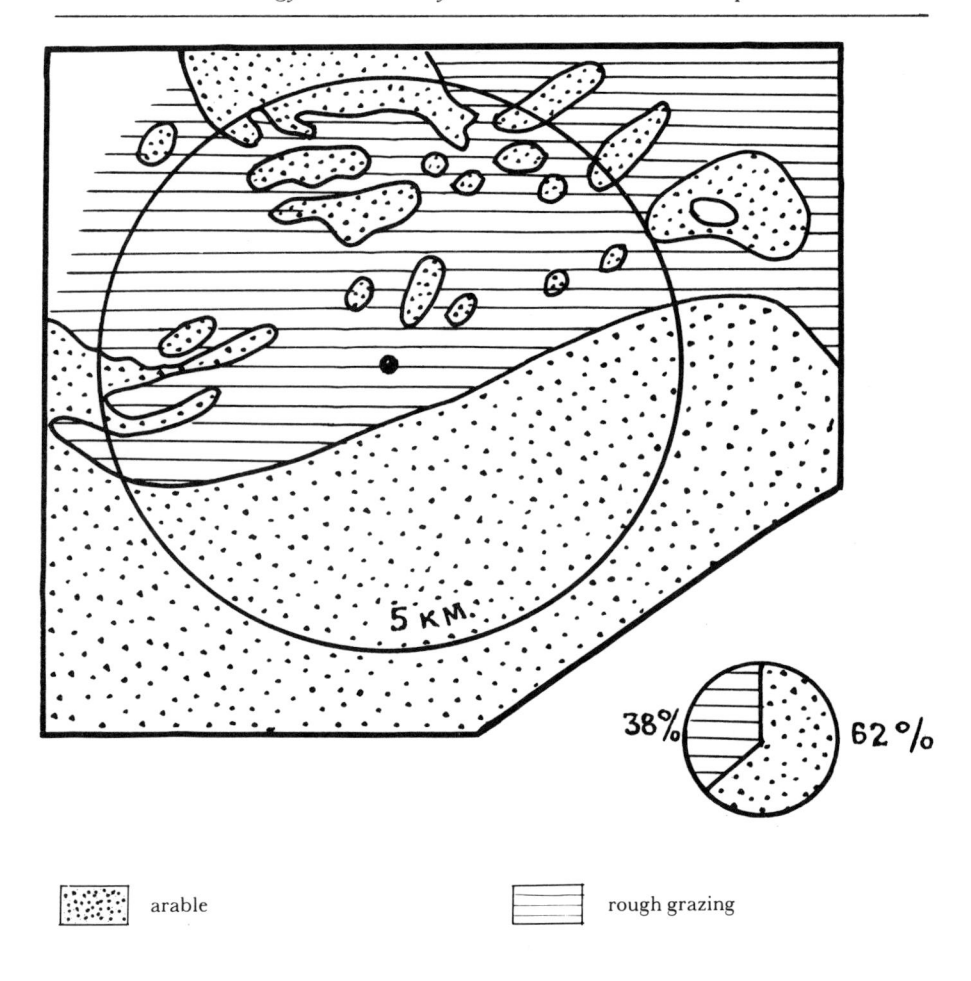

Figure 10 Site catchment of Djebel Quafzeh (after Vita-Finzi & Higgs, 1970; Note 2.22)

Jericho lie between 10,500 and 8,700 B.P.

To the same initial stage in the evolution of the farming communities belongs the settlement of Beidha near Petra, 200 miles south of Jericho.[24] The village, occupying an area of 1.5 to 2 acres, consists of houses similar in their plans to the Jericho A buildings. As in the case of Jericho, there existed an original Natufian site in the Beidha area. The subsistence pattern of the Beidha Neolithic settlement was fairly similar to that of Jericho A. Einkorn wheat and two-row barley were cultivated. Wild pulses and the seeds of some wild grasses were collected. It is possible (but not definitely proved) that there existed some form of goat-breeding. Even so the hunting of wild goat, aurochs and gazelle was of far greater economic significance.

After a short interval there followed a new wave of Neolithic dwellers in the Jordan valley, best known from the site of Jericho, where the layers belonging to this stage were labelled 'Pre-Pottery Neolithic B'.[25] Apart from Jericho, similar settlements are known in the valley (Tell Sheikh Ali I, Tell Munhatta) and on the slopes (Tell Far'ah, Wadi Shu'aib). The economic structure did not change very much compared with the previous stage. Cultivation of wheat and barley provided the bulk of vegetable food, and goat-breeding supplemented by hunting (gazelles, ibex, birds) provided the meat diet. There were changes, however, particularly in architecture and in tool-kits. The houses contained rectangular rooms with plaster floors. Urban planning was much more complicated: several houses were designed as shrines. In the stone inventory beautiful arrow-heads and long straight sickle blades are the most common. Radiocarbon dates of the Pre-Pottery B layers of Jericho lie in the range 9,300 to 8,500, B.P.

During the same stage the Neolithic settlers seem to have spread into a new natural zone, the Levantine coastland. One of the first settlements in this zone was Ras Shamra on the north Syrian coast.[26] In the aceramic layers of the site (Néolithique ancien, according to Schaeffer) there were traces of houses with rectangular rooms and with plaster floors. Radiocarbon dates of these layers are within the range 9,400-8,000 B.P. Another important coastal settlement, Byblos,[27] was located on a consolidated sand dune. The rooms of the houses in the Early Neolithic settlements were rectangular in plan with stone foundations and white plaster floors. The settlement was large, with several hundred houses. Little is known about the economy of the site. It is suggested that wheat and probably barley were grown and some domestic animals (probably goats and pigs) were kept. Hunting and fishing were also practised. Radiocarbon dates of the Early Neolithic layers in Byblos lie within the time span 7,500-6,000 B.P.

A new element in the socio-cultural systems of the Near East made its first appearance about 8,000 B.P.: the manufacture of pottery. Early stages in the production of pottery are represented in a group of sites situated in the 'Amuq area, near the border between Syria and Turkey. The sites, excavated by an American expedition led by Professor Braidwood,[28] are situated inside the plain of Antioch, a northern continuation of the Levantine rift valley. The economy of the Neolithic sites was based on effective food production. Grains of emmer wheat and of hulled barley have been found in the deposits together with the seeds of two common weeds, oat grass and rye grass, which infested the fields. Among the faunal remains, pigs, sheep or goats and cattle have been identified. No wild animals have been found. Minute stratigraphic excavations have enabled archaeologists to distinguish several phases in the evolution of the local archaeological sequence. The presence of handmade pottery sherds has been fixed from Phase A upward.

Braidwood differentiates three types of pottery present in the finds of Phase A. (1) Coarse simple ware: deep bowls, ovoid jars, collared jars with flattened bottoms made of orange-buff paste, bearing no decoration. (2) Dark-faced burnished ware making up the bulk of the pottery assemblage: hemispherical or vertical-sided bowls made of grey-brown buff paste. A small portion of the pottery of this type is decorated. In the words of the American archaeologist 'the decoration consists of impressions made with both sharp and blunt implements, possibly bird bones. The shapes of the impressions are lunate, elliptical, squarish ... those on any pot are quite consistent and tend to be ordered horizontally even if applied all over'. (3) The third type of pottery is called 'washed impressed ware'. These are hemispherical bowls with vertical rims made in brown-black, lightly-fired paste. Decoration is nearly the same as in (2). In addition 'short crescent-shaped impressions with dentations inside, similar to impressions made by a certain type of shell in soft clay' and 'impressions made with a rocker-like motion which results in a zigzag' have been reported (Fig. 11). In the pottery assemblage of Phase B, in addition to the above mentioned types, so-called 'coarse red slip ware' has been found. This addition of a red slip is characteristic. The pottery is ornamented with rows of vertical, horizontal or diagonal impressions.

These pottery ornamentation styles are vital for the reconstruction of cultural processes in the whole area under investigation. On the basis of the analysis of archaeological material found in the Early Neolithic sites of the Antioch plain and in the surrounding areas of the Near East, Braidwood singles out the so-called 'essential Syro-Cilician dark-faced burnished ware assemblage'. The hallmark of this assemblage is the presence of 'dark-faced burnished pottery'. The main interest of this assemblage is represented by the material of the 'Amuq, Phase A, by Mersin (Yümük Tepe) below level XXVII and, possibly, by Ras-Shamra. Similar pottery has been found at Tell Chaghir Bazar, Tell al-Halaf in the Jabail plain, Carchemish and Junus. This pottery has also been reported from three sites in the Upper Tigris basin: Tell Arpachiyah, Tell Hassuna and Nineveh. To the south, pottery of a similar type has been recorded in Hamah and in Byblos.

Asia Minor

Asia Minor[29] belongs to the gigantic Alpine folded zone that crosses the Eurasian continent. Within this area the following structural units can be distinguished: (1) the Black Sea coastland extending from the Caucasus to the Bosphorus; (2) the Aegean-Marmara coastlands; (3) the Mediterranean coastlands; (4) the central plateau; and (5) the eastern highlands, which include the Armenian highlands and the piedmont connected with the Zagros system.

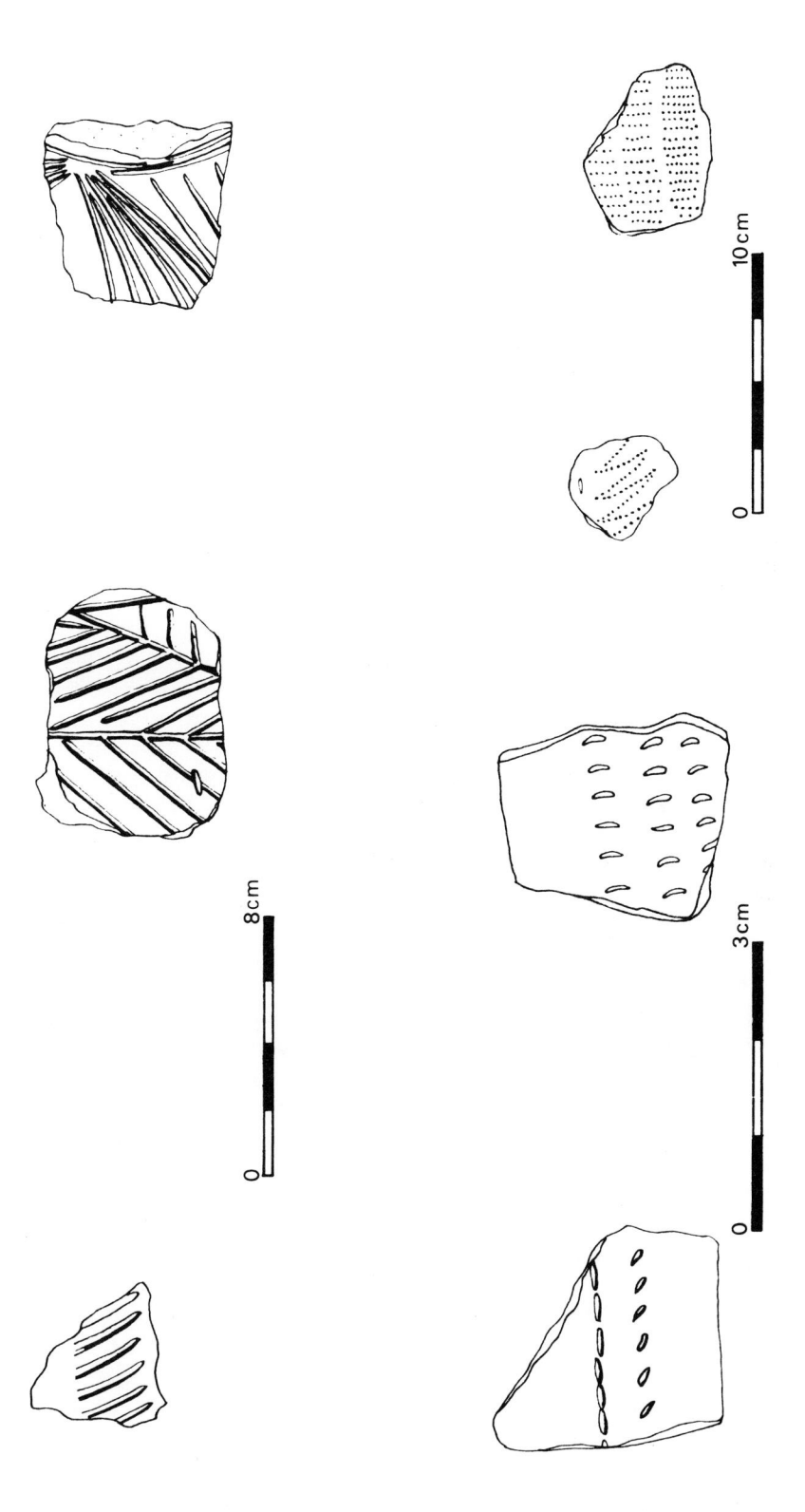

Figure 11 Ornamentations of Amuq A and B pottery (after R. & L. Braidwood 1960; Note 2.28)

The climatic conditions of Asia Minor are largely dependent on its position at junction of the Mediterranean and interior Asiatic climatic zones. The relief and the position of the sea are responsible for local peculiarities in the climate. In the Black Sea coastland, winters are mild and summers moderately hot. Rainfall is abundant, ranging from 600 mm. in the west to 2,500 mm. in the east. Similar conditions prevail in the Aegean coastland. In the south the temperature rises considerably. Rainfall ranges from 500 to 750 mm. per annum. In the Mediterranean coastland both summers and winters are much warmer; rainfall in the region ranges from 500 to 750 mm. annually, December and January being the wettest months. The central plateau is characterized by cold winters and hot summers and by greater aridity. The rainfall is between 250 and 525 mm. annually, May usually being the wettest month and July and August the driest. The climate of the eastern highlands is both varied and severe. Summers are hot and arid, winters are very cold. The total rainfall is between 450 and 600 mm., the wettest months being January to March in the south-west, May to June in the north-east.

Thick forests of alder, beech and pine cover the Black Sea coastlands. Mediterranean vegetation, including maquis and pine groves, covers the Aegean and Mediterranean coastlands. Steppe-like vegetation covers the greater part of the central plateau. Wooded areas are confined to the extreme north-east and north-west. Coniferous forests cover considerable parts of the eastern highlands while above the upper forest limits alpine pastures are found.

Little is known about the vegetational history of Asia Minor in late Quaternary times. Pollen analytical investigations of lake deposits in northern Anatolia[30] show that the vegetation of the Black Sea coastland has not changed very much during the last 5,000 years. The Dutch palaeobotanist van Zeist[31] suggests that forest vegetation also existed in that area during the cold phases of the Last Glaciation. He thinks that the mountains in south-western Turkey could have supported forest vegetation during the Ice Age. But the greater part of Asia Minor was covered by treeless vegetation. New evidence shows that treeless vegetation existed at that time in the Armenian highlands and in the vicinity of Lake Sevan. After 14,000 B.P. steppe-forest vegetation spread over the interior regions of Asia Minor. Later it resembled the present day forests.

New geological investigations have proved that the central plateau during the Ice Age consisted of a series of small inland drainage basins with no outlet to the sea. At least three such basins existed inside the Konya plain.[32] Around 10,000 B.P. the plain was drained and thus became suitable for human settlement, for the cultivation of crops and for pasture for domesticated animals. But even in the Early Holocene the plain was constantly affected by small-scale floods. There is reason to believe that the plain of Ararat in Armenia was covered with lake basins during the Ice Age.

Asia Minor is the natural habitat of all three important wild cereals. An important centre of wild einkorn wheat was found in western Anatolia, one predecessor of the tetraploid wheat – *Triticum diccocoides* – was found in south-east Turkey and another predecessor – *Triticum araraticum* – grew in south-east Turkey and in the Armenian highlands.[33]

The territory of Asia Minor was intensively populated by Palaeolithic man. The most densely populated areas were the mountainous coastlands and eastern highlands, including Armenia. Uninterrupted habitation from Upper Palaeolithic to Neolithic times was found in the Beldibi cave in a coastal range of the western Taurus, in the Antalya region of south Turkey.[34] The C layer of the cave contained microlithic tools and sickle blades similar to those found in the Levantine Natufian sites. Primitive pottery was found in the upper layer of the cave site.

During the initial phases of the Holocene the main area of human habitation shifted to the central plateau. Reliable palaeogeographical reconstructions show that this plateau was covered at that time with open grasslands; large areas were taken up by lake and swamps and low-lying lands were constantly being inundated.

An aceramic village at Hacilar[35] was situated on a high terrace of Lake Burdur. A comparatively small village (c. 150 sq.m.), it consisted of a number of rectangular mud-brick houses built on stone foundations. Seven habitation phases were identified, the duration of each being estimated at about 25 years.

Little is known about the economy of the site. Both stock-breeding and hunting were important for the meat supply and the bones of sheep or goats, cattle and deer, left from meals, were found. There was no proof of animal domestication, with the exception of the dog. That agriculture had existed was proved by finding two-row barley, emmer, wild einkorn and lentils. The cultural layer containing these remains was radiocarbon dated $8,700 \pm 180$ B.P.

The largest Neolithic site in Anatolia (and in the whole Near East), Çatal Hüyük,[36] lies within the lake depression of Konya-Eregli. Geologists suggest that the depression was completely covered with water during Upper Pleistocene times. The water level fell shortly before the site was established but even during the existence of the Neolithic site the surrounding plain was constantly flooded. The site covered an area of 32 acres (13.2 hectares) and was steadily inhabited for a millennium, between 8,500 and 7,600 years B.P. Detailed excavations, reports of which have been published in a number of books, revealed the existence of a sophisticated architectural construction of shrines, communication networks and defence systems. The population of the site at times reached a figure of about 8,000 persons.

The economy of Çatal Hüyük was based on intensive agriculture and stock-breeding. At the site grains of emmer and einkorn wheat and of naked wild barley were found, as were the remains of two varieties of peas and vetch. It has been calculated that about 91% of the meat consumed by the Çatal Hüyük settlers was supplied by stock-breeding, that of sheep and cattle probably being the most important. The hunting of aurochs, red deer, wild ass, boar and leopard was also an important source of food supply.

There is also evidence for the collecting of hackberries (for making wine and possibly beer), crucifers, almonds, acorns and pistachios (probably to obtain vegetable oil).

Summary

Taking the Near East as a whole, one may distinguish the following natural regions: (1) the Zagros mountains; (2) the high Zagros piedmont; (3) the low Zagros piedmont; (4) the Mesopotamian plain; (5) the Syrian and Arabian plateaux; (6) the rift valley; (7) the Levant mountains; (8) the coastal plain of the Mediterranean Sea; (9) the Black Sea coastlands; (10) the Aegean-Marmara coastlands; (11) the central Anatolian plateau; (12) the Anatolian highlands; and (13) the Armenian highlands.

20,000-10,000 B.P.

It is probable that the Zagros mountains and Armenian highlands were at least partially glaciated during the Ice Age. At a lower elevation there was a belt of Alpine vegetation. The high and low Zagros piedmonts, the Mesopotamian plain, the Syrian and Arabian plateaux, the Levant mountains and the central Anatolian plateau were covered with a treeless steppe-like vegetation. The central Anatolian plateau was partly covered by huge lake basins, and an enormous lake stretching from the Lake of Galilee up to the Dead Sea was situated within the rift valley. The slopes of the valley were covered with oak forests. Evergreen vegetation of the Mediterranean type spread along the Levantine coastland. During the Ice Age the level of the sea dropped considerably and the coastal area widened by up to 5 km. Forests are also presumed to have existed in the Black Sea and Aegean-Marmara coastlands.

The Upper Palaeolithic population in the Near East was concentrated mostly in the high Zagros piedmont, in the Levant mountains and in the Anatolian and Armenian highlands. Settlements were usually in caves. The subsistence pattern of the Upper Palaeolithic inhabitants of the Near East was based upon specialized hunting of herd animals. Thus the area of the Near East inhabited by Upper Palaeolithic men can be regarded as a single natural economic zone. Within this zone it is possible to distinguish several subzones, based on differences in hunting patterns. The Upper

Palaeolithic dwellers of the Zagros piedmont hunted bezoar goats and wild oxen. In the Judaean desert the bulk of the meat supply was provided by the specialized hunting of wild horse. Fallow deer and gazelle were the main sources of meat for the Palaeolithic hunters living in the caves in the mountains flanking the coastal area.

About 14,000 years ago there were marked changes in the environmental setting. These changes were shown by the spread of oak-pistachio savannah in the Zagros piedmont, the mountains of Levant and in the central Anatolian plateau. At the same time the forests covering the slopes of the rift valley grew thinner and the level of the lake in the rift valley dropped. Corresponding changes occurred in the economic structure and the material culture of the human groups. Environmental changes diminished the wild game supply and made it difficult to obtain sufficient meat through traditional hunting patterns. This led to the perfecting of hunting tools, including the use of complicated projectiles composed of inset geometric microliths. At the same time the growing scarcity of traditional hunting resources led to the more intensive exploitation of aquatic resources, fishing, hunting of waterfowl, collecting of edible molluscs, and to the more intensive gathering of edible plants.

The relative overpopulation of the main areas of Upper Palaeolithic settlement resulted in an overflow of part of the surplus population into the surrounding areas, and human groups penetrated the slopes of the rift valley and the valleys in the Zagros piedmont. Since these areas were the natural habitat of wild cereals, a new form of economic strategy, the collection of wild cereals, was made possible. Probably at the same time the first attempts at animal domestication took place. These new forms of economic strategy proved to be highly efficient and they triggered off processes with far-reaching consequences for the economy, demography, and social structure of the ancient population of the Near East (Fig. 12).

10,000-8,000 B.P.

At the initial phase of the Holocene the human population was concentrated in the same natural regions as in the Late Pleistocene, namely in the high Zagros piedmont, the rift valley and so on – areas covered with a savannah-like vegetation. The economy of the human groups in these areas was of a mixed character: hunting, fishing and food collecting, with elements of agriculture and of stock-breeding. The settlement pattern was also of a mixed character, with both cave and open-air settlements.

The acquisition of new stable sources of food and the amelioration of nutrition resulted in population growth. As a consequence further expansion of population into the surrounding areas took place. During this period Neolithic population appeared in the coastal area, in the lower Zagros piedmont and in the central Anatolian plateau.

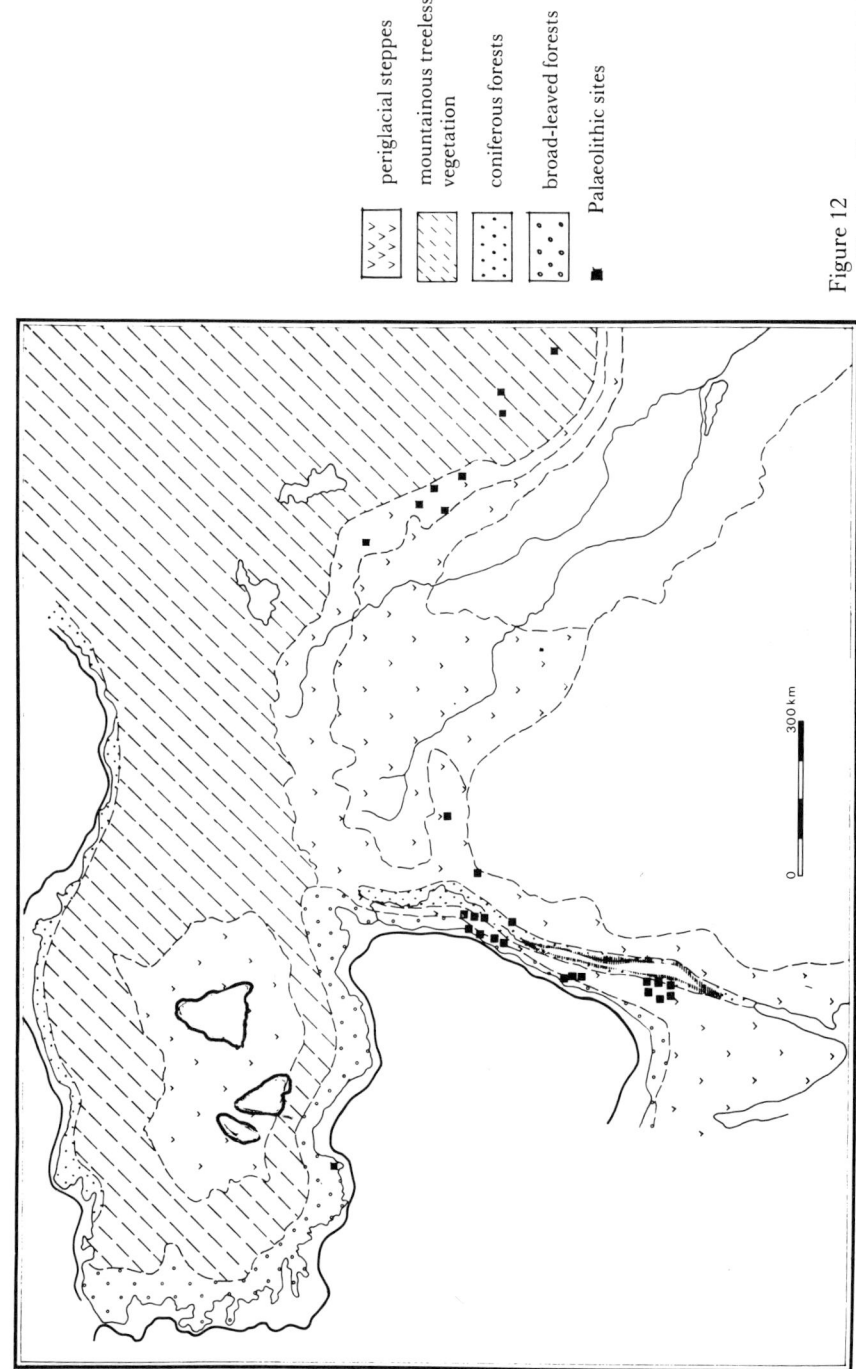

Figure 12
The Near East 20,000–10,000 B.P.

periglacial steppes

mountainous treeless
vegetation

coniferous forests

broad-leaved forests

○ Neolithic agricultural sites

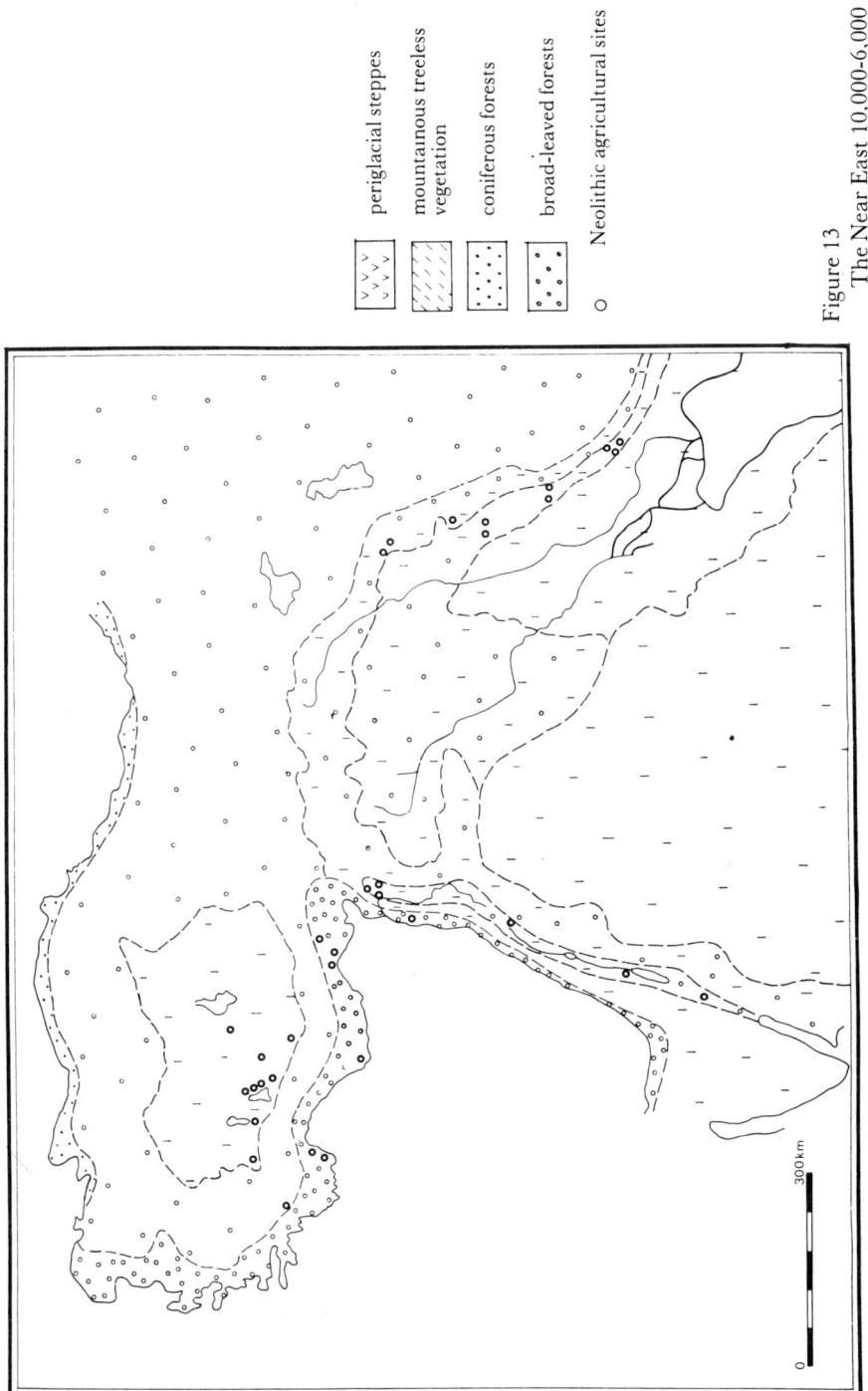

Figure 13
The Near East 10,000-6,000 B.P.

These areas, together with the rift valley, became the most important centres of human settlement in the Early Holocene. All these regions form a single natural economic zone within which the economy of the human groups was based upon both food-appropriation and food-production. Several subzones are distinguishable. They include: the low Zagros piedmont, with hunting (onager, gazelle, and water-fowl), fishing, collecting, agriculture and stock-breeding (goats, sheep); the rift valley, with hunting (wild goat, aurochs, gazelle), agriculture and stock-breeding (sheep, goats). Pottery manufacture was not known.

This mixed form of economic pattern was highly efficient in the local ecological setting. The population density of settled areas was relatively high (not less than one person per sq.km.). Large settlements with complicated structures appeared (Jarmo, Jericho, Beidha). The population of Jericho A is estimated to be of the order of 2,000 to 3,000 people.

8,000-6,000 B.P.

A further extension of the settlement area occurred, and the central Anatolian plateau was intensively populated. The subsistence pattern here was based upon stock-breeding (sheep, goats, cattle), agriculture (wheat, barley), hunting and collecting.

All the settled areas formed a unique natural economic zone where a mixed food-producing/food-appropriating economy was practised. The population density reached a value of no less than 10 persons per sq.km. Large settlements appeared: the population of Çatal Hüyük is estimated to have been about 8,000.

At this time pottery manufacturing made its appearance. Comparison of ornamental patterns on pottery makes it possible to distinguish several cultural zones. Within one zone pottery was decorated with shell and comb impressions and with incised lines, forming horizontal, vertical or diagonal rows and zigzag patterns. This pottery is referred to as 'dark-faced burnished ware'. It extended over the Syro-Cilician coastland, the northern part of the rift valley, northern Mesopotamia and in the low Zagros piedmont (Fig. 13).

NOTES

[1] The geological structure and the modern physical geographical setting are based on W.B. Fischer, *The Near East: A physical, social and regional geography* (6th edn.), London, 1971, pp. 16-100 and P. Birot, J. Dresch, *Le Mediterranée et le Moyen Orient*, 2, Paris, 1956, pp. 243-47.

[2] R.S. Solecki, 'Prehistory in Shanidar Valley, northern Iraq', *Science*, 139, 1963, pp. 179-92.

[3] W. van Zeist, 'Reflection on prehistoric environment in the Near East', *in* P.J. Ucko and G.W. Dimbleby (eds.), *The domestication and exploitation of plants and animals*, London, 1969, pp. 35-46.

[4] N.I. Vavilov's most important work concerning the origin of domesticated plants:

Centry proiskhozdeniya kulturniykh rastenii (*Izbrannye trudy* [*Collected Works*], 5), Moscow-Leningrad, 1965.

⁵ D. Zohary, 'The progenitors of wheat and barley in relation to domestication and agricultural dispersal in the Old World', *in* P.J. Ucko and G.W. Dimbleby (eds.), op. cit. (Note 3), 1969, pp. 47-66.

⁶ R.S. Solecki, *Shanidar: The first flower people*, New York, 1971; P.E.L. Smith, 'The palaeolithic of Iran', *Mélanges de préhistoire, d'archéocivilisation et d'ethnologie offerts à André Varagnac*, Paris, 1971, pp. 681-95.

⁷ Initial publication: D.A.E. Garrod, 'Palaeolithic in Southern Kurdistan: excavations in the caves Zarzi and Hazar Merd', *Bulletin of American School of Prehistoric Research*, 6, 1930, pp. 8-43; see also Smith op. cit. (Note 6), 1971.

⁸ Solecki op. cit. (Note 2), 1963, pp. 179-92.

⁹ D. Perkins, 'The faunal remains of Shanidar Cave and Zavi Chemi Shanidar, 1960 season', *Sumer*, 16, 1-2, 1960, pp. 77-8.

¹⁰ R. Braidwood, B. Howe, *Prehistoric investigations in Iraqi Kurdistan*, Chicago, 1960.

¹¹ J.M. Renfrew, 'The archaeological evidence for the domestication of plants: methods and problems', *in* P.J. Ucko and G.W. Dimbleby (eds.), op. cit. (Note 3), 1969, p. 156; Renfrew, *Palaeoethnobotany*, London, 1973, pp. 110, 113, 117, 157.

¹² F. Hole, K.V. Flannery, J.A. Neely, *Prehistory and human ecology of the Deh Luran Plain*, Ann Arbor, 1969.

¹³ The geological and physical geographical survey is based on Fischer op. cit. (Note 1), 1971, pp. 376-99 and Birot and Dresch op. cit. (Note 1), 1956, pp. 197-240.

¹⁴ M. Avnimelech, 'The main trends in the Pleistocene-Holocene history of the Israelian coastal plain', *Quaternaria*, 6, 1962, pp. 474-95.

¹⁵ D. Neev, K.O. Emery, *The Dead Sea*, Jerusalem, 1967.

¹⁶ Van Zeist, op. cit. (Note 3), 1969, p.43.

¹⁷ Zohary, op. cit. (Note 5), 1969, pp. 47-66.

¹⁸ D.A.E. Garrod, D.M.A. Bate, *The Stone Age of Mount Carmel*, I, Oxford, 1937.

¹⁹ D.A. Hooijer, 'The fossil verteberates of Ksar'Akil, a palaeolithic shelter in the Lebanon', *Zoologische Verhandlingen, Rijks museum voor natural historie*, 49, 1961.

²⁰ R. Neuville, *Le Paléolithique et le mésolithique du désert de Judée*, Archives de l'Institut de Paléontologie Humaine, 24, Paris, 1951.

²¹ J. Mellaart, *Earliest civilisations of the Near East*, London, 1965, pp. 22-32.

²² C. Vita Finzi, E.S. Higgs, 'Prehistoric economy in the Mount Carmel of Palestine: a site catchment analysis', *P.P.S.*, n.s., 36, 1970, pp. 1-37.

²³ K.M. Kenyon, 'Excavations at Jericho: 1957-1958', *Palestine Exploration Quarterly*, 92, 1960, pp. 88-108; D. Kirkbride, 'A brief report on the prepottery flint cultures of Jericho', *Palestine Exploration Quarterly*, 92, 1960, pp. 114-19; M. Hopf, 'Plant remains and early farming in Jericho', *in* P.J. Ucko and G.W. Dimbleby (eds.) op. cit. (Note 3), 1969, pp. 355-60; J. Mellaart, op. cit. (Note 21), 1965, pp. 32-8.

²⁴ D. Kirkbride, 'Beidha: early neolithic village life south of the Dead Sea', *Antiquity*, 42, 1968, pp. 263-74; P. Mortensen, 'A preliminary study of the chipped stone industry from Beidha', *Acta Archaeologica*, Copenhagen, 41, 1970, pp. 1-56; D. Perkins, 'The fauna from Madumagh and Beidha', *Palestine Exploration Quarterly*, 98, 1966, pp. 66-7.

²⁵ J. Mellaart, op. cit. (Note 21), 1965, pp. 39-46.

²⁶ J. Mellaart, op. cit. (Note 21), 1965, pp. 57-62.

²⁷ C.F.Q. Schaeffer, 'Les fondements pré- et proto-historiques de la Syrie, du néolithique précéramique au bronze ancien', *Syria*, 33, 1961, pp. 7-22.

²⁸ R.L. and L.S. Braidwood, *Excavations in the Plain of Antioch*, University of Chicago Oriental Publications, 56, Chicago, 1960.

²⁹ The geological and physical geographical survey of Asia Minor is given after Fischer op. cit. (Note 1), 1971, pp. 302-18, and Birot and Dresch op. cit. (Note 1), 1956, pp. 132-56.

³⁰ H.L. Beug, 'Contributions to the post-glacial vegetational history of Northern Turkey', *Revue paléobotanique et palinologique*, 2, 1967.

[31] van Zeist op. cit. (Note 3), 1969, p.43.

[32] H.R. Cohen, 'The palaeoecology of south central Anatolia at the end of the Pleistocene and the beginning of the Holocene', *Anatolian Studies*, 20, 1970, pp. 119-38.

[33] Zohary, op. cit. (Note 5), 1969, pp. 47-66.

[34] E.J. Bostanci, 'Research on the Mediterranean coast of Anatolia: A new palaeolithic site at Beldibi near Antalya', *Anatolia*, 4, 1959, pp. 129-78.

[35] J. Mellaart, 'Excavations at Hacilar, fourth preliminary report', *Anatolian Studies*, 11, 1960, pp. 39-75; J. Mellaart, 'Early cultures of the Southern Anatolian Plateau', *Anatolian Studies*, 11, 1961, pp. 159-84.

[36] J. Mellaart, '*Çatal Hüyük: A neolithic town in Anatolia*', London, 1967.

Chapter 3

SOUTH-EASTERN EUROPE

Greece

Geologists[1] distinguish three structural zones within peninsular Greece: (1) occidental Greece; (2) south-east Greece; and (3) the Peloponnese. In occidental Greece the main structural features are regular chains of folded mountains. Synclinal structures coincide with the main river valleys and lake depressions. So-called Red Beds, alluvial and fan deposits, formed in the period of intensive alluvial activity in the Upper Pleistocene period, developed in the valleys of the Pindhos Mountains. There is good reason to believe that the level of the rivers and lakes in central Greece during the last glacial period was much higher than it is today. It has been discovered that some 20,000 years ago the level of Lake Ioannina was at least 3.2 m. higher than it is now and that the Mediterranean at that time was some 90 m. below its present level. In south-east Greece the most elevated areas coincide with outcrops of crystalline basement. The elevated areas are separated by large depressions which coincide with important tectonic faults. In Quaternary times these depressions were filled with large lakes. At least four terraces of such lakes were found inside the Thessalian depression.[2] The drying up of these lakes occurred during the Riss-Würm interglacial period or during the Würm ice age. But even in Neolithic times the level of the lakes in the depression was much higher than it is now: Lake Karla was 20 m. above its present level. The complicated structure of the Peloponnese is mainly caused by the superimposition of Ionian and Pindus series rocks and by a combination of folded and fault structures.

In a biogeographical sense the Greek peninsula corresponds to two bioclimatic regions. The first region, the Mediterranean, is subdivided into two sub-regions: one of evergreen Mediterranean forests in low-lying valleys (annual temperatures +15 −18°C, annual rainfall 700-1900 mm., mostly in winter) and one of semi-arid open woodland in mountainous areas (annual temperatures +17 −19°C, annual rainfall 350-850 mm., mostly in winter).

North-eastern Greece is included in the sub-Mediterranean

bioclimatic region of deciduous xerothermophilous forests and shrub forests. The intermontane depressions are covered with dry oak forests (annual temperature 9.5-12°C, annual rainfall 500-800 mm., with a summer drought of up to two months).

New palaeobotanic evidence throws light on the vegetational history of Greece. Very interesting data were secured as a result of the pollen analytical investigation of a deep peat bog, Tenagi Philippon, on the plain of Drama in Greek Macedonia.[3] It was shown that during the period corresponding to the maximum advance of the Last Glaciation, this area was covered by treeless vegetation with isolated patches of pine forests. Some time after 11,200 B.P. the appearance of oak and lime was registered. Some time after 10,000 B.P. open mixed oak forests were established in the area. Similar evidence was recorded in the Ioannina depression: treeless vegetation between 40,000 and 10,000 B.P. and the establishment of open oak forests about 10,000 years ago.[4]

Palaeolithic sites in the Greek peninsula are concentrated in the mountainous regions. A number of Upper Palaeolithic sites have been found in Epirus. One of the sites, Asprochaliko, is a rock shelter in the Louros river valley, 50 feet above the valley bottom. Upper Palaeolithic tools have been found in Red Beds, but never more than 12 m. below their surface. It is thought that Upper Palaeolithic settlements appeared towards the end of the deposition of the Red Beds. Several Upper Palaeolithic sites have been discovered in the mountains of the western Peloponnese.[5]

Important evidence has been secured as a result of excavations by an American expedition of a cave site situated in the coastland of the southern Peloponnese.[6] This cave, known as the Franchthi Cave, is situated at the west end of a high headland, 12.5 m. above the present sea level. The following layers have been identified in a preliminary report: Palaeolithic, Mesolithic, aceramic Neolithic, Early Neolithic, Middle Neolithic and more recent. The faunal list shows that most of the bones found in the Mesolithic layer were those of red deer. The subsistence pattern of the Mesolithic dwellers was largely dependent upon hunting this animal. A small proportion of bones of foxes, wild pigs and bovids (aurochs or bison) are listed. An abrupt faunal change heralds the beginning of the next phase, that of aceramic Neolithic. Bones of sheep or goats form 70-85% of the faunal remains. Pigs are fairly common, red deer is rare. The Early Neolithic layer is characterized by the appearance of pottery while the subsistence pattern remains unchanged compared with the aceramic layer.

Some radiocarbon dates have been obtained from samples taken from the Franchthi Cave. Six dates obtained from the Mesolithic layer fall within the range 9,300-8,700 B.P. A date from the Neolithic aceramic layer is 7794 ± 140 B.P.; from the Early Neolithic layer is 7704 ± 81 B.P.

Since the post-war excavations of Vl. Milojčić the aceramic

Neolithic phase has been recognized in a number of tells in the plains of Thessaly. The tells are situated in the eastern part of the plains, lying upon a Late Quaternary terrace of lacustrine origin (Fig. 14).

The economy of the Thessalian aceramic Neolithic was based on food-production. Grains of einkorn and emmer wheat, six-row barley, broomcorn millet and lentils have been found in layers attributed to the aceramic Neolithic. The bulk of the faunal remains consisted of sheep bones. There was a small proportion of pig and cattle bones. Only a few bones of wild pig and of aurochs were discovered. Shells of edible molluscs were found in great quantity.

Remains of house constructions were unearthed in the aceramic layers, some with their floors below ground level, others with beaten earth floors on the surface. The superstructures were made of wattle and daub on a frame of posts. The aceramic layer in the Argissa Magula tell has been radiocarbon dated to 8,200-8,000 B.P.[8]

In a number of the Thessalian sites, layers containing numerous pot sherds are found above the aceramic Neolithic layers. These sherds made up hand-made hemispherical bowls and globular jars

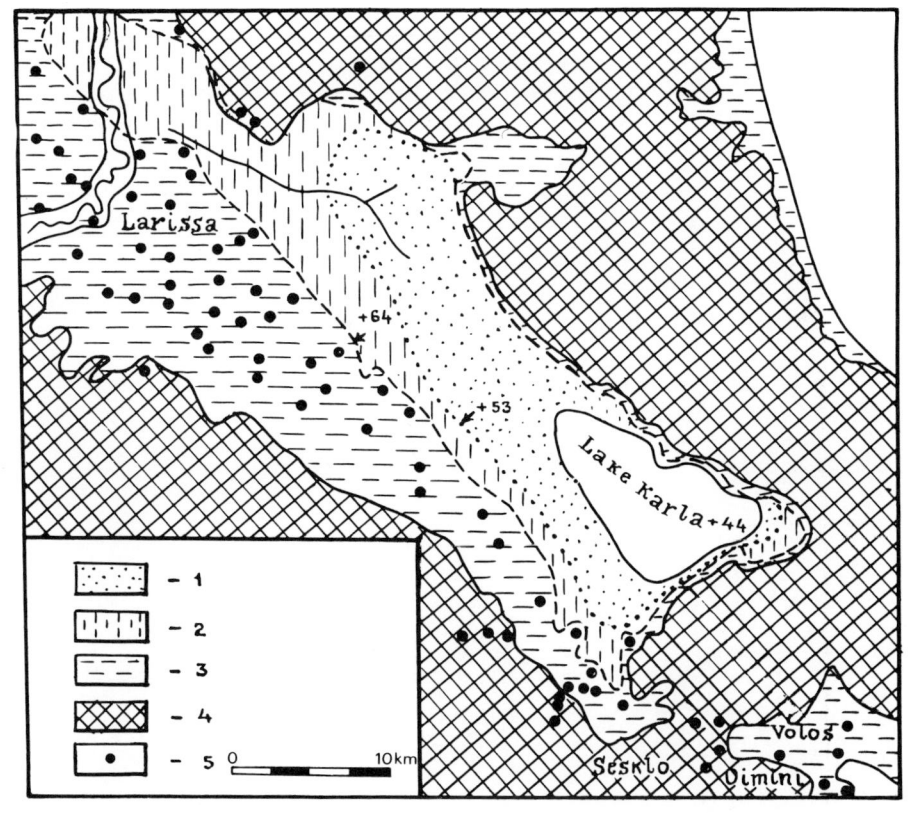

Figure 14 The Plain of Thessaly (after Milojčić, 1962; Note 3.7) 1 – terrace up to 53m; 2 – terrace up to 64m; 3 – terrace above 64m; 4 – tertiary deposits; 5 – Neolithic sites

with round or flat bases. Some had handles in the form of pierced lugs. Pots were made of well cleaned clay and were characteristically grey-black or dark brown. The appearance of the pottery did not change the economic structure of Neolithic settlement. In the numerically unimportant faunal remains found in the early pottery-bearing layer of Argissa Magula the bones of sheep, goats, cattle, wild pigs and red deer are present in equal proportions.

The next phase recognized in the Thessalian Neolithic tell sites is characterized by the appearance of painted decoration on pottery. The most common patterns were zigzags, chevrons, or hatched, cross-hatched or filled triangles and lozenges. In one case a pot was ornamented with a band displaying dancing human figures. Among the very few bones found in the layer attributed to this phase the same species as in the previous phase were present.

The next phase, known as Pre-Sesklo, manifested itself by the appearance of monochrome pottery. Two varieties are distinguishable: wares decorated in the so-called Barbotine technique and wares ornamented in the Cardium style. The Barbotine pottery is ornamented by impressions made by finger-nails and small bones so that some clay stands are in relief. The Cardium style is so named because the wares are decorated by rows of small dot impressions made by the edges of *Cardium edule* shells. But it is thought that in some cases these impressions were obtained by using a comb-like instrument (Fig. 15). These ornamentations were made on bowls and small jars with pointed or flat bases. There is an undoubted similarity

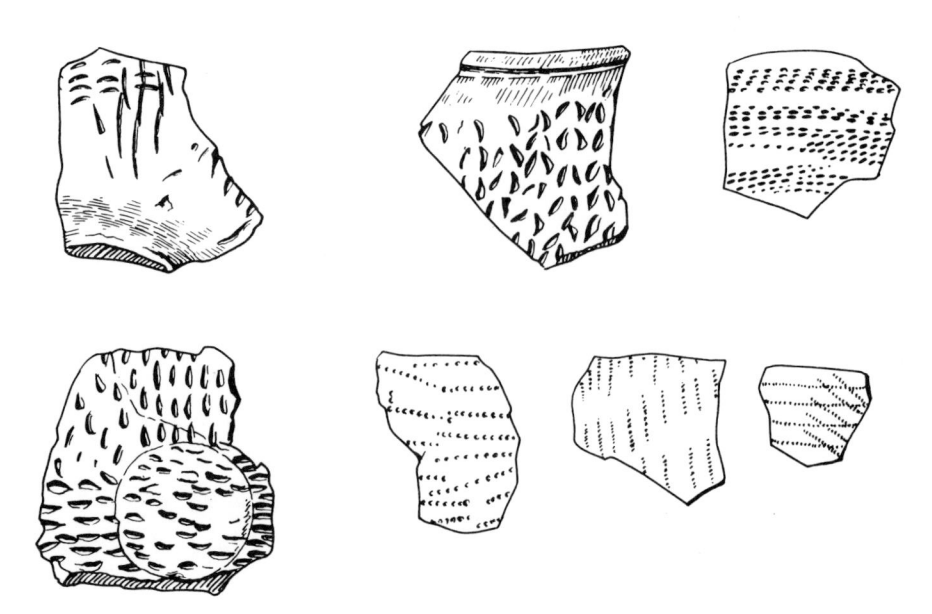

Figure 15 Ornamentations of the Vorsesklo pottery (after Milojčić, 1962; Note 3.7)

between the ornamental patterns of Barbotine and Cardium pottery and the dark-faced burnished ware of the Near East, which is unlikely to have been pure coincidence. Pottery similar to Barbotine and Cardium wares has also been found in Epirus and in the island of Levkas. This type of pottery seems to be the earliest in western Greece. No such pottery has been reported from southern Greece.

Numerous bones have been recovered from the Pre-Sesklo layers in the Tell Otzaki in Thessaly. The faunal list shows that the subsistence pattern of the Neolithic settlers of that time did not change compared with the previous Neolithic phase. The greater part of the fauna consisted of sheep and goats. The bones of cattle and pigs were found in considerably smaller numbers. A few red deer antlers and one hare bone have also been found. Radiocarbon dates obtained for the early pottery-using phases of Thessaly Neolithic vary between 8,000 and 7,400 B.P.

Important data have been secured from the excavation of Nea Nikomedeia,[9] an early Neolithic site in Greek Macedonia. The tell, 9 m. high, lies in the alluvial plain formed by the recent silting up at the mouth of the Haliakmon and Axios (or Vardar) rivers. It lies at the southern end of an important fault line that crosses the central Balkans. The site covers an area of between 110 and 220 m. The faunal remains reveal that stock-breeding was the main source of meat: 310 sheep or goat bones (a considerable part of both species belonging to immature animals) and 61 pig bones have been identified. Wild animals formed an unimportant part of the fauna. The sheep and goat group was the most important among the faunal remains. Cattle and pigs came next, in approximately equal proportions. Palaeobotanical investigations show that an open unwooded land existed at the time of the Neolithic settlement in the area.

Carbonized seeds found in the cultural layers have been identified. Emmer wheat, einkorn wheat and naked six-row barley were cultivated. Palaeobotanists think that the first and the third crops were economically the most important. Lentils have been found in great quantities, and were probably important in the diet; peas and bitter vetch were also grown. Food collecting was also of economic importance, as is shown by the presence of acorns and fruit stones.

The chipped stone industry is distinguished by the production of long thin blades. Some geometric microliths, notched blades and microburins are reported. Blade segments with a specific 'sickle gloss' are found, as well as querns and hammerstones.

The American archaeologist, Professor R.J. Rodden, who directed the excavations, distinguishes two groups in the pottery assemblage of the Nea Nikomedeia site: plain wares and decorated wares. Among the last the most interesting in our opinion is the so-called 'finger-tip and finger-nail impressed ware'. The pottery of this type was made of buff-brown, brown or greyish-brown paste. The most typical shape is an open-mouthed bowl with a small ring or flat solid-disk foot. Decoration consists of 'closely set finger-tip impressions or vertical (and horizontal) rows of finger-nail or pinched finger-nail motifs'.

A number of radiocarbon dates are available for the early Neolithic layer of the site: $8,180 \pm 150$; $7,555 \pm 90$; $7,280 \pm 75$ B.P.

Bulgaria, Romania, Yugoslavia

The central part of the Balkan peninsula[10] belongs to the Alpine folded zone. Three ancient massifs are situated here: Macedonian, Rhodopian and Pelagonian. All three massifs were formed in the Pre-Cambrian period and folded during the successive mountain-building episodes. The Dinaric folded system stretches along the Adriatic coast. The central part of the Balkans is formed of intensively folded deposits of the Mesozoic and Cenozoic age. The eastern part is a complicated folded system with a network of deep fault lines. A deep fault line, referred to as the Vardar axis, separates the Pelagonian and Macedonian massifs. A number of depressions developed north of the Rhodopian massif. In the north-eastern part of the Balkans lies a gigantic system of anticlines and synclines which includes both the southern and eastern Carpathians and the Stara Planina.

The following structural units may be distinguished within the area: (1) Stara Planina, a row of parallel mountain ranges and deep valleys; (2) intermediate fault zone, some depressions of which were covered with lake waters during the Quaternary; (3) the Rhodope mountains, the most elevated area in the central Balkans; (4) the Danube plain, which may be subdivided into (a) lower and (b) middle Danube plains; the plains are separated by a number of gorges, including the Iron Gate. The most elevated area in the whole of south-eastern Europe is the Carpathian mountain zone. Here one may distinguish: (5) the southern Carpathians or Banat, faulted folds of schists, sandstones and sandy clays, and (6) the eastern Carpathians – a composite anticline the cores of which are formed by granites and gneisses of the Pre-Cambrian age. The mountains are eroded by deep valleys.

To the east is situated (7) the Carpathian depression, filled with folded Tertiary deposits. Further to the east lie (8) the Moldavian highlands, formed of Tertiary limestones, sandstones and clays. The mean elevations here are 500-600 m. Enclosed by the Carpathians is (9) Transylvania, a hilly region with elevations of 250-500 m.; geologically it is a deep depression filled in by marine and continental deposits of the Tertiary.

The greater part of Yugoslavian territory is covered by mountains of low and medium height, a southern extension of the Alpine system. Here can be distinguished (10) the Dinaric Alps, high *Inselgebirge* separated by tectonic depressions; (11) the Dinaric Karst, uneven highlands with numerous karst-determined landforms; (12) the Dinaric maritime zone, monoclinal ridges separated by vast depressions; (13) the Albanian slope, young, intensively eroded mountains and littoral plains.

The bioclimatic structure of the Balkan peninsula is determined by the aridity, which increases towards the north-east. Only a narrow belt of the Adriatic coast is included in the Mediterranean bioclimatic region. The eastern slopes of the Dinaric Alps are included in the Sub-Mediterranean region (annual temperature 13-16°C, annual rainfall 1,350-1,250 mm., mostly in the autumn and winter). The rest of the Balkan mountainous area belongs to the European forest area. The Dinaric Alps are covered with mesophilous, deciduous, mixed forests with an admixture of firs. The mountains of southern Bulgaria are covered with forests. At elevations up to 600 m. there are mixed oak forests, at elevations between 600 and 1,700 m. these give way to beech forests. In the Rhodope mountains a belt of fir forests follows at a still greater height. The piedmont of the Carpathian mountains and the most elevated part of the Transylvanian and Moldavian highlands are covered with mixed oak forests; at elevations up to 1,000 m. beech forests prevail, while spruce and fir forests grow between 1,000 and 1,800 m. The original aspect of the vegetation in the Danube Plain has been established as meadow steppe and forest-steppe with oak groves. In the Bulgarian plains open oak forests originally existed.

New palaeobotanical evidence[11] shows that considerable parts of southern Europe during the time of the Last Glaciation had treeless vegetation. In the Dinaric Karst there existed treeless vegetation or rare pine forests. In all probability similar vegetation covered the Dinaric Alps. It has been established that treeless vegetation with a high percentage of steppe grass existed inside the intermontane plains. It is probable that a Mediterranean type of vegetation existed along the Adriatic coast during the Ice Age. It has been proved that deciduous oak forests already existed in the Dalmatian coastland 9,000 years ago. Treeless steppe-like vegetation covered the slopes of the Rhodope mountains at that time. Pine and birch forests appeared there[12] only 10,000 years ago.

New palynological data[13] show that the pine forests existed inside the Carpathian arc and in the Moldavian highlands during the last glacial period. Pine forests existed in the low belt of the southern Carpathians at least 10,000 years ago. The appearance of mixed broad-leaved forests (with a predominance of limes) is dated to about 8,000 B.P. The development of forest vegetation in the eastern Carpathians and in Moldavia probably followed the same lines.

There is some evidence that the central and northern Balkan territory supported a considerable Upper Palaeolithic population. The greater part of the known Upper Palaeolithic sites in Bulgaria are situated in the caves in the Stara Planina mountains. Open-air sites on high terraces are also known. The inventory of stone industries in these sites is characterized by a combination of Mousterian and Upper Palaeolithic tools (prismatic cores, long blades, keeled end scrapers, symmetrical points, backed knives).[14]

Nearly all the Upper Palaeolithic sites in Romania[15] have been discovered in mountain areas, in the southern and eastern Carpathians or in the Moldavian highlands. Both cave sites and open-air sites are situated on high river terraces. Towards the end of the Last Glaciation an expansion of the so-called Gravettian industry took place. Typical of this industry is a high percentage of prismatic cores, burins, backed knives and particularly of small points. The faunal evidence from the Upper Palaeolithic sites in the Bistriţa valley (in the western part of the Moldavian highlands) shows that the wild horse was the most intensively hunted animal there.

In Yugoslavia[16] nearly all the known Upper Palaeolithic sites have been discovered in caves situated in the mountains – in the Dinaric Alps, the Dinaric Karst and in the Dinaric maritime zone. The wide spread of 'Gravettian' industries took place towards the end of the Last Glaciation. Two existing radiocarbon dates make it possible to suggest that this extension took place between 18,000 and 12,000 B.P. Unfortunately we know practically nothing about the economy of the Upper Palaeolithic settlers.

A great number of Mesolithic sites have been discovered in the Balkan area. Three types of Mesolithic sites are known in Romania.[17] The first type (Swiderian) is characterized by the presence of tanged arrowheads, points and geometric microliths. Sites of this type have been found upon plateaux in the eastern Carpathians. A feature of the second type of Mesolithic site ('Azilo-Romanelli') is the presence of so-called Azilian points. A site of this type – the Cuina Turcului cave – has been found in the Iron Gate area of the southern Carpathians.[18] The inhabitants of the site hunted elk, roe deer, bison, bear, aurochs, wild goat and wild pig. The slopes of the mountains were heavily forested by pine and mixed oak woods. Radiocarbon dates of the two-layer site are 11,000-8,000 B.P. The third type of Mesolithic site (Tardenoisian) is characterized by the high percentage of geometric microliths in its inventory. These sites were found in Transylvania and in the Moldavian highlands where they are situated mostly on high river banks. Microlithic tools predominate in the tool-kit of the La Adam cave site in the mountains of Dobrugea, south of the Danube delta. Bones of wild goats and wild sheep have been found in association with the stone industry.[19]

In Yugoslavia an area of intensive Mesolithic habitation was concentrated along the Adriatic coast. A number of caves in the coastland were inhabited continuously from Upper Palaeolithic times. One example is Crvena Stena cave in the Montenegro coastal area.[20] A high percentage of geometric tools is typical of the Adriatic coastal Mesolithic. The subsistence pattern was determined by the hunting of forest animals: red deer, roe deer, wild pig, ibex and wolves. The collection of edible marine molluscs provided an important source of food.

After the appearance of Neolithic sites in the central Balkans, the settlement pattern changes abruptly. Neolithic sites were concentrated mostly in the intermontane plains and in the Danube valley. The oldest known Neolithic sites in Bulgaria are situated within a depression of the intermediate fault zones, namely in the Thracian depression. Open woodland has been the dominant type of vegetation here since the early Holocene. The Thracian depression was covered with lake waters in Quaternary times. Lacustrine terraces are visible on the flanks of the depression. At lower levels are situated the Maritsa river terraces. Nowadays Thrace is one of the most important agricultural regions of Bulgaria.

The Karanovo tell site lies[21] in the northern part of the depression. The depth of the cultural deposits here reaches 12.4 m., and the overall area is 1,700 sq.m. Seven phases, each including several construction levels, have been identified. The earliest Neolithic settlements in Thrace are usually referred to as Karanovo I. The layers belonging to this phase have been discovered at a number of sites (Karanovo itself, Tell Azmak and others).

Unfortunately, up to now it has been impossible to describe fully the economic structure of early Neolithic settlements in the area. Agriculture was of primary importance. Grains and impressions of wheat (emmer, einkorn) have been identified. No remains of barley have been found.[22] No faunal analysis is available, but there is no doubt about the economic importance of stock-breeding. The location of the site at Karanovo suggests that hunting did not play any major role in the economy.

Remains of houses have been found on the early Neolithic sites. These were small rectangular dwellings, averaging 8 m. long and 4 m. wide. They probably consisted of a framework of wooden posts on which thick walls of clay and chaff were built.

The stone industry found in the early Neolithic layers consists mostly of thin blades. Many blades have a specific gloss. Probably they were slotted compositely into hafts and were used for cutting grass, reeds or cultivated wheat.[23]

Three varieties of pottery have been found in the early Neolithic layers. The first variety consists of hemispherical, spherical or tulip-shaped bowls made of fine, well-fired paste. The surface is covered with a red or white slip and painted red, black or white. Geometric patterns (spirals, triangles, wavy lines) prevail. The second variety is made of fine well-fired paste of grey or buff colour and covered with a slip of the same clay. The pottery is usually undecorated. The shapes are the same as in the previous variety. The third variety (monochrome pottery) is made of thick, coarse chaff-tempered paste, poorly fired, of a buff or orange colour. The usual shapes are rounded or globular pots. The pottery is ornamented by finger-nail impressions or by patterns made by running the fingers over the surface while it was still wet (Barbotine technique). Some vessels were decorated with incised lines (cannelures) forming parallel lines and zigzag patterns.

The earliest Neolithic sites in Romania are referred to as belonging to the Criş culture.[24] The Criş sites are concentrated in three regions in Romania: the lower Danube Plain (Oltenia and Muntenia), Transylvania and the Moldavian highlands. The sites in the Danube plain are usually situated on low terraces. In Transylvania the sites are connected with the river systems: they are mostly situated either on low terraces or on flood-plains.

According to existing evidence the economy of the Criş sites was based on agriculture and stock-breeding. In at least one case, impressions of einkorn grains have been found on Criş pottery. In most known cases cattle predominated in the faunal remains of the Criş sites of the Danube plain and in Transylvania. It is noteworthy that in the Criş sites situated in the Moldavian highlands the number of wild animal remains, mostly red deer, increases.[25]

Remains of both rectangular and round dwellings have been found in Romanian Early Neolithic sites. The stone inventory is fairly typical of Balkan Neolithic, but in some cases the presence of geometrical microliths similar to those found in Mesolithic sites has been reported.

The multi-layered Criş site of Leţ has been intensively excavated. The pottery assemblage of the site is of particular importance for our study. The Romanian archaeologist E. Zaharia[26] distinguishes two varieties of pottery here: the fine (decorated and undecorated) and the coarse. The most characteristic shapes of the first variety are bowls on tall pedestals and with cylindric collars. Globular pots are typical of the second variety. The coarse pottery which makes up the bulk of the wares found in the lower level of the Leţ site is decorated in the Barbotine technique, by stamped impressions or by incised lines. Barbotine ornamentation is either applied without any visible pattern, or forms waved lines. Stamped impressions either cover the whole surface of a vessel or form vertical or horizontal lines. Incised lines form either zigzag or network patterns (Fig. 16). Radiocarbon dates of the Criş-Körös sites, rather few in number, lie in the range 6,700-6,200 B.P.

Early Neolithic settlements on Yugoslav territory are represented by the sites usually included in the Starčevo culture, and by the sites of the Adriatic coast usually included in the impressed-pottery Neolithic. Sites belonging to the Starčevo group may be easily divided into sites situated in the mountain zone and those lying on the plain. The sites of the mountain zone are often situated within geomorphological units connected with the so-called Vardar zone, a fault line crossing the central part of the Balkan peninsula. The valley could have provided a convenient route linking the plains of Greece and south Bulgaria with the middle Danube plain and with the Adriatic coast.

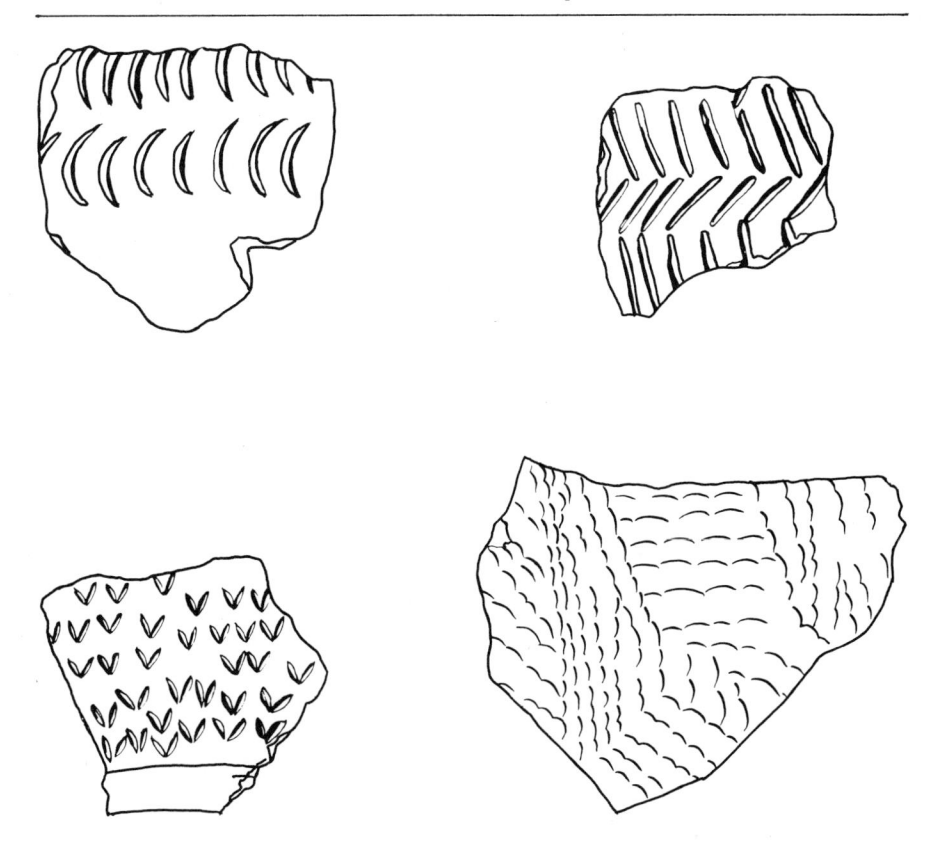

Figure 16 Ornamentations of the pottery from the site of Leţ (after Zaharia, 1962; Note 3.26)

Inside the Begalnitsa valley and the Ovče Polje depression, filled with lacustrine sediments of the Tertiary age, an important group of Early Neolithic sites has been discovered. This group is known as Anzabegovo-Vršnik.[27] In the pottery assemblages belonging to the first phase the most common types of pottery are light monochrome and painted white-on-red vessels. There are few specimens of coarse Barbotine and impressed pottery. The number of examples of coarse pottery increases considerably in the assemblage of the second phase. Palaeobotanic analysis shows that wheat (emmer and einkorn) was cultivated in the area.

The Early Neolithic sites of Serbia and Vojvodina are situated in most cases on the upper terraces of river valleys and on the edges of plateaux. Stable food-production was the basis of the economy of these sites. Existing osteological evidence, shows that cattle were more important here than sheep, goats and pigs.

Several phases are distinguishable in the evolution of local pottery assemblages. In the opinion of some Yugoslav archaeologists coarse monochrome pottery was typical of the earliest phase. Painted pottery only made its appearance during the next phase. Existing radiocarbon dates fall within the range 7,300-6,600 B.P.

Yugoslav archaeologists regard the Early Neolithic sites of the Adriatic coastland as belonging to an independent tradition.[28] The pottery of these sites is referred to as Cardium-impressed ware. It consists of hemispherical bowls with flat or concave bases decorated with impressions of trimmed or untrimmed shells, often of *Cardium edule*. These impressions either cover the surface of the vessels evenly or form horizontal rows. Incised lines often form a part of the simple patterns (Fig. 17).

It has been noted that the layers with Cardium pottery very often lie on top of Mesolithic layers in the same caves, for example at Crvena Stena and Jamina Sredi. It has also been noted that the introduction of pottery did not change the Mesolithic subsistence pattern. The economy of the Adriatic coastal Neolithic was based on hunting, fishing and collecting of edible molluscs. Even the tool-kit did not change compared with that of the Mesolithic layers; geometric microliths and flint blades are commonly found in the Neolithic layers.

Similar types of pottery are represented all along the Mediterranean coasts, in Italy, Spain and even in North Africa. The earliest radiocarbon dates belong to the 6th millennium B.C., the latest to the 4th millennium.[29] Comparison of pottery shapes and of ornamental patterns shows that the Cardium-impressed ware has much in common with the Pre-Sesklo pottery in Thessaly and with the dark-faced burnished ware of the Near East.

Important sites have been excavated in the Danube valley, near the Iron Gate. The most interesting site is Lepenski Vir.[30] The site is situated on a narrow bank of the Danube, between the river and a steep limestone slope. Three phases in the evolution of the material culture have been distinguished. The first two are wholly aceramic and contain evidence of a hunting and fishing economy. In the faunal remains red deer predominate (70-80%); then follow aurochs and wild pig. The stone inventory is microlithic in character. It is assumed that fishing (especially of a large species of carp) was economically very important.

Remains of numerous dwellings have been found in Lepenski Vir. Five habitation levels belonged to the first phase only. Each level consisted of about 20 dwellings uniformly constructed, trapezoidal in plan, with the wide ends towards the river. The size of the dwellings varied between 5.5 and 30 sq.m. Palaeobotanical analyses have shown that pine and birch forests covered the Danube slopes when aceramic settlements existed at the Iron Gate. Numerous radiocarbon dates have established that Lepenski Vir 1 was occupied between 7,500 and 6,600 B.P.

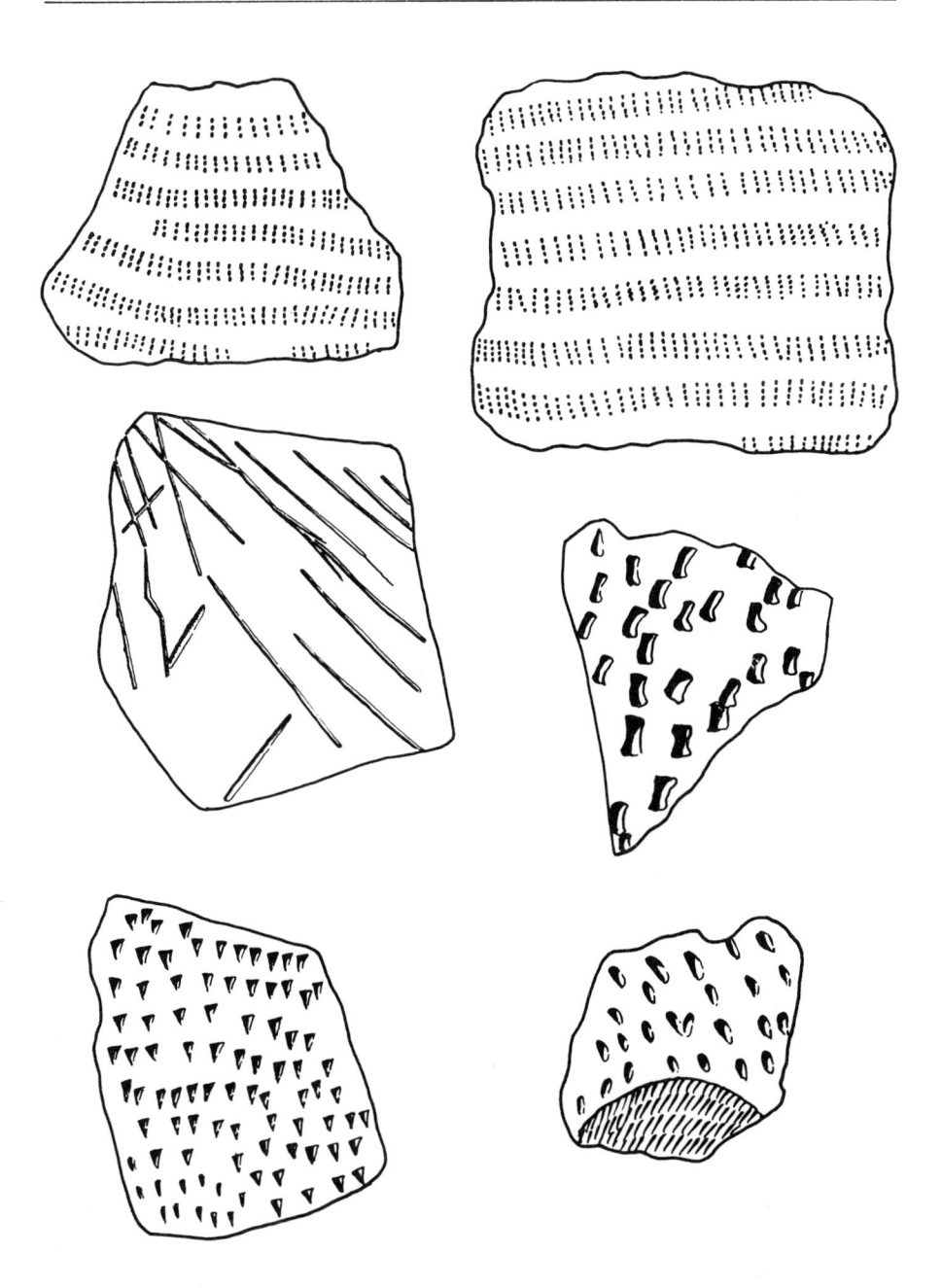

Figure 17 Ornamentations of the Cardium impressed ware from the Crvena Stena cave (after Benac, 1957; Note 3.20)

Summary

Taking south-eastern Europe as a whole, the following natural areas can be distinguished: (1) the coastlands of the Adriatic and Aegean Seas. (2) Mountainous regions: (a) the Ionian massif; (b) the mountains of eastern Greece and of the Peloponnese; (c) Thrace; (d) the Stara Planina; (e) the Rhodope mountains; (f) the southern Carpathians; (g) the eastern Carpathians; (h) Dobrogea; (i) the Dinaric Alps. (3) Plains and highlands: (a) the depressions and plains of central and north-eastern Greece; (b) the depressions and plains of south-western and central Bulgaria; (c) the central Danubian plain; (d) the lower Danubian plain; (e) Transylvania; (f) the Moldavian highlands.

20,000-10,000 B.P.

According to palaeobotanical evidence, a treeless steppe-like vegetation prevailed at this time in the depressions and plains of the Balkans; broad-leaved forests were confined to the coastland. In the Dinaric Alps sparse pine forests existed. In the lower belts of the southern and eastern Carpathians, in Transylvania and in considerable parts of the Moldavian highlands there were dense pine forests. In all probability pine forests also spread over the Stara Planina and the Rhodopes. Considerable areas of the lowlands in Greece and Bulgaria were covered by lakes.

The Upper Palaeolithic population was concentrated mostly in the mountainous regions – the Ionic massif, the Stara Planina, the southern and eastern Carpathians, and the Moldavian highlands – though settlements are also found in the coastal area. In most cases the settlements were in caves. Open-air sites were situated on the upper terraces of rivers and lakes. The subsistence pattern of the Upper Palaeolithic population was based entirely on the hunting of forest and steppe animals, on fishing and on food collecting. In this sense, the mountain regions containing the Upper Palaeolithic population may be regarded as a single natural economic zone (Fig. 18).

10,000-8,000 B.P.

The important change in the landscape that occurred c. 10,000 years ago considerably changed the face of south-east Europe. About that time a forest-type vegetation began spreading across the plains of Bulgaria and Greece. During this time numerous groups of people using Mesolithic tools were spread over south-eastern Europe. The settlement pattern of the Mesolithic population was mostly the same as that of the Upper Palaeolithic: the greater part of the Mesolithic

South-Eastern Europe

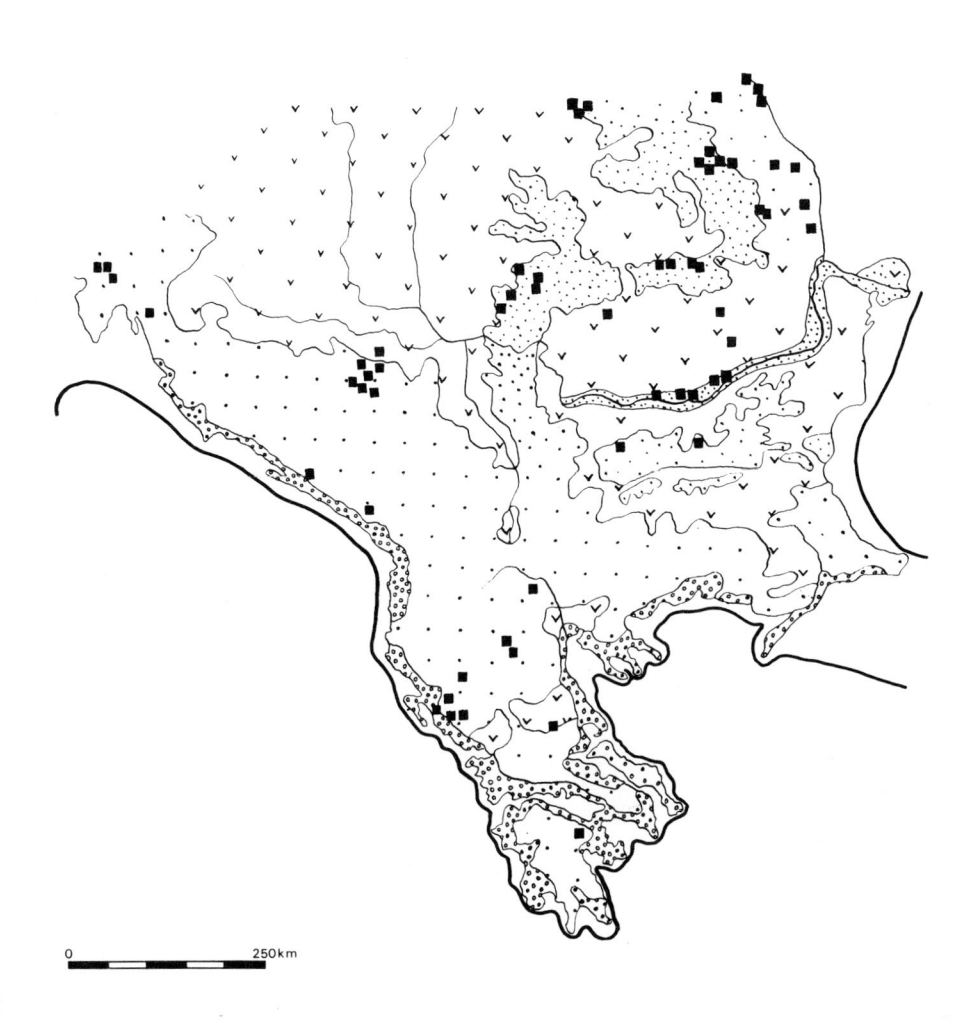

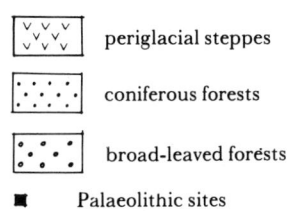

ᵛᵛᵛ	periglacial steppes
∴	coniferous forests
∴	broad-leaved forests
■	Palaeolithic sites

Figure 18 South-eastern Europe 20,000-10,000 B.P.

74   *Ecology and Economy in Neolithic Eastern Europe*

	steppes
	coniferous forests
	broad-leaved forests
▲	Mesolithic sites

Figure 19 South-eastern Europe 10,000-8,000 B.P.

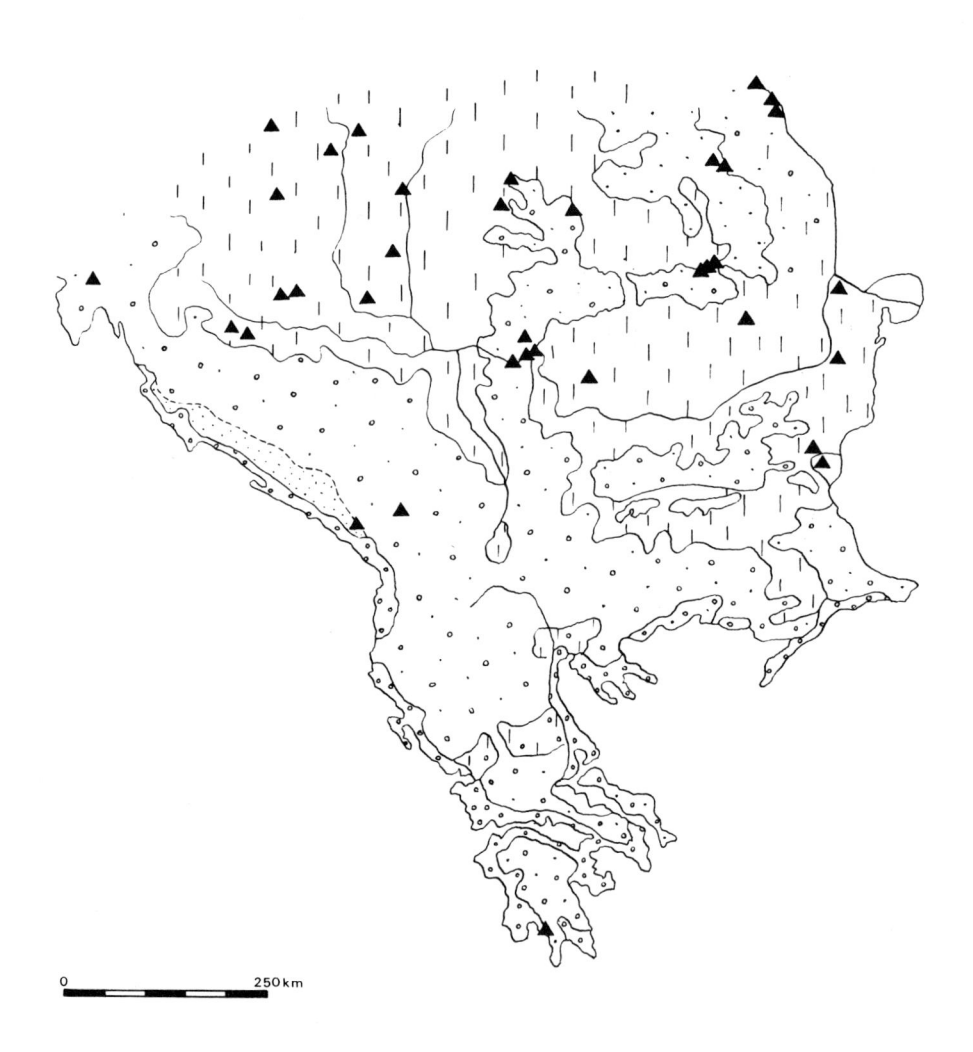

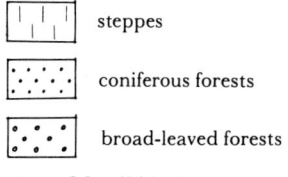

population was concentrated in the mountains and on the coastland. By the end of the Mesolithic period settlements had appeared on the plains, particularly in the middle and lower Danubian valley. The number of open-air sites increased.

The subsistence pattern of the Mesolithic groups was based on the hunting of forest animals (red deer, roe dear, aurochs, wild pig), and on intensive fishing and gathering. In this sense the area of Mesolithic settlement may be regarded as a single natural economic zone. Several sub-zones may be distinguished, according to distinctions in hunting patterns and in tool-kits. The Mesolithic groups spread over the southern and eastern Carpathians are characterized by the use of projectile points; whereas those Mesolithic groups living in the coastal area and in the plains used large numbers of geometric microliths (Fig. 19).

8,000-6,000 B.P.

This time-span is characterized by the spread in some areas of south-eastern Europe of settlements with a stable food-producing economy. The settlements with a farming economy were concentrated predominantly in the plains: the areas most intensively settled by farming communities were the plains of Thessaly and of Thrace, Macedonia, the Danube plains and the Moldavian highlands. In these areas intensive evolution of structures based on a food-producing economy took place.

The spread of farming economy in the plain of Thessaly occurred some 8,200-8,000 years ago. About a thousand years later, 7,200-7,000, food-producing communities appeared on the plains of southern Bulgaria, Macedonia and in the Danubian plains. The existence of aceramic Neolithic has been stratigraphically proved in two areas of Greece: in the tell sites of Thessaly and in the Franchthi cave. Judging from existing radiocarbon dates the period of aceramic Neolithic in the Balkans was of comparatively short duration, from 8,200 to 7,500 B.P.

The appearance of food-producing communities in the plains and depressions of the Balkan peninsula must be linked with the overflow of part of the surplus population from the earliest agricultural areas in the Near East. The independent appearance of agriculture and stock-breeding is improbable. The existing evidence of radiocarbon dates does not contradict this supposition: radiocarbon dates of aceramic Neolithic sites in the Near East lie within the period c. 11,000-8,000 B.P. It is also possible that after the initial spread of farming communities, a food-producing economy was adopted by some of the local Mesolithic groups.

In south-eastern Europe, during the period of time under discussion, there existed at least three natural economic zones: (1) a zone of food-producing economy covering the plains and depressions

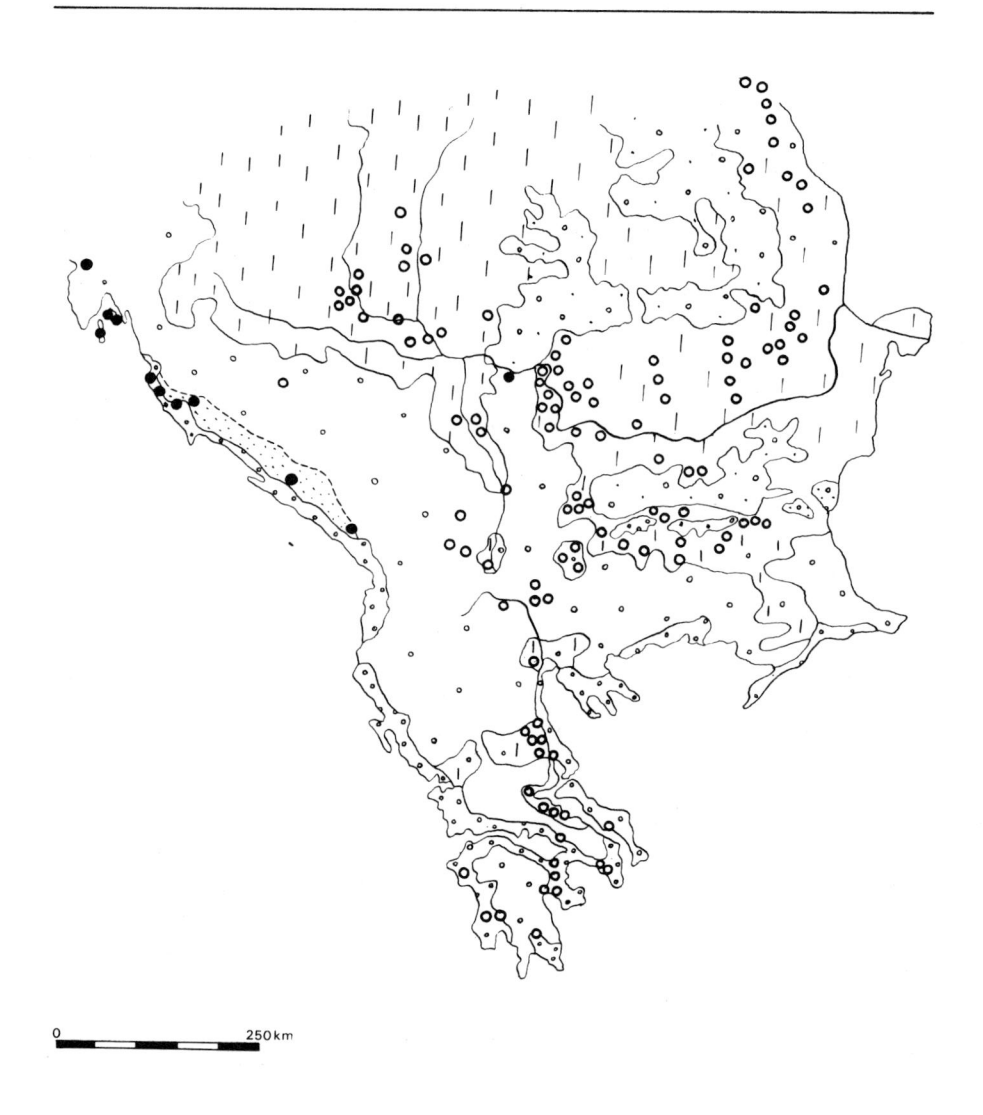

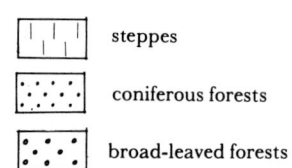

76 *Ecology and Economy in Neolithic Eastern Europe*

	steppes
	coniferous forests
	broad-leaved forests
●	Neolithic hunting/fishing sites
○	Neolithic agricultural sites

Figure 20 South-eastern Europe 8,000-6,000 B.P.

of Greece, Bulgaria and the middle and lower Danube; (2) a zone of mixing food-producing/food-appropriating economy in the Moldavian highlands and in Dobrugea; (3) a zone of food-appropriating economy in the Adriatic coastland and in the southern Carpathians. Neolithic settlements in the depressions and plains of Greece and Bulgaria were characterized by a stable food-producing economy based on agriculture (wheat, barley) and on stock-breeding (with a predominance of ovicaprids). The settlements were of a tell type and reached considerable size (100-200 persons). Stock-breeding in the lower Danubian plain was characterized by the predominance of cattle. The settlements of the middle Danube plain are characterized by the dominance of ovicaprids in the domestic animals and by the greater economic importance of hunting. The economic significance of hunting is still greater in the settlements situated in the Moldavian highlands and in Dobrugea. In both these regions the settlements were of much smaller size than those in Greece and southern Bulgaria. No tell sites are known.

Pottery manufacture in south-eastern Europe began some 7,500-7,200 years ago. Several cultural zones may be identified on the basis of similarities in ornamental patterns. In the pottery assemblages of the Early Neolithic settlements of the Balkans so-called monochrome pottery is widely represented. This pottery is ornamented with impressions of shells, combs, and finger nails, or with finger pinches and incised lines. These elements form the following patterns: horizontal rows, vertical rows, wavy lines, zigzags, networks. The pottery thus decorated is found in the Early Neolithic settlements in the depressions of central and north-eastern Greece and of southern Bulgaria, in the middle and lower Danubian plains, in Transylvania, in Dobrugea, in the Moldavian highlands and along the Adriatic coast. All the sites containing this pottery are regarded here as belonging to a single cultural zone.

Other cultural zones in the area are represented by the assemblages of painted pottery in the same territory and in southern Greece.

In the tell sites of Thessaly the monochrome Barbotine impressed pottery is situated stratigraphically above the Early Neolithic and the Proto-Sesklo pottery assemblages and below the painted Sesklo pottery. In the tell sites of Greek Macedonia and southern Bulgaria the monochrome pottery seems to be situated in the same layers as the painted pottery. In the sites of the middle Danube plains the monochrome pottery is situated below the painted pottery. At the site of Leţ in Romania the quantity of monochrome pottery diminishes and that of painted pottery increases in the upper layer. Monochrome Cardium-impressed ware is exclusively represented in the coastal sites of the Adriatic Sea. In general, it seems probable that the spread of painted pottery in the Balkan area occurred at a later stage than the spread of monochrome pottery.

There is a striking similarity between the ornamentation of the monochrome Cardium-impressed pottery of the Balkan sites, on the one hand, and that of the dark-faced burnished ware in the Near East on the other. This similarity cannot be accidental. In my view it reflects the migration of part of the surplus population from the initial agricultural centres in the Near East. The migrating population acquired economic strategies that could guarantee an optimal yield under local conditions. These optimum strategies were agriculture and the breeding of ovicaprids in the depressions of Greece and Bulgaria; agriculture and cattle-breeding in the lower Danubian plain and in Transylvania; agriculture, stock-breeding, hunting and fishing in the valleys of the Moldavian highlands and in Dobrugea; hunting, fishing and food gathering in the forested valleys of the southern Carpathians and along the Adriatic coast.

Existing radiocarbon dates do not contradict the suggested scheme. The dates of Near Eastern sites containing an initial assemblage of dark-faced burnished ware lie in the time span of 8,500-7,000 B.P. and the Early Neolithic sites in the Balkan area containing monochrome pottery are dated 7,500-6,500 B.P. (Fig. 20).

NOTES

[1] The geological and geographical survey of Greece is based on P. Birot, J. Dresch, *Le Mediterranée et le Moyen Orient*, 2, Paris, 1956, pp. 28-44, 57-62, and M.V. Muratov, *Tektonika i istoriya razvitiya al'piyskoi geosinklinalnoi oblasti na yugye yevropeiskoi časti SSSR i sopredelnykh stran*, Tektonika SSSR, 2, Moscow-Leningrad, 1949.

[2] D. Jung, H. Schneider, 'Beiträge zur Quartärgeologie Ostthessaliens', *in* Vl. Milojcič (ed.) *Die deutsche Ausgrabungen auf der Argissa Magula in Thessalien I*, Beiträge zur Ur- und Frühgeschichtliche Archäologie des Mitterlmeer-Kulturraumes, 2, Bonn, 1962.

[3] T.A. Wijmstra, 'Palynology of northern Greece', *Acta Botanica Neerlandica*, 18, 4, 1969, pp. 511-27.

[4] E.S. Higgs, C. Vita Finzi, 'The climate, environment and industries of Stone Age Greece', Part II, *P.P.S.* n.s., 32, 1966, pp. 1-29.

[5] E.S. Higgs, C. Vita-Finzi, D.R. Harris, A.E. Fagg, 'The climate, environment and industries of Stone Age Greece', Part III, *P.P.S.* n.s., 33, 1967, pp. 1-30.

[6] T.W. Jacobsen, 'Excavations at Porto Cheli and vicinity, preliminary report II: The Franchthi cave, 1967-68', *Hesperia*, 38 (3), 1969, pp. 343-81.

[7] Vl. Milojčić, 'Die Hauptergebnisse der deutschen Ausgrabungen in Thessalien 1953-1958', *Jahrbuch des Römisch-Germanischen Zeutralmuseums*, 6, Mainz, 1959, pp. 1-33; Milojčić, 'Präkeramisches Neolithikum auf der Balkanhalbinsel', *Germania*, 38, 3/4, 1960, pp. 320-35; Milojčić, op. cit. (Note 1), 1962; M. Hopf, 'Berich über die Untersuchungen von Samen und Holzresten aus der präkeramischen bis mittelbronzezeitlichen Schichten, *in* Milojčić op. cit. (Note 1), 1962, pp. 101-12; J. Boessneck, 'Zu den Tierknochen aus neolithischen Siedlungen Thessaliens', *Berichte der Römisch-Germanischen Komission*, 36, 1955 (1956), pp. 1-51; Boessneck, 'Die Tierreste aus der Argissa-Magula vom Präkeramischen Neolithikum bis zur mittleren Bronzezeit', *in* Milojčić, op. cit. (Note 1), 1962, pp. 27-100.

[8] Radiocarbon determinations of collagen, extracted from bones of domesticated animals (sheep, dog, cattle, pig) originating from aceramic layers of Argissa-Magula revealed dendrochronologically calibrated dates: 7200-7000 B.P. (Protsch and

Berger; *Science*, 179, pp. 235-9), which roughly correspond to an uncalibrated age of 8200-8000 B.P. It should be noted that collagen based radiocarbon dates are often regarded as unreliable (see comment by S. Bökönyi, R. Braidwood and Ch. Reed in *Science*, 182, pp. 1161). The aceramic layer was dated at Tell Sesklo: 7483 ± 72; 7755 ± 97 and 7300 ± 93 B.P. Two dates were obtained from Early Neolithic layers of the same site: 7611 ± 83 and 7427 ± 78 B.P. (B. Lawn: *Radiocarbon*, 15, 1973, pp. 369-370).

[9] R. Rodden, 'Excavation at the early neolithic site at Nea Nikomedeia, Greek Macedonia', *P.P.S.* n.s., 26, 1962, pp. 267-88.

[10] The geological and geographical description of the Balkan peninsula is based on Birot and Dresch, op. cit. (Note 1), 1956, pp. 3-28; 57-62; I.P. Gerasimov, Ž.S. Glebov, (eds.), *Geografiya na Blgaria*, Sofia, 1966; Muratov, op. cit. (Note 1), 1949.

[11] A. Šerclj, *Würmska vegetacija in klima v Slovenje*, Ljubljana, 1970; H.J. Beug, 'On the forest history of the Dalmatian coast', *Revue paléobotanique et palynologique*, 2, 1967, pp. 271-9.

[12] Ye. D. Božilova, *Ksnolyednikova i syedlyednikova istoriya na rastitelnostta v Rila Planina*, Sofia, 1972.

[13] E. Pop, *Mlaştinile de turba din Republica Populara Romîna*, Bucharest, 1960; E. Pop, N. Boşcaiu, V. Lupşa, 'Analisa sporopolinaca a sedimentelor de la Cuina Turcului-Dubovica', *Studii şi cercetări de istorie veche*, 21, I, 1970, pp. 31-34; N. Boşcaiu, 'L'évolution postwürmienne de la végétation du défilé du Danube', *3rd International Palynological Conference*, Novosibirsk, 1971; N. Boşcaiu, V. Lupşa, V. Boroneaţ, 'Analisa sporo-polinica a sedimentelor din pestera lui Climente (Defileul Dunarii)', *Studii si cercetări de biologie, Seria botanica*, 23, 5, 1971, pp. 401-3.

[14] P.I. Boriskovsky, 'Očrerki po paleolitu central'noi i yugovostocnoi Evropy', Part I, *S.A.*, XXVII, 1957, pp. 29-70, and Part II. *S.A.*, XXIX, 1959, pp. 5-41; G. Georgiev, 'Die Entwicklung der älteren prähistorischen Kulturen Südbulgariens', *in* V.I. Georgiev (ed.) *Ethnogenèse des peuples balkaniques, Studia Balkanica*, 5, Sofia, 1965, pp. 21-35.

[15] C.S. Nicolaescu-Plopşor, 'Le paléolithique dans la R.P. Roumanie à la lumière des dernières recherches,' *Dacia*, n.s. I, 1957, pp. 41-60; A. Păunescu, *Evoluţia uneltelor şi armelor de piatră cioplită descoperite pe teritoriul Românei*, Bucharest, 1970.

[16] M. Malez, F. Osole, 'Paléolithique et mésolithique', *in* G. Novak (ed.) *Epoque préhistorique et protohistorique en Yougoslavie: Recherches et resultats*, Beograd, 1971, pp. 245-67; M. Brodar, 'Olschewien; die Anfangsstufe des Jungpaläolithikums in Mitteleuropa', *Actes du VIIIe Congrès des sciences pré- et protohistoriques*, I, Beograd, 1971, pp. 43-52.

[17] A. Păunescu, op. cit. (Note 15), 1970.

[18] A. Păunescu, 'Epipaleoliticul de la Cuina Turcului-Dubovica', *Studii şi cercetări de istorie veche*, 21, I, 1970, pp. 3-48; A. Bolomey, 'Citeva observatii asupra faunei de mammifere din straturile romanello-aziliene de la Cuina Turcului', *Studii şi cercetări de istorie veche*, 21, I, 1970, pp. 37-9.

[19] Vl. Dumitrescu, 'Le début du néolithique en Roumanie', *Actes du VIIIe Congrès International des sciences pré-et protohistoriques*, 1, Beograd 1971, pp. 85-96.

[20] A. Benac, 'Crvena Stena – 1955 (I-IV stratum)', *Glaznik Zemaljskog muzeja u Sarajevu*, ns., XII, 1957, pp. 15-50.

[21] G. Georgiev, 'The Azmak mound in southern Bulgaria', *Antiquity*, 39, 1965, pp. 6-8; Georgiev, 'Kulturgruppen der Jungstein- und Kupferzeit in der Ebene von Thrazien (Südbulgarien)', *in* J. Böhm and S. de Laet (eds.) *L'Europe à la fin de l'Âge de la Pierre*, Prague, 1961, pp. 45-100.

[22] J.M. Renfrew, *Palaeoethnobotany*, London, 1973, p. 203.

[23] R. Tringham, *Hunters, fishers and farmers of Eastern Europe 6000-3000 B.C.*, London, 1971, pp. 68-114.

[24] E. Comşa, 'La civilisation de Criş dans le territoire de la R.P. Roumanie', *Acta Archeologica, Carpatica*, 1, 2, 1960, pp. 173-90; D. Berciu, *Contributii la probleme neoliticului in Rominia in lumina noilor cercetari*, Bucharest, 1961; R. Tringham, op. cit. (Note 23) 1971, pp. 95-6.

[25] O. Necrasov, 'Sur les restes des faunes subfossiles datant de la culture Starčevo-Criş et le problème de la domestication' – *Analele Stiintifice ale Universitaţii din Jaşi*, n.s. 11, 10, 1964, pp. 167-81.

[26] E. Zaharia, 'Considération sur la civilisation de Criş à la lumière des sondages de Let,' *Dacia*, n.s. VI, 1962, pp. 5-51.

[27] M. Garašanin, 'Genetische und chronologische Probleme der frühkeramischen Neolithikums auf dem mittleten Balkan', *Actes du VIIIe Congrès international des sciences pré et protohistoriques*, 1, Beograd, 1971, pp. 73-84. A series of C14 dates was obtained for Anzabegovo recently. Phase Ia was dated to 7,300-7,100 B.P., phase Ib to 7,140-7,000 B.P., phase II to 7,000-6,700 B.P.: C.W. Ferguson, M. Gimbutas, H.E. Suess, 'Historical dates for neolithic sites of southeast Europe', *Science*, 191, 1976.

[28] A. Benac, 'Le néolithique ancien dans les Balkans du nord-ouest et ses relations avec les régions voisines', *Actes du VIIIe Congrès international des sciences pré et protohistoriques*, I, Beograd, 1971, pp. 97-108.

[29] J. Guilaine, A. Calvet, 'Nouveaux points de la chronologie absolue pour le néolithique ancien de la Mediterranée', *L'Anthrópologie*, 74, 1-2, 1971, pp. 85-92.

[30] D. Srejović, *Lepenski Vir*, Beograd, 1969.

Chapter 4

THE SOUTH RUSSIAN PLAIN

Geological background

Crossing the national boundary of the USSR formed by the Prut river, we enter a structural zone quite different from those dealt with in the previous chapter. This is the Russian platform or plain.[1] The difference between the highest and lowest points of the Russian plain never exceeds 800 m.

In the evolution of a platform one can always distinguish two stages: the stage of the formation of the folded basement and that of the formation of sedimental cover. The formation of the folded basement of this platform ended in the Proterozoic era. Since that time the formation of sedimental deposits upon the denuded folded basement has proceded steadily. The major mountain-building cycles directly affected the character of the sedimentation. At the end of each cycle large portions of the platform were elevated and huge peneplains were formed.

The main structural units in the southern part of the Russian plain are determined by the relief of the folded basement and by the peculiarity of its evolution in the post-proterozoic time. These units are: (1) the Pontic depression; (2) the Ukrainian shield; (3) the Volyno-Podolia plate and (4) the Moldavian plate.

The Pontic depression forms part of a gigantic Alpine trough. It separates the folded chains of the Crimea and of the Carpathian mountains from the Russian platform proper. The formation of the depression began in the Cretaceous period and the most intensive downward bending took place in the Mid-Tertiary. The Proterozoic basement is broken by faults into separate blocks; it has been proved that the major river valleys of the Pontic depression follow the fault lines. Geomorphologically the depression is an accumulative plain with an altitude of from 0 to 200 m. above sea level. The plain is cut by the broad valleys of the major rivers and there are networks of ravines on the watersheds.

The fluctuations of the Black Sea coastline in the Late Quaternary era were an important factor in the evolution of the land forms in the coastal area. During the maximum stage of the Last Glaciation the sea level was much lower than it is now. According to the most reliable calculations the sea level at that time was 24-26 m. below the present one (the so-called Neo-Euxine regression). In the Early and Middle Holocene a rapid rise in sea level took place (the so-called New Black Sea transgression). This transgression reached its maximum (4-5 m. above the present level) during the third and fourth millennium B.C. A new regression followed, which reduced the level to 7-9 m. below the present level, in the middle of the first millennium B.C. (the Phanagoraea regression). After a short-lived Nymphaeum transgression the Black Sea reached its present level.[2]

During the Neo-Euxine regression large and deep estuaries and limans, due to intensive erosion, were formed in the low stretches of major rivers. During the New Black Sea transgression the estuaries and limans were filled with marine deposits. In some cases these deposits reached a depth of 25 m.[3]

The Ukrainian shield is one of the most important structures of the Russian plain. Here the Proterozoic basement is situated above the modern basis of erosion. In the central part of the shield are situated depressions bounded by fault-lines. The depressions are filled with sedimentary deposits and through them flow modern rivers. Morphologically the Ukrainian shield is an elevated plateau cut by deep terraced river valleys. The ravines have numerous watersheds.

The Volyno-Podolia plate is the western continuation of the Ukrainian shield. Here the crystalline basement is submerged under sedimentary deposits of the Lower Palaeozoic age. Intensive accumulations of alluvial and marine deposits took place during the Tertiary; at that time a number of erosional plains were formed. These plains are cut by deep river valleys, some of them resembling canyons.

Undulating, intensively eroded hills are typical of the modern relief of the Moldavian plate. Here the most elevated areas are the mountain ridges of medium height running parallel to the Prut river, an elevation west of the middle Dniester river and the central Moldavian heights or Kodry. The rest of the territory is taken up by intensively eroded plateaux.

Considerable territory in the south Russian plain is taken up by river systems. Deep and important rivers run here; the Danube, the Prut, the Dniester, the southern Bug and the Dnieper. In its middle stretches the slopes of the Dniester river are steep, and the river cuts through thick carbonate marine sediments of the Cretaceous and Tertiary age. The river valley here is V-shaped, meanders are cut in it, and there are numerous rapids and waterfalls. In its lower stretches the valley widens and both the accumulative terraces and the flood-plain increase in width. Geologists[4] now distinguish ten terraces in the Dniester valley; the first terrace (9-15 m. high in the middle stretches) corresponds to the Upper Pleistocene; the upper (5-6 m.) and the lower (1-2 m.) flood-plains were formed during the Holocene.

One of the peculiarities of Quaternary deposition is the large-scale formation of loesses in south and central Europe. It is now accepted that loesses were formed during ice ages, in an arid and cool climate south of the ice-sheet. The onset of the loess formation coincides with the first important cooling of the climate. In the opinion of Ukrainian geologists[5] the oldest loess formation in the south Russian plain should be dated to the time of the Günz glaciation.

A rhythmic succession of cold and warm phases is one of the main features of the Quaternary era. This succession is clearly visible in the loess sequences. Thick yellow layers of loess deposited during the ice ages are separated by brownish or reddish horizons of buried soils which were formed during warmer, interglacial or interstadial intervals.

According to a stratigraphical scheme widely accepted in the USSR,[6] at the bottom of the Upper Pleistocene deposits of the south Russian plain is the so-called Mezin soil. This soil corresponds to the last interglacial phase (Riss-Würm or Eemian) and to the initial stages of the Last (Würm) Glaciation. Stratigraphically above this lies the Loess 1 formation which was deposited during the first cool stage of the glaciation. Overlying it is the Briansk soil, which corresponds to a lengthy Würmian interstadial. The soil is radiocarbon dated to 25,000-24,000 B.P. Stratigraphically above the Briansk soil lies the most important loess formation, the Loess II. It was formed during the coldest stage of the Last Glaciation, roughly between 20,000 and 10,000 B.P. About 10,000 B.P. the formation of loesses ceased throughout Europe.

Climate and vegetation

The climate of the south Russian plain resembles the continental climate of temperate Europe. Warm and cloudless weather is typical for the summer. The average July temperature is 18-23°C. Sometimes the summer temperature exceeds 40°. Cloudless cold weather prevails in the winter. The average January temperature is 2-4°C below 0. The rainfall never exceeds 474 mm. annually. Precipitation falls mostly in winter, in the form of snow.

Two vegetational zones cover the south Russian plain: the steppe and the forest-steppe. Before cultivation, herb bunch-grass steppe prevailed in the northern part of the steppe vegetation region. Shrubs and small oak groves still exist on valley slopes and in ravines. Feather steppe is characteristic of the southern region. Salt steppes spread along the Black Sea coast, particularly within the estuaries and limans. Water-meadows are the typical vegetation for the vast flood plains of the major rivers. Inside the forest-steppe zones the steppes are broken by woods on the watersheds. Hornbeam-oak forests dominate in the western part; oak-lime-maple forests spread over the eastern part of the forest-steppe zone. Numerous oak forests grow on the flood-plains.

Palaeobotanical evidence makes it possible to reconstruct the vegetational cover of the Upper Pleistocene and Holocene epochs. It seems certain that treeless vegetation prevailed here during the time of the Last Glaciation. Palaeobotanists suggest[7] that during the period of loess formation the vegetation in the middle Dnieper area was similar to that of present-day western Siberian forest-steppe. Steppe vegetation covered the watersheds during the period when the Briansk soil was formed. Pine and birch forests were concentrated inside the river valleys. Open birch forests grew in the northern part of the zone.

There is some reason to believe that pine formations covered slopes of the Dniester river valley and those of other rivers crossing the Moldavian highlands. Some palaeobotanists suggest that even broad-leaved species survived the cold of the glaciation inside the deep river valleys.

In Early Holocene times pine and birch forests rapidly spread over the sandy terraces of the major rivers. Elms and a deep undergrowth of nut-trees formed part of the vegetation cover of the river slopes. Steppe vegetation remained on the watersheds.

In Middle Holocene times corresponding to the Atlantic period of northern Europe, oak forests spread over these areas. These forests were widespread both on the watersheds (where the area covered by steppe-like vegetation diminished) and inside the river valleys. In the Late Holocene the forest vegetation on the watersheds diminished in size. There is evidence that forest-like vegetation existed in the river valleys and in the limans of the steppe zone up to classical times.

The soils of the south Russian plain are predominantly of the chernozem varieties. These soils developed in the watershed area, mostly on loess formations. The most fertile soils, with the highest humus content, are found in the forest-steppe zone. Southern chernozems, with the humus content reaching 5.5%, developed in the steppe regions. Alluvial and meadow soils with a low humus content are found in the river flood-plains.

Palaeolithic sites

Judging from the number of Upper Palaeolithic sites found in the area, the Upper Palaeolithic population concentrated in two regions, the Moldavian plate and the Pontic steppes.

Two varieties of Upper Palaeolithic sites, cave sites and open-air sites, are known inside the Moldavian plate. Cave sites are particularly numerous in the limestone cliffs along the left bank of the Prut river. Faunal remains show that the Palaeolithic cave dwellers hunted mammoth, wild horse, bison, reindeer, red deer and rhinoceros. The open-air sites are situated inside the valleys of the Dniester and its right-hand tributary, the Reut.[8] The valley of the Dniester had been inhabited by primitive men since the Middle Pleistocene, but it was most intensively populated in Upper Palaeolithic times. The Upper Palaeolithic sites are situated on the high river terraces, not lower than the second terrace. In some cases such sites were found on the watershed level, in the parts adjoining the valley. The greatest number of Palaeolithic sites are situated in the most elevated parts of the Moldavian plate, where the Dniester valley is deep and V-shaped.

In analysing the environmental setting of the Upper Palaeolithic settlements it should be kept in mind that the river at that time was much deeper than it is now. All rivers flowing in a southerly direction were carrying masses of melt water accumulated in the basins in front of the ice-sheet. The second important factor was that the valley was intensively forested. The sandy terraces were covered with pine forests. It is probable that even broad-leaved forests survived the cold conditions there. At the same time the steppe-like vegetation spread over the watersheds. The variety of natural landscape within the catchment areas of the sites resulted in the existence of different forms of hunting activity. Among the faunal remains discovered in the Upper Palaeolithic layers were bones of mammoth, wild horse, red deer, bear, elk and reindeer.[9] The range of environments rich in game made the middle Dniester valley very attractive for the Upper Palaeolithic hunting groups. This is clearly shown by the great number of sites found in the valley. Some sites situated in areas particularly suitable for hunting were inhabited by many generations of Palaeolithic hunters for tens of thousands of years.

The fullest stratigraphical sequence covering the time from the Mousterian up to the end of the Upper Palaeolithic has been obtained from the multi-layer site of Molodova V, in the middle Dniester area.[10] The site is situated in a deluvial cone deposit on the second terrace of the Dniester river. Twelve cultural layers were distinguished, the lower two belonging to the Mousterian, the rest to the Upper Palaeolithic.

Two lower Upper Palaeolithic layers are connected with buried soil which corresponds to the time of the Würm interstadial. These layers are C14 dated from 30,000 to 24,000 B.P. The next layer is dated to the final phase of the same interval, some 23,000 B.P. Thereafter there was a break in the habitation of the site; the upper six Palaeolithic layers, according to radiocarbon dating, were deposited between 17,000 and 10,000 B.P.

One may judge from the faunal evidence that the subsistence pattern of the Upper Palaeolithic hunters during that whole time was more or less the same. They hunted mostly reindeer and wild horses. In all the layers, with the exception of the upper two, mammoth bones were found, although in small quantities. In the upper layers (from

c. 17,000 B.P. onwards) nearly all the faunal remains consist of reindeer bones only.

It is thought that the greater part of the Upper Palaeolithic sites were seasonal hunting camps. The remains of oval-shaped dwellings were found in only a few cases.

The tool-kits of the Upper Palaeolithic sites found in the Moldavian highlands have many common traits. Their main characteristics are the prevalence of burins over scrapers, and the large quantity of retouched blades and backed knives. In the upper layers the number of retouched blades and of backed knives increases. In Molodova and in other Upper Palaeolithic sites in this area a number of 'axe-like' or 'hoe-like' implements were found. These tools are made of bone or of antler. In the same sites stone querns were present. In all probability these artifacts were used for the gathering and preparation of vegetable food. The importance of food-collecting is also shown by the great number of *Helix* shells in the Palaeolithic layers.

The Upper Palaeolithic sites are concentrated in two areas inside the Pontic depression. These are the northern shores of the Azov Sea and the north-western Pontic area – the region of Odessa. The morphological situation of the Palaeolithic sites in both areas is similar. They are situated upon high terraces or upon highlands jutting into valleys or into ravines. Again, one should remember that the volume of water these rivers carried during Upper Pleistocene times was much greater than it is now. The slopes were covered by forest-like vegetation. The valley slopes in the western part of the steppe zone were particularly densely forested. The periglacial steppes of the Pontic depression contained large herds of animals, bison, aurochs and wild horse being the most numerous. Upper Palaeolithic camp-sites were situated in the area best suited for hunting.

The Upper Palaeolithic economy of the steppe zone was based on specialized hunting of herd animals. The hunting of bison and of aurochs was economically the most important and was very efficient. Bones belonging to no less than a thousand individuals of bison were found in the cultural layer of Ambrosievka,[11] an Upper Palaeolithic site north of the Azov Sea. In some cases these were entire skeletons, with the bones lying in anatomical order. Palaeolithic hunters massacred more animals than they could eat. A similar subsistence pattern was typical of all Upper Palaeolithic sites discovered in the steppe zone. Edible molluscs were found in great numbers: food gathering was also an important factor. Archaeologists think that all Upper Palaeolithic sites excavated in this zone are the remains of seasonal hunting camps.

The tool-kits of these sites have many common traits. Burins of different kinds, end scrapers, retouched blades and backed knives are the most common types of flint tools. The similarity of their tool-kit, of their economic pattern and of their ecological setting has led some archaeologists to suggest that these sites formed a particular province in Upper Palaeolithic Europe, the 'steppe province'.

Mesolithic sites

During recent years a considerable number of Mesolithic sites have been discovered in the south Russian plain.[12] Inside the Pontic depression Mesolithic sites are distinguishable on typological grounds. The number of end scrapers made on long blades diminishes; the number of short, rounded scrapers increases compared with the Upper Palaeolithic layers. Geometric tools appeared in the Mesolithic sites, trapezes being the most numerous. The Mesolithic sites in the area may be divided into two groups: the sites situated on high terraces and the sites found on flood-plains and low terraces.

The change in the settlement pattern was of vital importance for the evolution of economic and cultural processes in the south Russian plain; it should be considered together with the important events taking place in northern Europe. This period corresponds to the breaking up of the last glacier. The vast glacio-lacustrine basins which had existed in front of the retreating glaciers, dried up. There was a drop in the levels of the rivers which carried the water from these basins towards the southern seas. Lower river terraces and flood-plains became available for human habitation. These low-lying areas inside river valleys were particularly suitable for hunting, fishing and food gathering. The slopes of the valley were covered with pine forests; the mixed forests spread over the flood-plain and later appeared on the watersheds. Rivers were rich in fish and in edible water molluscs. All these factors made the low terraces and flood-plains of the major rivers very attractive places for hunters, fishers and food-collectors for many thousand years. In the Atlantic period, when the waters of the New Black Sea transgression submerged the mouths of rivers, the low flood-plains were temporarily deserted, but not for long.

An example of a Mesolithic site situated on a high terrace is Girževo, west of Odessa.[13] The site is located on a terrace-like platform in the valley of the Kučurgan river, at an altitude of 41 m. above the river. The valley is deep and wide; without doubt it was formed by a river much deeper than the present stream. Among the faunal remains identified here were aurochs, wild horse and the European ass. Little round scrapers predominate in the chipped stone inventory and there are numerous geometric microliths, mostly trapezes.

An example of a Mesolithic site situated on a flood-plain is Mirnoye, east of Ismail. The site is on the flood-plain of a wide liman which now opens up into the Danube delta. In the past, as the valley was forming, the stream ran directly into the Black Sea. The cultural layer is situated in sandy loam which is overlaid by silty clay. I suggest that this silty clay was deposited as the waters of the New Black Sea transgression reached the area during the Atlantic period. Pollen analysis showed the presence in the cultural layer of pollen grains of pine, fir, spruce, oak and nut-trees. There is a large quantity of grass pollen. The pollen analysis proves that the slopes and terraces were forested while steppe-like vegetation covered the watersheds. Preliminary faunal analysis shows that the Mesolithic dwellers hunted aurochs and wild horse. Little round scrapers, trapezes and retouched blades are the most characteristic types of chipped stone tools.

Neolithic sites

Very important data have been secured from the Kamennaya Mogila site, north of Melitopol, in the Azov Sea coastal area.[14] The site is situated in the valley of the river Moločnaya. The valley is typical of the steppe zone rivers, being wide with gentle slopes. In the middle of the valley there is a hill composed of limestone blocks, on several of which were found carvings of wild animals. Archaeologists suggest that this hill was a sacred place for the local tribesmen (Fig. 21).

Excavation of the flood-plain revealed the existence of several cultural layers. Three thin aceramic Neolithic layers have been established in the lower portion of loam, about 2 m. below the surface. Nearly 90% of all faunal remains discovered in these layers belonged to domesticated animals. Cattle was the commonest, followed by horses, sheep/goats and pigs. Among the wild animals were identified red deer, wild pigs and bison. There were numerous bones of fishes and birds. Blades are the most common tools in the chipped stone inventory. Rounded scrapers and burins of various types are also present. There is a complete absence of geometric microliths.

In the upper portion of the loam an early pottery layer was found. The pottery sherds belonged to oval-shaped jars with pointed bases, made of clay mixed with shell particles. No ornamented sherds were found. The animal remains are almost the same as in the aceramic layers. The number of wild species decreases, only aurochs being left. The chipped stone inventory is also the same as in the lower levels.

A considerable number of pollen grains belonging to trees have been identified in the loam deposits, comprising single grains of birch, alder, lime, elm and hornbeam. But the pollen of steppe grasses predominates. In the upper layers the tree pollen disappears completely.[15]

There are several layers of later date in the Kamennaya Mogila sequence, but they correspond to other cultural traditions which are not dealt with in the present book. What is important for us is that Kamennaya Mogila shows the early appearance of stock-breeding in the eastern part of the steppe zone. The specific environmental

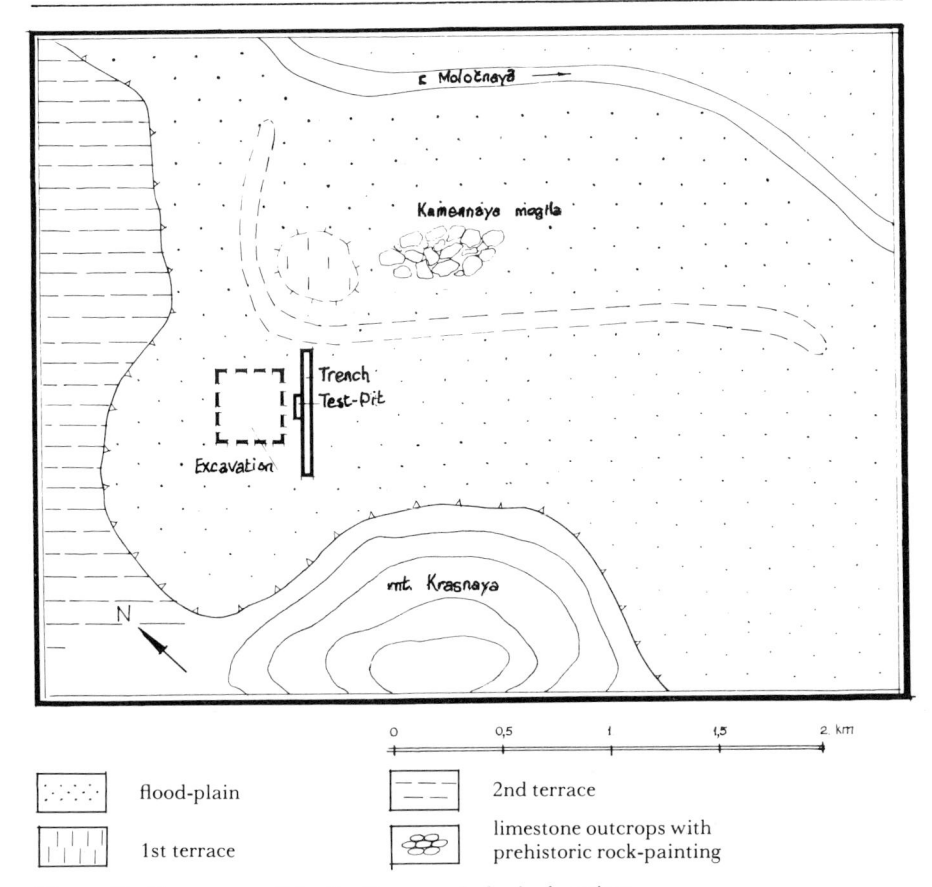

Figure 21 Kamennaya Mogila. Geomorphological setting

conditions of this area caused the early onset of a crisis in the hunting economy. On the other hand these conditions prevented the establishment of economic patterns based on agriculture. A stockbreeding economy with a preponderance of cattle was the only efficient economic strategy here. At the same time it should be noted that this economic pattern was not particularly stable. There are very few known Early Neolithic sites in the eastern part of the steppe zone. Population density would probably have been very low. No radiocarbon dates are available for these sites.

The evolution of economic patterns inside the Volyno-Podolia and the Moldavian plate was quite different. As we have seen, the valleys of the major rivers here were intensively populated, at least from Upper Palaeolithic times. The diversity of the environments within the catchment areas made these valleys extremely attractive for hunting communities. The density of the Upper Palaeolithic population within the valleys must have been high. Up to the upper limit of the Pleistocene epoch only the upper terraces (not lower than the second terrace) were populated. The change in environmental conditions about 10,000 years ago made the lower terraces, including the flood-plain, accessible for habitation. From this time the hunting and fishing population in the area was concentrated almost exclusively upon the low terraces and on the flood-plain. For instance, one of the oldest Mesolithic sites found on a low terrace of the Dniester river is Ataki VI, in the middle Dniester area, where the faunal remains consist of broken bones of red deer, wild horses and bison. The chipped stone inventory consisted mostly of scrapers, including little rounded ones, and single geometric tools, triangles, trapezes and tanged points were also discovered.[16]

The largest sequence of Early Holocene sites was investigated downstream in the vicinity of Soroki.[17] The sites are situated in the middle stretches of the Dniester on the right bank of the river. The right slope of the valley is steep: the river cuts through Tertiary limestone. The steep slopes are now covered with dense oak forest. The bank is cut by the deep valleys of numerous streams which fall into the Dniester (Fig. 22). All the sites are situated on the terrace, which is a flood-plain 6 m. high. The terrace is narrow, its width varying from 1 to 100 m., and it is built of alluvial loams and of clay deposited during the last phases of the Last Glaciation. The cultural layers are found in the so-called cover deposits which occur above alluvial loam and clay.

The Soroki sites can be divided into two groups: the older sites without pottery and the younger ones with pottery. Two aceramic layers were discovered at the Soroki sites. The cultural layers are found in sandy loam, with numerous blocks of broken pebbles, deposited above the alluvial deposits of the upper flood-plain. The two cultural layers are separated by sterile loam.

Remains of two oval-shaped semi-subterranean dwellings were discovered in the lower level. The dwellings measured 3.5 to 6 m. and 3.2 to 5.1 m. In the chipped stone inventory end and side scrapers on blades and on flakes are the most numerous. Long blades are also met with in great numbers. Several trapezes and one triangle were found. Two blades with a sickle gloss were reported. The results of faunal studies are of great significance: 83% of all identified bones belong to wild animals. Among these the bones of roe deer predominate (47%); red deer come next (24%). Among the domesticated animals pigs are the most important (12 bones, which make up 14% of all bones). Two cattle bones were identified. In the cultural level 841 fragments of fish bones were counted. Several hundred fragments of *Unio* shell were collected.

In the upper aceramic layer of the same site, the faunal evidence reveals a similar subsistence pattern. Bones of wild species form 81% of all the bones found. Here red deer are the most important with 55%; roe deer come next with 10% and wild pigs occupy third place with 8%. Nearly all the bones of domesticated species belong to pigs.

Another site attributed to the aceramic Neolithic is in the lower

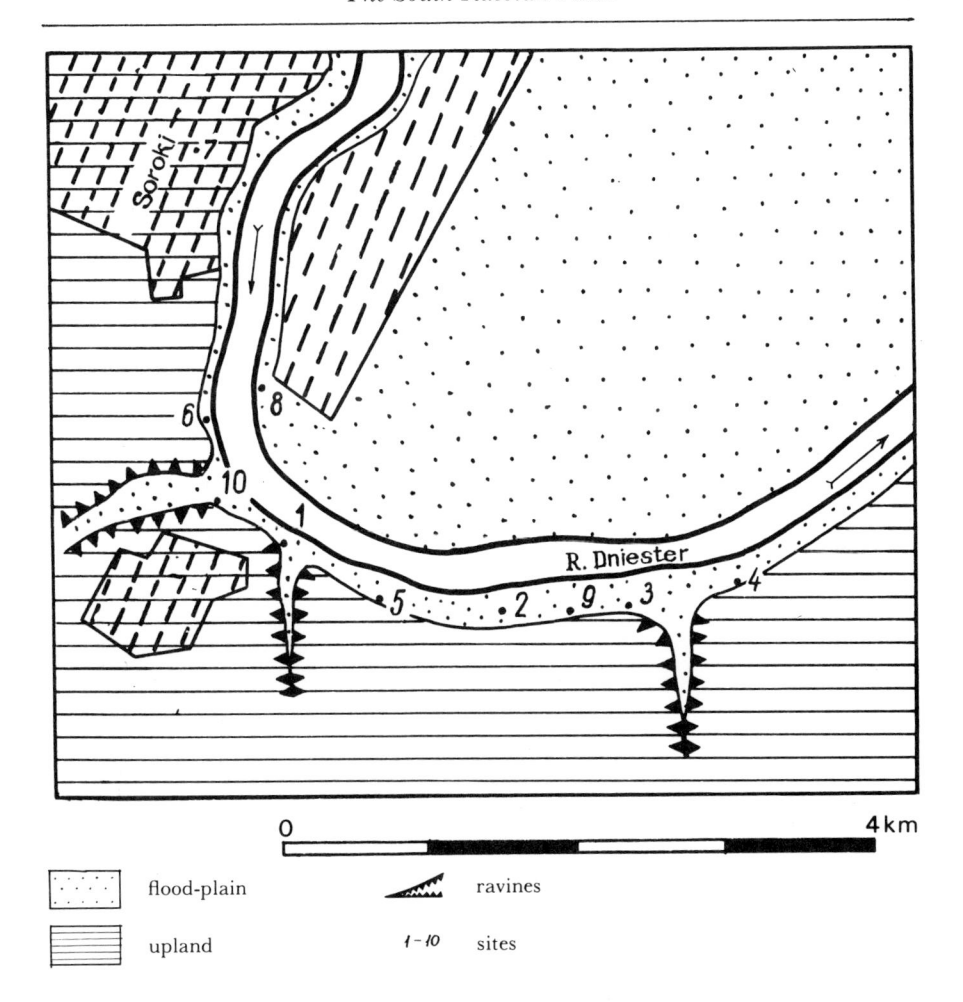

Figure 22 Soroki sites. Geomorphological setting

layer of Soroki I. Here 90% of all bones belong to wild animals. Red deer and roe deer are represented in equal proportions; wild pigs makes up 10%. Among the 10% belonging to domesticated animals pigs and cattle are present in equal quantities.

The lower and upper aceramic layers of the Soroki II sites have been radiocarbon dated to 7,515 $\pm$ 120 and 7,420 $\pm$ 80 B.P.

The earliest pottery-bearing site is Soroki I. Here in two pottery-bearing levels were found remains of both oval-shaped semi-subterranean huts and rectangular surface dwellings. The stone tool-kit is the same as in the aceramic layers – thin blades, end scrapers and trapezes – and two blades show sickle gloss. Of the bones found, 66% are of wild animal species, 27% belonging to roe deer and 24% to red deer. Among the domesticated animals cattle and pigs are equally represented. In the upper horizon of the same site the number of bones belonging to domesticated animals increases, reaching 50% (of which cattle make up 15% and pigs 35%). Roe deer predominate among the wild animals, red deer being the second most important. In the uppermost layers of Soroki II, the faunal remains consist almost entirely of wild animal species. Roe deer and red deer form 54% and 35% respectively, only 6% belong to domesticated pigs and 4% to cattle. In the Soroki I layer 1,166 fragments of fish bones were collected. Among them were identified roach (which predominates), wels (*Siluris glanis*) and pike. Among the bird bones two species of birds of prey (sparrow hawk and honey buzzard) and wood pigeons were identified. Impressions of three varieties of wheat were found on pot sherds; emmer, einkorn and spelt.

All the existing evidence indicates that the Neolithic dwellers of the Soroki area developed an effective economic pattern based on the exploitation of the rich natural resources in the Dniester valley. The subsistence pattern was based upon hunting of large forest animals (roe deer and red deer being the most important), on fishing and on food-collecting. Hunting provided the bulk of the meat diet. It is interesting to compare the hunting pattern with that of Late Palaeolithic sites. In the Molodova V Late Palaeolithic layers 80-90% of all faunal remains belonged to reindeer. Late Palaeolithic men hunted tundra herd animals, while Soroki tribesmen hunted the roe deer, red deer and wild pig which inhabited the Holocene mixed forests. Fishing and gathering edible molluscs were also very important food sources.

The morphological situation of the sites ruled out the possibility of effective agriculture and stock-breeding in the area. The upper floodplain, where all the sites are situated, is narrow and the soil covering is poor in humus content.[18] The nearest arable lands are more than 5 km. away and cut off by the steep and almost impassable slopes of the valley. The occurrence of domesticated animal bones and impressions of wheat grain may be attributed to the existence of economic contacts with agricultural tribes in other ecological zones. Not far from the Dniester, in the Moldavian highlands, there existed at the same time sites with a stable food-producing economy. Economic exchanges between social groups with different economic structures seem probable.[19]

The pottery assemblage of the Soroki sites is of particular importance. The number of pot sherds is very few and often it is very difficult to reconstruct the actual shapes of the vessels. The Soviet archaeologist V.I. Markevič reconstructed the following vessels: three-quarter spherical bowls, low biconical bowls, egg-shaped biconical bowls, spherical bowls with beaded rims and with flat bases. The most common decorative pattern consists of horizontal rows of shell (*Unio*) impressions or of comb stamp impressions. Some sherds are ornamented with finger-nail impressions, using a technique similar to Barbotine. Many sherds are decorated with incised lines, often forming zigzag patterns. Some are ornamented with 'wheat-ears' formed by complicated patterns of incised lines and rows of shell impressions. The pottery is made of grey or buff paste tempered with vegetable material or with sand. The radiocarbon date of the pottery-bearing layer in the Soroki II site is 6,835 ± 150 B.P.

In the pottery assemblage of the Soroki V site, some Linear pottery sherds were associated with sherds similar to those found in earlier sites. The stone inventory and the faunal remains are almost the same as in earlier sites (red deer 50%; roe deer 30%; cattle 12%; pigs 8%). The occurrence of Linear pottery proves the existence of intensive economic and cultural contacts with settlements situated in other ecological zones and with different subsistence patterns. The radiocarbon date of this site is 6,425 ± 100 B.P.

Another area with an intensive concentration of Neolithic sites in the south Russian plain is the valley of the southern Bug.[20] A number of sites are situated in the middle stretches of this river, where it crosses the structure of Kazatino. The valley here is deep and asymmetrical. Outcrops of crystalline rocks form narrow canyon-like passes, with numerous rapids.

The greater part of the sites excavated by the Soviet archaeologist V.N. Danilenko are now submerged due to the construction of a hydro-electric power dam. I was able to see and examine one of these sites, that of Pečera, south of Vinnitsa, before it was inundated. The valley of the southern Bug here has an asymmetrical character. The right bank is high, and here the river has broken through the Archaean age granite. Loess deposits were formed on the watershed level, above the granite. Above the loesses, modern chernozem soils developed. On this watershed level, near the outskirts of a modern village, a late Tripolye settlement was found and excavated (Fig. 23).

Two flood-plain levels and one terrace were traced within the valley. The Neolithic site was situated on the higher flood-plain, some 3.5-4 m. above the present mean river level. The cultural deposits were found in buried soil, 0.6 to 1.0 m. below the surface.

The level of the river in Early and Middle Holocene times was lower than it is now. In all probability many islets where Neolithic remains were found then formed part of the shore. At the same time the flood-plain, the slopes of the valley and even the watersheds were intensively forested.

The subsistence pattern of the southern Bug Neolithic settlers may be reconstructed on the basis of the faunal evidence available. The faunal lists of three southern Bug sites are known. These are: Baz'kov Island (lower level), Mit'kov Island, Baz'kov Island (middle layer) and Mikolina Broyarka. In all four occupation deposits the bone remains of wild animals predominate. They form 97.3%, 95%, 95% and 91% respectively of all the bones found. The hunting pattern is nearly the same in every case. The red deer is the most important animal hunted. It forms 53%, 54%, 66% and 60% of all bone remains. The wild pig is

Figure 23 Pečera. Geomorphological setting

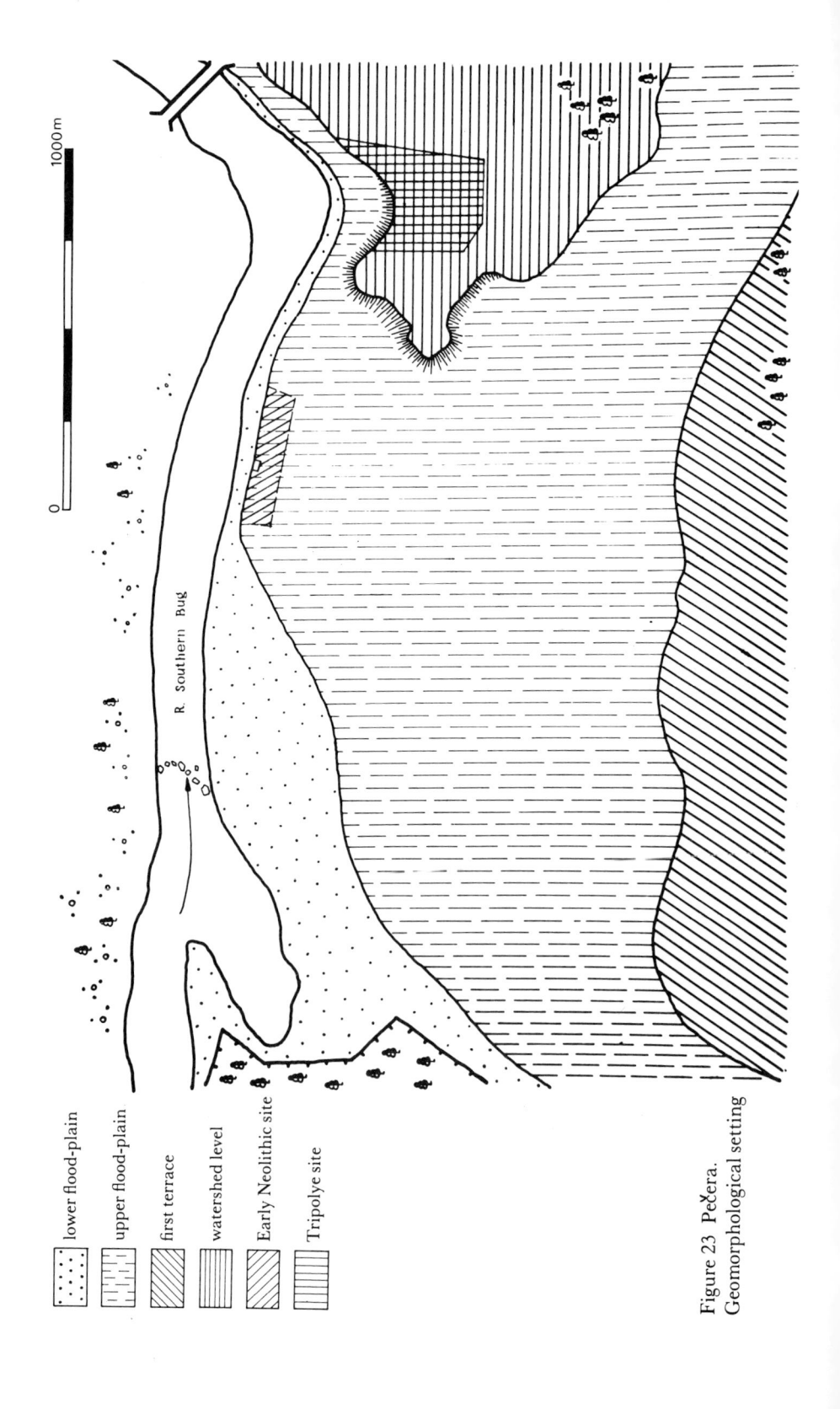

in second place and roe deer in third. In two cases (Mit'kov Island and Baz'kov Island, middle layer) a few elk bones were found. In one case (Mikolina Broyarka) wild horse bones were identified. Among the domesticated species only cattle were identified. Dr Bibikova, who carried out the faunal analysis, has suggested that the cattle bones denote an early phase of domestication. It seems certain that the hunting of forest game was practically the only source of meat food for the southern Bug Neolithic dwellers. Economically the most important animals were red deer, roe deer and wild pigs.

Food collecting was also economically important. The cultural layers of the southern Bug sites are filled with hundreds of *Unio* shells. In the layer of the Mikolina Broyarka site 240 tortoise shells have been found. That fishing played an important part in the economy of these sites may be deduced from the numerous fish bones found in the Neolithic layers.

A large number of hoe-like or axe-like implements made of red deer antler, of bones and of wild pig tusks were found at the Bug sites. There are several varieties of such implements, some with perforated holes in them, some similar to adzes, some resembling hoes (Fig. 24). Querns were also found on a number of sites. Some flint blades have a specific sickle gloss. According to V.N. Danilenko, the presence of these implements proves that agriculture was practised on the southern Bug flood-plains in Neolithic times. But I do not find this argument convincing. As we have seen earlier, hoe-like implements were discovered in the Upper Palaeolithic layers of the Molodova V site, though it is hardly possible that any kind of agriculture was practised in the Dniester valley during Upper Pleistocene times. Blades with a sickle gloss were discovered in the Soroki sites, where no agriculture was possible. Again, sickle blades are present in great number at the Natufian sites of Palestine where, according to the site catchment analysis, the available arable lands were very limited. All these examples seem to me to prove that stone tools taken alone cannot be used for the reconstruction of the economic activities of the prehistoric population. The environmental setting of the southern Bug sites is not favourable for farming activity. The low-lying flood-plains are covered with meadow soils with a very low humus content. The nearest arable soils are on the watersheds; Tripolye settlements with a stable food-producing economy appeared in the area many thousand years later. The hoe-like tools, querns and blades with a sickle gloss could all have been used for different kinds of gathering and preparing of vegetable food. Gathering of vegetable food had been economically important in the valleys of the south Russian plain since Upper Palaeolithic times. No palaeobotanical data to support or disprove Danilenko's theory are so far available.

In the chipped stone inventory blades, retouched knives and backed knives are the most numerous. Short and round scrapers are also present in large number. Some trapezes, triangles and tanged points

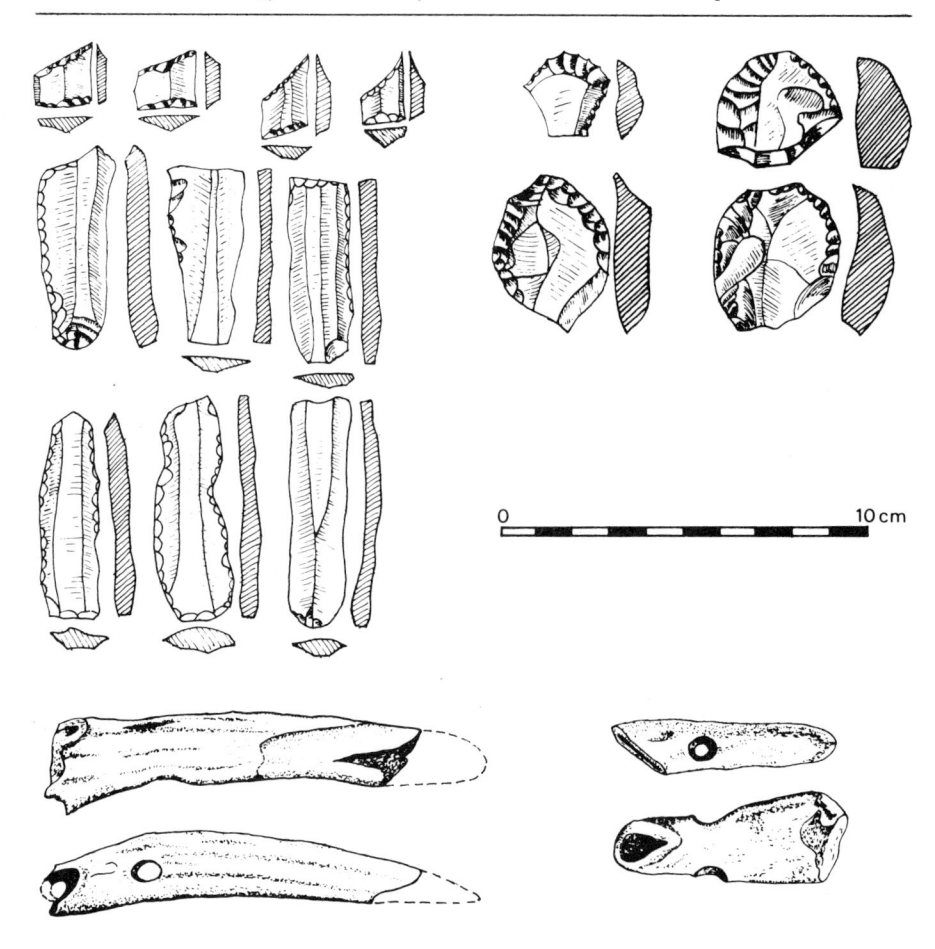

Figure 24 The Neolithic sites of the southern Bug: working tools (after Danilenko, 1969; Note 4.14)

are also reported. Danilenko discovered the remains of dwellings in the southern Bug Neolithic sites. According to him, these were surface houses of one or two rooms with stone-laid hearths.

Danilenko distinguishes five stages in the evolution of southern Bug Neolithic, based on stratigraphical and typological evidence: (1) Savran; (2) Samčincy; (3) Pečera; (4) Sokol'cy; (5) Skibency. In Table 8 I have tried to show the occurrence of these phases at specific sites. As the Table shows, the first two phases are represented at two sites and at a single site respectively. The three later stages are represented at a considerable number of sites.

Stratigraphical evidence shows that the cultural layers of the southern Bug Neolithic sites are in most cases 10-20 cm. thick. The difference in depth between the layers in multi-layered sites is very small.

Table 8. The phases of the Bug-Dniester culture as represented at the sites of southern Bug valley (after V.N. Danilenko). (X) denotes presence at a site of materials attributed to the phase indicated

Sites	Savran	Samčincy	Pečera	Sokol'cy	Skibency
Baz'kov island	X			X	X
Mit'kov island	X		X	X	X
Sokol'cy II		X		X	X
Sokol'cy VI			X	X	
Šimanovskoye			X	X	
Glinskoye			X	X	
Mel'nična Kruča			X		
Gayvoron Poližok			X		
Pečera			X	X	
Šurovčy				X	
Samčincy				X	
Žakčik				X	
Zaval'ye				X	
Ladyžin				X	
Čyernyatka					X
Savran'					X
Vladimirovka					X
Mikolina Broyarka					X
Gard					X

The pottery assemblages are of particular importance to our study. According to Danilenko, deep bowls with slightly everted rims and conical bases are the most common pottery types for the Samčincy phase (Fig. 25). The paste is tempered with organic material and shell particles. Decorative patterns include: finger impressions using a technique similar to Barbotine; incised lines forming zigzags and nets; incised lines forming volute patterns filled with cross-hatching. As we saw, all these patterns, with the exception of the last one, were in use in the monochrome pottery of the Balkan Neolithic.

For the Sokol'cy phase Danilenko reconstructed conical bowls with S-profile walls, hemispherical bowls with flat bases and conical vessels with vertical walls. The ornamentation patterns consist mostly of incised lines forming zigzags, networks and volute patterns.

For the Pečera phase S-profile bowls and deep bowls are the most common forms. Hemispherical bowls and beakers with flat bases are also often found. Decorative patterns consist of incised lines forming zigzags and volutes; finger impressions are also common.

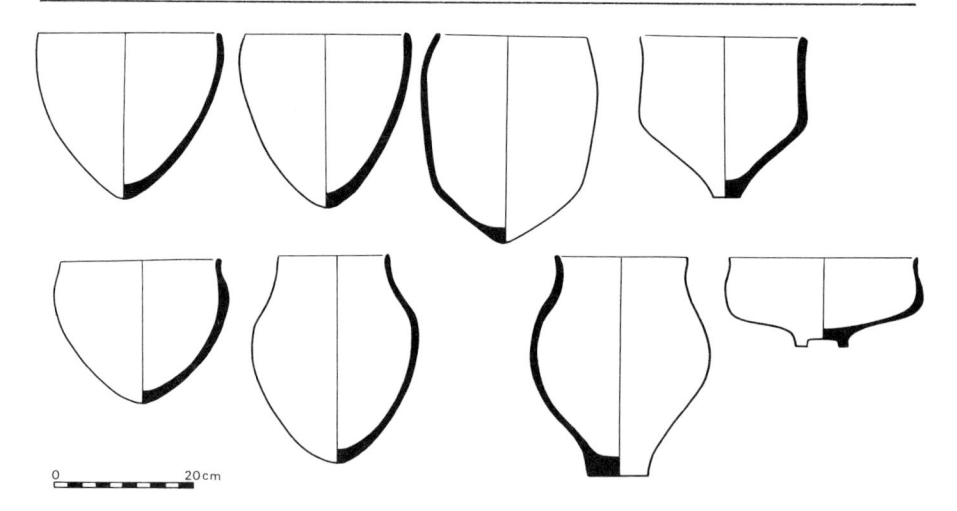

Figure 25 The Neolithic sites of the southern Bug: shapes of vessels (after Danilenko, 1969; Note 4.14)

In the pottery assemblage of the Samčincy phase, which is represented at most of the southern Bug Neolithic sites, conical S-profile bowls are the most common type. The ornamentation consists mostly of horizontal rows of comb-like impressions. Incised lines forming vertical or horizontal lines or voluted patterns are also common, and there are patterns consisting of combinations of incised lines and comb impressions. In several cases in the pottery assemblage of the Samčincy phase, sherds of Linear pottery (with 'music-note' or *Notenknopf*-type ornamentation) have been found.

In the pottery assemblage of the late (Savran) phase flat-based forms are the most common, with S-profile conical bowls represented to a lesser extent. In the ornamentation incised lines forming horizontal, vertical and voluted patterns were often used. Geometrical patterns consisting of broad chevrons and triangles appear (Fig. 26). As may be seen from this description, there is usually very little difference in the pottery shapes and in the decorative patterns between the phases of southern Bug Neolithic. New elements are recognizable only in the Savran phase.

Nearly all the most commonly used ornamentation patterns may be found also in Dniester Neolithic and in the monochrome wares of Balkan Early Neolithic. The only exception is the voluted pattern, which is missing in both the Dniester assemblages and the Balkan pottery. We shall meet this motif later on in the Neolithic pottery of the Dnieper area. It is possible that the voluted pattern was a local invention.

In my opinion, the Bug Neolithic sites are the remains of temporary seasonal hunting camps left by a culturally similar population. This population consisted of small hunting groups with a subsistence

Figure 26 The Neolithic sites of the southern Bug: pottery ornamental patterns; (a) (above) after Markevič, 1974; Note 4.17; (b) (overleaf) after Danilenko, 1969; Note 4.14.

Note: Solid lines correspond to incised lines, dotted lines and semi-circles to stamp or shell rim impressions, and small circles or triangles to strokes, in this figure and Figs. 40a and b, 48, 49 and 54.

Figure 26b.

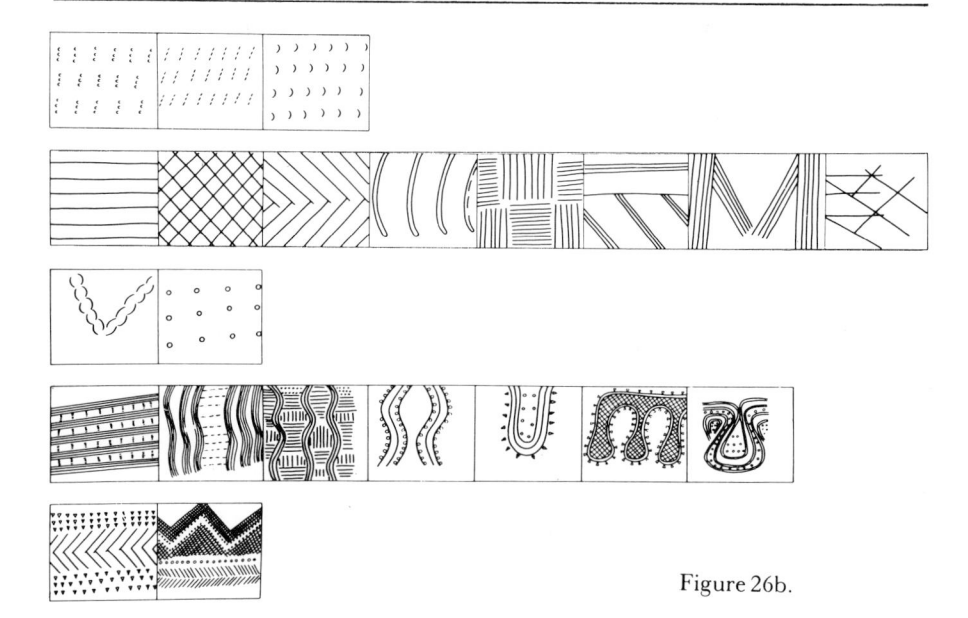

pattern based on the exploitation of the rich natural resources of the southern Bug valley – hunting of red deer, wild pig and roe deer, and intensive fishing and food collecting. The gap between the deposition of the different layers on multi-layer sites is insignificant.

We have so far no radiocarbon dates for the southern Bug sites, but the radiocarbon dates for pottery-bearing sites in the Dniester valley (which as we saw are very similar to those of the southern Bug) may be $6,825 \pm 150$ (Soroki II) and $6,495 \pm 100$ (Soroki V). Numerous dates of Linear pottery sites in Europe may be used as a reference since Linear pottery was found in the sites of the Samčincy phase. These dates lie in a maximum time-span of 6,700-5,800 B.P. The upper time limit for southern Bug Neolithic is set by the lower limit of the Tripolye settlements; the early Tripolye sites are dated to 5,600-5,500 B.P. Summing up, we may say that the broadest possible time-span of the southern Bug Neolithic sites lies within 6,900-5,500 B.P. In reality, the time-span was probably much narrower.

As we have seen, there is reason to suggest that the sites of the pottery-using hunters and fishers in the valleys of the south Russian plain were at least partly contemporaneous with the Linear pottery sites in central Europe. The spread of settlements with Linear pottery was an event of the utmost importance in the economic prehistory of Europe. As is shown from numerous radiocarbon dates during a comparatively short period of time, 6,700-5,800 B.P., settlements of this type spread over a very large part of Europe, from the Moldavian highlands northwards to Holland and Belgium. Nearly everywhere these settlements were situated on rich chernozem soils developed over the loess deposits. Detailed mapping has shown[21] that the Linear pottery sites in central Europe were situated mostly on parabrown soils (a variety of chernozems developed on thin loess deposits) in the marginal zones of loessic massifs, adjoining river valleys. The central parts of loessic massifs were practically devoid of such settlements. Palaeobotanists[22] have established that at a time corresponsing to the massive spread of Linear pottery sites the loessic massifs of central Europe were covered with open mixed oak forests.

The economy of the Linear pottery settlements had a stable food-producing character. The faunal remains consist almost entirely of domesticated species. Hunting was of no economic significance. In most cases the stock-breeding structure is fairly uniform. Cattle breeding held first place, ovicaprids were the second most important and pigs always retained third place among the faunal remains. There is no evidence of fishing. Agriculture as well as stock-breeding was vitally important for the Linear pottery-using settlers: numerous ovens for drying grain and storage pits have been discovered, and cereal remains have been identified as emmer and einkorn.

The stone inventory of the Linear pottery sites includes numerous querns, rubbers and sickle blades. At Bylany in Czechoslovakia these constitute 16% of all stone implements.

The stable food-producing economy of the Linear pottery settlements led to the development of complicated social and demographic structures. The houses uncovered at the Linear pottery sites are distinguished by their large dimensions, and their uniformity of proportion and of ground plan. These houses were rectangular; their width was 6 m. and their length varied from 8 to 45 m. Heavy oak posts supported a framework of wattle walls covered or daubed with clay. It is thought that these houses sheltered several families, and a correlation has been noted between the length of the house and the number of hearths. The Polish archaeologist S. Tabaczyński[23] has suggested that a house with a length of 6-9 m. sheltered one family; 11-16 m., two families; 18-23 m., three families; and 23-27 m., four families. The longest known house, of 45 m., could have sheltered five families.

The Linear pottery settlement at Bylany western Czechoslovakia has been intensively excavated by the late Professor B. Soudsky.[24] On the basis of these excavations 21 habitation phases have been distinguished, the general duration of which covered about 700 years. It has been proved that during this time the Neolithic settlement was constantly shifting in a circular pattern to allow the soil to regain its fertility, returning to its original place every 30-50 years. It has been calculated that the basic settlement consisted of five or six houses. It is thought that the Linear pottery settlements of central Europe were bigger than the Criş-Körös sites of Hungary and Romania, and could have been as large as the Early Neolithic settlements of south Bulgaria.

The problem of the origins of Linear pottery is central to European archaeological discussion. Many scientists note a similarity between the early Linear pottery and the coarse monochrome pottery of Starčevo and Criş-Körös. This similarity concerns the paste, an organic-tempered fabric. The shapes of vessels are also identical: hemispherical bowls, bottles with cylindrical or flaring necks, ribbon lugs, globular bowls with flat or ring bottoms. There are some similarities in the ornamental patterns formed of incised lines.

The Moldavian plate and the valleys of the Prut and Dniester are the south-eastern extremities of the distribution area of Linear pottery sites.[25] The spread of Linear pottery sites in this area took place at a later stage of its evolution, when *Notenknopf* ornamentation had appeared on the vessels. The forested valleys of Moldavia were extremely rich in natural resources suitable for a hunting and fishing economy, and the subsistence pattern of the Linear pottery sites in this area is different from that of those in central Europe. Hunting and fishing were much more important here. For example at the Trojan settlement (Moldavian highlands) 34.7% of all animal remains belong to wild species. At the site of Floreşti situated on the Reut river (the right-hand tributary of the Dniester) the proportion of wild animals was 26.2% (wild pigs 17%, red deer 2%, roe deer 1%). Domesticated animals are represented mostly by cattle.[26] The mixed character of the economy is reflected in the settlement pattern. The greater part of the Linear pottery settlements within the Moldavian plate are situated either on flood-plains or on low river terraces.

A stable food-producing economy is typical of the Gumelniţa settlements, which spread over the area between 5,800 and 5,300 B.P. Bones of domesticated animals form from 90% to 98% of all faunal remains at the Gumelniţa settlements. Cattle breeding was the most important branch of the economy. Impressions of cultivated cereals have been found on pottery. These include three varieties of wheat, einkorn, emmer and spelt. Apart from wheat, six-row barley, oats and broom-corn millet have been identified. Neither hunting nor fishing were of any economic importance.[27] The Gumelniţa settlements are situated in the areas most suitable for a farming economy, on high promontories of loessic plains flanking limans or lakes (Oziornoye, Bolgrad) or in river valleys (Vulkaneşti). The remains of complex houses have been discovered on the Gumelniţa sites. According to reliable reconstructions, some of these houses were of two-storeys.

Between 5,500 and 4,500 B.P. sites of another type spread over the plains of Romania, Moldavia and the Ukraine. They are usually referred to as belonging to the Cucuteni-Tripolye culture.[28] Investigations by Soviet archaeologists have made it possible to follow the economic and cultural evolution of these sites within the Dniester and the southern Bug basins. It now seems certain that the economy of the initial phases of the Tripolye site had a mixed character. Hunting and fishing were important parts of the economy. A considerable part of meat consumption was provided by hunting red deer, roe deer, wild pig and elk. Fishing and food gathering were also important sources of food. Only in the final stages of Tripolye does stock-breeding become a leading part of the economy (Table 9). According to osteological determinations, about one-third of the herds were cattle, pigs were the second most numerous and ovicaprids the third. Horse bones are always found at the late Tripolye sites in the Ukraine.

Table 9 Percentages of wild and domesticated animals in the Tripolye sites (after T.S. Passek, 1961:99)

Period	Site	Wild	Domesticated
A	Luka Vrublevetskaya	47.6	52.4
A	Bernevo-Luka	38	62
A	Lenkovcy	42	58
A	Sabatinovka II	69.2	30.8
B/I	Polivanov-Yar	60	40
B/II	Vladimirovka	76	24
B/II	Kolomiyščina II	79.5	20.5
CI	Kolomiyščina I	80	20
D/II	Usatovo	88.4	11.6

The faunal remains of the sites belonging to the Usatovo group of the steppe zone, often regarded as belonging to the final stage of Tripolye culture, display a predominance of sheep and goats over cattle and horses. The number of pigs was very small. Agriculture was a very important economic factor at the late Tripolye settlements. Grains of wheat, barley, oats, broom-corn millet and of pulses have been identified in the cultural layers.

The change in the economic patterns of the Tripolye sites is clearly reflected in the change of settlement pattern. The greater part of the early Tripolye sites are situated either on flood-plains or on low terraces. An example of this is the early Tripolye site of Klišcev, south of Vinnica. The site is situated on the high flood-plain level, 4-5 m. above the actual river level. Only in the Late Tripolye period did the settlements shift on the watershed levels. The Late Tripolye sites are situated in the marginal zones of the loess plain adjoining the river valleys.

The Late Tripolye settlements were of considerable size. According to calculations made by S.N. Bibikov,[29] a late Tripolye settlement (of the Kolomiyščina I type) had some 500 inhabitants or 80 families. Such a population needed, according to Bibikov, about 250 hectares of arable land. About the same amount of land would have been allowed to lie fallow. According to the same authority, the mean population density in the area where the Late Tripolye sites are found amounted to 19 persons per sq.km. It is possible that these figures are slightly exaggerated because Bibikov assumes that all dwellings found at the settlement were inhabited simultaneously.

Summary

The territory of the south Russian plain may be divided into two zones, (1) the steppe and (2) the forest-steppe. Within zone (2) one can distinguish three units on morphological and structural grounds: (a) the Ukrainian shield, (b) the Volyno-Podolia plateau and (c) the Moldavian plate. The valleys of the major rivers, the Prut, the Driester and the southern Bug, may be classified as interzontal units.

20,000-10,000 B.P.

During the time corresponding to the maximum spread of the ice-sheet of the Last Glaciation, periglacial hyperzonal landscapes were dominant in the south Russian plain. Treeless steppe-like vegetation covered huge areas. There is reason to believe that forest-like vegetation covered some areas in the Moldavian plate, the sandy slopes of valleys and of ravines.

The rivers which carried water from the glacial lakes to the sea were large and deep. The level of the Black Sea at that time was at least 25 m. below the present. The Upper Palaeolithic population was concentrated mostly in the Moldavian plate and in the steppic zone. The cave sites were situated along the Prut valley while open-air settlements existed in the Dniester valley and in the steppic zone. Open-air settlements were situated upon the upper terraces of rivers or ravines or on loessic uplands in areas adjoining valleys or ravines.

The subsistence pattern of the Upper Palaeolithic groups was based upon specialized hunting and on food gathering. Thus the area of Upper Palaeolithic habitation may be regarded as a single natural economic zone. At least two subzones may be distinguished: the Palaeolithic inhabitants of the Moldavian plate hunted wild horses and reindeer while the Palaeolithic inhabitants of the steppic zone hunted mostly bison and aurochs. There are differences in the stone inventories in these subzones (Fig. 27).

10,000-8,000 B.P.

The marked change in the evolution of the earth's surface that took place about 10,000 years ago directly affected the south Russian plain. By that time the hyperzonal periglacial zone had disintegrated into two zones: steppe and forest-steppe. Forests consisting of pine, birch, spruce and elm with an undergrowth of nut-trees spread in the forest-steppe area and covered the slopes of major river valleys, reaching the

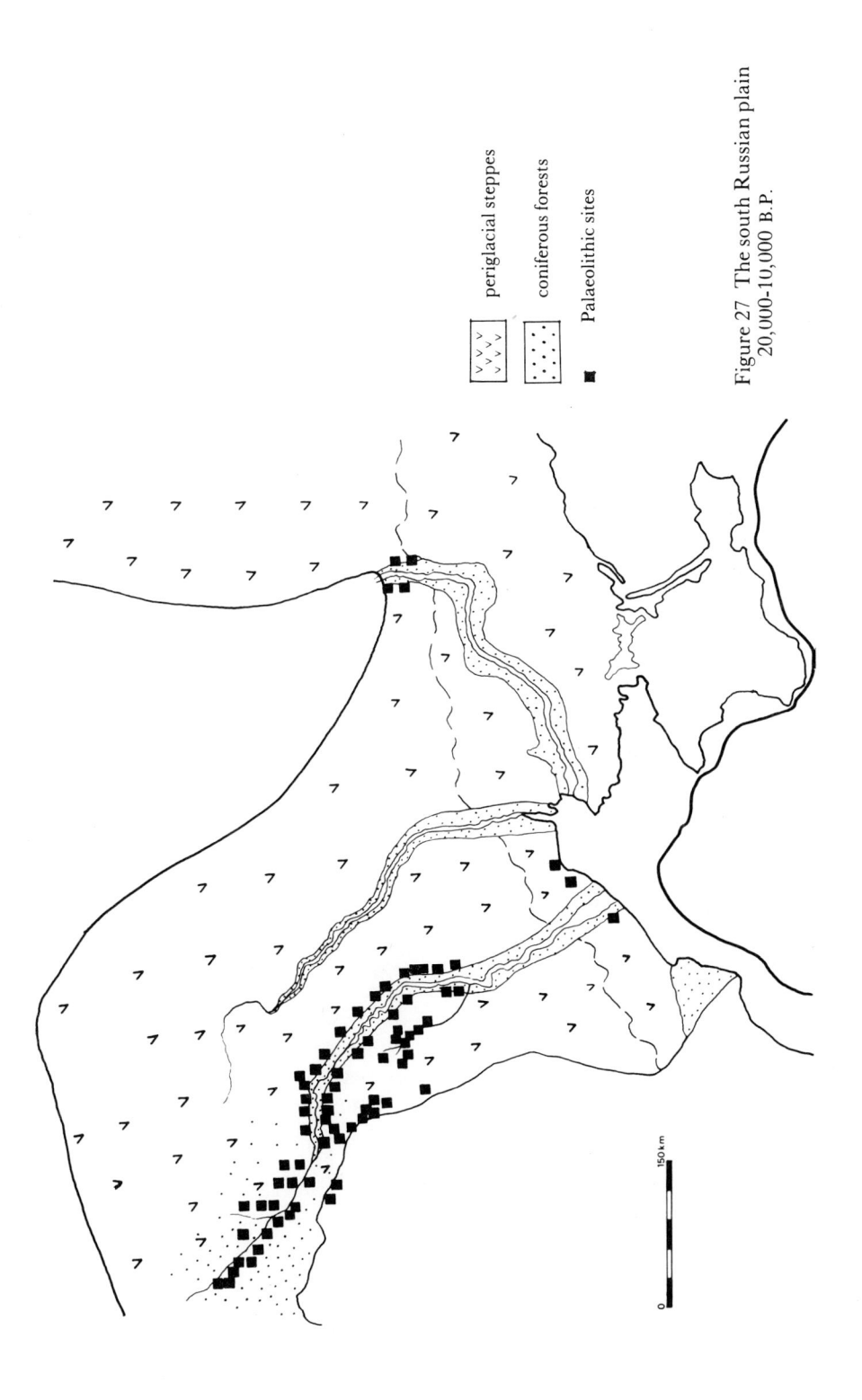

Figure 27 The south Russian plain 20,000–10,000 B.P.

Black Sea. By the end of the period the vegetation of the forest-steppic zone had become mixed coniferous/broad-leaved 'island' forests containing a high biomass. At the beginning of the Holocene the levels of the rivers fell, making low terraces and flood-plains available for human habitation.

During the whole of this period the territory was inhabited by human groups using a Mesolithic stone inventory. At the initial stage of the Holocene the settlement pattern of the Mesolithic groups was the same as that of the Upper Palaeolithic. Later, due to the fall in the river levels, the low river terraces, flood-plains and limans became the most important areas of human settlement. The greater part of the Mesolithic settlement was concentrated in the valley of the Dniester and in the western part of the steppe zone.

The subsistence pattern of the Mesolithic groups was based upon fishing, food gathering and on hunting of forest and steppe animals. Thus, a territory inhabited by Mesolithic groups formed a single natural economic zone with subzones. The Mesolithic people who settled in the Dniester valley hunted roe deer, red deer and wild pig while the Mesolithic groups of the steppe zone hunted wild horses and aurochs. In all probability at the same time in the eastern part of the steppe zone a stock-breeding centre began to be formed (Fig. 28).

8,000-6,000 B.P.

During this time the formation of modern natural zones continued. Islands of mixed oak forests were widely spread over the forest-steppe zone. Dense coniferous broad-leaved forests covered the slopes of the major river valleys, the Prut, the Dniester and the southern Bug.

At that time at least four different natural economic zones were formed in the south Russian Plain and in adjacent areas of Europe. The valleys of the Dniester and of the southern Bug were populated by human groups with an economy based on fishing, hunting and gathering. This economic strategy provided the optimum yield of products in densely forested valleys rich in natural resources.

The Moldavian highlands and part of the Dniester valley were settled by a population with a mixed food-producing/food-appropriating economy. The marginal areas of loessic uplands in the south-east and in central Europe were settled by a population with a stable food-producing economy based on agriculture and on stock-breeding. The eastern part of the steppe zone was occupied by human groups with a food-producing economy based upon stock-breeding.

About 6,800-6,500 years ago pottery manufacturing spread over the south Russian plain. The elements of decoration commonly used by the Neolithic dwellers of the Dniester and the southern Bug valleys were impressions of shells and finger nails, comb stamps, incised lines and finger pinches. The ornamental patterns consisted of horizontal, vertical and wavy lines, volutes or chevrons, zigzags and networks.

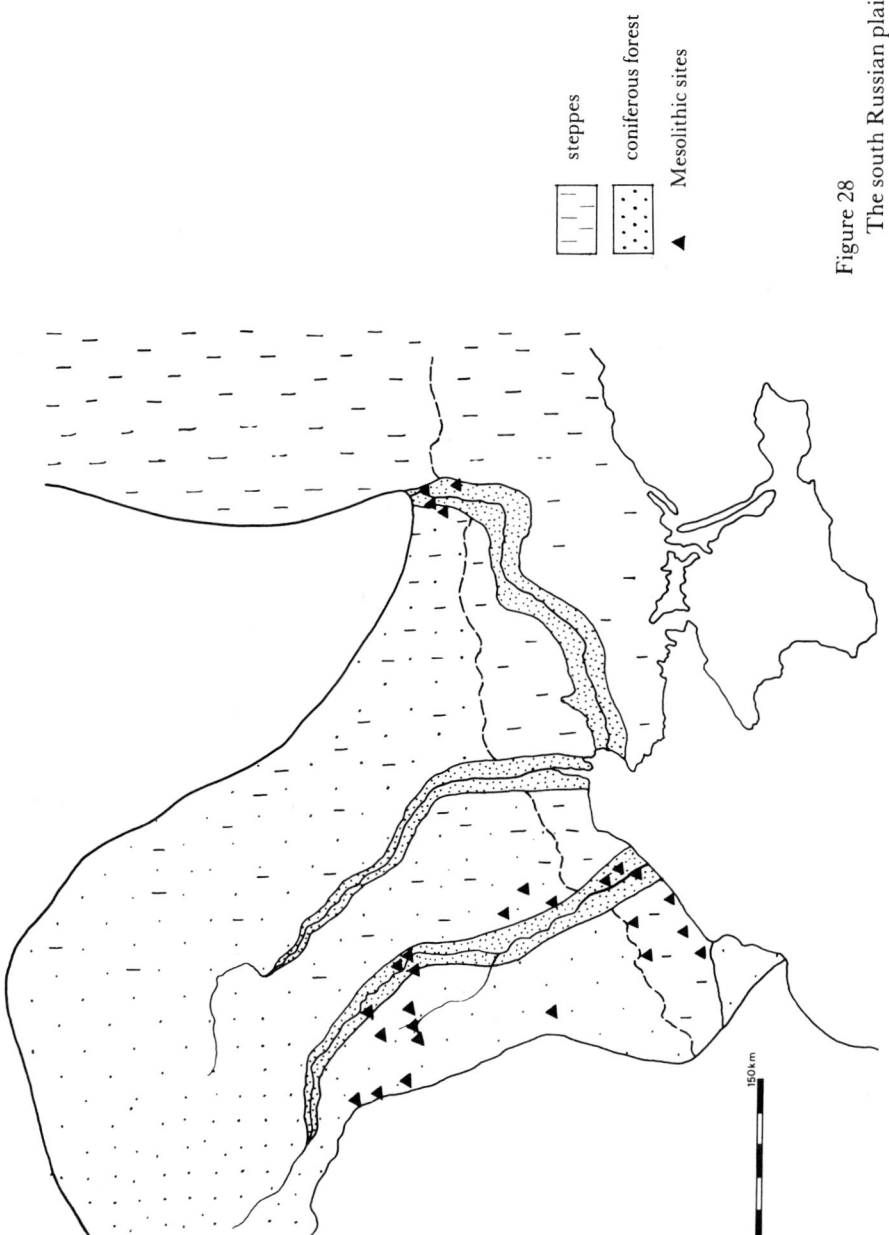

Figure 28
The south Russian plain 10,000-8,000 B.P.

The greater part of these ornamental patterns were directly analogous to the Early Neolithic monochrome Barbotine or impressed pottery of the Balkans. On this basis I include the Neolithic sites of the Dniester and of the southern Bug, on the one hand, and the Neolithic sites with monochrome pottery, on the other, in a single cultural zone. Apart from that, other cultural zones may be distinguished in the south Russian plain, represented by a zone of Linear pottery, a zone of Gumelniţa culture, and zones of Neolithic cultures in the eastern part of the steppe zone.

The emergence and evolution of cultural zones may be explained by the following processes. Population stress in the agricultural zone in the Balkan peninsula (due to an intrinsic rise of population and to extensive forms of agriculture) led to a hiving off of part of the surplus population. This splitting up proceeded in three directions and led to the realization of different economic strategies: (1) outflow of population into the loessic plains of south-eastern and central Europe, with a retention of an agricultural economic strategy; (2) outflow into the coastal area of the Mediterranean, with the acquisition of a fishing, hunting and gathering economic strategy; (3) outflow into the forested valleys of the Dniester and the southern Bug where fishing, hunting and food collecting guaranteed the optimal yield. In the second and third cases the migrating population was at least partially absorbed by the native one, originally occupying the sites most suitable for a food-appropriating economy (Fig. 29).

6,000-4,000 B.P.

During this time a further consolidation of natural zones took place. Open mixed oak forests spread in the forest-steppe zone, while coniferous/broad-leaved forests remained in the valleys. By the end of the period the area covered by forests had diminished.

The natural economic zone of the food-producing economy spread considerably, embracing the western parts of the steppe and forest-steppe zones. This part of the natural economic zone of the food-producing economy coincides with the Tripolye cultural zone.

Early Tripolye settlements, situated on lower terraces and on flood-plains, had a mixed food-producing/food-appropriating economy. Later Tripolye settlements, situated in most cases on loessic uplands, were characterized by a stable food-producing economy. These settlements reached considerable size.

At about 4,200-4,000 B.P. the spread of human groups with a predominantly stock-breeding economy began in this area. This spread is due partly to the exhaustion of arable lands by intensive forms of agriculture, partly to the overflow of surplus population from stock-breeding areas in Europe (Fig. 30).

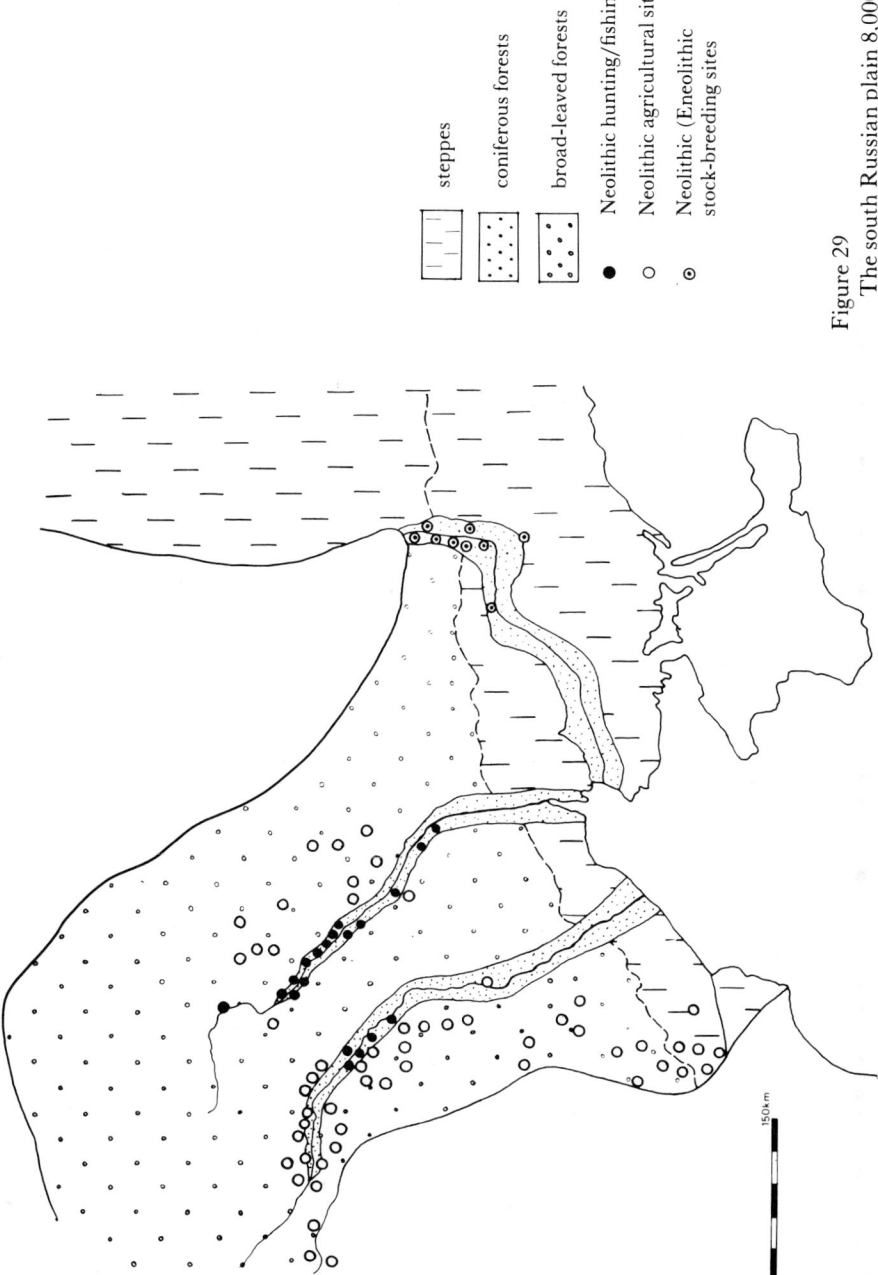

Figure 29 The south Russian plain 8,000-6,000 B.P.

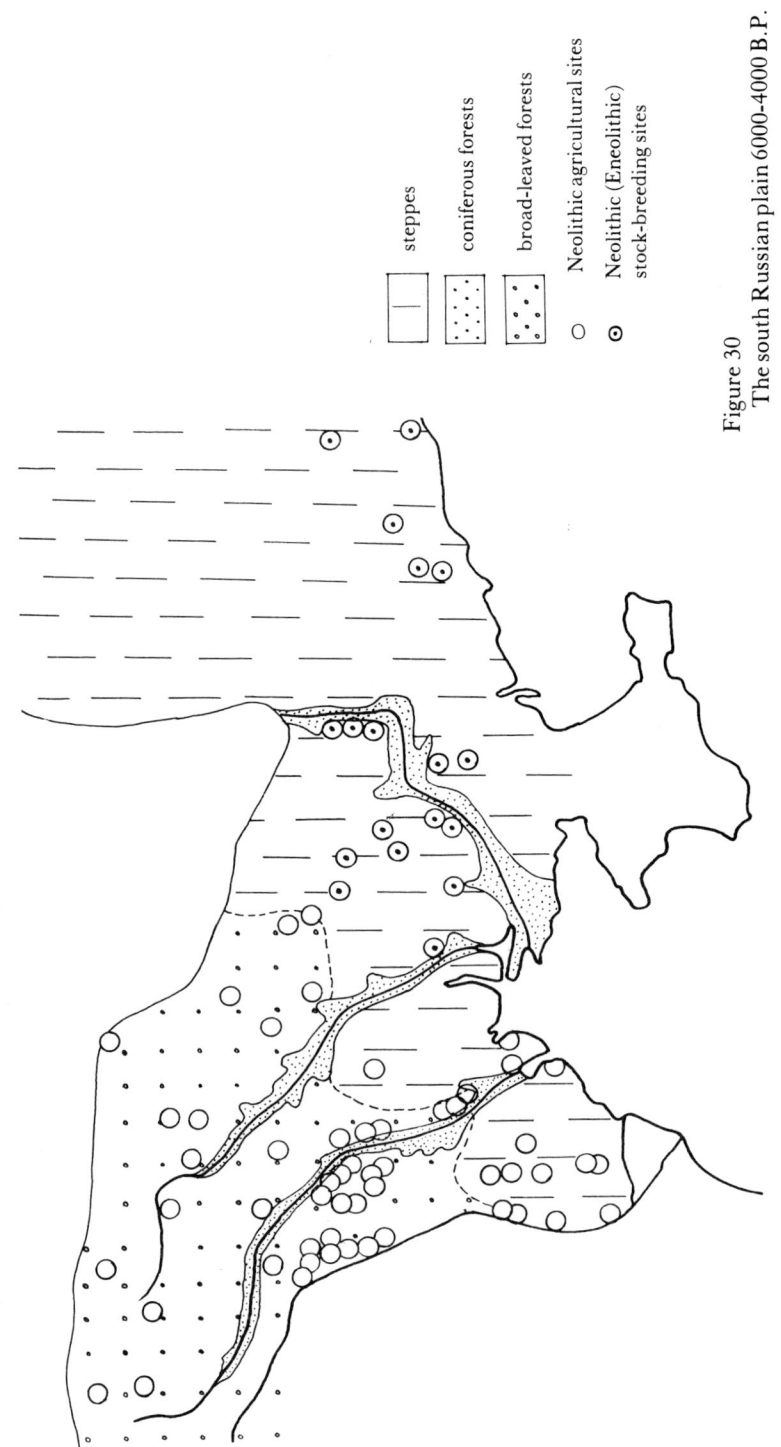

Figure 30
The south Russian plain 6000–4000 B.P.

NOTES

[1] The geological and physical geographical survey of the south-western part of the Russian Plain is based on M.V. Muratov, *Tektonika i istoriya razvitiya al'piyskoi geosinklinalnoi oblasti na yugye yevropeiskoi časti SSSR i sopredyel'nykh stran*, Tektonika SSSR, 2, Moscow-Leningrad, 1949; V.G. Bondarčuk, *Geologiya Ukrainy*, Kiev, 1959; I.P. Gerasimov (ed.), *Ukraina i Moldaviya. Prirodnyye usloviya i yestyestvennyye resursy*, Moscow, 1965.

[2] A.B. Ostrovsky, 'Regressivnyye urovni Černogo morya i ikh svyaz' s pyeryeuglublyeniyem ryečnykh dolin kavkazskogo pobyeryežya', *Izvyestiya AN SSSR, seriya geografičyeskaya*, 1, 1967; K.K. Šilik, 'Opryedyelyeniye vysoty i absolyutnogo vozrasta novočyernomorskoi terrasy v Olvii', *Doklady AN SSSR*, 203, 5, 1972, pp. 1157-9.

[3] D.A. Lilenberg, 'Osnovnyye čerty geomorfologii i paleogeografii yugo-zapadnogo pobyeryežya Černogo morya', in Yu. D. Boulanger, N.S. Blagovolin (eds.), *Kompleksnyye isslyedovaniya černomorskoi vpadiny*, Moscow, 1970, pp. 82-114.

[4] K.N. Negodayev-Nikonov, P.V. Yanovsky, *Četvyertičnyye otloženiya Moldavskoy SSR*, Kishinev, 1969.

[5] M.F. Veklič, *Stratigrafiya lesovoi formacii Ukrainy i sosednikh stran*, Kiev, 1968.

[6] A.A. Velička, *Prirodnyi process v pleistocenye*, Moscow, 1973; A.A. Velička, T.D. Morozova, 'Osnovnyye gorizonty lesov i iskopayemykh počv Russkoi ravniny', in A.A. Velička (ed.), *Lëssy, pogryebyennyye počvy i kriogennyye yavlyeniya na Russkoi ravninye*, Moscow 1973, pp. 5-25.

[7] V.P. Gričuk, 'Rezul'taty paleobotaničeskogo izučyeniya lesov Ukrainy i yuga Sryednyerusskoi vozvyšyennosti,' in A.A. Velička (ed.), *Lëssy, pogryebyennyye počvy i kriogennyye yavlyeniya na Russkoi ravninye*, Moscow, 1973, pp. 26-48; A.T. Artyušenko, *Rastityel'nost' lyesostepy i stepi Ukrainy v četvyertičnom periodye (po dannym sporo-pyl'cyevogo analiza)*, Kiev, 1970.

[8] N.A. Ketraru, *Arkheologičeskaya karta Moldavskoi SSSR, Čast' I, Paleolit*, Kishinev, 1973.

[9] A.I. David, N.A. Ketraru, 'Fauna mlyekopitayuščikh paleolita Moldavii', in K.N. Negodayer-Nikonov (ed.), *Fauna kainozoya Moldavii*, Kishinev, 1970, pp. 3-53.

[10] A.P. Černyš, 'Pozdnii paleolit Sryednyego Pridnyestrovya', *Trudy komissii po izuceniyu četvyertičogo perioda*, XV, 1959; I.K. Ivanova, 'Geologičeskiye usloviya nakhoždyeniya paleolitičeskikh stoyanok Sryednyego Pridnyestrovya', in Černyš, op. cit. (Note 10), 1959, pp. 215-78.

[11] P.I. Boriskovsky, N.D. Praslov, 'Paleolit basseina Dnyepra i Priazovya', in B.A. Rybakov (ed.), *Svod arkheologiceskikh istočnikov*, A1-5, Moscow, 1964. G.V. Grigor'yeva, *Pozdnyepaleoliticeskiye pamyatniki syevero-zapadnogo Pričernomorya*, Leningrad, 1968.

[12] P.I. Boriskovsky, 'Quelques problèmes du Mésolithique de l'Ukraine', *Mélanges ... offerts à André Varagnac*, Paris, 1971, pp. 75-81; V.N. Stanko, *Mezolit severo-zapadnogo Pričernomorya*, Kiev, 1967.

[13] The sites of Girževo and Mirnoye were geologically investigated by the author in 1970. A pollen analysis was made by Dr Levkovskaya, Leningrad, and Dr Paskevič, Kiev. The archaeological description is based on Stanko, op. cit. (Note 12), 1967 and Stanko, 'Mezolit Dnyestro-Dunayskogo myežduryeč'ya', in P.O. Karyskovskiy (ed.), *Materialy po arkheologii syevernogo Pričernomorya*, Odessa, 1971, pp. 93-117.

[14] V.N. Danilenko, *Neolit Ukrainy*, Kiev, 1969.

[15] The pollen analysis was made by Dr G.A. Paškevič, Kiev.

[16] A.P. Černyš, 'Khronologiya mezolitičeskikh pamyatnikov Podnestrovya', *Sovetskaya Arckheologiya*, I, 1970, pp. 9-18.

[17] V.I. Markevič, *Bugo-Dnyestrovskaya kul'tura na territorii Moldavii*, Kishinev, 1974.

[18] The humus content in the modern soil layer in the profile of the Soroki 5 site is 2·3-3·4%; that in the cultural layer in 0·44-0·69%. The humus content of the modern chernozem soil developed over the loessic deposits in the Dniester valley is 5·75-5·88% (analysed at the laboratory of soil sciences, Leningrad State University).

[19] Existence of trading connections between prehistoric communities is usually proved by findings of imported goods in the assemblages. The identification of obsidian tools made it possible to follow up neolithic trading links covering the Near East and south-eastern Europe. As J. Mellaart wrote recently, obsidian acts as a guide fossil in recognizing trade, most of which may have been in perishable products, such as domestic grain, and animals, woven cloth, etc.: J. Mellaart, 'Anatolian Neolithic settlement pattern', in P.J. Ucko, K. Tringham, J. Dimbleby (eds.), *Man, Settlement and Urbanism*, London, 1972, p.281.

[20] Danilenko, op. cit. (Note 14), 1969.

[21] H. Quitta, 'Zur Lage und Verbreitung der bandkeramischen Siedlungen in Leipziger Land,' *Zeitschrift für Archäologie*, 4, 1970, pp. 155-76.

[22] E. Rybníčková, K. Rybníček, 'Pollen diagram from Vracov and the problem of the origins of the southern Moravian steppe', in M.I. Neistaat (ed.), *Palynology of Holocene and Marine Palynology*, Moscow, 1973, pp. 33-39.

[23] S. Tabaczinski, *Neolit srodkowoeuropejski. Podstawy gospodarcze*, Wroclaw-Warsaw-Cracow, 1970.

[24] B. Soudsky, *Bylany*, Prague, 1966; B. Soudsky, I. Pavlu, 'The Linear pottery culture settlement problems in Central Europe, in P.J. Ucko, et al, op. cit. (Note 19), 1972, pp. 317-28.

[25] T.S. Passek, Ye. K. Černyš, 'Pamyatniki lineino-lyentocnoi kyeramiki na territorii SSSR', in B.A. Rybakov (ed.) *Svod arkheologičeskikh istočnikov*, BI-II, Moscow, 1966.

[26] V.I. Calkin, *Drevneišiye domašniye životnyye Vostočnoi Yevropy*, Moscow, 1963.

[27] Z.V. Yanuševič, V.I. Markevič, 'Espèces des plantes cultivées des stations primitives au sud-ouest de l'URSS', *VIIIe Congrès international des sciences pré- et protohistoriques, Rapports des archéologues soviétiques*, Moscow, 1971.

[28] T.S. Passek, *Rannyezemlyedyel'českiye (tripol'skiye) plyemyena Podnyestrovya*, Materialy i isslyedovaniya po arkheologii SSSR, 84, Moscow, 1961.

[29] S.N. Bibikov, 'Khozyaistvenno-ekonomičeskii kompleks razvitogo Tripol'ya (opyt izučeniya pyervobytnoi ekonomiki),' *S.A.*, 2, 1965.

Chapter 5

THE WEST RUSSIAN PLAIN

Geological background

The huge territory referred to here as the west Russian plain[1] has one common feature: it was directly affected by the ice of Quaternary glaciations. Landforms connected with the activities of ice-shields are widely spread over the area: terminal moraines, glacio-lacustrine basins, and so on. In the full sequence of Quaternary deposits the sediments formed during cold phases, often in glacial conditions, are interstratified with deposits which were formed during mild interglacial periods, when the climate was much warmer than it is now. In the Quaternary deposits of the west Russian plain geologists have established the existence of nine climatic fluctuations, each including cold (glacial) and warm (interglacial) phases.[2]

The Dnieper glaciation was the maximal one in eastern Europe. The ice-sheet of this glaciation, usually correlated with the Saale glaciation of central Europe, reached the middle stretches of the Dnieper. After a short interglacial interval there followed the Moscow (Warthe) glaciation when the ice-sheet reached the vicinity of the Soviet capital. During the following interglacial epoch, known as Mikulino (Riss-Würm or Eemian), considerable parts of the north-western Russian plain were submerged by the waters of a marine transgression. This interglacial phase lasted from 100,000 to 70,000 B.P.

The history of the Last Glaciation, which is known in the Russian plain as Valdai (Würm or Weichselian in western Europe), has been studied in much more detail than the older section of the Quaternary deposits. The formations of the Last Glaciation, which lasted from 70,000 to 10,000 B.P., may be subdivided into three sections: Early Valdai, Middle Valdai and Late Valdai.

During the Early Valdai there were three cold intervals separated by mild climatic phases of an interstadial character. The first mild phase is known as the Upper Volga interstadial – and it is usually correlated with the Amersfoort interstadial in Holland. In one case it was radiocarbon dated to more than 55,000 B.P. The second mild phase is correlated with the Brörup interstadial known in Denmark and in Holland. The radiocarbon age of this deposit in Estonia is about 52,780 B.P.

During the next period, the Middle Valdai the territory of Europe was practically free of ice. This interval was not particularly warm; treeless vegetation of a periglacial character covered the continent up to its southern limit. These deposits are found in stratigraphically good condition in borings studied in Leningrad. Here bog and lake deposits lie stratified between two morainic layers. These deposits were radiocarbon dated to 40,000-39,000 B.P.

A period of climatic cooling preceding the onset of the subsequent ice advance was revealed by pollen analysis and by radiocarbon dating as occurring between 21,000-20,000 years ago. Similar dates have been obtained in other parts of Europe and in America. It now seems certain that the last important cooling of the climate, which caused the last advance of the ice-sheet, occurred throughout the world about 21,000-18,000 B.P.

Quaternary geologists have proved that the advance of the ice-sheet during the Late Valdai was the maximal one for the last 70,000 years. About 18,000 years ago the ice-sheet reached the Valdai upland and northern Byelorussia and covered the north European plain.

The retreat of the ice-sheet proceeded by means of rhythmic oscillations. Phases of retreat alternated with renewed advances. The chronology of the last glacial episodes in the Russian plain is as follows:

Rauñis warm episode: 13,700-13,200 B.P.
Luga re-advance: 13,200-12,400 B.P.
Bölling: 12,400-12,000 B.P.
Middle Dryas: 12,000-11,800 B.P.
Alleröd: 11,800-11,000 B.P.
Salpausélkä (Younger Dryas): 11,000-9,800 B.P. (Fig. 31).

The existence of numerous glacio-lacustrine basins was an important feature of the landscape of the glacial age.[3] These basins were created when the advancing ice-sheet blocked the valleys of rivers flowing in a north-westerly direction. An enormous dam of pressed ice and soil prevented the river waters from following their courses. The levels of the dammed rivers rose rapidly, and the low-lying depressions of the ice-sheet were filled with water. The levels in these basins continued to rise until the height of the watershed was reached. At this point the waters of the glacial lakes obtained access to the valleys of rivers flowing in a southerly direction. These valleys became channels which drained the excess waters from the glacial lakes into the southern seas. Land forms connected with the activity of the glacio-lacustrine basins – terraces and depressions filled with sands and varved clays – are widespread in the west Russian plain. Geologists have been able to follow the evolution of these basins during the course of the Last Glaciation.

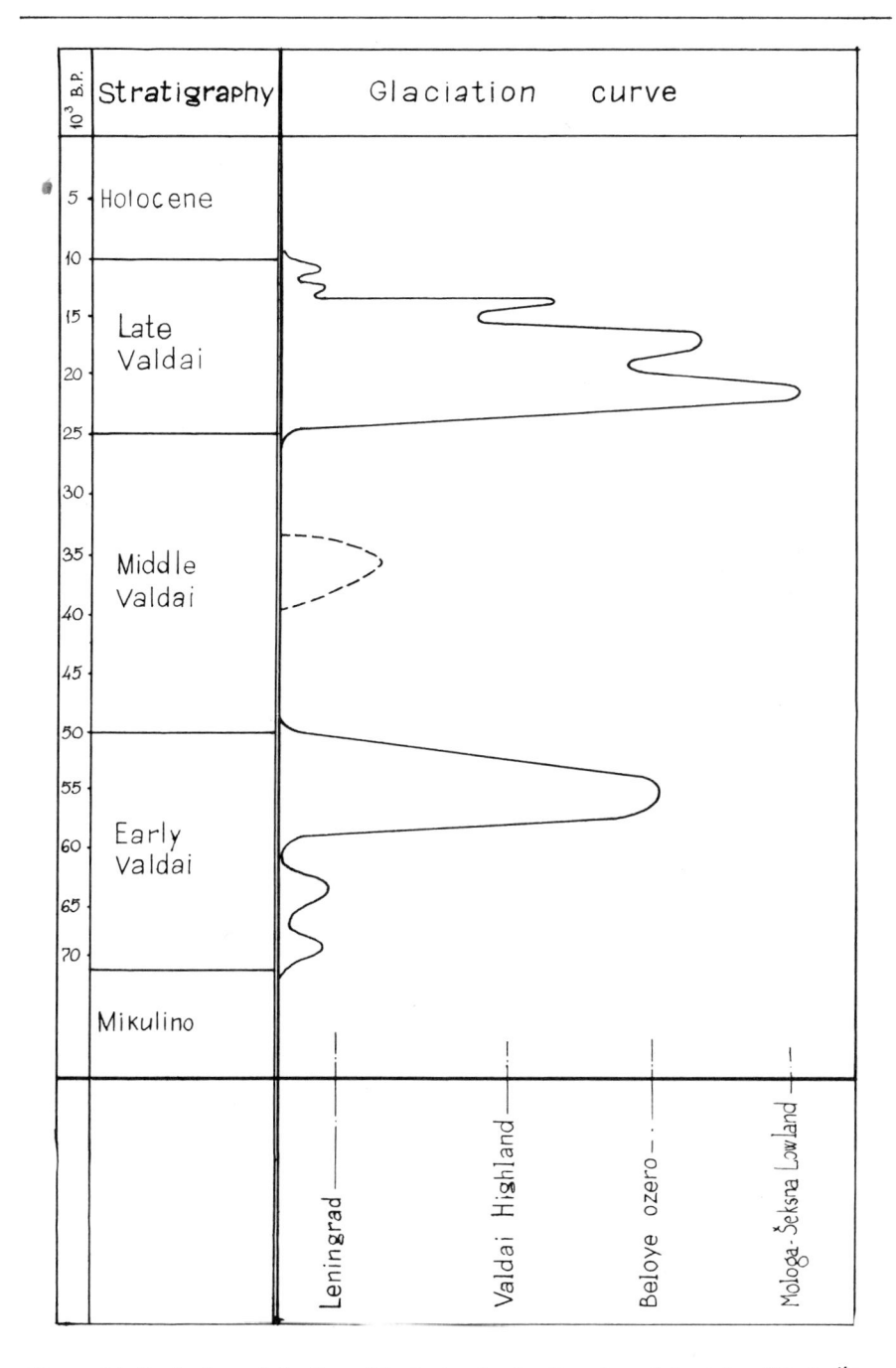

Figure 31 Evolution of the Last Glaciation in the Russian plain (after Vigdorčik et al., 1971; Note 5.2). The curve shows the displacement of the ice-sheet in the course of time; the vertical column is the time scale; the horizontal scale displays geographical points in the Russian plain attained by the glacier in the course of its advance and retreat

The evolution of the natural environment in northern Europe during the Holocene was determined to a large extent by the evolution of the Baltic Sea.[4] The size, salinity and temperature of the Baltic Sea were undergoing changes during the Holocene. Two important factors were responsible for these changes: the eustatic rise of the sea level and tectonic movements of the Earth's crust. Tectonic movements in northern Europe were mostly due to the so-called glacial rebound or to isostasy. The masses of ice, pressed snow and boulders forming the body of the glacier were very heavy. Their weight caused a depression of the crust, which was most marked in the areas where the glacier was thickest. When the glaciers retreated the crust straightened itself, causing land upheaval. Investigations by Soviet geologists[5] of the river valleys in the north-western part of the Russian plain revealed the existence of tilting, due partly to isostatic upheaval and partly to the development of geological structures inherited from older geological times.

The first major basin situated within the Baltic depression is referred to by geologists as the Baltic glacial lake. This basin was dammed by a huge morainic belt stretching from middle Sweden (middle-Swedish moraines) to south-eastern Finland (Salpauselkä). This basin had no connection with the ocean; its level was much higher than that of the open sea. The retreat of the glacier from the Mount Billingen area in central Sweden led to the formation of a strait, and to the linking-up of the Baltic basin with the North Sea. The absolute date for this event has been established as 10,189 B.P. by the sophisticated counting of varves. This date is often used to mark the beginning of the Holocene.

After these dramatic events in central Sweden the level of the Baltic Sea dropped. The level of the ocean at that time was about 30 m. below the present one. The first Baltic marine basin has been labelled by geologists the Yoldia Sea; according to radiocarbon datings this basin existed between 10,189 and c. 9,200 B.P. The level of the Yoldia Sea rose between 9,700 and 9,200 B.P. Isostatic upheaval gradually led to the closing of the strait in middle Sweden which connected the Yoldia Sea with the ocean. Thus the freshwater Ancylus lake was formed in the Baltic depression.

Many geologists distinguish two stages in the history of this lake: Lake Echineis, a brackish lake which existed between 9,200 and 9,000 B.P., and Lake Ancylus, a freshwater lake, existing between 8,900 and 8,000 B.P. The two stages were separated by a marked regression. We found indication of this regression during our investigations at the Sarnate site on the western Latvian shoreland. Two layers of sea marl were separated here by the thin layer of peat which was deposited when the level of the lake dropped. The C14 date of this peat layer was 8,900 ± 90 B.P.[6]

About 7,900 B.P. tectonic movements in southern Scandinavia led to the formation of the present straits linking the Baltic Sea with the ocean, the Kattegat and Skagerrak straits. A new marine basin came into being. The linking up of the Baltic Sea with the ocean led to a long regression. The sea-level dropped considerably, and numerous sea lagoons were separated from the sea and turned into peat bogs, which were the favourite dwelling places of Mesolithic and Neolithic hunters and fishers in the Baltic area. Numerous radiocarbon dates indicate that the regression continued from 7,900 to 7,100 B.P.

About 7,100 years ago a new rise in the sea level occurred. This time it was directly connected with the eustatic rise of the ocean level. The marine basin which was formed in this way in the Baltic Sea is referred to as the Littorina Sea. The period of the Littorina Sea in the Baltic was of importance for human settlement. During this period the shores of the Littorina Sea were intensively populated by groups of primitive hunters and fishers.

Geological investigations have shown that during the stage of the Littorina Sea several fluctuations of its level occurred. These fluctuations, which were in all probability worldwide, are visible in the terraces of the northern Baltic and in the stratigraphy of the off-shore peat bogs. The Swedish geologist N.A. Mörner,[7] summing up his own investigations and those of other scientists, distinguishes the following fluctuations between 7,100 and 2,000 B.P.:

7,100-6,900: transgression;
6,500-6,300: regression;
6,300-5,900: transgression;
5,900-5,600: regression;
5,600-4,600: transgression;
4,600-4,300: regression;
4,300-4,000: transgression;
4,000-3,700: regression;
3,700-3,300: transgression;
3,300-3,000: regression.

During the regressions the dwellings of hunters and fishers appeared in the peat bogs near the sea. During the transgressions these areas were submerged by rising sea waters. This peculiarity of the evolution of the Baltic Sea makes it possible to correlate, the late Stone Age sites in the Baltic area. It was during the regression between 5,600 and 5,000 B.P. That the group of Ertebølle sites in the south-western Baltic area originated. These are Buddelin (6,192 ± 120 B.P.) and Augustenhof (5,496 ± 100 B.P.), both on the island of Rügen; and Elinelund in south Sweden (5,410 ± 210 B.P.). A group of sites appeared in off-shore lagoons during the regression that took place between 4,600 and 4,300 B.P. These were the Sarnate site in western Latvia and the Šventoji site in north-western Lithuania. The site on a floating island in a peat bog near Muldbjerg, Zealand, probably came into being during the same regression. A number of

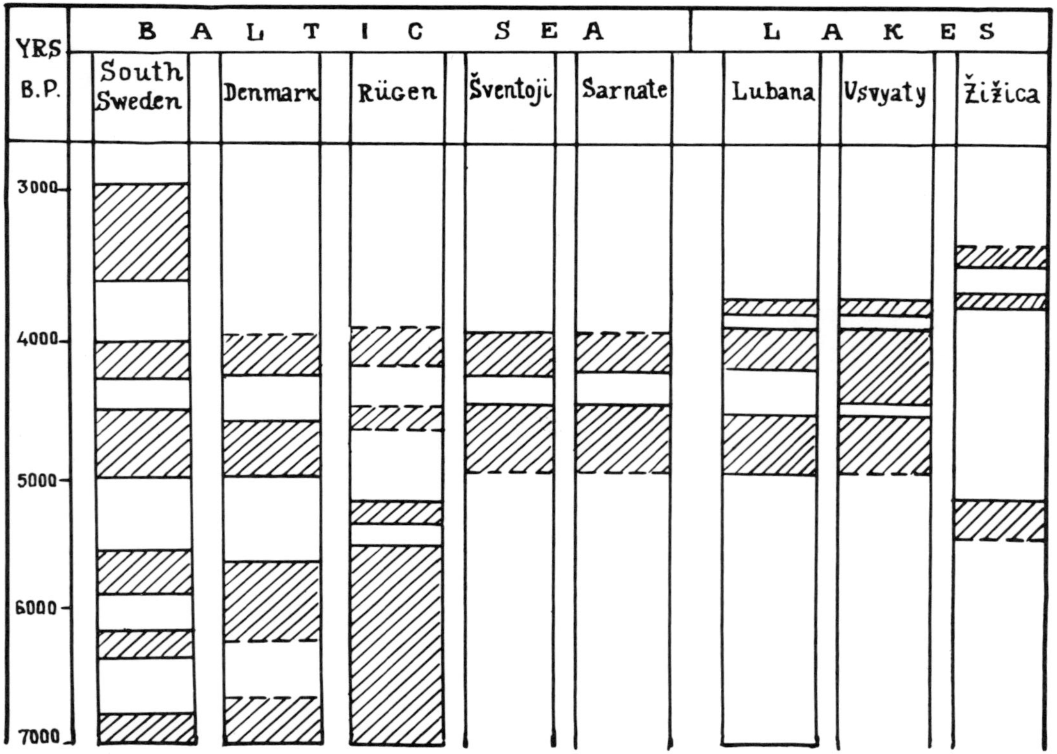

Figure 32 Transgressions of the Baltic sea and inner lakes during the Holocene. Shaded rectangles correspond to transgressions, solid lines to solid dates, and broken lines to provisional dates.

sites in off-shore lagoons appeared during the regression that took place between 4,000 and 3,700 B.P. During this regression the upper cultural layer at the Šventoji site was formed. This layer contains corded wares (Fig. 32).

As we have seen, there is reason to believe that fluctuations in the sea level of the Littorina Sea were caused by worldwide eustatic fluctuations. It is interesting to note that investigations of the so-called Flandrian transgressions in the British Isles have revealed that these transgressions were almost synchronous with the Littorina transgressions of the Baltic. British geologists[8] distinguish the following transgressions: 7,000-6,700; 6,450-6,200; 5,700-5,500; 5,000-4,700; 4,100-3,900 (this particular transgression is doubtful, it is based on one date of a buried peat layer in the Forth valley in an uncertain stratigraphic position); 3,700-3,500; and 3,200-3,000 B.P. Very similar fluctuations of the sea level have been established in the North Sea southern coastal area. The beginning of the sea ingressions along the western coast of Schleswig occurred between 7,200-7,000 B.P. Important regressions took place between 6,500-6,000 and about 5,000 years ago.[9] The onset of the marine transgression along the Dutch coast took place about the same time as in other parts of Northern Europe. Important regressions of the sea took place between 6,200-6,000; about 4,800; between 4,500 and 4,000; about 3,800 B.P. and after 3,400 B.P.[10]

The actual heights of the Littorina-Flandrian transgressions may be deduced on the basis of the altitudes of terraces and cliffs formed during these transgressions in tectonically stable areas. The highest Littorina terrace in the Lithuanian coastal area has an altitude of 6 m. above sea-level.[11] The bottom of the Littorina strand wall on the island of Rügen is only 2 m. above the present sea-level.[12]

Small lakes, the remnants of huge glacial lakes, still exist in some of the depressions formed by glacial lacustrine basins in the west Russian plain. These lake depressions were just as important as centres of primitive hunting and fishing as were the off-shore sea lagoons. They were probably particularly suitable for economic strategies based on hunting, fishing and food collecting. The water-levels of glacial lacustrine basins dropped as the ice-sheet retreated towards the north, and such basins dryed up completely during the terminal phases of the last glaciation, the Alleröd or the Younger Dryas. In other places only small lakes were left.

New investigations have produced evidence that the levels of these lakes fluctuated during the Holocene. Geological investigations, supported by radiocarbon datings and by pollen analysis, have shown that these fluctuations in most cases synchronized with those of the Baltic Sea.[13] This was true even for the lakes lying some 500 km. from the shores of the Baltic. The phenomenon has been established for three lake depressions: Lubana in eastern Latvia; Usvyaty in the south of the Pskov district; and Žižica in the western part of the same district. Summing up the results of our recent investigations, we may distinguish the following fluctuations of lake levels which more or less synchronize with the Littorina-Flandrian coastline displacements:

transgression: 7,200-6,000;
regression: 6,000-5,000;
transgression: 5,000-4,500;
regression: about 4,500-4,000;
transgression: 4,000-3,800 B.P.;
regression: after 3,800 B.P.

Fluctuations in the levels of lakes situated within the glacio-lacustrine basins were not restricted to the western part of the Russian plain. Similar fluctuations have been noted in lakes in the northern part of East Germany, in the marshes of north Friesland in West Germany, and in the north of Holland, though they probably reflect the short-term rhythms of natural processes caused by variations of solar radiation or other factors unknown to us.

The numerous sites of fishing and hunting communities found within the lake depressions coincide in most cases with periods of lake regression. By correlating the periods of lake and sea regression, it has been possible to synchronize the evolution of primitive sites over a vast territory (Fig. 33).

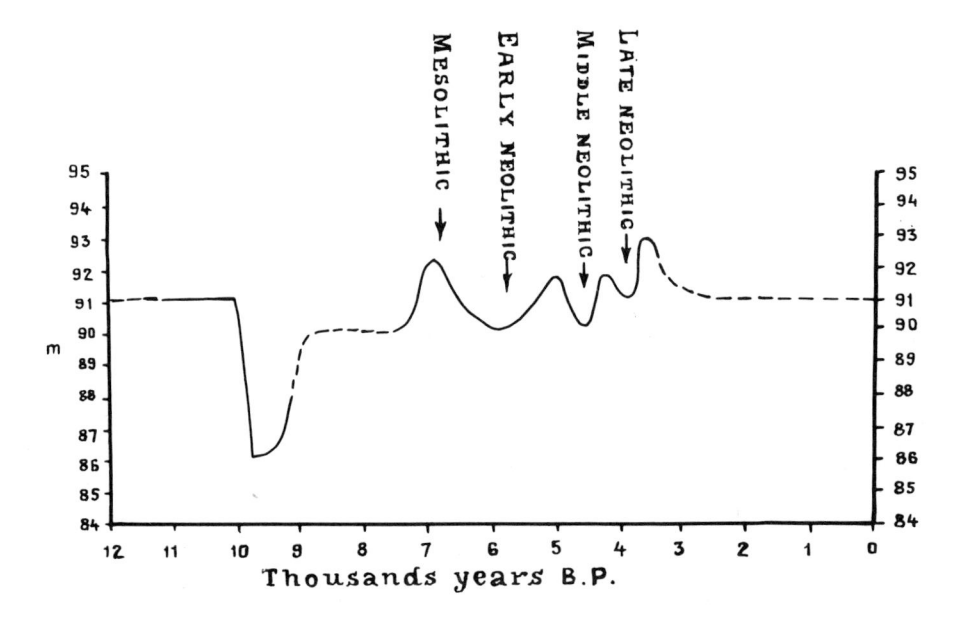

Figure 33 Fluctuations of the level of the Lubana Lake (eastern Latvia) during the Holocene. The solid line corresponds to firmly established displacement of the shore level in metres above the present shore level; the broken line corresponds to provisionally established displacement

The west Russian plain may be conveniently divided into two geomorphological zones: (1) the zone of the Middle Pleistocene (Dnieper and Moscow) glaciations, and (2) the zone of the Upper Pleistocene (Last, Weichselian or Valdai) glaciation. The first zone is characterized by the predominance of erosional forms over glacial ones and by the denudation of land-forms created by the glacial accumulation. The second zone is characterized by the freshness of the glacial topography and by the predominance of glacial forms over erosional ones.

The Middle Pleistocene zone, zone (1), includes the middle Dnieper, the Polessye and the Byelorussian provinces. The valley of the middle Dnieper is typical of the central Russian plain. Its maximum width is 125 km. The fourth terrace of the middle Dnieper is the widest; it is covered by the washed morainic clays of the Dnieper glaciation. Some parts of the valley consisted of chains of lakes at the time of the Last Glaciation; during that time the second and first Dnieper terraces were formed. The watershed plain is covered with thick loesses.

The Polessye[14] consists of two parts: the western part, the Pripyat valley, and the eastern part, the Desna valley. The Pripyat valley is situated in the central part of an intensively depressed geological structure. It is characterized by the smoothness of its relief and the width of its terraces. The swampy flood-plain of the Pripyat in several cases reaches 22 km. in width and there are numerous sand dunes within the flood-plain. The width of the first terrace, which is 5-8 m. high, varies from 10 to 15 km. The second terrace is 10 to 20 m. high and from 8 to 24 km. wide. The terrace slopes are extremely gentle. The exact attribution of the terraces is sometimes very difficult. Both the first and second terraces were formed during the Last Glaciation. They are built of sand carried by the waters from huge glacial lacustrine basins. In some areas of the watershed plain adjoining the valley on the south and on the north, relics of glacial landforms are visible: morainic belts, eskers and kamms of the Dnieper and Moscow glaciations. The eastern part of the Polessye, the Desna valley, is extremely wide in its lower and middle stretches. Geologists[15] distinguish a flood-plain 3-4 m. high, the first terrace being 10-12 m. high and the second terrace reaching 20-25 m. above the mean river level. The watershed level is at an altitude of 30-50 m. above the river. The first terrace was formed during the time of the Last Glaciation.

The zone of the Upper Pleistocene glaciation, zone (2), may be conveniently divided into three main provinces: (a) The outer province, which is characterized by large areas of accumulative fluvio-glacial plains which existed south of the ice sheet limits. The number of lakes here is few. (b) The main (central or morainic) province, which features morainic belts situated close to one another. This is the most elevated part of the Last Glaciation area. The high morainic belts surround deep lake depressions. The great number of lakes of different sizes and shapes is characteristic of the province. (c) The inner province, which covers the northern part of the zone of the Last Glaciation. Vast territories here are taken up by glacial lacustrine plains. Here are also situated terminal moraines of the last glacial stages. The number of lakes is comparatively few. This province includes the maritime area, where land forms connected with the activity of the Baltic Sea are represented.

Climate and vegetation

The modern climate of the west Russian plain is affected by atmospheric circulation. Masses of moist air are carried in from the Atlantic by cyclones moving east from Iceland. These cyclones occur frequently in winter. These intrusions of moist west winds are usually followed by intrusions of cold north winds, carried from the Arctic by anticyclones moving in a south-easterly direction. The moist Atlantic winds ensure that the west Russian plain receives more than 600 mm. of rain annually. The high ground in Lithuania and Latvia receives even more, about 800 mm. annually. The prevailing westerly winds penetrate a long way eastwards, causing repeated thaws with wet snow and mists. The coldest weather, with temperatures reaching minus 20-25°C, is caused by the intrusion of Arctic air. In the middle of May the day time temperature exceeds 10°; in July and August the day time temperature reaches 20° or even higher. The wettest months are July and August (75-100 mm. per month). In early October the day time temperature falls below 10° and the first frosts occur. The prevailing Atlantic cyclonic circulation again causes very rainy weather which continues until the beginning of the cold season.

Forests are the most common type of vegetation in the west Russian plain. Geobotanists distinguish several types of forests within the territory. Mixed oak forests were widespread in the area in early historic times, being common on watersheds and on the upper terraces of major rivers. Oak forests also grew on the boulder clays of the terminal morainic belts. In the Polessye, Latvia and Lithuania, mixed forests consisting of oak, hornbeam, ash-tree and alder are found on flood-plains. Coniferous oak forests grow in the same habitats; they are distinguished from the true mixed oak forests by an admixture of spruce. Pine forests are most common in the glaciated area of the Russian plain; they grow on sandy plains filling glacial lacustrine depressions, on the sandy terraces of major rivers and on sandy morainic plains. Spruce forests are usually found at the bottom and on the slopes of morainic belts, and are also often met with inside lacustrine depressions in areas where boulder clay overlies lake sediments. Birch forests are most common in the flood-plains of small rivers and on the edges of large peat bogs. Alder forests grow in the moistest areas of the west Russian plain, often on the flood-plains of large rivers and in depressions separating morainic hills where the ground water level is high enough.

Meadows are common in the territory under investigation. They usually occupy the low-lying portions of the flood-plains of major rivers and low terraces in the lacustrine basins. Large areas of the Russian plain are taken up by peat bogs, which are particularly common in the outer province of the Upper Pleistocene glaciation; they occupy considerable portions of the flood-plains of the Pripyat and of the middle Dnieper. Great numbers of peat bogs are also found in the inner province of the Last Glaciation area, being situated within glacial lake depressions. Peat bogs are also numerous in the maritime area of the Baltic Sea. Podsolic soils are widespread in the west Russian plain, being typical of the morainic deposits found all over it. Brown soils are characteristic of the sandy river terraces and sand filled lake depressions; and swampy soils are widespread in floodplains and on the low terraces of lake depressions.

The history of the vegetation of the west Russian plain is now more intensively studied than that of any other part of Europe. This is partly due to the fact that peat and lacustrine deposits are widely spread over this area and pollen grains are beautifully preserved in these sediments. At the same time the high content of organic matter in the deposits makes it possible to use radiocarbon dating. In many cases it has been possible to link the evolution of the vegetation cover with the development of human settlements.

One of the achievements of modern palaeobotany is the discovery of a particular type of vegetation that existed during the Last Glaciation, with no direct analogies in present-day vegetational cover. Plant species which now grow in areas with a semi-desert climate (*Artemisia, Chenopodiaceae*) coexisted side-by-side with plants now growing north of the Arctic Circle (*Betula nana*, an arctic birch).

A detailed palaeobotanical analysis has enabled the Soviet scientist V.P. Gričuk[16] to distinguish two types of glacial floras, the first with a high content of moisture-loving plants, and the second with a high content of drought-resisting plants. The first type is characteristic of the vegetation found during the first half of the Last Glaciation, while the second type is more characteristic of the end phases. As a result Gričuk has suggested that the glaciation consisted of two periods with different climatic patterns: the first period, when the ice-sheet was advancing was cold and wet, and the second period, when it was retreating, was cold and dry.

In the areas directly affected by the ice-sheet, ice-age vegetation is known mostly from the deposits laid down during mild intervals, when bogs and lakes were formed in the depressions. The palaeobotanical evidence shows that during the first mild intervals of the Last Glaciation the vegetation here resembled that of present-day moss tundra. The deposits of a subsequent mild interval were similar to present-day forest tundra: treeless vegetation and open spruce woodland. Forest vegetation spread anew over the area only during the Bölling oscillation that occurred between 12,400 and 12,000 B.P. At that time pine and birch-pine forests appeared in the northern parts of the plain, while spruce forests were more common in the southern regions. But the climate, judging from the plant remains, was still comparatively cold.

During the Middle Dryas, forest formations disappeared almost completely. During the Alleröd oscillation a new growth of forests is recorded in the whole area. Birch, pine and spruce formations were dominant in the vegetational cover. Broad-leaved plant species penetrated into the south-western regions. Thereafter, a cold Younger Dryas interval followed, the last episode of the glacial epoch. The forests diminished and polar birch and treeless tundra plant communities covered the area. But the cold episode did not last long. The spread of pine and birch forests at about 10,000 heralded the end of the Ice Age and the beginning of the Holocene.

The history of Holocene vegetational cover in the west Russian plain has been studied in detail. In many places radiocarbon dates have made it possible to date the stages of vegetational history in absolute figures. The Holocene vegetation in the area is determined by the dominance of forest formations. But within individual zones and provinces, and even within separate morphological units, the vegetation developed differently, directly affecting the evolution of human settlements.

The most detailed information about the history of Holocene vegetational cover in the zone affected by the Last Glaciation has been secured as a result of pollen analytical investigation of sediments from the glacial lacustrine basins. A number of pollen diagrams were compiled after investigations of these depressions in the outer province. In many cases, these investigations were carried out in connection with the study of Mesolithic and Neolithic sites in the basins.[17] The first stage of the history of the vegetation, corresponding to the Pre-Boreal period, is characterized by the spread of both pine and birch forests within these depressions.[18] The high percentage of grasses in the pollen spectra in the Pre-Boreal period confirms that treeless vegetation with tundra and steppe grasses covered the loess plains and morainic uplands. The treeless vegetation almost completely disappeared during the next stage, the Boreal period, when pine forests dominated the vegetation. The third stage, corresponding to the warm Atlantic period, was distinguished by the maximum spectrum of broad-leaved trees in the vegetation. The pine still dominated in sand-covered depressions but mixed oak forests were widespread over the loess plains and on the morainic hills. During this phase a great number of prehistoric sites appeared in the depressions. In several cases these sites are radiocarbon dated, indicating that the maximum spread of the mixed oak forests in this area took place between 5,500 and 5,000 B.P. During the next stage (the Sub-Boreal zone) the number of warmth-loving trees sharply diminished; spruce forests spread inside the low-lying terraces and in the depressions of the morainic landscape. Judging from the radiocarbon dates, the spread of spruce forests occurred about 3,600 years ago. The final stage is characterized by the gradual decrease of spruce forests and by the increase of birch forests.

A great number of pollen diagrams illustrate the development of the vegetational cover in the inner province during the Last Glaciation. In most cases this evidence is supported by radiocarbon dates. Palaeobotanists distinguish eleven phases in the evolution of vegetation in eastern Latvia.[19] In the Pre-Boreal phases birch forests predominate. A marked increase in pine and spruce forests is a feature of the Boreal period; towards the end of the period alder forests spread and a deep undergrowth of chestnut was formed. In the first half of the Atlantic period pine and alder forests predominate, and an increase in spruce forests is also noticeable. A number of broad-leaved trees appeared. The spread of alder and spruce forests was probably connected with the transgression of lakes inside the glacial lacustrine depressions. At this time the lake depressions began to be intensively populated by Mesolithic hunters and fishers. Radiocarbon dates indicate the time of this vegetational zone as 7,200-6,500 B.P. During the second half of the Atlantic period, pine and alder forests still dominated. Broad-leaved species attained their maximum spread (elm, lime, hornbeam and sometimes oak). Spruce forests increased. During this phase a considerable number of Neolithic hunting and fishing sites appeared inside the lake depressions. The radiocarbon dates of the layers corresponding to this vegetational zone lie in the period 6,500-4,500 B.P. The beginning of the Sub-Boreal period was marked by a decrease in the numbers of broad-leaved species, elm in particular; alder and pine forests were dominant. This period is radiocarbon dated from 4,500 to 4,000 B.P. The second half of the Sub-Boreal period was heralded by the massive spread of spruce forests. Their maximum spread is radiocarbon dated to 4,000 B.P. The Sub-Atlantic period is characterized by a gradual decrease of spruce forests and an increase of birch and pine forests.

In Estonia[20] the Atlantic period is characterized by the dominance of pine forests; oak pollen was present in negligible amounts; broad-leaved communities were formed by lime and elm with an undergrowth of chestnut, and alder forests were widespread. The spread of spruce forests occurred in Estonia earlier than in the southern regions. In south-eastern Estonia the beginning of the appearance of spruce is dated to 4,500 B.P. In the south-eastern Baltic region, in western Latvia and in Lithuania[21] the Atlantic period is characterized by the dominance of alder forests. In the second half of the Atlantic period oak, elm and lime attained their maximum spread. Some time after 4,500 B.P. the number of broad-leaved species fell. During the second half of the Sub-Boreal period, spruce forests spread in western Latvia and in northern Lithuania. In the Sarnate peat bog the maximum extent of spruce is dated to c. 3,100 B.P.[22]

Palaeolithic sites

Within the zone of the Middle Pleistocene glaciations, Upper Palaeolithic sites are concentrated in the middle Dniester valley and in the Polessye. Palaeobotanical investigations carried out in the classical Palaeolithic region of the Russian plain, Kostenki on the Don, have shown[23] that during the initial Upper Palaeolithic phases the slopes of the Don valley were covered with spruce trees. During Upper Palaeolithic times open steppe forests with pines, birch, and larch groves covered the area around the sites. The periglacial landscape contained large herds of herbivorous animals, mammoths, wild horses, saiga and reindeer. At the same time there were no animals trophically connected with forests – no elk, red deer or roe deer.

The basis of the Upper Palaeolithic economy was the specialized and highly effective hunting of periglacial herd animals. The effectiveness of Upper Palaeolithic hunting may be seen from Table 10, showing the number of animal species found at the Upper Palaeolithic sites on the Russian plain.

Table 10   (after N.K. Vereščagin[24])

Site	Species	Number of individuals
Byzovaya, Pečera river	Mammoth	32
Yeliseyeviči	Mammoth	60
Mezin, Černigov oblast'	Mammoth	116
Goncy, Poltava oblast'	Mammoth	25
Kirillovka, Kiev	Mammoth	70
Dobraničevka, Kiev oblast'	Mammoth	18
Mezerici, Čerkassy oblast'	Mammoth	95
Anosovka, river Don, Voronež oblast'	Mammoth	32
Ambrosyevka, Doneck oblast'	Bison	c. 1,000
Starosel'ye, Crimea	European ass	

The considerable biomass at the disposal of the Palaeolithic hunters and the effectiveness of their hunting pattern could have supported a substantial population. This suggestion is based on the fact that a large number of dwellings which were lived in all the year round have been discovered at Upper Palaeolithic sites. These sites are usually found in similar geomorphological situations. They are situated on the edges of watershed plains adjoining river valleys or upon high terraces, not lower than the second terrace. They are often found on promontories formed by deep ravines cutting the slopes of valley. These were probably the places most suitable for hunting. It should be remembered that in the Upper Pleistocene the rivers were much deeper and wider than they are now, and some parts of the valleys were chains of lakes.

In the middle Dnieper[25] valley, two groupings of Upper Palaeolithic sites are known. The southern group is represented by a group of sites known as Kaistrova Balka I-IV. The sites are situated on the slopes of a ravine cutting a high terrace of the Dnieper. Among the faunal remains bison predominates. The chipped stone inventory contains a large number of long blades and backed knives, and burins predominate over scrapers. No traces of dwellings have been discovered. A numerous group of Upper Palaeolithic sites is known upstream, in the area of Kiev and north of Kiev.[26]

The cultural deposits of the Fastov site are situated on the slope of the second terrace of the Irpen river, the right-hand tributary of the Dnieper. The cultural layer of the Kirillovskaya site was found under loess deposits 10 m. thick on the upper terrace of the Dnieper. The layers of the Dobraničevka and Goncy sites were found in the cover deposits of the second terraces of the Supoi and the Udai, tributaries of the Dnieper.

The hunting pattern of the middle Dniester Upper Palaeolothic dwellers was similar to that of the middle Dnieper dwellers. Nearly all their meat supply was provided through the highly efficient hunting of mammoths.

At Kirillovskaya, Goncy and Dobraničevka the remains of permanent dwellings made of mammoth bones have been discovered. According to reconstructions made by the Soviet palaeontologist I.G. Pidopličko, these were oval dwellings similar to the yarangas of modern tundra reindeer hunters, and did not exceed 23 sq.m. in size.

A number of Upper Palaeolithic sites are known in the eastern Polessye in the Desna valley. According to geological investigations[27] all the sites, with one exception (the site of Mezin), have a similar morphological position. The sites are situated at the edges of plateaux adjoining the valleys (Fig. 34). Geologists think that in Upper Palaeolithic times the level of the Desna river was 15-20 m. higher than at present.

The Soviet archaeologist I.G. Shovkoplyas[28] attributes two sites, Puškari I and Pogon, to early Upper Palaeolithic times. The cultural layers of both these sites are found in the upper horizons of the Briansk buried soil. At the Puškari I site the remains of three oval-shaped dwellings 3 to 3.5 m. long have been found. In the stone inventory there were a great number of cutting tools (retouched blades and points). An axe-like tool made of mammoth rib bone was found. Shovkoplyas has investigated a further site, near the town of Novgorod Severski. Its inhabitants hunted mammoth, woolly rhinoceros, wild horse, reindeer and bear. Mammoth hunting was

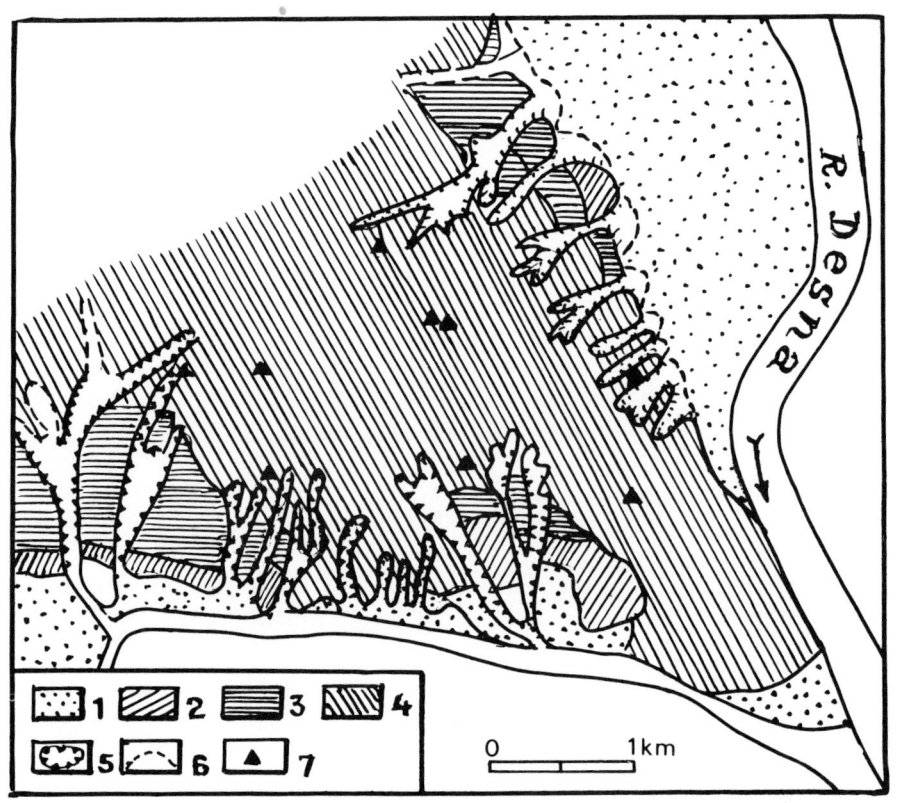

Figure 34 Upper Palaeolithic sites in the Desna River valley (after Veličko, 1969; Note 5.15). 1 – flood-plain; 2 – 1st terrace; 3 – 2nd terrace; 4 – plateau; 5 – ravines; 6 – dejection cones; 7 – sites

economically the most important. The stone inventory contains a large proportion of long, wide retouched blades and of large axe-like tools.

The Mezin site is the only one situated at a low level. The site lies on the first terrace of a huge ravine. The Soviet palaeogeographer A.A. Veličko is of the opinion that the site came into being after the river dropped to its flood-plain level. The cultural layer is buried under alluvial loess, 5 m. thick. Faunal determinations show that the subsistence pattern of the Mezin Palaeolithic inhabitants was determined by the efficient hunting of mammoth, with reindeer the second most important animal. The remains of five round dwellings made of mammoth bones were found. According to Pidopličko these dwellings, like those in the middle Dnieper area, resembled the northern yarangas. The foundation size is 23 sq.m.

The upper Dnieper and its tributaries were also inhabited by Upper Palaeolithic men.[29] The sites were discovered on the river Sož (a tributary of the Dnieper) and the river Sudost (a tributary of the Desna). Here, too, the sites are situated on levels higher than the second terrace. The Berdyž site belongs to an early phase of the Upper Palaeolithic. The site was found on a slope of a ravine at a level corresponding to the second terrace of the Sož river. The cultural layer was buried in stratified loess-like deposits, which are regarded by the geologist L.N. Voznyačuk[30] as belonging to the period preceding the maximum ice advance of the Last Glaciation. The geological date has recently been confirmed by C14 evidence: a mammoth tooth from the site was radiocarbon dated 23,430 ± 180 B.P. Remains of three oval dwellings made of mammoth bones have been uncovered, with dimensions of 4.5 and 3.4 metres.

The Yeliseyeviči site belongs to a later stage. The cultural layer of the site was found in stratified loess-like deposits developed on the second terrace of the Sudost river. According to geological investigations carried out by L.N. Voznyačuk, this site existed during the maximum phase of the Last Glaciation. Two radiocarbon dates were obtained for this site, 14,470 ± 100 (mammoth tooth) and 12,970 ± 140 (bone coal). Burins of various types are most numerous in the stone inventory of the Yeliseyeviči site. Scrapers form the next most numerous group. A large number of retouched blades and points has been recovered and a series of large axe-like and hoe-like stone tools have been reported.

The site of Yudinovo has been attributed to a still later stage (mostly on typological grounds). The cultural layer was found under the loamy loess of the second terrace of the same river. Two radiocarbon dates have been obtained for the site, 14,470 ± 100 (mammoth tooth) and 13,830 ± 850 (bone coal) the remains of a large dwelling were uncovered at the site. The dwelling, the size of which was 17 by 10 m., consisted of six sections, and was adjoined by another construction of 5.5 by 4.5 m., which consisted of two sections. The remains of another many-chambered dwelling were reported.

The subsistence pattern of all the Palaeolithic sites in the Sož and Sudost valleys was much the same. The bulk of the meat was supplied by the specialized hunting of mammoth. At the sites of Berdyž, Yeliseyeviči and Yudinovo 50, 80 and 100 individual mammoths have been identified. Woolly rhinoceros, aurochs, bear, wolf, arctic fox and reindeer were hunted too. Numerous axe-like tools found at the sites prove the existence of various forms of food gathering.

During the late glacial stages of the Last Glaciation there took place a spread of birch, pine and spruce forests in the ice-free localities of northern Europe. At the same time changes occurred in other elements of the ecosystem. The gigantic herbivorous mammals such as mammoth and woolly rhinoceros became extinct. The wild horse migrated to more continental areas. Corresponding changes took place in the subsistence patterns of the Palaeolithic hunting groups. The economy of the Late Palaeolithic human groups of northern Europe was based primarily on the hunting of reindeer. The groups of reindeer hunters penetrated deep into the north, building hunting camps on the sandy shores of glacial lakes and on the banks of the deep channels which carried the waters of these lakes toward the sea. These were the most suitable places for hunting.

A group of such Late Palaeolithic sites is known in the vicinity of Hamburg.[31] The sites were situated on the shores and islets of a gigantic tunnel-like valley, which drained the waters from the glacial lakes into the distant sea. The pollen analytical evidence shows that the shores of the tunnel valley were covered with open pine and birch forests. Judging from the radiocarbon dates, Palaeolithic sites existed there between 13,700 and 13,100 B.P. These sites belonged to hunters who were specialists in reindeer hunting. At two Hamburgian sites respectively 105 and 265 individual reindeer have been identified.

Later, during the Alleröd warm oscillation and the following cold interval, the Younger Dryas, another group of Late Palaeolithic sites spread over the German Plain. In the stone inventory of these sites minute retouched points are common. They are somewhat similar to pen-knife blades and were labelled pen-knives or *Federmesser* points in German. This label was later used for this whole group of Palaeolithic sites. The *Federmesser* sites are situated in settings typical of the Late Palaeolithic hunting camps – the sandy shores of glacial lakes (Fig. 35) and the banks of rivers carrying the waters from glacial lakes. The radiocarbon dates obtained for the *Federmesser* sites in West Germany, Holland and Belgium lie within 11,500-10,500 B.P.

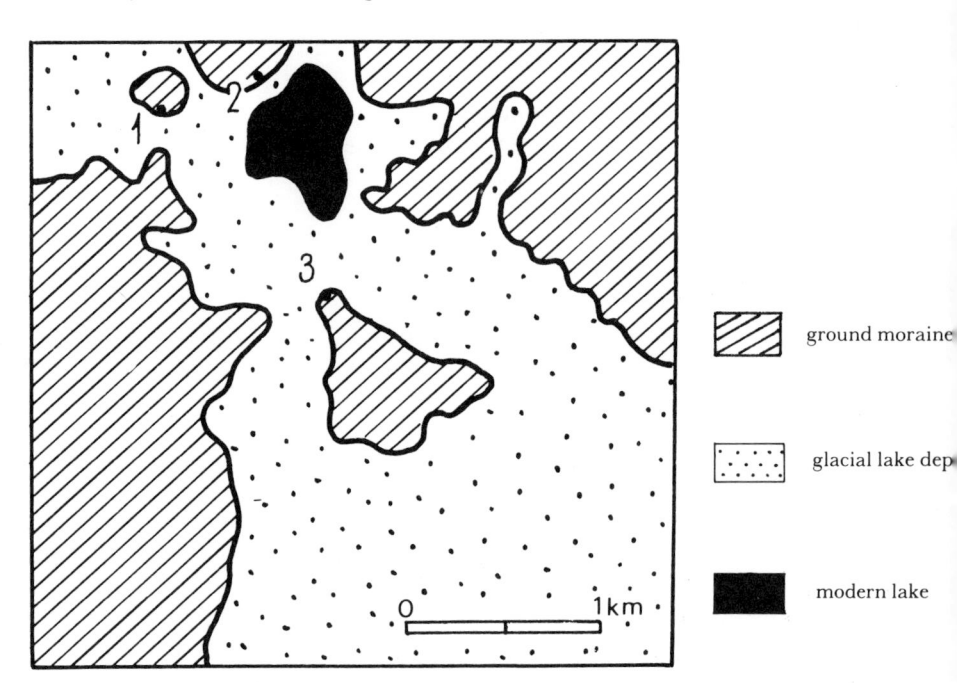

Figure 35 Juhnsdorf group of sites (after Taute, 1968; Note 5.32). 1 – Mesolithic; 2 – Federmesser; 3 – Tanged Points

Later a new variety of Late Palaeolithic sites appeared on the plains of West Germany, East Germany, Poland and Byelorussia. These sites have one common feature: in their chipped stone inventory there are many tanged points which were probably used as arrowheads. Archaeologists[32] distinguish several varieties of these tools, which are found in different regions of northern Europe. These are the Lyngby point in Denmark; the Ahrensburg point in classical sites near Hamburg; the Swiderian points in Poland, Byelorussia and Lithuania; the Hintersee point in the German plain; and the Chwalibogowice point in Poland.

The geomorphological situation of these sites does not differ from that of other late glacial sites. The sites are in most cases on the sandy shores of glacial lakes. In many cases they are found buried inside wind-blown dunes which were formed upon the shores of glacial basins. The greater part of the sites with tanged points were temporary hunting camps. Remains of dwellings were found in only two cases. In both cases these were comparatively small oval dwellings 3 by 4 m. in size. The subsistence pattern of the Late Palaeolithic sites with tanged points was typical of the late glacial period. The dwellers in the Hamburgian tunnel valley retained their specialization of reindeer hunting. In the Ahrensburg site there, 650 individual reindeer have been identified. A similar hunting structure was probably characteristic of all the sites with tanged points.

The evolution of late Stone Age industries with tanged points has been followed up in detail in Poland.[33] On typological grounds, from the change in the forms of tanged points found, several phases in this industrial evolution have been distinguished. In several cases it was possible to link this evolution with the development of sand dunes. The formation of wind-blown dunes was particularly intensive during the colder Dryas stages, when treeless vegetation was predominant. During the warmer oscillations, when pine and birch forests covered the sandy shores of glacial lakes, the layers of buried soils were formed. On the basis of these geological considerations the Swiderian industries of central Poland were dated to a time span corresponding to the Alleröd and to the Younger Dryas. The Swiderian site of Witów, in the district of Lęczyca in central Poland, was radiocarbon dated to 11,020 + 170 B.P.[34] Industries containing tanged points similar to the Swiderian ones have been met with in Byelorussia,[35] and on geological grounds these sites are also dated to the Alleröd and to the Younger Dryas.

A number of Swiderian-like sites have been discovered on the terraces of the upper Dnieper (Podluž'ye, Grensk, Latki) and of its tributaries (Sož, Iput', etc.). In most cases the layers of these sites have been found inside the dune formations developed at the first terrace of these rivers. It was often possible to correlate the sites with the formation of dunes and buried soils. In the chipped stone inventory tanged points resembling the Swiderian ones coexist with burins, small rounded scrapers and with *Federmesser* points.

A site with Swiderian points has been discovered in clear stratigraphic conditions in the shore deposits of lake Naroč in north-western Byelorussia. The site, referred to as Studenec,[36] was found on a terrace 2 m. high. The cultural layer was discovered in a peat layer covered by thick layers of lake sand and wind-blown sand. The radiocarbon date of the site is 10,810 ± 100 B.C. Pollen analysis shows that at that time pine forests predominated on the sandy shores of the lake.

The valleys of the Niemen basin in Lithuania were intensively populated in the late glacial period. On morphological grounds the Soviet Lithuanian archaeologist R.K. Rimantiene[37] suggests that all these sites go back to the Alleröd and Younger Dryas times. They are always situated upon the second and third terraces of the Niemen system. Tanged points are numerous, and Rimantiene distinguishes types similar to Ahrensburg, Lyngby and Swiderian points.

Further to the east, Swiderian points have been found in the dunes surrounding the Usvyaty lake depression in the southern part of the Pskov region.[38] According to firm geological evidence, the dunes were developed upon the shore formations of a lake that existed during the Alleröd and Younger Dryas times.

Mesolithic sites

Sites attributed to the Mesolithic period are known throughout the west Russian plain but they are not numerous in the zone of the Middle Pleistocene glaciations. Mesolithic sites are found in the middle Dnieper valley, south and north of Kiev.[39] In every case they are on sand dunes developed on the first terraces. The stone inventories are all much the same: short rounded scrapers and geometrical microliths are always present, including trapezes of an elongated form (in some cases similar to the 'transverse arrow-heads' of northern Europe). Retouched and unretouched blades are very common. Axe-like tools made of huge flakes are systematically present. In some cases points resembling Swiderian ones have been reported.

A considerable number of Mesolithic sites are found in the western Polessye, in the Pripyat valley.[40] Most of them are situated on the dunes developed on the first terrace of the Pripyat. Some have been found on the remnants of morainic hills on low terraces. A few sites were situated on upper terraces (Fig. 36). The stone inventory of the Mesolithic sites is different in the western and eastern parts of the Pripyat valley. Axe-like tools (core-axes and flake-axes) are particularly typical of the western area, being very numerous at the more recent sites. Apart from these tools, tanged points, retouched blades and scrapers are present. In the eastern part of the Pripyat valley microlithic tools are the most characteristic. These tools include

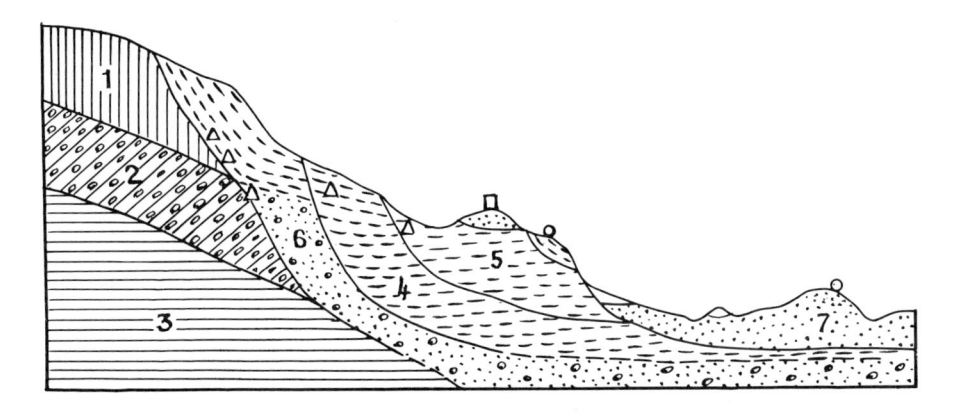

Figure 36 Stone Age sites in the Pripyat River valley (after Isaenko, 1971; Note 5.40).
1 – loess; 2 – ground moraine; 3 – solid rocks; 4 – deluvium drift; 5 – redeposited alluvium; 6 – gravels; 7 – flood-plain alluvium

geometric microliths: trapezes, rectangles, microblades, points. At a later stage axe-like tools appeared (Fig. 37).

It has been noted that all Mesolithic sites in the north German plain are connected with lakes or river valleys. It was also noted that in most cases these sites are situated on sand deposits. The Mesolithic sites are situated on the sandy banks of lakes or rivers, on sandy hills or dunes within lake depressions or within river valleys. Similar situations are typical of Mesolithic sites in southern Scandinavia. The evolution of Mesolithic assemblages in the north German plain covers the Pre-Boreal, Boreal and Early Atlantic vegetational zones.

The earliest Mesolithic sites in the area date from the Pre-Boreal. There are two important sites in the area of the north German plain which are pollen analytically dated to this time. These are Pinnberg[41] in the Hamburg tunnel valley and Klosterlund[42] in Denmark. The Pinnberg site is situated on a low (1.5 m.) sandy hill inside the Hamburg valley. The pollen analysis shows that open birch and pine forests covered the slopes of the valley. Remains of an oval-shaped dwelling (2.5 x 1.5 m.) have been found in the deposit. In the stone industry, as in previous cases, both axe-like tools (core-axes) and microlithic tools were found. Microlithic points are the most typical.

During the Boreal vegetational zone at least three different Mesolithic groups are distinguishable in the north German plain and in southern Scandinavia. One distinct group is referred to as Maglemose.[43] The sites attributed to this group are known in Jutland, Zealand and Scania. Special investigations show that the greater part of the Maglemosian sites are connected with lakes, the sites being situated either on lake shores or within lake depressions.

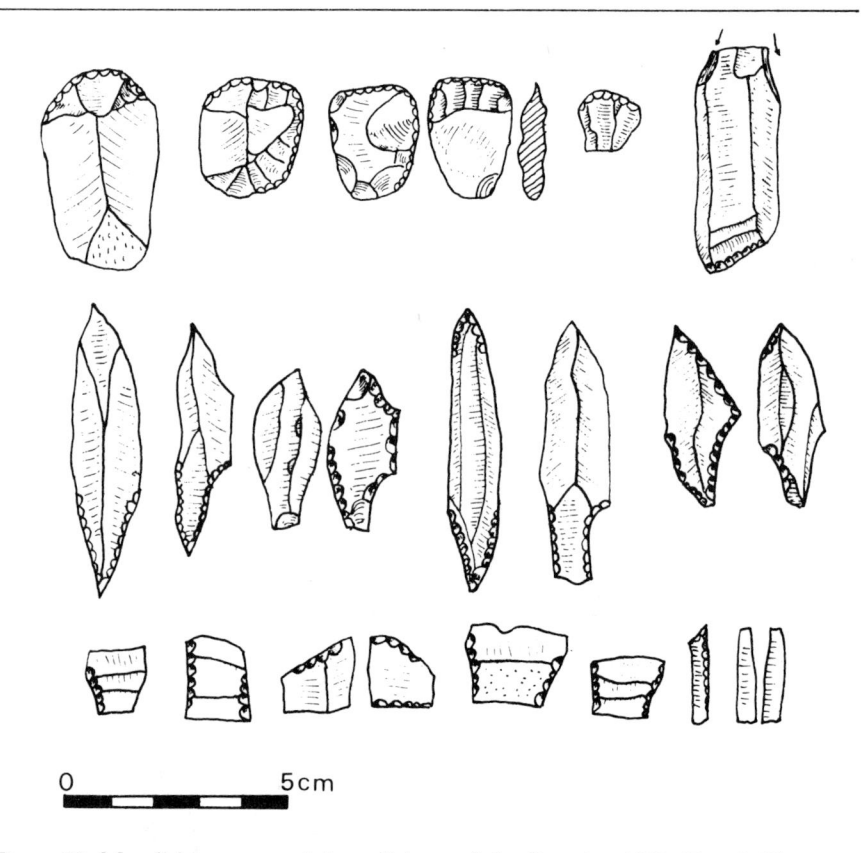

Figure 37 Mesolithic stone tools from Polessye (after Isaenko, 1969; Note 5.40)

The subsistence pattern of the Maglemosian sites was based upon hunting, fishing and food gathering. In the hunting structure the most important hunting was of red deer, wild pigs and roe deer. Among the faunal remains the bones of aurochs are present in lesser quantities. In earlier sites the bones of elk are present but in later sites they disappear.

The stone inventory of the Maglemosian sites is characterized by the presence of axe-like tools (core- and flake-axes). Microlithic tools – points and triangles – were found. Trapezes appeared at later stages. The bone inventory is remarkably rich. It includes harpoons, fishhooks, arrow-heads, shafts into which geometric microliths were inserted and socketed chisels. Pollen analysis shows that the areas around Maglemosian sites were covered with birch and pine forests with heavy chestnut undergrowth and with mixed oak forests (probably spread over morainic belts). The radiocarbon dates indicate that the Maglemosian sites existed between 9,000 and 7,500 B.P.

Further to the south and to the south-east there was spread another Mesolithic group known as Duvensee. Typologically and economically this group was fairly similar to the Maglemose. The stone inventory includes both core and flake-axes and microliths. Among these there are points, triangles and a few trapezes. The settlement pattern is nearly the same as that of the Maglemose. At the site of Hohe Vicheln situated on the Schwerin lake, East Germany, the following animal bones have been identified: roe deer (33 individuals); red deer (19 ind.); wild pigs (7 ind.); aurochs (3 ind.); elk (2 ind.). It has been noted that the Duvensee sites are situated in the regions immediately south of the young morainic zones. In Boreal times this area was covered predominantly with pine forests with a low content of chestnut undergrowth and of broad-leaved species.[44]

The third Mesolithic group distinguished on the north German plain during the Boreal period is referred to as Haltener.[45] The stone inventory of this group is characterized by the complete absence of axe-like tools and by the dominance of microliths: rectangles, triangles and points with retouched bases. Geomorphologically this group is distinguished from others by the fact that its sites are situated outside the morainic belt, in the plain between the lower Elbe and the lower Rhine. According to palaeobotanists, this area in the Boreal period was covered by pine and birch forests with dense chestnut undergrowth. Later, alder forests spread in this area.

A similar pattern of Mesolithic group distribution existed in Early Atlantic times. Dr B. Gramsch,[46] from East Germany, distinguishes the following axe-bearing assemblages in the early Mesolithic sites of the northern part of East Germany: an Oldesloe-Kobrow group, a Jühnsdorf group and an Ahlbeck group. All these groups are characterized by the presence of core- and flake-axes in their inventories. Geometric microliths, including triangles and trapezes of different shapes, are also present. The mapping of these sites and their correlation with geological maps and with pollen analytical data show that their distribution area coincided with areas of predominantly pine forests with an admixture of mixed oak forest elements on richer soils.

At the same time the sites of the so-called Ahlbeck group were spread over dunes between the lower Elbe and the lower Rhine. These sites were surrounded by predominantly mixed oak forests. The stone inventory of the Ahlbeck group is characterized by the total absence of axe-like tools.

At the beginning of the Atlantic zone, roughly between 7,500 and 6,300 B.P., another Mesolithic group appeared in Denmark. This group is referred to as 'Kongemose'. Two types of settlement pattern are known for these sites. The inland sites are found under nearly the same conditions as the Maglemosian ones. These were small seasonal hunting camps inside the swamps. The other settlement type is represented by coastal sites. The sites were situated in ancient sea lagoons (fjords), close to the shore.

The settlement pattern of the Kongemose sites was determined by hunting forest game, by fishing and by food collecting. Exploitation of marine food resources was particularly characteristic of the coastal sites. In the faunal remains of the Kongemose sites red deer, roe deer, elk, wild pigs, aurochs, bears, wolves, beavers and dogs have been identified. The presence of at least two species of seals (harp seal and grey seal) testifies to an intensive exploitation of marine resources and among numerous fish bones spur dog, tench, wels (*Siluris glanis* L.), coalfish and flounder have been identified. Numerous remains of oysters show the significance of food collecting in the coastal area.

According to investigations by Polish archaeologists[47] there were several distinct Mesolithic groups in Polish territory. In central and southern Poland are situated the sites referred to as the Komornica culture. The assemblages are characterized by the presence of short and round-end scrapers, of core- and flake-axes (in small numbers), of triangle points, backed points and triangles and are dated 9,300-9,200 B.C. The Janislawice culture is represented in eastern Poland. The stone assemblage is characterized by the presence of short round scrapers and by the absence (with one exception) of axes; at a later stage trapezes (transverse arrowheads) are present. Chronologically this group corresponds to the time span from the second half of the Boreal up to the end of the Atlantic period. The third Mesolithic group in Poland, the Chojnice-Pienki culture, is regarded as an eastern continuation of the Jühnsdorf group of East Germany.

A considerable number of Mesolithic sites have been discovered on Lithuanian territory, mostly due to intensive investigations carried out by Dr Rimute Rimantiene.[48] They are situated on the lower terraces of the Niemen and its tributaries and were found either on the flood-plain or on the first terrace.

The chipped stone inventory of the Lithuanian Mesolithic sites is characterized by the presence of arrow-heads, scrapers, burins and axe-like tools. In the inventory of the late Mesolithic sites trapezes and axe-like tools (both core- and flake-axes) were numerous (Fig. 38).

Large and important Mesolithic sites are known in the northeastern part of the Baltic Sea area, particularly in Estonia. One of the largest sites is situated in the northern part of the republic, near the town of Kunda.[49] It is situated on the shore of a huge peat bog. South of the bog is a shore terrace of the Baltic glacial lake. To the north of it a number of strand-walls belonging to the later stages of the Baltic Sea are visible. Mesolithic remains have been discovered upon a hill (Lammasmägi) in the middle of the peat bog and inside the bog itself, in the layer of lake marl. Another important Mesolitic site is situated several miles to the east. In the sand deposits forming the bank of the Narva river three Mesolithic layers separated by thin sterile deposits have been uncovered. At both Mesolithic sites the large number of the faunal remains makes it possible to carry out a reconstruction of the subsistence pattern. This pattern was quite different from those of the south Baltic Mesolithic sites. The difference was due to the fact that

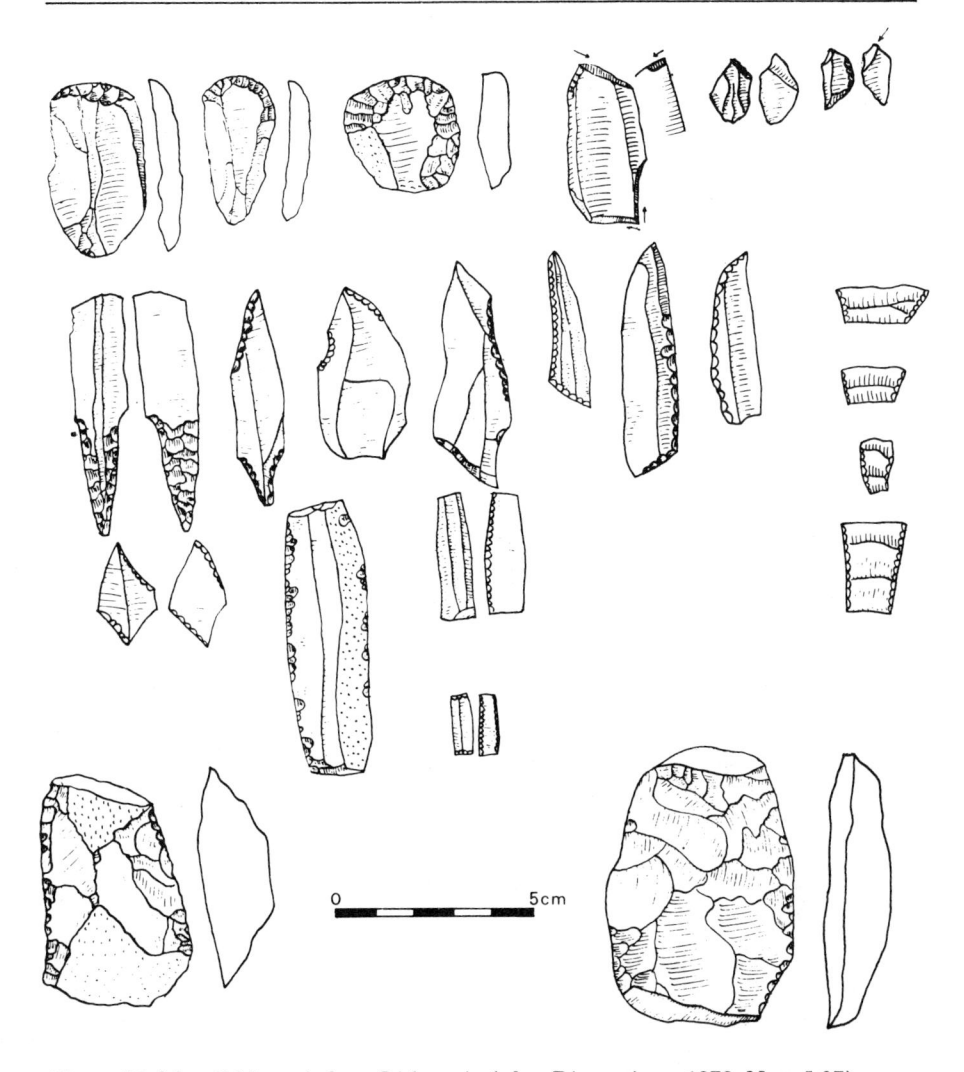

Figure 38 Mesolithic tools from Lithuania (after Rimantiene, 1972; Note 5.37)

the bulk of the meat supply was obtained by the hunting of a single species of animal. In this respect the hunting pattern of the eastern Baltic Mesolithic was similar to that of the Upper Palaeolithic. But here animals living in the Holocene woods were hunted; i.e. elk.

In the Mesolithic layer of Kunda the bones of elk form 96% of all faunal remains. The rest is formed by bear (1.5%); wild pig (1%); wild horse (0.5%) and by seal (1.5%). The hunting of sea animals, such as seals, is a characteristic feature of the sites situated in the maritime zone of the Baltic area.

The hunting pattern of Estonian Mesolithic sites belonging to later phases becomes more complicated. The hunting of red deer and particularly of wild pigs gains in importance. The following faunal remains have been identified in Mesolithic layers of the Narva site (individuals):

Narva, third and second layers: elk, 55%; red deer, 11%; wild pig, 25%; roe deer, 3%; bear, 3%; seal, 3%.
Narva, first layer: elk, 37%; red deer, 4%; wild pig, 43%; roe deer, 1.2%; bear, 8%; seal, 4.4%.

A rich collection of implements made of flint, quartz, bone and antler have been obtained from the Mesolithic sites of Estonia. Among the stone implements of Kunda large axes are numerous, some specimens being similar to those of the south Baltic areas. Stone arrowheads are present, including tanged points similar to the Swiderian ones. Microlithic tools are also present, triangles made both of flint and quartz being particularly common. Burins, scrapers and retouched blades are numerous.

In the Kunda assemblage implements of bone and of antler are the most typical. Among these there are axes of different shapes, including an implement similar to a 'Lyngby' antler axe found at the Jutland and Holstein sites. There are also numerous fish-hooks, plummets, picks for breaking ice, harpoons and arrowheads. Bone and antler implements, including harpoons and knives, are numerous in the Mesolithic layers of Narva. The stone industry contains perforated axes, scrapers of different types, burins and retouched blades. Tools are made both of flint and of quartz. The inventories of all three Mesolithic layers are similar.

There are radiocarbon dates which may determine the time when Mesolithic hunting sites were in operation in the north-eastern Baltic area. The two radiocarbon dates obtained for Kunda are 8,340 $\pm$ 280 and 6,015 $\pm$ 210 B.P. The radiocarbon dates obtained for the third Mesolithic layer of Narva lie in the time span 7,800-7,000 B.P. The dates for the second layer lie between 7,500 and 6,000 B.P. The first Mesolithic layer of the site was dated at 5,300 $\pm$ 250 B.P.

A new Mesolithic site has been discovered recently in Estonia, Pulli.[50] The site is situated on the bank of the Pärnu river in south-western Estonia. The cultural layer was found in a buried humus layer covered with stratified peat and deposits formed in a lagoon of the Yoldia Sea. In their turn these deposits are overlaid by sands accumulated during the Ancylus transgression. According to a preliminary report bones of elk, bears and beavers were found in the cultural layers. Bone and antler implements include points and adzes. Stone scrapers, blades and fragments of tanged points were also discovered. A fragment of wood from the cultural layer was dated 9,600 $\pm$ 120, B.P. Overlying peat revealed its age as 9,300 $\pm$ 75 B.P.

An important Mesolithic site has been uncovered in the depression of Lubana, in eastern Latvia.[51] As we saw earlier, a large glacial lacustrine basin existed there in the late glacial period. The present lake, surrounded by a large peat bog, is a relic of a huge glacial lake. Borings carried out in the peat bog and inside the lake enable us to follow up the fluctuations of the lake level during the Holocene. Archaeological prospecting and excavations carried out by the Latvian archaeologists Dr F. Zagorskis and Dr Ilze Loze have revealed the existence of a number of sites within the lake depression.

Mesolithic and Early Neolithic sites have been found on the sandy shore of the ancient lake. A peat layer has been found under sand deposits one metre thick. In this layer Early Neolithic archaeological and faunal remains have been uncovered. Below were sands and loam. The lower sandy deposits were interlayered with thin layers of peat. In these deposits Mesolithic implements of bone and antler and numerous animal bones were discovered. Of all faunal remains 40.5% belonged to wild pig and 24.5% to elk. The Mesolithic assemblage included numerous tools made of bone and of antler: spear- and arrow-heads, harpoons, knives, adzes.

Pollen analysis shows[52] that the vegetation around the site was typical of the first half of the Atlantic period. The sandy shores were covered with pine forests while alder forests covered the wet floodplain of the lake. The remains of wooden constructions unearthed in the Mesolithic layers have been radiocarbon dated. The three dates obtained were $6,960 \pm 80$, $6,760 \pm 80$ and $6,580 \pm 70$ B.P. Geological investigations show that the Mesolithic site existed during the first important transgression of the Lubana lake in the first half of the Atlantic period.

Neolithic sites

Neolithic sites in the west Russian plain appeared during the second half of the Atlantic period, when the mixed oak forests attained their maximum extent there. It should be remembered that in most cases these were the sites of pottery-using hunters and fishers. The spread of pottery production did not coincide with any noticeable change in the subsistence pattern. Nor was there any change in the settlement patterns. The pottery-using Neolithic hunters were settled in the same areas as their Mesolithic aceramic predecessors – the areas most suitable for their hunting economy.

1. The zone of Middle Pleistocene glaciations

As in the preceding Mesolithic epoch, the Neolithic sites in the zone of the Middle Pleistocene glaciations concentrated in two major areas, the middle Dnieper area and the Polessye. The Neolithic sites in the middle Dnieper valley[53] are found in the same morphological setting as the Mesolithic ones. They are situated on the sand dunes of the flood-plain or of the first terrace. The same conditions obtained for the sites found in the valley of Severski Donetz. It has been noted that the Early Neolithic sites are situated on higher levels than the Middle or Later Neolithic sites. Hydrological observations show that the levels of the middle Russian rivers fell during late Atlantic and early Sub-Boreal times.

The cultural layers of the dune sites are usually found in the lower portion of the soil or in the subsoil developed upon the dune sand. The situation of the Pogorelovka site in the middle Desna stretches is typical.[54] The cultural layer of the site was found in sandy cover deposits upon flood-plain alluvial deposits. The height of the cultural layer of the site above the actual level of the river was 3 m.

The lake depressions in the zone of the Middle Pleistocene glaciation were intensively populated by Neolithic hunters. A lake widening of a flood-plain in the basin of the upper Dnieper was used for a long time by Late Neolithic hunters and fishers. A hill in the midst of a big peat bog, in former times a lake, near Mostva, west of Žitomir, was continuously inhabited in Middle and Late Neolithic times.

In the eastern Polessye, in the valley of the Pripyat, the Neolithic sites are situated on dunes on the flood-plain and on the first terrace. The altitude of the Neolithic sites there does not exceed 2-3 m. above the river in the upper Pripyat and 8-12 m. in the lower stretches of the river.[55]

Pollen analysis shows that in most cases the appearance of Neolithic sites in the area coincided with the maximum spread of broad-leaved species in the pollen diagrams. So the level of the Neolithic deposits of Pogorelovka on the Desna river flood-plain corresponds to the maximum extent of oak, alder and chestnut. In all probability, at that time mixed oak forests with chestnut undergrowth were widely spread over the watersheds. Oak and alder forests grew in the flood-plain, and birch forests also existed there. The sandy first and second terraces were covered with pine forests. The economy of the Neolithic sites in the northern part of the forested area may be evaluated on the basis of the faunal remains of the Pogorelovka sites.[56] These are characterized by the following figures: wild pig, 9 individuals; wild horse, 7 individuals; red deer, 2 individuals; elk, 3 individuals; bear, 3 individuals; roe deer, 2 individuals.

The presence in considerable quantity of wild horse remains distinguishes the faunal list of Pogorelovka from those of other sites situated to the west and to the north. It should be noted that the wild horse is not necessarily connected with steppic landscapes. Bones of wild horses are often found in the Holocene deposits of the Baltic area where steppic landscapes hardly existed. According to the palaeozoologist K. Paaver[57] the wild horse was typical of the forest zone. The banks of lakes and of rivers and the vicinity of large peat bogs were the favourite ecological setting for the wild horse in this area.

The subsistence pattern of the Neolithic sites in the Dnieper valley may be distinguished from the following faunal evidence.[58] The sites are listed from north to south.

Igren' 8: Wild: aurochs, 93 bones; red deer, 11; roe deer, 3; wild pig, 2. Domesticated: cattle present.
Sobački: Wild: aurochs, 1%; red deer, 4%; wild pig, 1.5%. Domesticated: cattle, 28%; sheep/goat, 27%; pig, 5%; horse, 24%; dog, 4%.
Sredni Stog: Wild: red deer, 12%. Domesticated: cattle, 23%; sheep/goat, 39%, pig, 1%; horse, 9%; dog, 12%.
Buz'ki: Wild: red deer, 11%; elk, 1.5%. Domesticated: cattle, 28%; sheep/goat, 2%; pig, 2.5%; dog, 6%.

On the basis of the high proportion of horse in the faunal remains (particularly in those of Buz'ki) Ukrainian archaeologists and palaeozoologists have come to the conclusion that in the steppic zone of the Ukraine there existed one of the most important centres of horse domestication.[59] However, in the opinion of palaeozoologists it is very difficult to recognize the domesticated horse from bone remains, and as noted earlier wild horses were not necessarily restricted to steppic landscape.

The economy of the Neolithic sites in the forest-steppes and in the steppes of the South Ukraine was a complicated one. Stock-breeding was an important economic factor. Fishing was also important: numerous fish bones have been found at Neolithic sites in the Dnieper area. The importance of food-gathering is emphasized by the large number of *Unio* shells found at the Dnieper sites. At the Buz'ki site 126 turtle shells were found.

Controversy has arisen over the problem of the existence of agriculture in the Dnieper Neolithic. An impression of barley (*Hordeum sativum*) has been identified on a potsherd from the Vita Litovska site, near Kiev. On this basis it was argued that agriculture was widely practised by the Neolithic tribesmen of the Dnieper. However, the morphological situation of the Dnieper sites makes me doubt the validity of this suggestion. The size of the arable lands within the catchment area of these sites is negligible. As with the Neolithic sites of the southern Bug, the presence of grain should in my opinion be attributed to economic ties with other cultural and economic groups. Contacts with the Tripolye population are the most probable.

There are many reasons for believing that the greater part of the Neolithic sites found in the area of the Middle Pleistocene glaciations are the remains of seasonal hunting camps. Relics of dwellings have been found in very few cases. The remains of eight oval-shaped dwellings have been established at the Mněvo site in the middle Dnieper.[60] The minimum size of the dwellings is 2.4 by 1.8 m.; the maximum size is 8.5 by 7.4 m. The site contained pit-and-comb decorated pottery of a late phase.

The chipped stone inventory of the Neolithic sites in the Dnieper and Donetz valleys have many common traits with those of the Mesolithic sites. Axe-like large tools of core-axe and flake-axe types, similar to those of the Mesolithic age, are common at the Neolithic sites. Microlithic tools are always present. Among these trapezes are particularly numerous. Blades and retouched blades are common. Large retouched knives made of long and wide blades are typical of the sites. In addition scrapers and projectile points are nearly always present in the stone inventory.

Ukrainian archaeologists attribute the sites of so-called 'Strumel-Gastyatin' group[61] to the earliest phase of the local Neolithic. These sites are situated on the slopes of the first terrace and on sand dunes within the flood-plain in the vicinity of Kiev. The pottery found at the sites was made of clay with a small admixture of vegetable matter. The pot sherds are coarse and thick, they come from large conical vessels with straight sides, poorly decorated. The only ornamental pattern consists of rows of comb impressions on the upper part of the vessel (Fig. 39). There are neither radiocarbon dates nor pollen analytical data for the Strumel-Gastyatin sites.

All the Neolithic sites in the territory of central, northern and eastern Ukraine are often regarded as belonging to two distinct cultures, namely the Dnieper-Donetz culture and the culture of pit-and-comb decorated pottery. The economic structure and the settlement pattern of both cultures are practically identical. There are many common traits in their tool-kits (Fig. 42). The principal distinctions are restricted to the ornamental patterns of ceramic vessels.

To take the Dnieper-Donetz culture first, several phases may be singled out in its evolution. Two leading archaeologists dealing with the Neolithic of the Ukraine, Dr Telegin and Dr Danilenko, have put forward two quite different schemes for the evolution of this culture. I shall not go into this controversy here, as it mainly concerns minute differences between phases, but shall simply outline the general characteristics of the pottery assemblage of the Dnieper-Donetz Neolithic sites.

According to Telegin,[62] wide-mouthed pots are the most typical of the Dnieper-Donetz culture. Four varieties of these pots are distinguishable: (1) an egg-shaped wide-mouthed pot with a pointed base and with a straight or slightly flaring rim; (2) a wide-mouthed pot with a pointed base and with a straight rim; (3) a spherical bowl with a pointed bottom, a short cylindrical neck and a straight or outbent rim; (4) a hemispherical bowl with a flat bottom and with a straight rim (Fig. 40).

Decorations on the Dnieper-Donetz pottery contain the following elements: impressions of combs, notches, incised lines and strokes.

The West Russian Plain 143

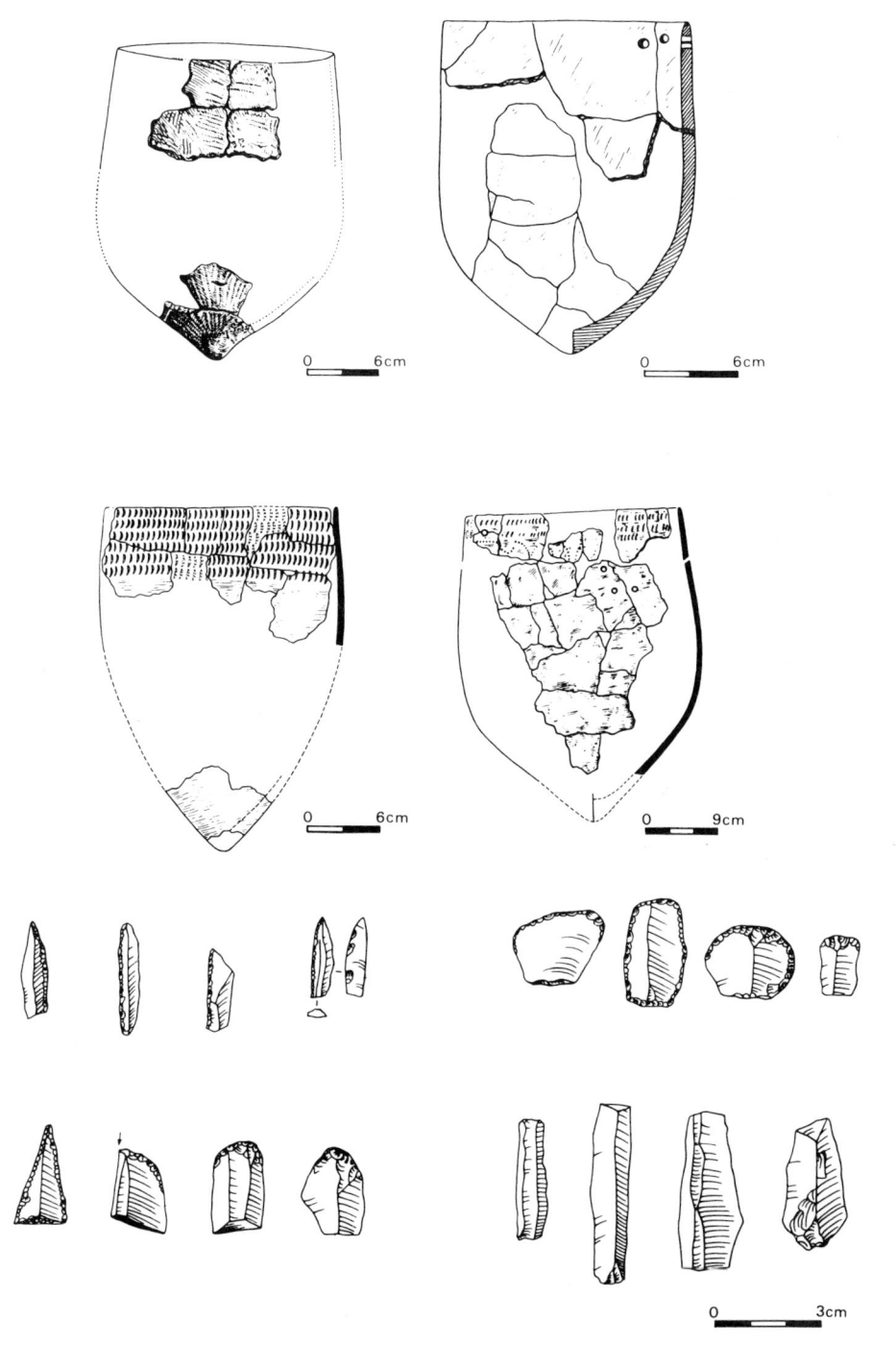

Figure 39 Strumel-Gastyatin sites: pottery and working tools (after Telegin, 1970, Note 5.53)

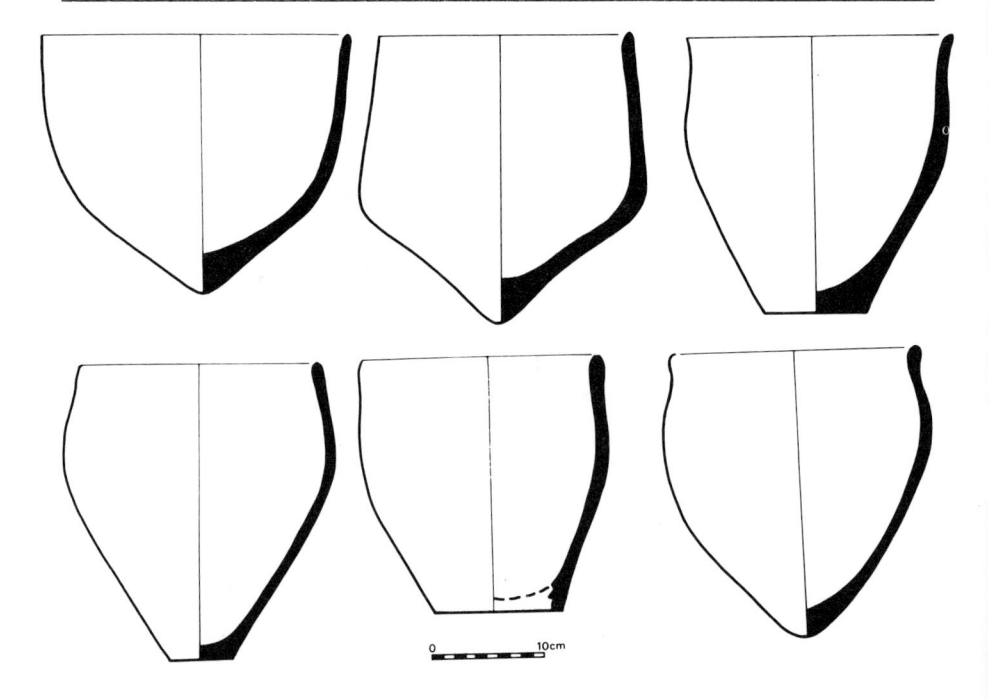

Figure 40 Dnieper-Don Neolithic sites: shapes of vessels (after Telegin, 1968; Note 5.53)

Comparison with Bug-Dniester pottery ornamentation shows that the strokes are the only new element. The stroke impressions were made by thin bone points or by the edges of broken blades. The most commonly used ornamental patterns were horizontal rows of comb impressions or notches. In some cases rows of comb impressions alternated with incised horizontal lines. Incised lines form vertical and curvilinear patterns, zigzags and nets. Incised lines and notches sometimes form complicated patterns similar to the 'volutes' of Bug-Dniester pottery. Of particular interest are the so-called geometric patterns which consist of triangles, rhombs and rectangles. Comparison with Bug-Dniester pottery shows that these are the only new patterns; other patterns, such as rows of comb impressions, zigzags, nets, curvilinear patterns made of incised lines, and 'volutes', have counterparts in the ornamental patterns of the Bug and Dniester Neolithic pottery. The two new characteristics, strokes and geometric patterns, are closely linked with one another: all the geometric figures consist of closely-set strokes (Fig. 41a).

The evolution of ornamentation in Neolithic pottery has been followed up in the western Polessye.[63] The pottery of the earliest Neolithic sites there is fairly similar to those of the Strumel-Gastyatin sites in the middle Dnieper valley. It is made of coarse orange buff

The West Russian Plain 145

Figure 41a Dnieper-Don Neolithic sites: pottery ornamental patterns (after Telegin, 1968; Note 5.53). (See Fig.26)

paste with a rich admixture of vegetable material; the pots are conical with straight sides and rims. Ornamentation is simple, the most common pattern consisting of rows of comb impressions. Other ornamental motifs are rows of small pits and networks of incised lines (Fig. 41b).

In the eastern Pripyat valley, three Late Neolithic sites of the Litvin type are situated on sand dunes within the flood-plain. On typological grounds the Byelorussian archaeologist V.F. Isaenko regards them as belonging to a local variant of the late phase of the Dnieper-Donetz culture. The most common shape in the Litvin pottery is a widemouthed pot with a pointed base. The elements of ornamentation are comb impressions, incised lines and strokes. The ornamental patterns are very similar to those on the Dnieper-Donetz vessels, with some differences. Nearly all the vessels are decorated with rows of large beads below the rims, and some have cord impressions, which suggests that the Litvin sites were at least partly contemporaneous with corded ware pottery sites.

Similar Neolithic sites have been found in the western part of the Pripyat valley and in the Niemen valley;[64] in both valleys the sites are found either on the first terrace or on dunes within the flood-plain, and there are neolithic sites on almost every large dune there.

Some differences are noticable in the pottery between the Early and Late Neolithic sites. At the earlier sites large, wide-mouthed pots with pointed bases are found, and the elements of decoration are comb impressions, notches, incised lines and large round or oval pits. The ornamental patterns are horizontal rows (using comb impressions,

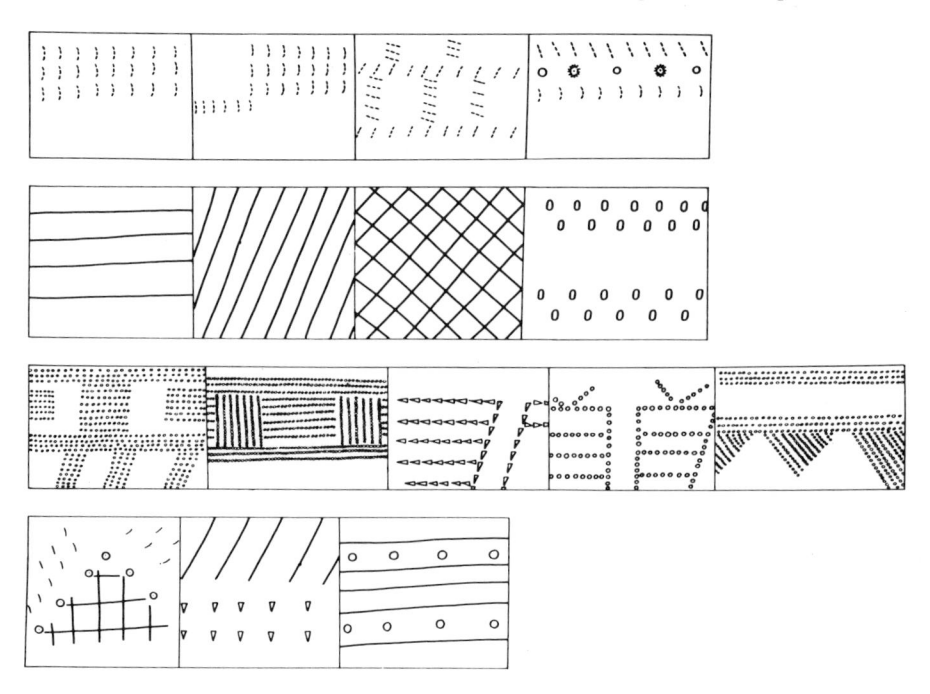

Figure 41b Dnieper-Don Neolithic sites: pottery ornamental patterns (after Isaenko, 1970; Note 5.63). (See Fig.26).

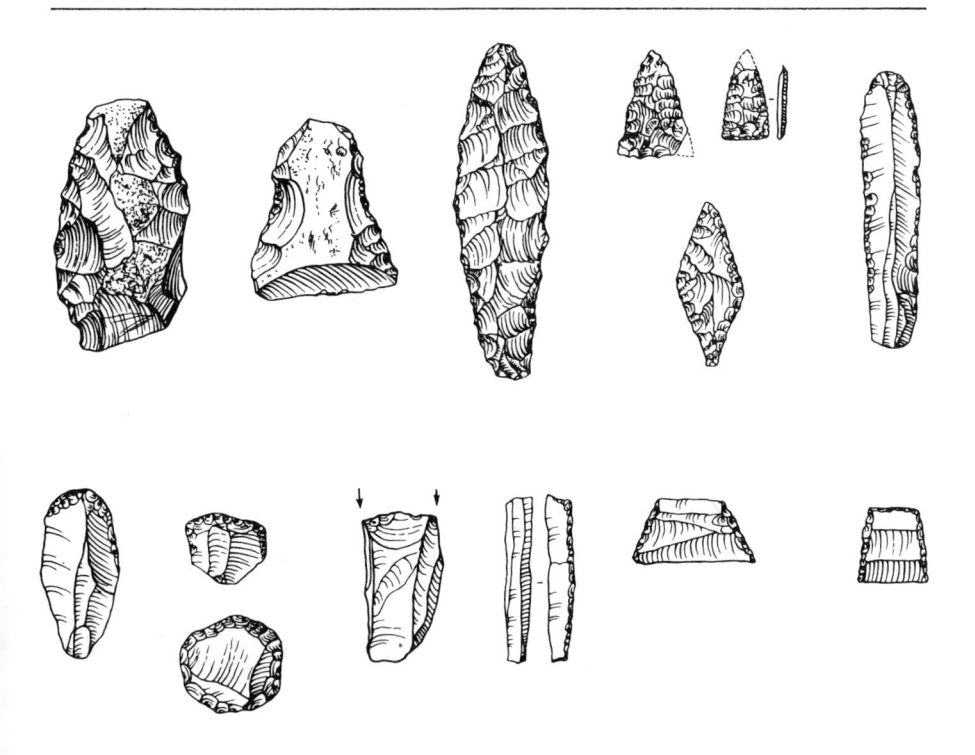

Figure 42 Dnieper-Don Neolithic sites: working tools (after Telegin, 1973; Note 5.53)

notches and pits) and nets (composed of incised lines). The site of Dubičiai in south-eastern Lithuania[65] probably belongs to this early phase of the Neolithic. At the later Neolithic sites, large pots with pointed bases are found, and the basic elements of decoration are much the same as in the earlier phase, with the difference that strokes are often used. The ornamental patterns are similar to those of the Dnieper-Donetz pottery, with the addition of some local patterns (Fig. 41b).

The chronological position of the Neolithic sites in the valleys of the Dnieper, Donetz, Pripyat and Nieman is not altogether clear. So far no radiocarbon dates have been obtained, but some conclusions can be drawn from radiocarbon datings of similar sites in other territories. The time of the initial spread of pottery over these areas is suggested by the dates of the following early pottery-bearing sites: Soroki II in the Dniester valley (6,825 ± 150 and 6,495 ± 100), and the early comb-decorated pottery assemblages at Zacenye in central Byelorussia (5,530 ± 60 B.P.), and Osa, eastern Latvia (5,730 ± 50 B.P.). From these, the initial spread of Early Neolithic pottery in the central and northern Ukraine and in Byelorussia can be roughly dated to between 6,500 and 5,500 B.P. Another chronological guide is the presence in many Dnieper-Donetz sites of the pottery of Tripolye phases B-2 and C-1. At the Tripolye sites these phases are radiocarbon dated to 5,000-4,700 B.P.; the maximum spread of the Dnieper-Donetz sites probably occurred during this time-span. In some areas, such as parts of the western Polessye, sites of this type could have survived until 4,000 to 3,800 B.P.

A third source of evidence about the age and formation of these settlements is the funnel beaker culture of central Europe. This culture spread over a vast territory of Europe, from Bohemia in the south to southern Sweden in the north and from the Rhineland in the west to the western Bug in the east. Settlements with funnel beakers in central Europe have been radiocarbon dated to 5,500-4,500 B.P. Mapping of the funnel beaker sites[66] shows that they were situated on the margins of loessic plains. At the south-eastern end of the distribution area, in the western Bug basin, funnel beaker settlements are found on the high loess-covered banks of the western Bug and its tributaries.[67]

The funnel beaker culture had a stable food-producing economy centred on cattle-breeding, with pigs usually more important than ovicaprids but both being of secondary importance. Hunting was usually of little economic importance. Among the faunal remains red and roe deer, aurochs, wild pig, bear, wild horse, seal (in the coastal area), birds and fish have been identified.[68] Agriculture was a very important factor in the economy: einkorn and emmer wheats were the main crop in the greater part of the distribution area, and club wheat, bread wheat, spelt, barley, millet and flax were also cultivated. In southern Sweden, probably due to climatic conditions, six-row barley became the dominant crop. Large houses have been established at the funnel beaker settlements. In Denmark a house 50 m. long, consisting of six sections, has been uncovered; in Poland a house 15 m. long, consisting of two sections, has been found. In the funnel beaker sites in the western Bug basin remains of both rectangular and oval-shaped dwellings have been discovered. Special corrals for stock-keeping have also been found. In some cases the remains of large settlements consisting of two rows of houses have been excavated.

The most characteristic feature of this culture is its pottery. Within the distribution area of this cultural group the pottery was very similar: the commonest shapes of the vessels were funnel beakers, collared flasks and amphorae. Ornamental patterns were also very similar. On the basis of the pottery many theories have been put forward about the origin of this culture; I will quote only one here, that of Professor Behrens[69] of East Germany. According to him the funnel beaker culture originated in Bohemia and Moravia, evolving from the local Danubian civilization. The cultures of Lengyel and Rössen played a considerable role in its formation; the role of the Rössen culture was particularly important, and Behrens attributes to this influence the S-shaped form of funnel beakers and the appearance of some ornamental patterns including strokes and geometric patterns. These elements and patterns are particularly common in a variant of the funnel beaker culture found mostly in West Germany and known as stroke-ornamented ware (Fig. 43). Strokes and geometrical patterns are also quite common in northern funnel beaker sites. Geometric patterns are known among the funnel beakers of Poland, being particularly numerous in the assemblages of the early (Wjorek) phase of the eastern variety of Polish beakers. Geometrical patterns are completely absent in later phases of the southern group, for instance in the western Bug-Volynian funnel beaker sites.

As we saw, the new decorative element in the Dnieper-Donetz Neolithic pottery, compared with the decorations of the Bug and Dniester ware, consisted of geometric patterns, usually filled with strokes. A detailed comparison with funnel beaker ornamentations shows the coincidence of at least two ornamental patterns. These are precisely the elements which Professor Behrens ascribes to Rössen influence. Is this similarity purely accidental, or is it a reflection of some fundamental process? In my opinion the coincidence of such ornamental patterns cannot be accidental. In favour of this suggestion the following arguments may be put forward: (1) the funnel beakers of central Europe are roughly contemporaneous with the Dnieper-Donetz Neolithic; (2) the distribution areas of the two cultures had a contact zone in eastern Poland/western Byelorussia.

It should be remembered that the similarity between the funnel beakers and the Dnieper-Donetz Neolithic pottery concerns only one element in the cultural system, the ornamentation of pottery. Even the pottery shapes are different. The subsistence patterns are quite different: stable food-producing at the funnel beaker sites, and hunting and fishing with elements of stock-breeding in the south at the Dnieper-Donetz sites. The stone tool kit is also quite different, with a typical agricultural inventory on one side, and a typical hunting and fishing inventory, with axes and geometric microliths, on

Figure 43 Rössen pottery (after Behrens, 1961; Note 5.69); stroke-ornamented pottery (after Knöll, 1959; Note 5.69)

the other. But according to the monothetic classification principle formulated in the first chapter of this book, one group of attributes can be used to distinguish classification units. On the basis of the similarity in pottery ornamental patterns we can postulate a huge cultural zone which embraces both the distribution area of the funnel beaker settlements and the area of the Dnieper-Donetz Neolithic sites in the Polessye, in the valley of the Dnieper and in the Severski Donetz.

The formation of this cultural zone, in my opinion, is similar to the processes which occurred during the Early Neolithic. An intrinsic rise in the population density in agricultural zones led to population pressure in the funnel beaker area in central Europe. The hiving off of the surplus population became unavoidable. A part of the surplus population moved to areas rich in natural resources; to the valleys of the Pripyat, Desna, Dnieper and Donetz, rich in wild game and in aquatic resources. Here the new population intermixed with the local Early Neolithic one and gradually acquired the local subsistence pattern based on hunting, fishing and food collecting. This was the optimal economic strategy in the conditions of the dense mixed forests of eastern Europe. Essentially analogous processes probably occurred in southern Scandinavia, on the periphery of the northern domain of the funnel beakers, where an area of Scandinavian pitted pottery with a predominantly hunting and fishing economy was formed.[70] Here, too, part of the surplus population probably overflowed into an area rich in natural resources and acquired a hunting and fishing economy as the best possible strategy under local conditions.

The second culture represented in the Neolithic period of the central, northern and eastern Ukraine, that connected with pit-and-comb decorated pottery, is distributed over a vast territory.[71] As so often, conflicting suggestions have been put forward by different archaeologists, and the attribution of many sites is a subject of controversy. The oldest varieties of pit-and-comb decorated pottery are found in central Russia. It is not the oldest pottery found there: in recent excavations carried out in central Russian sites (Ivanovskoye, Yazykovo, Borinka and others) ceramic-bearing layers have been found below the oldest layers containing pit-and-comb decorated pottery.[72] This oldest type of pottery from the central regions of Russia is decorated with impressions of combs and small pits, but the ornamental patterns are similar to those used in the Dnieper-Donetz pottery. In all probability this pottery assemblage reflects the earliest penetration of a pottery-using population from the valleys of the south-western Ukraine into the river valleys and lake depressions of central Russia.

The earliest assemblages of pit-and-comb decorated pottery are usually referred to as the Lyalovo culture.[73] The Lyalovo type of pottery is usually decorated with conical pits forming chequer-board patterns, with horizontal rows of pits, or with lunate and comb impressions. Archaeologists distinguish at least three stages in the evolution of the Lyalovo culture. Pottery of the early stage is ornamented almost exclusively with round pits; comb impressions are rare. In the pottery of the middle phase the comb impressions are used more often, though pits still dominate the pattern. Comb impressions are the most commonly used decoration in the pottery of the late phase. Pit-and-comb impressions often form rhombic patterns.

The original area of the oldest Lyalovo pottery embraces the upper Volga basin and its tributaries, the valley of Klyazma being particularly rich in sites. The economy of the sites was based exclusively on hunting, fishing and food collecting. There are now at least two radiocarbon dates for sites with early assemblages of pit-and-comb decorated pottery. For the site of Berendeyevo in the Yaroslavl region the date is 5,730 ± 120 B.P., and for that of Zarečye in the Moscow region, 5,670 ± 50 B.P. During the following millennia pit-and-comb decorated pottery spread intensively to the south, west and north. The date of the southern penetration may be estimated on the basis of the date 4,770 ± 60 B.P.[74] obtained for a pit-and-comb pottery assemblage at Podzorovo, in the Tambov region. The sites with pit-and-comb pottery in the Ukraine also contain imported goods from the late Tripolye settlements.

2. The zone of the Last Glaciation

In the zone of the Middle Pleistocene glaciations Neolithic sites were situated mostly inside river valleys, but in the area of the Last Glaciation they are usually found within the lacustrine basins. The lake depressions, relics of huge glacial lacustrine basins, are particularly numerous in the outer and inner provinces of the glaciated zone. These lake depressions are almost absent in the middle morainic belt, and there are practically no Neolithic sites there. While the sites in the valleys were in most cases seasonal hunting camps, the lake dwellings were inhabited all the year round. The dwellings were constructed on piles in the water near the shore. Many sites were inhabited by different cultural groups after interruptions caused by lake transgressions. The economic strategy of the Middle Holocene lake dwellers was highly effective. Some of these sites attained considerable size: several Late Neolithic sites in the zone of the Last Glaciation extended over as much as one hectare.

There are comparatively few Neolithic sites in the outer provinces of the Last Glaciation, but an important site, Zacenye, was discovered in central Byelorussia in the Minsk region. It is situated within a lake-like depression now drained by the river Cna.[75] During the Early and Middle Holocene there was a lake there, the level of which fluctuated, possibly in accordance with the rhythms established in other lake depressions. A considerable fall in the level occurred (according to a radiocarbon date) in 5,530 ± 60 B.P. At that time an early Neolithic site came into existence there. The cultural layer found in the peat deposits contained coarse grey pot sherds with shell particles in the paste. The sherds belonged to wide-mouthed hemispherical pots with pointed bases. A row of widely-spaced round pits was placed below the rim and rows of comb impressions or notches decorated the upper parts of the vessels.

A number of Late Neolithic sites have been discovered in a huge Krivina peat bog in north-eastern Byelorussia.[76] At the time when the sites existed there was a large lake there. All the sites were situated offshore, and piles were used in the construction of the dwellings. The subsistence pattern of the lake sites can be determined from the faunal list of the Osovec I site: Wild: elk, 48%; wild pig, 21%; red deer, 13%; roe deer, 1.4%; bear 6%. Domesticated: cattle, 11%; sheep/goats, 1.4%. The list shows that the bulk of the meat diet was supplied by hunting. Fishing was also very important. In the cultural layer remains of mushrooms, berries, acorns, water-chestnuts and hazelnuts were discovered. All this underlines the importance of food gathering.

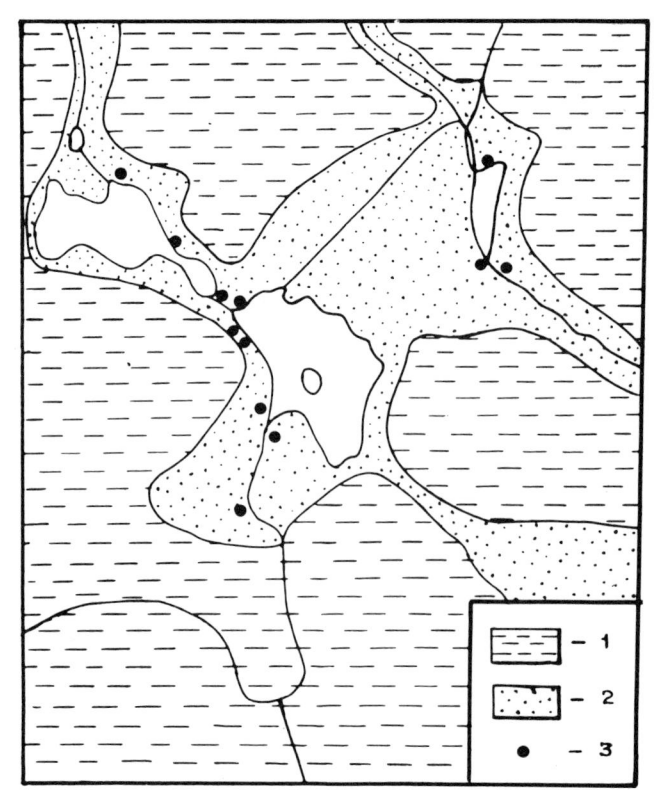

Figure 44 Usvyaty sites: geomorphological setting; 1 – morainic upland; 2 – glacial lake depression; 3 – sites

The sites situated in the inner province of the Upper Pleistocene glaciation are much more numerous. Here glacial lacustrine basins were widespread, and many of their depressions are filled by modern lakes. In the Usvyaty depression in the south of the Pskov region, detailed investigations of lake dwellings in the western part of the Russian plain have been carried out for the first time.[47] The following problems were dealt with: the fluctuations of the lake levels during the Upper Pleistocene and the Holocene; the evolution of human settlements in connection with the fluctuations of the lake level; the evolution of vegetational cover; the absolute chronology of human settlements and of environmental history.

The glacial lacustrine basin in the Usvyaty area came into being soon after the ice-sheet receded from its maximum extent. In all probability the glacial lake existed at least until the Younger Dryas. Pollen spectra of this type were established in an upper portion of glacial lacustrine deposits. Late Palaeolithic industries with tanged points have been discovered in sandy dunes formed upon shore terraces, fixing the maximum extent of the glacial lake. On a lower terrace of the same glacial lake tools of an early Mesolithic type have been found (blades and axe-like tools). A break in the sedimentation followed. At the beginning of the Pre-Boreal period the lake level fell abruptly, and during the Pre-Boreal and Boreal period the level was much lower than it is at present. An important rise in the lake level took place during the second half of the Atlantic period and the following periods. During this Late Holocene transgression, deposits 1.5 m. thick were laid down and a low (1.3 m. high) terrace was formed. Neolithic and Bronze Age sites are connected with these formations (Figs. 45, 46). On the basis of geological investigations it has been established that during the first (late Atlantic) transgression the level of the lake rose by at least 0.8 m. During this transgression a thick layer of fine sand was deposited. A piece of wood from this deposit was radiocarbon dated to 5,530 ± 90 B.P.

Later the water level fell; during this regression the first lake settlement appeared. Diatom analysis has shown that at that time the lake was shallow and stagnant. The off-shore area where the settlement was built was overgrown with pond vegetation. Radiocarbon evidence reveals that the earliest pile constructions in the lake appeared some 4,500 years ago. The analysis of the pile constructions shows that during the existence of the first settlement the level of the lake ceased to fall and again rose steadily. The lake dwellers several times rebuilt their houses on higher levels. A pile belonging to a later construction was radiocarbon dated 4,110 ± 70 B.P. This pile crushed another one belonging to an earlier period of construction, its date being 4,230 ± 70 B.P. During this period, while the water was rising, there occurred a fire which completely destroyed the settlement. A burnt pile was radiocarbon dated 3,920 ± 70 B.P. The burnt site was covered by the lake water which deposited upon it a

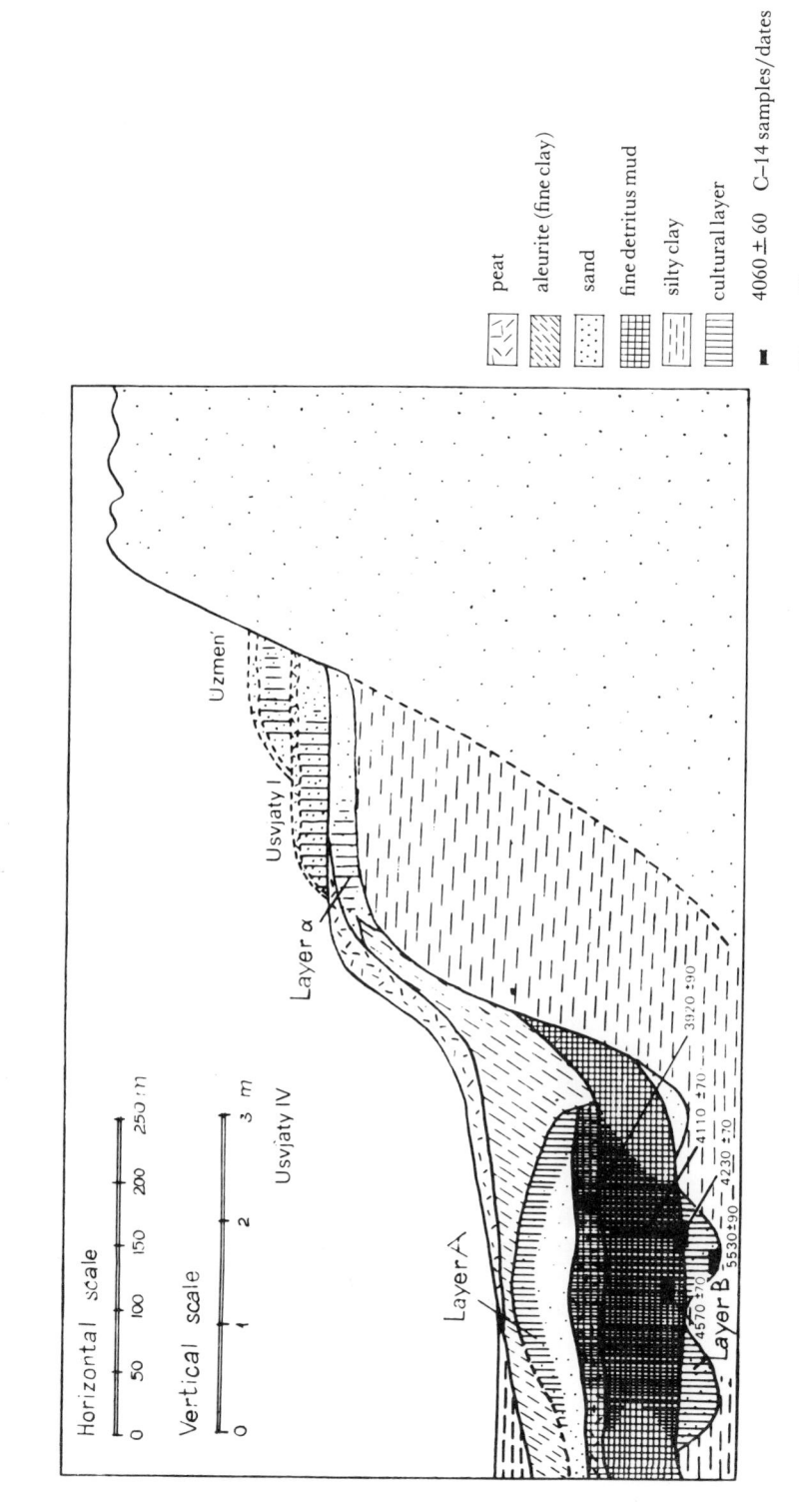

Figure 45 Usvyaty depression: cross-section

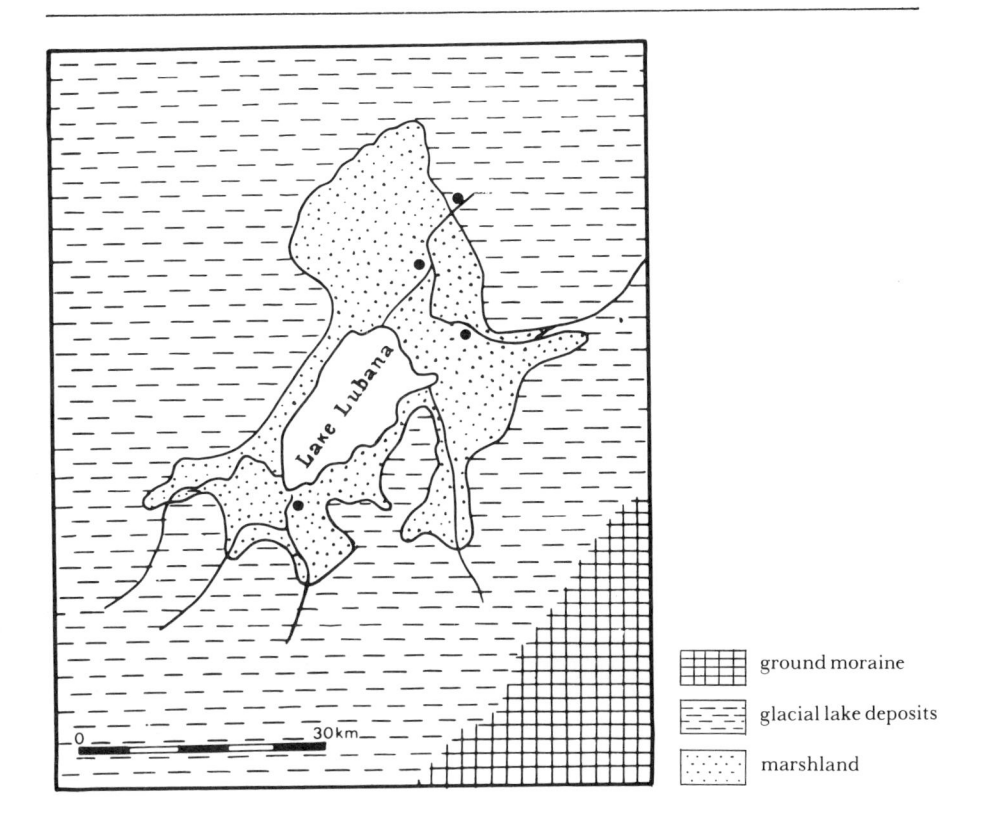

Figure 46 Lubana depression: geomorphological setting

layer of grey sand. Summing up the radiocarbon dates obtained for the first settlement in the Usvyaty lake, its duration may be estimated at some 500 years, roughly from 4,500 to 4,000 B.P. Pollen analytical data show that the settlement corresponded to the maximum spread of broad-leaved three species in the area. Forests consisting of oak, elm and lime probably grew on the morainic hills surrounding the lake depression. Birch and alder forests as well as spruce woods spread over the peaty shores of the lake.

Some time after, the transgression reached its highest point and there was another fall in the lake level. During that regression the layer of grey sand emerged from the water and on it a new settlement appeared. This regression did not last long. It was succeeded by a new, significant rise in the lake level, measuring at least 2 m. The low terraces were covered with water which deposited a thick layer of sandy clay. Pollen analysis shows that this lake transgression took place during the massive spread of spruce forests in the vicinity of the lake. A group of Bronze Age settlements appeared during the regression which succeeded the maximum rise in the lake level.

The subsistence pattern of the Usvyaty lake sites is shown by the results of faunal analysis (individuals):

Usvyaty, first settlement: elk, 45%; bear, 15%; wild pig, 13%; hare, 8%; beaver, 2%; roe deer, 1%; aurochs, 3%.
Usvyaty, second settlement: Wild: elk, 32%; bear, 36%; wild pig, 13%; aurochs, 3%. Domesticated: pig, 9%; cattle, 5%; sheep/goat, 1%.
Usvyaty, late settlement: Wild: elk, 17%; bear, 12%; wild pig, 24%; aurochs, 3%. Domesticated: pig, 8%; cattle, 8%; sheep/goat, 1%.

There are numerous bird bones at all the sites. The large number of fish-bones testifies to the great importance attached to fishing. Among the fishes have been identified pike, pike-perch, bream and carp. Food gathering was very important, too. In the cultural layers were found numerous acorns, chestnuts, water-chestnuts and *Unio* shells. Summing up, one may state that the subsistence pattern of the Usvyaty lake dwellers was primarily based upon the hunting of forest animals, fishing and food collecting. The existence of domesticated animals, the number of which rises at later sites, may be ascribed to economic contacts with stock-breeding communities. The pottery assemblages of these sites reflect the influence of corded ware cultures.

Pottery sherds are extremely numerous. In the pottery assemblage of the first settlement large pots with conical and pointed bases are the most common. The paste in most cases had an admixture of shell particles; in some cases organic matter was added. The most commonly used elements of ornament were comb impressions, incised lines and strokes. The comb impressions usually form horizontal rows; the incised lines usually form nets; strokes and incised lines together form geometric patterns. In most cases these patterns are simple zigzags and triangles, but in several cases the geometric motifs are very complicated. In the latest construction level of the first

Table 11

Dates B.P.	Fluctuations of lake-level	Vegetational	Sites
3,800	Regression		Abora
	Transgression		
4,000	Regression	Sub-Boreal	Sulka, Eini
	Transgression		
4,500	Regression		Piestina
4,800	Transgression		
	Regression	Late Atlantic	
6,000			Osa, Early Neolithic
	Transgression	Early Atlantic	Osa, Mesolithic

The West Russian Plain

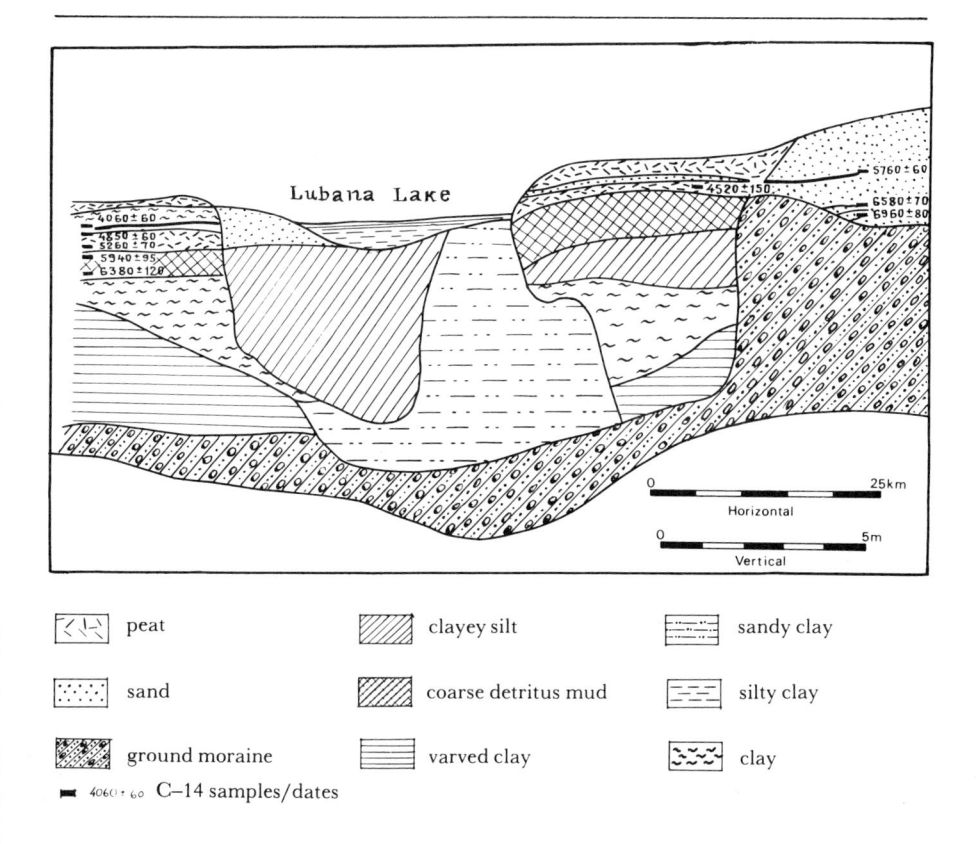

	peat
	sand
	ground moraine
	clayey silt
	coarse detritus mud
	varved clay
	sandy clay
	silty clay
	clay
4060±60	C–14 samples/dates

Figure 47 Lubana depression: cross-section

settlement there appear pot sherds decorated with cord impressions. The number of these sherds rises in the second settlement layer. But here, too, the simple rows of comb impressions and geometric patterns formed by the incised lines and strokes continued to predominate.

The most interesting information about lake basin settlements has been obtained as a result of archaeological, palaeogeographical and geochronological investigations carried out in the Lubana depression, in the eastern part of Latvia.[78] Huge glacial lacustrine basins were formed in the Lubana depression and in the middle stretches of the Zapadnaya Dvina valley during the final stages of the glacial retreat. The actual lake is a relic of a huge late glacial basin and it occupies only a small portion of the depression, two-thirds of which is taken up by peat bogs. Nine rivers fall into Lake Lubana and only one flows out of it, the Aiviekste, the right tributary of the Daugava (Zapadnaya Dvina). The slopes of the depression and the surrounding morainic hills are covered with pine forests and dense shrubs (Figs. 46, 47). Intensive land-reclamation is now being carried out in the Lubana depression, in the course of which numerous archaeological sites have been brought to light.

On the basis of geological, geomorphological and geochronological data the evolution of the Lubana depression during the Holocene appears to be as in Table 12. As we have seen, the first traces of human settlement there were found in the Mesolithic layer of Osa. The site is situated on the northern sandy shore of the depression. The Mesolithic site was inhabited during the first Atlantic transgression of the lake, between 7,000 and 6,500 B.P. A layer containing an Early Neolithic pottery assemblage was found at the same place, in sandy peat, under a thick cover of stratified sand. Three radiocarbon dates were obtained from samples of wood extracted from the Early Neolithic layer: $5,730 \pm 50$; $5,880 \pm 80$; $5,780 \pm 70$ B.P. The practically identical dates show that the site was inhabited 5,800-5,700 years ago.

The pot sherds found in this layer are made of paste with vegetable matter or with particles of shells. The sherds belonged to large vessels with pointed bases (Fig. 48). The rims were either straight or sloping inside. A peculiarity of the pottery assemblage of the Early Neolithic Osa site was the presence of small oval troughs similar to the Ertebølle 'blubber lamps'. The most commonly used ornamentation consisted of horizontal rows of comb impressions on the upper part of the pot. In some cases the rows of comb impressions formed diagonal lines or triangles. In rare cases sparsely set pits and incised lines were used (Fig. 49).

Bone and antler implements were numerous. They included antler adzes, epiphyses of bones sawn at an angle of 45°, bone adzes, awls, bone arrow-heads, uniserially barbed harpoons. The stone industry included polished axes, small scrapers and blades. Among the faunal remains the following species have been identified (individuals): wild

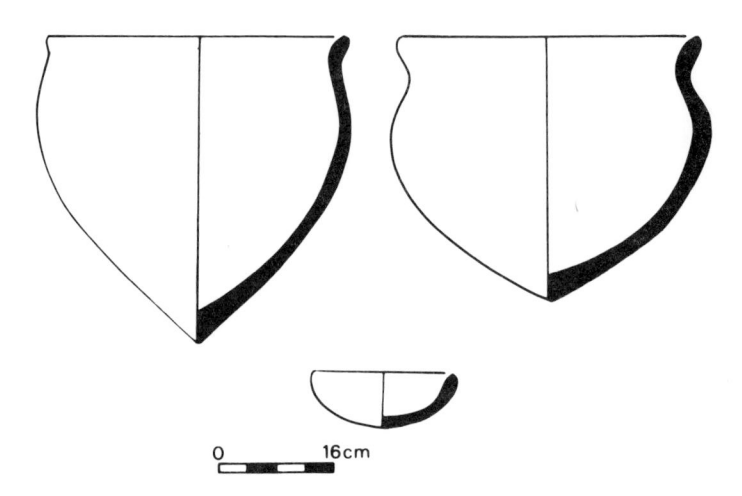

Figure 48 Neolithic sites of eastern Baltic area: shapes of vessels

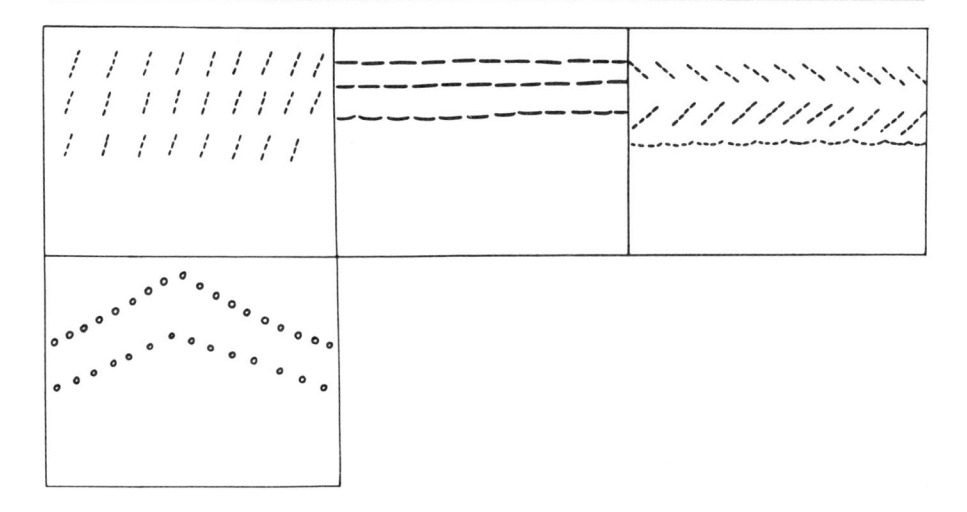

Figure 49 Early Neolithic of eastern Latvia: pottery ornamental patterns (see Fig.26)

pig, 49.7%; marten, 20%; elk, 17%; bear, 4.6%; aurochs, 2%; red deer, 2%; wild horse, 1.3%; beaver, 4.6%; badger, 2%; otter, 1.3%; dog, 6.6%.

Three km. west of the Osa site, within the peat-covered flood-plain of the Lubana lake, on the shore of a small stream, another important site, Piestina, is situated. The cultural layer lies in the peat, buried between two layers of sand. Special analysis has shown that it was a grass fen peat containing remains of water-lilies, reeds and cane. Three radiocarbon dates have been obtained from the samples of wood and peat taken from the cultural layers: 4,670 ± 150; 4,520 ± 120 and 4,250 ± 50 B.C.

The pottery assemblage discovered in the Piestina site is of particular importance. According to the Latvian archaeologist Dr F. Zagorskis, two varieties of pottery are represented there. The first is typical pit-and-comb decorated pottery; the second belongs to the so-called Piestina type. The fabric of this second variety contains particles of shells and organic matter. The pots are large hemispherical bowls with pointed bases. The rims are either straight, or cut inside or slightly thickened. The elements of ornamentation are comb impressions, notches, incised lines, strokes and cord impressions. The most commonly used patterns are horizontal or diagonal rows of comb impressions or notches, incised lines or cord impressions. All these patterns are found in the ornamentations of the Early Neolithic pottery assemblage at Osa; but Piestina ware also includes geometric motifs – triangles, rhombs, and rectangles made of strokes and incised lines – and also more complicated patterns made by combinations of these elements (Fig. 50). The Piestina pottery

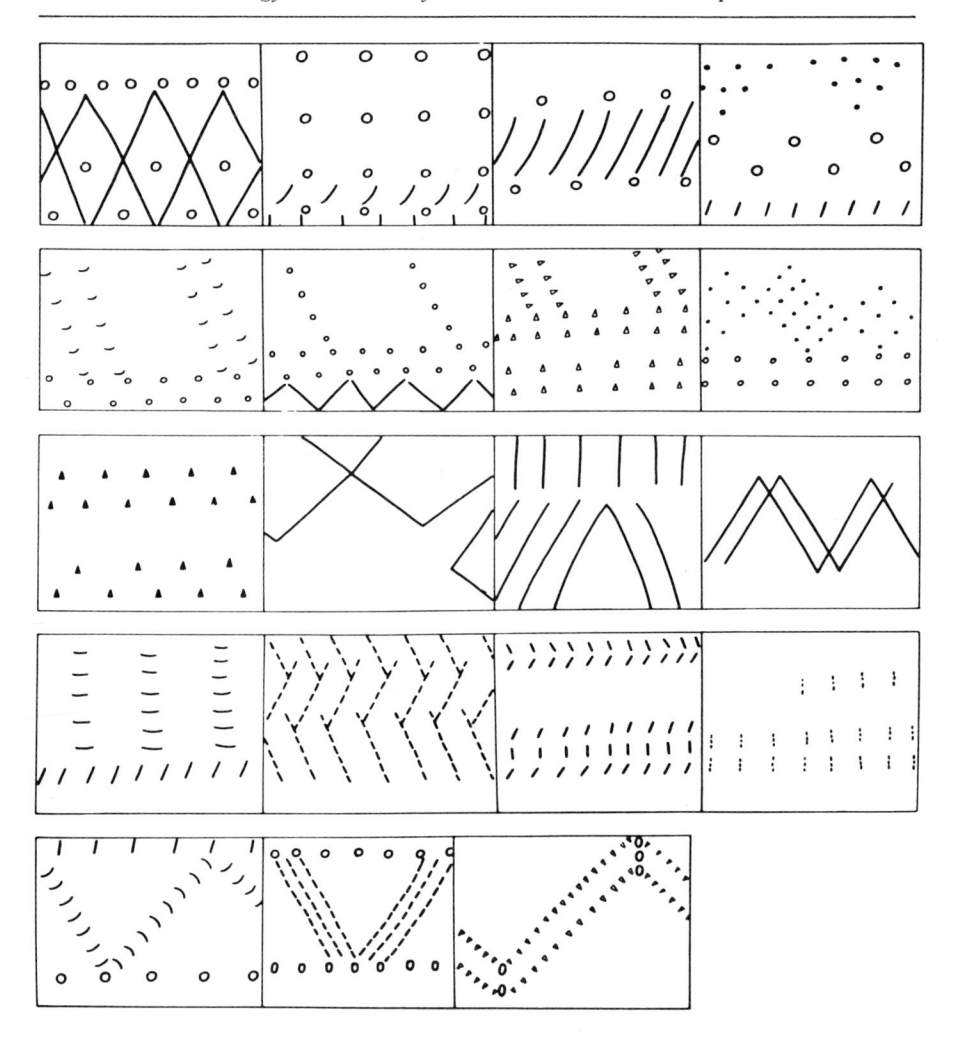

160   *Ecology and Economy in Neolithic Eastern Europe*

Figure 49 Middle Neolithic of eastern Latvia: pottery ornamental patterns (see Fig.26)

assemblage reflects the penetration of elements of the funnel beaker culture in the eastern Latvian lake depressions. These elements interacted with the local ones, with the early comb-decorated pottery (which in its turn reflected the penetration of southern elements), and with the local Mesolithic substratum.

Investigations carried out in the south-eastern corner of the lake depression are of great significance. Here a site known as Sulka was situated. This site lies on the flood-plain, on the banks of the river Sulka, not far from the point where it falls into the Lubana lake. The following stratigraphy has been established: the upper 0.6 m. was occupied by diatomic *gyttja* – mud deposited in a shallow stagnant lake. Below this a sandy *gyttja* was situated which contained cultural deposits. Then followed a layer 0.4 m. thick of grass fen peat. Below this there were 0.5 m. of a fine detritus *gyttja*, and below that lay blue clay.

The pottery of the Piestina and Sulka sites is different. The pit-and-comb decorated pottery, which formed less than 10% of all the pot sherds found at Piestina, makes up the bulk of the pottery assemblage of the Sulka site. The pots were made of clay with an admixture of sand or of small pottery particles, rarely with an admixture of shells. The most frequent forms were bowls with rounded bases. The rims were thickened and cut inside. The ornamental patterns consisted of horizontal rows of comb impressions and pits, or pits forming geometric figures, triangles and rhombs. Both patterns are known in the later stages of the Lyalovo pottery.

The Neolithic sites of the Lubana depression contained rich industries of stone, bone and antler. There were flint and bone arrow- and spearheads and harpoons, stone axes and bone adzes, and numerous scrapers on thick flakes and on the ends of blades (Fig. 51).

Another group of sites in the area is classified by Latvian archaeologists as belonging to the Late Neolithic. In most cases these sites were inhabited during the lake regressions which occurred in about 4,000 B.P. and after 3,800 B.P. The site of Eini is situated on the flood-plain terrace of lake Lubana. The cultural deposit was in the peat layer above the layer of *gyttja* and overlaid by fen peat. Numerous piles have been found in the layers: pile lying horizontally has been dated 4,000 ± 60 B.P. Another Late Neolithic site is situated in the north eastern part of the depression inside the flood-plain of the Aiviekste river. The cultural deposits were found in the peat above *gyttja* and sand. Samples of wood and peat have been radiocarbon dated 3,860 ± 100 and 3,870 ± 70 B.P. Other Late Neolithic sites in the Lubana lake depression have the following radiocarbon dates:

Nainiekste (peat): 4,170 ± 130 B.P.; Kreiči (wood): 4,020 ± 300 B.P.; Leimaniški (wood): 3,970 ± 250 B.P.; Leimaniški (bone): 3,770 ± 200 B.P.

According to pollen analytical evidence the Late Neolithic sites existed at a time when the area in the vicinity of the lake was covered by mixed oak forests. Pine forests were spread over the sandy shores; pine and alder forests covered the low terraces.

The subsistence pattern of these Late Neolithic sites may be reconstructed on the basis of the faunal evidence[79] (individuals):

Eini: Wild: elk, 40.7%; wild pig, 22.8%; aurochs, 14.7%; red deer, 3.6%; bear, 1.8%; roe deer, 0.9%; marten, 0.9%; beaver, 10.5%; otter, 0.3%; badger, 0.3%. Domesticated: cattle, 1.2%; horse (domesticated?), 0.3%; dog, 1.8%.
Abora: Wild: elk, 37%; wild pig, 26%; aurochs, 10.8%; bear, 1.9%;

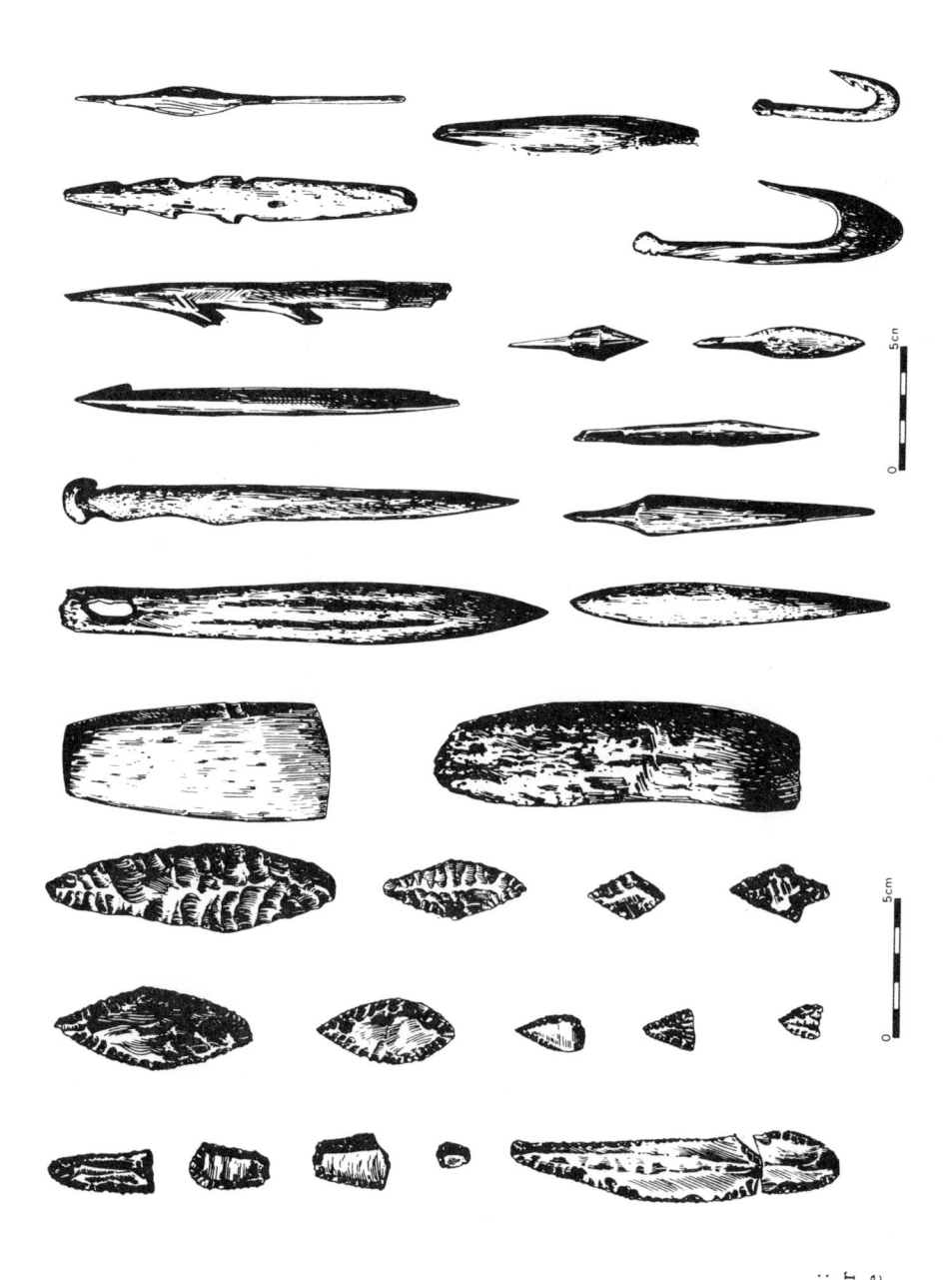

Figure 51 Neolithic sites of eastern Baltic area: working tools (after Jaanits, 1973; Note 5.80).

red deer, 3.9%; marten, 0.9%; beaver, 13.8%; otter, 0.6%. Domesticated: cattle, 1.1%; horse (domesticated?), 0.9%; dog, 2.0%.

From this faunal list it becomes quite clear that the economy of the Lubana Late Neolithic sites was based entirely on hunting. Stockbreeding was of no importance at all. Fishing and food collecting were probably important sources of food.

Remains of dwellings have been discovered at several sites. At the Late Neolithic site of Lagaža the remains of a rectangular house built on piles have been found. The size of this house was 10 by 4 m. At the same site a copper furnace has been unearthed.

The number of sites here belonging to the Late Neolithic is greater than those belonging to earlier periods. Such sites are much bigger than those of earlier stages. The size of the Lagaža site, for example, reaches one hectare.

The Latvian archaeologist Dr Ilze Loze distinguishes three groups in the pottery of the Late Neolithic sites. So-called Abora pottery is made of a porous mass; shells and grass were added to the clay. The vessels in most cases had flat bases, but some with rounded or pointed bases were also met with. The pots were decorated with comb and cord impressions, incised lines, strokes, pits and round impressions. The most common motives were horizontal lines, zigzags, nets, triangles and rhombs. The last two patterns are the same as in the Piestina pottery. 'Textile' pottery is very similar to the Abora pottery; the only distinction is that the outer and inner surfaces of the pots were covered with textile fabric impressions. Corded ware is less numerous in the Lubana Late Neolithic pottery; it includes beakers, bowls and amphorae. The beakers had S-shaped profiles and funnel-like necks, and were decorated with cord impressions and incised lines forming zigzags. The bowls were decorated with a prominent line on the neck; the amphorae were decorated with vertical, parallel groups of incised lines flanked with comb impressions. Similar vessels are known in the groups of corded ware in north-eastern Poland notably in the Zlota and Rzucewo cultures.

Estonian Neolithic sites show a striking consistency of subsistence patterns from Early Neolithic right up to the first half of the second millennium B.C.; they had a stable hunting economy based on the hunting of elk, wild pig and aurochs. Examples of Estonian Early and Middle Neolithic sites are Akali in the flood-plain of the Eimajõgi river and Kääpa in north-eastern Estonia.[80] Three radiocarbon dates are available for the Kääpa site: peat taken from the layer with Narva-type pottery (described below), 4,850 ± 235 B.P.; bone extracted from the layer with pit-and-comb pottery, 4,480 ± 225 B.P.; charred wood from the same layer, 4,350 ± 220 B.P. The economic structure of the Early Neolithic sites of Estonia may be deduced from the following faunal determinations[81] (individuals):

Akali, lower layer: elk, 48%; wild pig, 33%; aurochs, 22%; roe deer, 1%; bear, 11%; beaver, 10%.
Kääpa: elk, 22%; wild pig, 15%; aurochs, 5.5%; wild horse, 2.2%; red deer, 2.2%; bear, 6.6%; beaver, 33%; marten, 3%; dog, 44%.

The faunal identifications obtained for two Late Neolithic sites in the same area, Tamula and Villa, both containing corded ware pottery, are very similar. (All figures are for individuals):

Tamula: Wild: elk, 20.4%; wild pig, 11.2%; aurochs, 7.5%; red deer, 3.8%; roe deer, 2.3%; bear, 3.2%; beaver, 29.2%; marten, 8.4%; otter, 5.0%. Domesticated: pig, 0.5%; sheep/goat, 0.1% (2 bones; 1 individual); cattle, 0.1% (1 bone, 1 individual); dog, 3.6%.
Villa: elk, 19%; wild pig, 99%; aurochs, 9%; red deer, 3%; roe deer, 4.5%; bear, 3%; beaver, 37%; marten, 4.5%; otter, 6%; dog, 4.5%.

Another highly efficient economic strategy lasting for millennia is that of the sites in the Baltic coastal area, where the subsistence pattern was based on the exploitation of land and sea food resources. This area is included in the zone covered by the ice-sheet of the Last Glaciation, and contained numerous off-shore peat bogs, which were turned into sea lagoons when the sea level rose and became marshy swamps when it retreated. These marshy lagoons were intensively settled by hunting groups along the Baltic coastal area. The earliest settlements of this kind are situated in the south-western part of the Baltic Sea: along the coasts of Jutland and the Danish islands, and in the maritime areas of southern Sweden and East and West Germany.

These sites are usually referred to as belonging to the Ertebølle culture. The settlements were surrounded by mixed oak and alder forests and dense hazel groves.

Two important Ertebølle sites, Buddelin and Augustenhof, were situated on the island of Rügen, on the Baltic coast of East Germany. In recent years these sites have been studied by Dr B. Gramsch, the archaeologist, and by Professor H. Kiewe, the Quaternary geologist.[82] Both sites were located on the coastal formations of the inner bays of the island. The site of Buddelin was situated on the northern shore of Kleiner Jasmunder Bodden. The site of Augustenhof lay on a narrow isthmus which separated Kleiner and Grosser Jasmunder Bodden (Fig. 52). Both Boddens were deep gulfs of the Littorina Sea. Rügen island itself was at that time an archipelago of small islets. The cultural layers of both sites were buried in the shore deposits and covered by sands deposited during the later stages of the Littorina Sea transgressions.

At the bottom of the Holocene sediments at the site of Buddelin lay coarse sand with pebbles. Here artifacts were found belonging to the lower cultural layer. The radiocarbon date of this layer is $5{,}815 \pm 100$

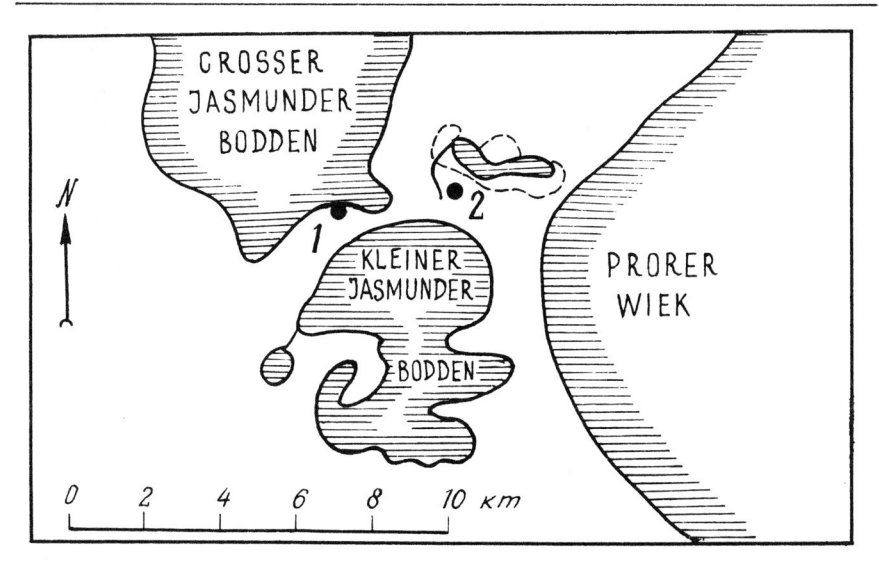

Figure 52 1 – Buddelin site. 2 – Augustenhof site. Island of Rügen (after Kliewe und Lange, 1968; Note 5.86). - - - - Limits of an early Holocene lake

B.P. Above it was situated a layer of washed peat which was deposited during a transgression. Above this again was a peaty layer containing artifacts of a second cultural layer, dated to 5,192 ± 120 B.P. This layer was covered with sand deposited during the following Littorina transgression, in which pot sherds belonging to the Middle Neolithic age have been found.

At the Augustenhof site the cultural layer was discovered in a layer of buried soil deposited upon marine sand and covered with the sands of a strand wall of a later Littorina transgression. Charcoal from the cultural layer gave the age of 5,496 + 100 B.P. The bottom of the strand wall fixing the maximum height of the Littorina transgression in the south Baltic area stands at 2.35 m. above the present sea level.

A considerable number of Ertebølle sites are known in the coastal area of Jutland and of the Danish isles. Danish archaeologists[83] distinguish two varieties of Ertebølle sites: the kitchen middens (huge shell heaps) and the so-called coastal plain sites. The large coastal sites were occupied all the year round. The small sites were seasonal camp sites. The Ertebølle sites were very numerous along the coasts of narrow fjords or on the small islands of lakes separated from the sea.

The faunal evidence reveals that the subsistence pattern of the Ertebølle sites was based on the exploitation of both marine and land food resources. The proportion between the two was approximately fifty-fifty. Among the mammalian land fauna were identified elk, red deer, roe deer, wild pigs, aurochs, bear, foxes, beavers, wolves and dogs. The hunting of sea mammals was widely practised. At least four species of seal were identified: common seal, ringed seal, harp seal and grey seal. Whale bones have been found at many sites. In most cases these bones belonged to comparatively small animals, but at one site in Jutland bones belonging to a stranded blue whale no less than 20 m. long were found. The hunting of birds and of waterfowl in particular provided an important source of meat. Among the many bones of birds found on the Ertebølle sites divers, gulls, grebes, duck and many other species have been identified.

Fishing at the Ertebølle sites was both intensive and effective. Among the fish bones the following species were identified: spur dog, salmon, pike, roach, wels (*Siluris glanis* L.), eel, garfish, cod, haddock, coalfish, perch, mackerel, sea scorpion, flounder. Thousands and thousands of sea shells fill the cultural layers of the Ertebølle kitchen middens. At least six species of molluscs typical of the Littorina Sea have been identified here: common and flat periwinkles, netted dog whelk, cross-cut carpet, pullet carpet and golden carpet shells. The shells of the European tortoise have also been found.

Some archaeologists are of the opinion that stock-breeding was economically important at the Ertebølle sites. Bones of cattle have been identified at the Ertebølle site of Saturper Moor on the West German coast near Hamburg. At the late Ertebølle site of Muldbjerg on Zealand bones of both cattle and sheep/goat radiocarbon dated to 4,860 – 4,700 B.P. have been found. According to a reconstruction made by the Danish archaeologist and palaeogeographer J. Troels-Smith, the site was built on a floating island in a small lake. There were no suitable pastures in the vicinity of the site and J. Troels-Smith has put forward the hypothesis that plants growing near by, elm, ivy and mistletoe, were used as fodder plants.[84] In my opinion, however, the presence of small numbers of domesticated animals at sites with a predominantly hunting and fishing economy may, as in the cases previously discussed, be attributed to economic links with settlements having a predominantly food-producing economy.

The bulk of the inventory of the Ertebølle sites consists of stone tools. As J. Troels-Smith[85] has convincingly shown, the tool-kit of the Ertebølle sites is a direct continuation of earlier Mesolithic stages, in particular those of Kongemosen. At the Rügen sites (which Dr B. Gramsch treats as belonging to the Litzow culture) the greater part of the stone inventory consists of large axe-like tools, core- and flake-axes. The second most important group of the stone inventory was made up of trapezes or transverse arrow-heads. Among other tools scrapers and retouched blades are reported. There were numerous tools of bone and antler: points, harpoons, axes and adzes.

The pot sherds found at the Ertebølle sites are of particular interest. They belonged to two types of vessels: thick-walled, coil-built, pointed-based jars with crude rim decorations, and troughs or blubber lamps. The West German archaeologist H. Schwabedissen sees in the Ertebølle pots analogies to the pottery of the Michelsberg culture of West Germany and the adjacent regions of France and Switzerland.[86] He also considers that one particular form of stone axe has analogies in the culture of Rössen. The East German archaeologist B. Gramsch[87] believes that pottery manufacturing appeared among the Ertebølle people as a result of contacts with the Danubian (Linear pottery) population. A triangle-ornamented plate found at a Rügen site has a direct analogue in the assemblage of the Brzesc-Kujawski group of the Lengyel culture in Poland. Troels-Smith[88] thinks, however, that pottery manufacturing appeared among the Ertebølle population independently, and even believes that funnel beakers developed from the Ertebølle pottery (among the Ertebølle pot sherds at Muldbjerg early types of funnel beakers were found).

In my opinion, the Ertebølle sites along the south Baltic coast were not homogeneous. The off-shore lagoons and fjords were very rich in natural resources and were highly suitable for hunting, fishing and food collecting. For a very long time these lagoons absorbed the surplus population from different agricultural communities in central and northern Europe. To this constant process of absorption may be ascribed the presence of imported goods from the Lengyel and Rössen cultures and of Michelsberg pottery and funnel beakers, and also of a small number of domesticated animals.

The Neolithic sites of the northern Baltic, on the shores of Estonia, Latvia and Lithuania, have a subsistence pattern similar to that of the Ertebølle sites in the southern Baltic, with a few local differences due to the more severe conditions. Three sites, Narva-Riigiküla I, II and III, have been excavated and studied by Dr N.N. Gurina.[89] They are situated on the left bank of the Narva river, between ranges of high dunes, wind redeposited strand walls which separated a shallow lagoon of the Littorina Sea from the open sea (Fig. 53). The subsistence pattern of the Narva sites is made abundantly clear by the faunal analysis (all individuals).

Narva-Riigiküla I: elk, 12.5%; wild pig, 18%; aurochs, 19%; seal, 12.5%; bear, 5%; beaver, 7%; dogs, 19%.
Narva-Riigiküla II: elk, 1; wild pig, 3; aurochs, 3; seal, 3; bear, 1; beaver, 1; dog, 3.
Narva Riigiküla III: elk, 7; wild pig, 3; aurochs, 6; seal, 9; bear, 2; beaver, 3; dog, 3.

The faunal lists are fairly typical of Neolithic sites with a stable hunting and fishing economy. Marine food resources were intensively exploited: apart from numerous seal bones, medium-sized whale bones were found. Numerous bones indicate the intensive hunting of waterfowl. Among the bird bones were identified those of duck, swan and Great Northern divers. Bird bones were particularly numerous at the Narva Riigiküla III site. Among the extremely numerous fish bones pike, perch, salmon and sheat-fish have been identified.

The remains of dwellings have been discovered at the Narva sites. These were oval and semi-subterranean, 6 by 7 m. across. The

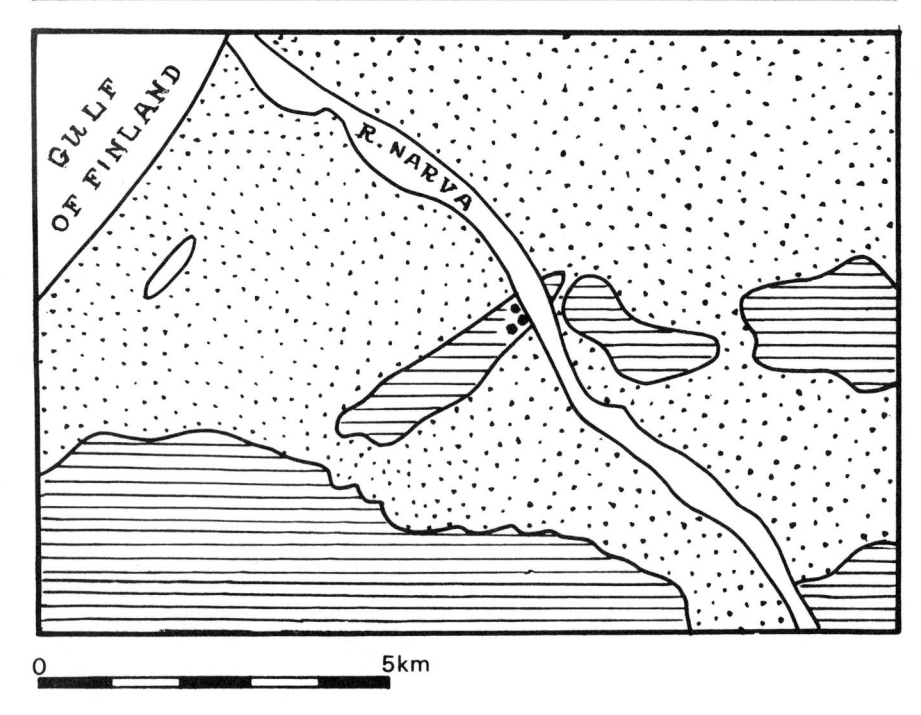

Figure 53 Geomorphological setting of the Narva-Riigiküla sites. The dots show the area submerged by the sea in the course of the Littorina transgression. Lines show dunes, strand walls and shore formations. Big black dots show Neolithic sites.

chipped stone inventory included numerous arrow- and spearheads, large scrapers and axe-like and adze-like tools. A large number of tools made of bone and antler have been found. These were arrow- and spearheads, harpoons, axes, adzes, hoe-like tools, fish hooks. Particular interest is attached by archaeologists to strange-looking tools consisting of the metapodia of elk and red deer cut at an angle of 45 degrees. Such tools, whose use is unknown, were widespread over the Early Neolithic sites of the northern Baltic area.

Numerous pot sherds have been found at the Narva sites. An Early Neolithic pottery assemblage distinct from pit-and-comb decorated pottery has been recognized for the first time in the northern Baltic area, and has been labelled Narva pottery. This type of pottery made up 96.7% of pottery finds at the Narva Riigiküla III site, 26.7% at Narva Riigiküla I and only 3% at Narva Riigiküla II. It was made of clay with the addition of shells and organic matter. The bases of the pots were either pointed or rounded; the rims in most cases were slightly thinner than the walls, and were either straight or slightly cut inside. The decorative motifs used were comb impressions, notches, strokes and little pits. The most common ornamental patterns were horizontal rows of comb impressions (the comb impressions in several cases forming zigzags) and horizontal rows of strokes or dots. Most of these ornamental patterns have parallels in the pottery assemblages of Estonia and Latvia, though there are some differences, such as the absence of incised lines, the lack of geometric patterns and the use of pits.

Very interesting material has been secured after intensive excavations of the site of Sarnate, in the coastal area of Latvia, south of the town of Ventspils.[90] The site is situated in a marginal zone of a huge fen peat bog, lying on a low terrace of the Littorina Sea. The peat bog is separated from the sea by a high range of dunes (Fig. 54). Inside the bog more than 40 Neolithic dwellings have been found. The dwellings were built upon sandy foundations, the size of which varied from 3 to 15 sq.m. and piles were largely used in their construction.

Control excavations carried out in the dwelling area have revealed the following stratigraphy. The cultural layer was found in a layer of fen peat at a depth of 0.4-0.6 m. Below the cultural layer a thick layer of *gyttja* was found. Under the *gyttja* was a layer of sedge peat, and below this was a thick layer of sea marl, separated by a thin horizon of sedge peat. On the basis of intensive analytical investigations the Holocene history of the Sarnate peat bog appears to be as follows. The deposition of the sea marl took place during the time of the Ancylus lake. The horizon of sedge peat was deposited during the regression which separated the two Ancylus transgressions. The layer of sedge peat above the sea marl was deposited during a lengthy regression

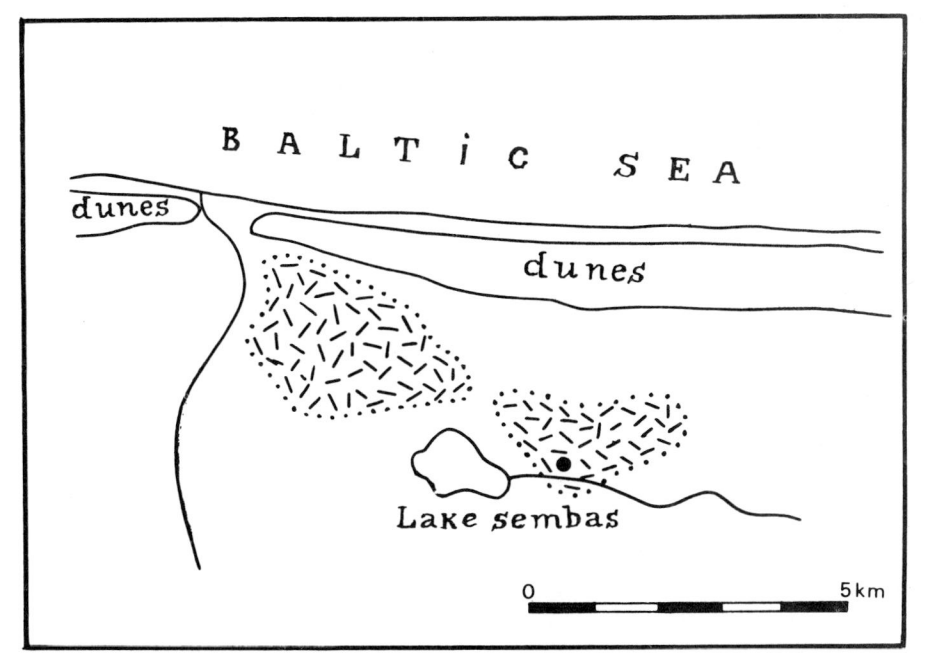

Figure 54 Geomorphological setting of the Sarnate sites. The stroked areas show present-day peat bogs – ancient lagoons of the Littorina Sea. Black dot shows the area of Neolithic settlements.

which preceded the Littorina Sea transgressions. The layer of *gyttja* was formed during one of the late Littorina transgressions (there was a break in sedimentation due to an abrasion). The cultural layer was formed during one of the late Littorina regressions.

Samples of peat and of wood taken from the cultural layer have revealed the following age: 4,539 ± 100 and 4,500 ± 110 B.P. Earlier the following radiocarbon dates were obtained for the Sarnate Neolithic dwellings: 4,490 ± 250; 4,700 ± 250; 4,630 ± 70 B.P. All the dates obtained lie within a narrow time span and may be regarded as corresponding to a regression of the Littorina Sea that took place c. 4,500-4,200 B.P.

Among the faunal remains (rather few in number) were identified: 2 elk bones; 10 wild pig bones; 4 seal bones; 13 beaver bones. Fishing was of major importance. A pit discovered inside one of the excavated dwellings was completely filled with fish bones. The enormous amount of nut-shells found in all the excavated dwellings testifies to the significance of food collecting.

Two varieties of pottery have been found at the Sarnate dwellings. The first variety is typical pit-and-comb decorated pottery. The second variety was labelled Sarnate pottery by the excavator, the Latvian archaeologist Mrs L. Vankina. Typical of this pottery are hemispherical pots with conical or round bases and straight or S-shaped rims. Some oval troughs have been found (similar to the blubber lamps found at Piestina in eastern Latvia). Some pots were ornamented by wavy lines apparently made by fingers applied to the wet surface of vessels. The most commonly used horizontal patterns were rows of comb impressions, notches or pits. Some pots were decorated with geometric patterns, triangles and rhombs made of strokes and incised lines. A peculiarity of the Sarnate pottery is the use of pits in ornamental patterns. They were used in combination with other elements or formed independent patterns (Fig. 55).

Another interesting site, Šventoji, situated some 100 km. to the south in the coastal area of north-western Lithuania, was discovered and excavated by Dr Rimute Rimantiene of Vilnius.[91] The site is situated inside the Pajuris peat bog lying on the terrace of the Littorina Sea. As in the previous case the peat bog is separated from the sea by a range of dunes. The general stratigraphy of the site is as follows. Under a thin layer of peat a layer of clay loam was situated containing the material of an upper cultural layer. Below was situated a fine detritus *gyttja*, with numerous plant remains, in the upper portion of which artifacts of a lower cultural layer were found. Pollen analysis has shown that during the existence of both the settlements in this area the swampy lagoon was covered with alder and spruce forests. Pine forests grew on the sandy terraces. There were mixed oak forests further to the east on morainic hills.

Some radiocarbon dates have been obtained for both the layers. The four dates available for the lower layer are 4,400 ± 55, 4,400 ± 90,

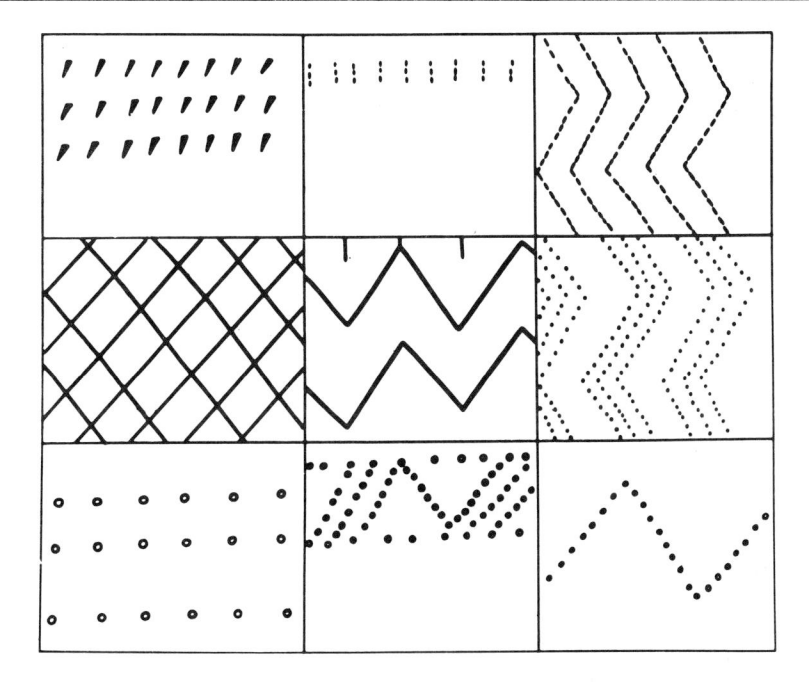

Figure 55 Sarnate Neolithic pottery ornamental patterns (after Vankina, 1970; Note 5.90) (See Fig.26)

4,250 ± 60 and 4,100 ± 60 B.P. The three dates obtained for the upper layer are 4,120 ± 80, 4,100 ± 100 and 3,860 ± 50 B.P. In all probability the site corresponding to the lower cultural layer existed during a Littorina Sea regression which occurred between 4,500 and 4,200 B.P. and the second site existed during the following regression between 4,000 and 3,800 B.P.

According to Dr Rimantiene the pottery assemblage of the lower layer corresponds to the western group of the Narva-Niemen culture; it has common traits with both Narva and Sarnate pottery. The second cultural layer contains pottery attributed to the Vistule-Niemen group of corded ware.

Some of the pottery assemblages at Neolithic sites in the eastern Baltic area reflect the influence of corded ware pottery. The influence of corded ware is noticeable in the Late Neolithic sites of Lithuania, Latvia, Estonia, the Pskov region and Byelorussia. None of these sites actually belongs to the corded ware culture, because they do not contain the basic features typical of that culture, defined by J. Machnik[92] as 'the appearance in the graves of beakers, amphorae and stone battle axes'. We can only speak of some elements of the corded ware culture penetrating the Russian plain.

European archaeologists usually divide the corded ware culture into two phases. The first phase is also known as the general

European horizon. In Poland a feature of this phase is the homogeneity of its cultural manifestations. The sites of the first phase are represented by small barrows and the grave furniture usually comprises one or two vessels, two-handed amphorae or beakers decorated with vertical lines and strokes forming zigzags, and stone axes of an older type. The radiocarbon dated sites of this first stage usually lie in the period 4,600 to 4,300 B.P. The homogeneity typical of the first phase was completely lost during the second phase. During the second phase there appeared various local groups frequently mixed with other cultures. The spread of the influence of corded wares noticeable in the Neolithic sites of the Russian plain may be dated to the second phase in the evolution of the corded ware culture.

The economic structure of the groups belonging to the corded ware culture is not yet clear. The majority of archaeologists are of the opinion that the people who left behind the barrows and sites with corded ware were pastoral, warlike nomads. This suggestion is supported by the fact that there are practically no settlements belonging to the early phase and that a great quantity of horse remains and weaponry is usually found on their sites. There are, however, opposing views. There is evidence that many corded ware groups supported themselves by agriculture and stock-breeding.[93] In all probability the economic structure of the corded ware groups depended largely on local natural resources. As in the other cases discussed, the population groups chose the optimal strategies for the local ecological setting. For instance, in south-eastern Poland are situated sites of the so-called Zlota culture, which is related to the corded ware culture complex. The settlements are situated on the loess upland near the Vistula valley, and the economy of the settlements was based on agriculture and stock-breeding, only depending to a small extent on fishing, hunting and gathering.[94] On the other hand the Rzucevo culture of north-eastern Poland,[95] also related to the corded ware culture, has an economy based mainly on hunting and fishing; the sites are situated on a narrow coastal strip of the Baltic Sea, from the Hel bar along Gdansk bay and Vistula bar and further to the north-east along the Sambia and Kursh spits. According to the faunal evidence, the economic strategy included the hunting of land animals (bison, bear, boar, wolf, wildcat, roe deer, beaver, fox); the hunting of sea animals (seals); the hunting of waterfowl (wild geese, swans); and fishing (pike, sheat-fish, perch-pike, tench, bream, perch, roach). Among the domesticated animals were identified pigs (the most numerous), cattle, sheep/goats and dogs.

The spread of corded ware in Europe may be regarded as a process similar in its essence to the processes which helped to determine the spread of comb-impressed and stroke-decorated pottery in earlier times. Extensive stock-breeding practised by the communities using corded ware led to the exhaustion of local pastures and to population pressure. Part of the surplus population moved into surrounding territories and developed economic strategies which were optimal in the local ecological setting. On loessic upland these were agriculture and stock-breeding, while in off-shore swampy lagoons and lake depressions the optimal strategies were hunting, fishing and food collecting.

It should be noted that the spread of the corded ware culture in Europe did not affect the economic and cultural systems in the west Russian plain to any great extent. The subsistence pattern here remained practically unchanged, although limited influence is noticeable in the pottery assemblages.

Summary

Within the west Russian plain the following regions have been distinguished: (1) the zone of Middle Pleistocene glaciations; (2) the zone of Late or Upper Pleistocene glaciation or Last Glaciation. The first zone includes three provinces: (a) the Middle Dnieper valley; (b) the Polessye; (c) the Byelorussian highlands. The second zone can also be divided into three provinces: (a) the outer; (b) the central (or morainic); (c) the inner. Within the last may be distinguished the maritime area of the Baltic Sea.

20,000-10,000 B.P.

During this time there occurred the maximum extent of the ice-sheet of the Last (Würm, Weichselian, Valdai) Glaciation and the recession which followed it. The ice-free area was characterized by the dominance of periglacial or hyperzonal landscapes: light birch and larch forests, open woodlands and periglacial steppes. A characteristic feature of periglacial landscapes was the presence of numerous lakes and large, deep rivers. A system of huge glacial lacustrine basins was situated off the ice-sheet. Numerous waterways drained water from the glacial basins towards the southern seas; these waterways were much larger and deeper than the present rivers. In some cases chains of lakes were formed in the valleys.

The periglacial landscapes contained a comparatively high biomass. Large herds of mammoths, woolly rhinoceros, wild horses and, later, reindeer were widespread there. The periglacial landscapes of the Russian plain supported a comparatively dense Upper Palaeolithic population. This population was concentrated almost exclusively within the middle Dniester province and in the Polessye. The settlements were situated on the edges of loessic plains adjoining river valleys and on the upper river terraces. The subsistence pattern of the Upper Palaeolithic population was based upon the specialized and highly efficient hunting of periglacial herd animals, primarily mammoths. In this sense the territory of the Upper Palaeolithic settlements formed a single natural economic zone. The comparatively high biomass at the disposal of the Upper Palaeolithic hunters permitted the existence of stable settlements inhabited all the year round. The remains of such settlements have been discovered at a number of sites in the middle Dnieper valley and in the Polessye (Mezin, Mežerici, Kirillovskaya, Goncy, Berdyž, and others).

About 12,000 B.P. marked changes occurred in the structure of the periglacial landscapes: the retreat of the ice-sheet, the deglaciation of vast territories, the amelioration of the climate and the gradual spread of forest vegetation. The levels of glacial lacustrine basins fell. The gradual extinction of periglacial herd animals (mammoths, woolly rhinoceros) took place. The area of human settlement expanded and settlements appeared in the ice-freed zone on the banks of glacial lakes and along waterways. The subsistence patterns of the late glacial communities were based mostly on the specialized hunting of reindeer. The massive spread of tanged points and of retouched blades in the stone inventory of Late Palaeolithic hunters is remarkable. (Fig. 56).

10,000-6,000 B.P.

The profound changes that occurred on the surface of the Earth about 10,000 years ago were particularly evident in the area directly affected by the ice-sheet of the Last Glaciation. The ice-sheet disintegrated, a marine basin was formed in the depression of the Baltic Sea and glacial lakes were drained; forest vegetation was formed, and the periglacial faunal complex disappeared, to be replaced by fauna consisting of forest non-herd animals (elk, red deer, roe deer, wild pig, bear, aurochs, and others). During the Early Holocene birch and pine spread over the ice-freed zone, and later forests of broad-leaved trees made their appearance there.

Throughout this period populations using tools of a Mesolithic type existed in the west Russian plain. The settlement area was much larger than that of the Upper Palaeolithic, practically all the territory under investigation being inhabited. The settlement pattern was slightly different from that of the Upper Palaeolithic; low terraces, flood-plains and lake depressions were intensively populated. Human settlements appeared in the coastal area of the Baltic sea.

The subsistence pattern of the Mesolithic settlements was based on the hunting of forest game, fishing and food gathering. Thus the area settled by the Mesolithic groups formed a single natural economic zone. Within this area it is possible to distinguish several subzones taking into account differences in the hunting structure. In the area where mixed oak forests grew extensively (the middle Dnieper, the Polessye, Lithuania) the hunting of red deer and of wild pig was economically the most important. In the inner province of the Last

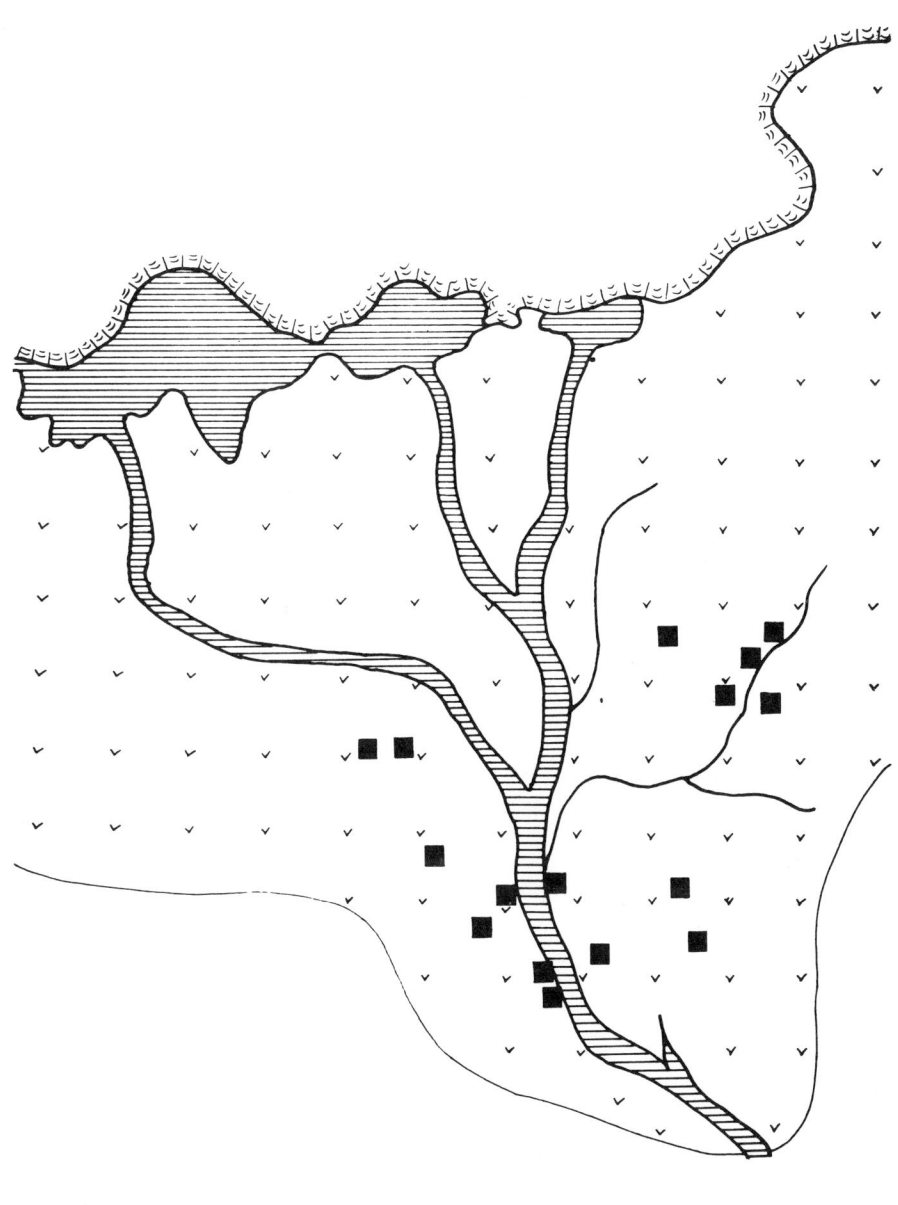

The West Russian Plain

     limit of Last Glaciation

     glacial lakes and river valleys

     periglacial steppe

     Palaeolithic sites

Figure 56 The west Russian plain 20,000-10,000 B.P. (Palaeogeographical setting corresponds to c. 20,000-18,000 B.P.)

	periglacial steppes	▲	Mesolithic sites
	coniferous forests	― ― ―	limit of Last Glaciation
	broad-leaved forests	------	southern limit of the middle morainic area
		_._._	southern limit of the inner morainic zone

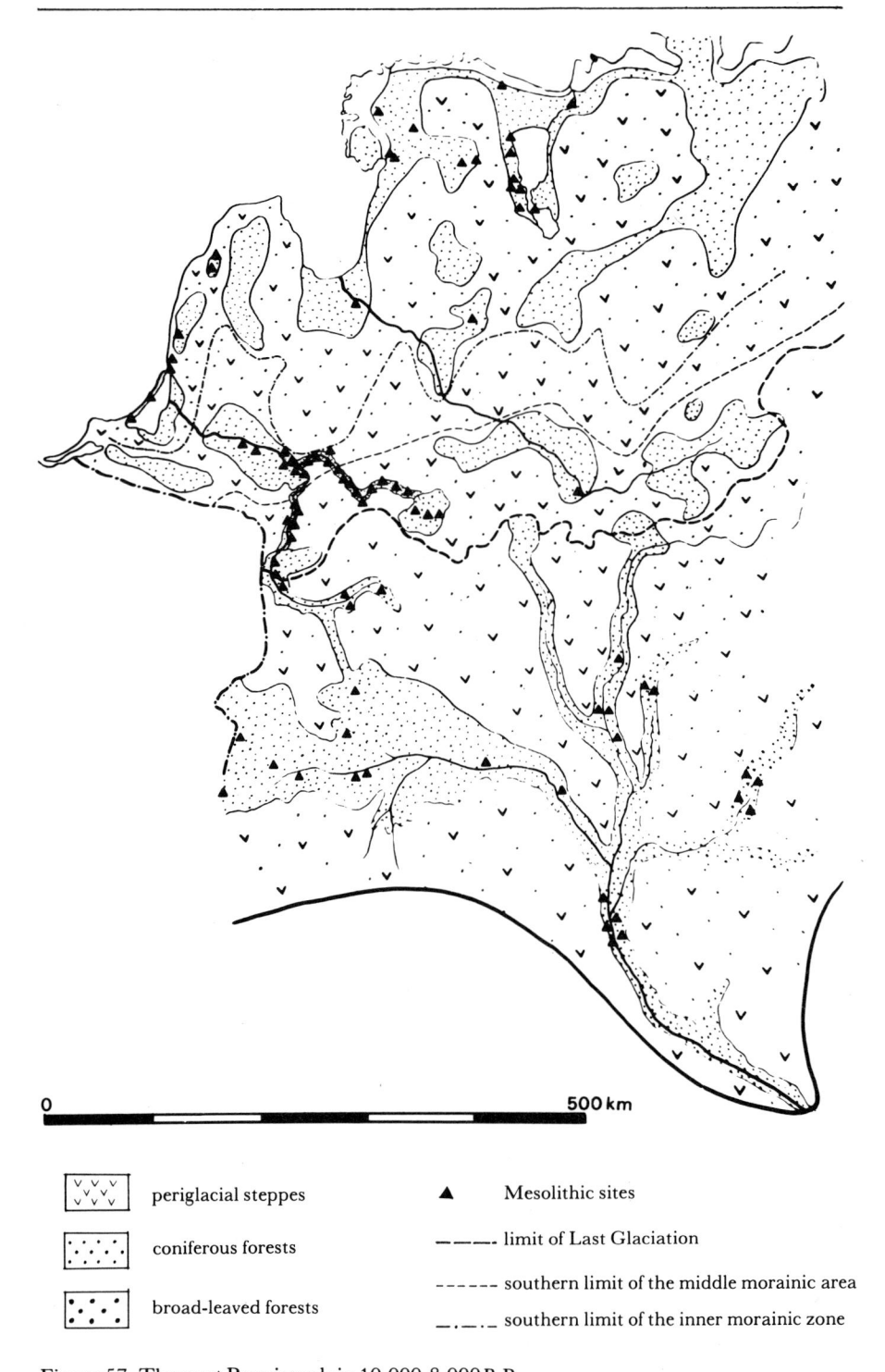

Figure 57 The west Russian plain 10,000-8,000 B.P.

Glaciation zone the hunting of elk held a dominant position in the hunting structure. In the coastal area the exploitation of marine resources (the hunting of sea animals and of waterfowl, fishing, and collecting of sea shells) was very important. In the first subzone the use of geometric microlithic tools is an important feature. In the second subzone these tools were less common. In both subzones stone axe-like tools were widely in use (Fig. 58).

6,000-4,000 B.P.

During this time interval a further transformation of the ecological setting took place along the lines determined during the initial Holocene phase. Mixed oak forests were widespread on the watershed uplands and in the flood-plains of rivers and lakes. Mixed coniferous broadleaved forests, containing a relatively high biomass, were the dominant type of vegetation during this period.

The settlement pattern was essentially the same as during the Early Holocene. A more intensive occupation of the flood-plains in the zone of the Middle Pleistocene glaciations took place; in the zone of the Last Glaciation human settlements concentrated within the lake depressions and off-shore lagoons in the maritime area. The economic pattern of the greater part of the settlement area was based upon hunting, fishing and food collecting. The only exception was formed by the southern part of the middle Dnieper area, where, since the Early Neolithic, there had been pronounced elements of stock-breeding (cattle, horses). Thus the greater part of the settlement area formed a natural economic zone with a food-appropriating economy. The southern part of the middle Dnieper province belonged to a natural economic zone with a mixed food-appropriating/food-producing (stock-breeding) economy.

Within the first natural economic zone two subzones can be distinguished. In the first subzone, which embraces mostly the middle Dnieper area and the Polessye, the hunting of red deer, wild pig and aurochs was the most important part of the hunting pattern. Within the second subzone, which roughly coincides with the area of the Last Glaciation, the hunting of elk, wild pig and bear dominated. In the coastal area of the Baltic Sea, the exploitation of marine resources was economically very important.

The study of pottery ornamentation makes it possible to distinguish several cultural zones within the area under investigation. The earliest pottery assemblages in the western Russian plain are represented at some sites in the middle Dnieper area (Strumel-Gastyatin), in the Polessye, in the outer province of the Last Glaciation (Zacenye, Dubičiaj) and in the inner province (Osa). The dominant ornamental patterns of this pottery were made up of horizontal rows of comb impressions or notches and of incised lines. These patterns are similar to the ornamentation of pottery used in the Dniester and southern

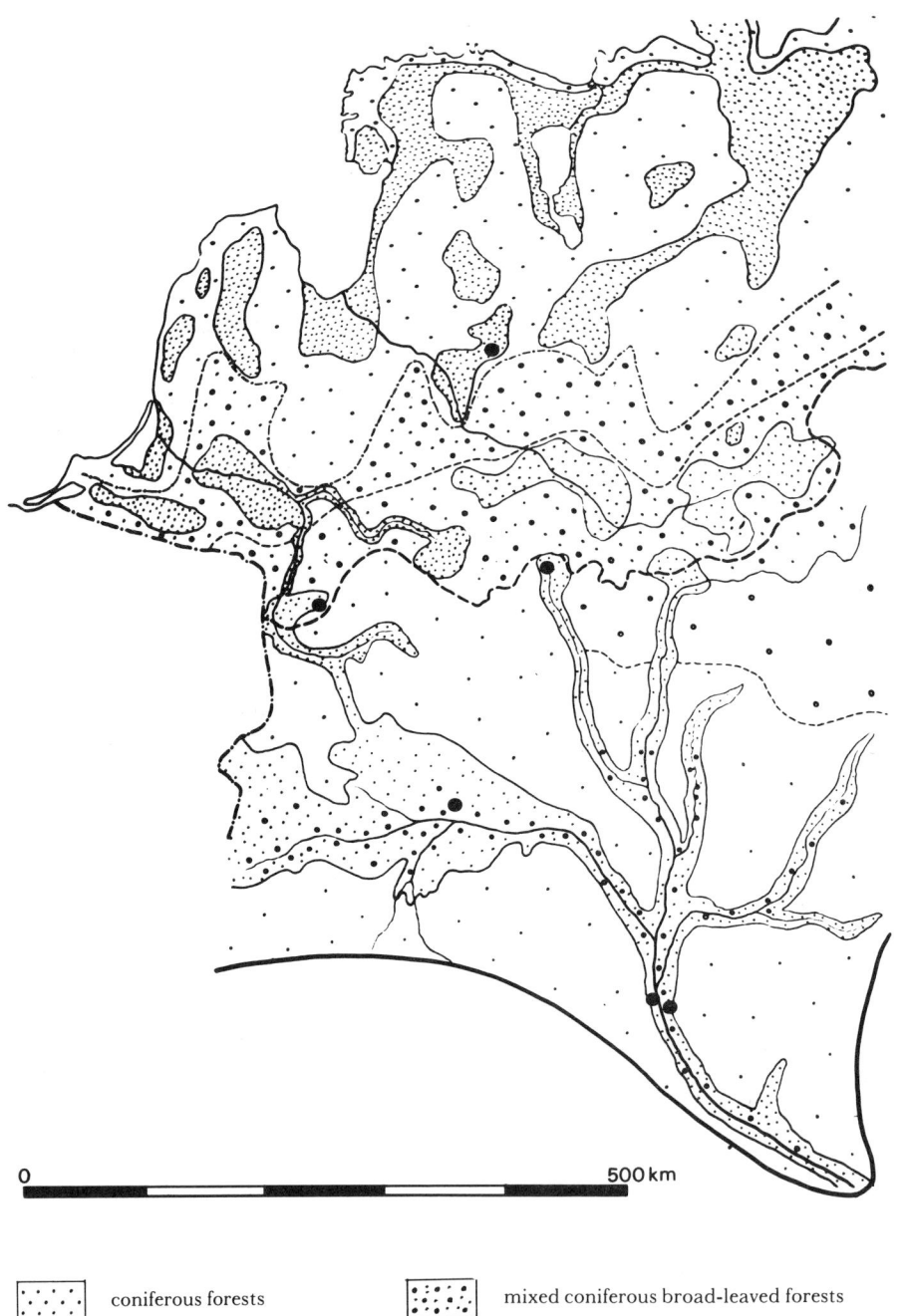

178 *Ecology and Economy in Neolithic Eastern Europe*

Figure 58 The west Russian plain 8,000-6,000 B.P.

Bug Neolithic. On this basis the Early Neolithic assemblages of the western Russian plain and the Neolithic assemblages of the Dniester and southern Bug are regarded as belonging to a single cultural zone. The cultural unity of this zone reflects, in my opinion, a gradual penetration into the north of the forest zone by a part of the surplus population originating in the agricultural area of the Balkans. This new population acquired a hunting, fishing and food-gathering subsistence pattern as the most effective economic strategy under local conditions. The new population was spread over the landscapes previously occupied by local Mesolithic groups and in all probability was gradually absorbed by them. Finally they adopted the subsistence patterns and tool-kit used by the Mesolithic groups. The time of the initial spread of the pottery-using Neolithic groups may be dated to 6,500-5,500 B.P. (Fig. 59).

At a later stage the number of Neolithic sites in the west Russian plain increased considerably. To this stage, usually referred to as Developed Neolithic, we attribute the sites of the Dnieper-Donetz culture in the middle Dnieper and in the Polessye, the sites of Developed Neolithic in the Niemen valley and in the south of the Pskov region, the Piestina-type sites in eastern Latvia, the sites with Narva pottery in Estonia, and the Sarnate and Šventoji (lower level) sites in the Baltic coastal area. The pottery assemblages of all these sites have marked differences, but some common ornamental patterns may be singled out. First of all, patterns typical of the Early Neolithic assemblages persist. Among new features the most remarkable is the widespread use of strokes forming geometric patterns of triangles, rhombs and rectangles. These elements and patterns were widely spread throughout some groups of the funnel beaker culture of central Europe. The suggestion has been made that this similarity reflects the migration of a part of the surplus population from the agricultural zone of central Europe into the forested valleys of the middle Dnieper and the Polessye and into the lake depressions and off-shore lagoons in the zone of the Last Glaciation. These areas, containing a high biomass, were very favourable for hunting, fishing and food-gathering activities. As in the previous case, the migrating population was gradually absorbed by the local population. The new population acquired the subsistence patterns of the local tribes (since these were optimal in local conditions), the tool-kit used by the local groups and even some elements of their cultural system, as expressed in the ornamental patterns.

One of the peculiarities of an economy based on hunting and food gathering is the relative constancy of population density, which is subject to feedback regulations and limited by the food resources available. This inevitably led to the territorial isolation of hunting groups. Studies of modern hunting and gathering communities show that the territory exploited from a site lies within certain well-defined limits, usually within a radius of 10 km.[96] Therefore the single

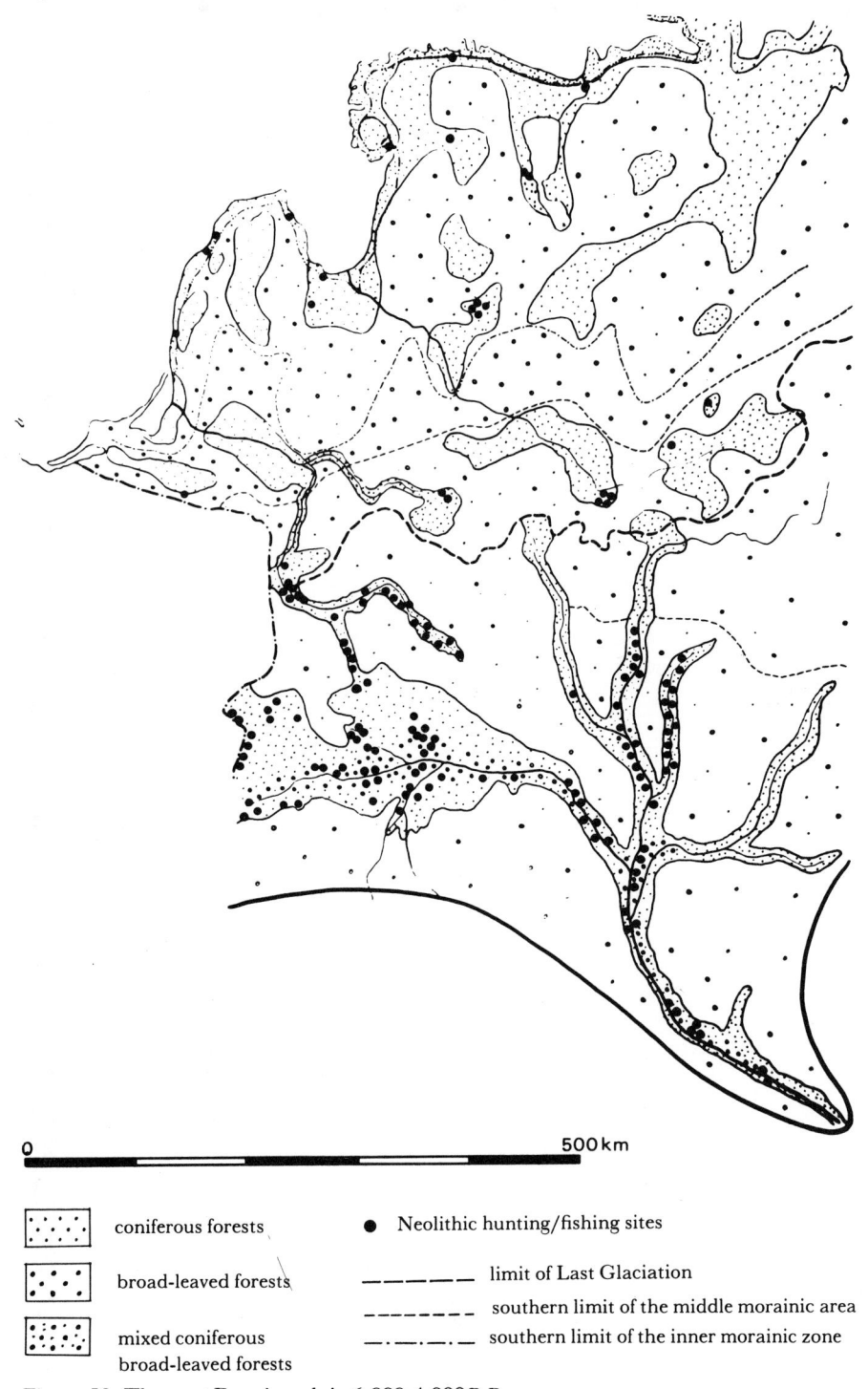

180 *Ecology and Economy in Neolithic Eastern Europe*

Figure 59 The west Russian plain 6,000-4,000 B.P.

- coniferous forests
- broad-leaved forests
- mixed coniferous broad-leaved forests
- ● Neolithic hunting/fishing sites
- ‒ ‒ ‒ limit of Last Glaciation
- ‒ ‒ ‒ ‒ southern limit of the middle morainic area
- —·—·— southern limit of the inner morainic zone

landscape unit suitable for hunting activity (a medium-sized lake depression) could have harboured no more than one hunting group. The size of this hunting group never exceeded 100 individuals (the optimum size of modern hunting groups is 20-30 people).[97] The existence of territorially isolated hunting groups led to the growth of local peculiarities in the sphere of spiritual culture, reflected in the pottery ornamental patterns. Taking into account the uncertain criteria which archaeologists usually use to define archaeological cultures, every single hunting group could be regarded in principle as forming a separate culture. But some attributes exist which may be used to distinguish cultural zones of a higher order. Such a higher order cultural zone might include for instance both the distribution area of funnel beakers in central Europe and that of the Neolithic groups in the Russian plain. The formal attributes for distinguishing this cultural zone are the use of strokes and of geometric patterns in the ornamentation on pottery. This cultural zone includes two natural economic zones, one with a food-producing and one with a food-appropriating economy. Its period is between 5,500-4,000 B.P.

Another cultural zone which can be distinguished in the west Russian plain includes the distribution area of pit-and-comb decorated pottery. The earliest sites belonging to this zone in the central part of the Russian plain are dated to 5,800-5,600 B.P. The spread of sites with pit-and-comb decorated pottery into the Ukraine and into the Baltic area occurred about 4,700-4,500 years ago. The subsistence and settlement patterns of pit-and-comb decorated pottery sites did not differ from those of the sites of stroke-ornamented pottery. This led to the appearance of sites with hybrid pottery in the upper Dnieper basin.

About 4,200-4,000 B.P. the pottery assemblages of the sites within the cultural zone of stroke-ornamented pottery showed the influence of corded ware. This influence may be regarded as reflecting the infiltration of populations originating in the predominantly stock-breeding zones of Europe. The penetration of this population did not lead to any marked changes in the economic structures of the western part of the Russian plain, which were based on effective hunting, fishing and gathering. Moreover in most cases it did not change the stable cultural systems as reflected in the ornamental patterns on pottery. In most cases some new ornamental patterns were added to the dominant motifs in the zone of stroke-ornamented pottery (Fig. 57).

NOTES

[1] The geological and physical geographical description of the north-western part of the Russian Plain is based on Yu. A. Mesčeryakov, *Strukturnaya geomorfologiya ravninnykh stran*, Moscow, 1967 and I.P. Gerasimov (ed.), *Srednyaya polosa yevropeiskoi časti SSSR, Prirodnyye usloviya i yestyestvennyye resursy*, Moscow, 1967.

[2] The quaternary history of the north-western part of the Russian Plain is outlined on the basis of D.B. Malakhovsky and K.K. Markov, *Geomorfologiya i četvyertičnyye otlozeniya Syevero-Zapada yevropeiskoi časti SSSR*, Leningrad, 1969; M. Ye. Vigdorčik, P.M. Dolukhanov et al., 'Geokhronologiya i periodizaciya pleistocena Syevero-Zapada Russkoi ravniny', in V.A. Zubakov (ed.), *Problemy periodizacii pleistocena*, Leningrad, 1971.

[3] D.D. Kvasov, *Pozdnyečetvertičnaya istoriya krupnykh ozyor i vnutryennikh moryei Vostočnoi Yevropy*, Leningrad, 1976.

[4] The holocene history of the Baltic Sea is outlined on the basis of P.M. Dolukhanov, *Istoriya Baltiki*, Moscow, 1969; P.M. Dolukhanov, 'Die Spiegelschwankungen der Ostsee und der Seebecken während des Holozäns', *Petermanns Geographische Mitteilungen*, 117, 3, 1973, pp. 169-79.

[5] B.G. Vasileyev, M.E. Vigdorčik, 'Earth's crust undulations in the region of the slope of the Baltic Shield during Late and Post-Glacial times', *Baltica*, 4, Vilnius, 1970, pp. 285-96.

[6] P.M. Dolukhanov, op. cit. (Note 4), 1973, pp. 171-2.

[7] N.A. Mörner, 'The Late Quaternary history of the Kattegat sea and the Swedish West Coast', *Sveriges Geologiska Undersökning*, 63, 3, Stockholm, 1968.

[8] R.E. Binns, 'Flandrian strandline chronology for the British Isles and correlation of some European postglacial strandlines', *Nature*, 235, 1972, pp. 206-10.

[9] B. Menke, 'Vegetationsgeschichtliche Untersuchungen und Radiocarbondatierungen zur holozänen Entwicklung der schleswigholsteinischen Westküste', *Eiszeitalter und Gegenwart*, 20, 1969, pp. 35-45; W. Prange, 'Uber die Beziehungen zwischen Schichtenfolge und Meeresspiegelanstieg in Holozän der Nordseemarschen', *Geologische Rundschau*, 57, 1967, pp. 709-26.

[10] S. Jelgersma, Holocene sea level changes in the Netherlands, *Mededelingen van de Geologische Stichting*, C, VI, 7, The Hague, 1961.

[11] V.K. Gudelis, 'Drevnelednikovye obrazovaniya na territorii sovetskoi Pribaltiki i Leningradskoi oblasti,' in I.P. Guerassimov (ed.), *Posledniy lednikovyi pokrov na Syevero-Zapadye yevropeyskoi časti SSSR*, Moscow, 1969, pp. 142-50.

[12] H. Kliewe, 'Zum Littorinamaximum aus südbaltischer Sicht', *Wissenschaftliche Zeitschrift der. Er.-Schiller-Universität Jena, Mathemathisch-Naturwissenschaftliche*, 14, 4, 1965, pp. 85-94.

[13] Dolukhanov, op. cit. (Note 4), 1973, pp. 173-9.

[14] A.M. Marinič, *Geomorfologiya Yužnogo Polesya*, Kiev, 1963.

[15] A.A. Veličko, 'Paleogeografiya stoyanok pozdnego paleolita basseina srednyei Desny', in I.P. Guerassimov (ed.), *Priroda i razvitiye pyervobytnogo obščestva na territorii yevropeyskoi časti SSSR*, Moscow, 1969, pp. 88-97.

[16] G.A. Paškevič, 'Istoriya rastitel'nosti Cernogovskogo Polesya v pozdnye- i poslelednikovoye vremya', in D.K. Zerov (ed.), *Problemy palinologii*, Kiev, 1971, pp. 188-99.

[17] N.A. Makhnač, *Etapy razvitiya rastitel'nosti Belorussi v antropogene*, Minsk, 1971; P.M. Dolukhanov, 'Paleogeografiya Usvyatskikh stoyanok', *Arkheologičeskiy sbornik gosudarstvennogo Ermitaža*, II, 1969, pp. 41-7.

[18] P.M. Dolukhanov, 'The Holocene history of the Baltic Sea and ecology of Prehistoric settlement', *Baltica*, 6, Vilnius, 1977.

[19] I.J. Danilans, V.J. Stelle, 'O pyl'cevykh zonakh golocena i nekotorykh ikh regional'nykh osobennostyakh na territorii Latvii', in T.D. Bartoš (ed.), *Palinologičeskie issledovaniya v Pribaltike*, Riga, 1971, pp. 67-97; P.M. Dolukhanov, G.M. Levkovskaya, 'Istoriya razvitiya prirodnoi sredy i pervobytnykh kul'tur na vostokye Latvii, in M.I. Neištadt (ed.), *Palinologiya golocena*, Moscow, 1971, pp. 53-62.

[20] A.A. Sarv, E.O. Ilves, 'Geokhronologiya i stratigrafiya golocenovykh ozyerno-bolotnykh otloženii Estonii (po dannym radiouglerodnogo metoda)', in M.I. Neištadt (ed.), *Palinologiya golocena*, Moscow, 1971, pp. 33-42.

[21] M.V. Kabailiene, 'O vosstanovlenii sostava golocenovykh lesov Litvy setočnym metodom', in T.D. Bartoš (ed.), *Palinologičeskie issledovaniya v Pribaltike*, Riga, 1971, pp. 111-26.

[22] Dolukhanov, op. cit. (Note 4), 1973, pp. 170-1.
[23] V.P. Gričuk, 'Rasityel'nost' na Russkoi ravninye v pozdnyem paleolite', in I.P. Guerassimov (ed.), Priroda i razvitiye pyervobytnogo obščestva na territorii yevropeiskoi časti SSSR, Moscow, 1969, pp. 58-67.
[24] N.K. Vereščagin, 'Okhoty pyervobytnogo celovyeka i vymiraniye pleistocenovykh mlyekopitayuščikh v SSSR', in N.K. Vereščagin (ed.), Materialy po faunam antropogena SSSR, Trudy Zoologičyeskogo Instituta, 49, Leningrad, 1971, pp. 200-32.
[25] P.I. Boriskovsky, N.D. Praslov, 'Paleolit Basseina Dnyepra i Priazovya', in B.A. Rybakov (ed.), Svod arkheologiceskikh istočnikov, A1-5, Moscow, 1964.
[26] The stratigraphy, fauna and reconstruction of dwellings of the upper palaeolithic sites in the Middle Dnieper area are outlined on the basis of I.G. Pidoplicko, Pozdnyepaleolitičeskiye žilišča iz kostyei mamonta na Ukrainye, Kiev, 1969.
[27] Veličko, op. cit. (Note 15), 1969, pp. 88-97.
[28] I.G. Šovkoplyas, Mezinskaya stoyanka, Kiev, 1965; Šovkoplyas, 'Do pitannya pro kharakter rozvitku kul'tury pizn'yogo paleolitu (na materialakh Ukrainskoi RSR i susidnikh territorii)', Arkheologiya, 22, 1969, pp. 31-54.
[29] V.D. Bud'ko, 'Paleolit', in V.F. Isaenko (ed.), Ocerki po arkheologii Belorussii, 1, Minsk, 1970.
[30] V.D. Bud'ko, L.N. Voznyačuk, 'Paleolit Belorussii i smežnykh territorii', in V.D. Bud'ko (ed.), Drevnosti Belorussii, Minsk, 1969, pp. 4-27; L.N. Voznyačuk, Kh. A. Arslanov, 'K paleogeografii i geokhronologii epokhi valdaiskogo oledeneniya na territorii Belorussii', in V.A. Zubakov (ed.), Khronologiya lednikovogo veka, Leningrad, 1971, pp. 73-8. In recent years a number of radiocarbon dates has been obtained for bones from Upper Palaeolithic sites in the area. The earliest date has been secured for Yurevichi site: 26470 ± 480 B.P., the end of the Bryansk interval. A number of sites correspond to the coldest phase of the Last Glaciation; Pogon: 18690 ± 770 B.P.; Yeliseyeviči: 17470 ± 100; 17340 ± 170; 12940 ± 140 B.P. To the phases of deglaciation correspond the following sites: Timonovka II: 15110 ± 530 B.P.; Yudinovka: 15660 ± 180; 13830 ± 530; 13650 ± 200 B.P. (A.A. Veličko, Kh. A. Arslanov, Ye. I. Kurenkova, 'Radiouglerodnye opredeleniya vozrasta verkhnepaleolitičeskikh stoyanok Centra Russkoi ravniny', Doklady AN SSSR, 228, 3, 1976, pp. 713-16.
[31] A. Rust, Die steinzeitliche Renntierjägerlager bei Meiendorf, Neumünster, 1937; Rust, Die alt- und mittelsteinzeitliche Funde von Stellmoor, Neumünster, 1943; Rust, Die jungpaläolithische Zeltanlage von Ahrensburg, Offa-Bücher, 15, Neumünster, 1958.
[32] W. Taute, 'Die Stielspitzengruppen im nördlichen Mitteleuropa', in H. Schwabedissen (ed.), Fundamenta: Monographien zur Urgeschichte, A, 5, XXX, Cologne-Graz, 1968.
[33] R. Schild, 'The final Palaeolithic settlement of the European plain', Scientific American, 234, 2, V, 1976, pp. 88-99.
[34] On the basis of investigations of stratified sites Witów and Calowanie, distr. Otwock, R. Schild distinguishes several phases in the evolution of 'tarnovian' and 'witowian' complexes in Poland ranging from ca. 11,400 to 10,500 B.P.: R. Schild, 'Późny paleolit', in W. Chmielewski, H. Hensel (eds.), Paleolit i Mezolit, Wroclaw-Warsaw-Cracow, 1975, pp. 159-336.
[35] Bud'ko, op. cit. (Note 29), 1970.
[36] L.N. Voznyačuk, V.D. Bud'ko, O.P. Leonovič, J.-M. Punning, 'Geologo-geomorfologičeskie usloviya nakhoždeniya i vozrast pozdnepaleoliticeskoi stoyanki Studenec na ozyere Naroč', Doklady AN SSSR, 13, 4, 1969. It should be noted that new excavations carried out on the site have failed to produce any artifact in the peat layer or beneath it (M.M. Čiernyavsky, 'Issledovaniya Niemanskogo arkheologičeskogo otryada', in B.A. Rybakov (ed.), Arkheologičeskiye otkrytiga 1975 goda, Moscow, 1976, p.428).
[37] R.K. Rimantiene, Paleolit i mezolit Litvy, Vilnius, 1971, pp. 19-94.
[38] A.M. Miklyayev, 'Pamyatniki Usvyatskogo mikroryona,' Arkheologičeskiy Sbornik gosudarstuennogo Ermitaža, II, 1969, pp. 18-40; P.M. Dolukhanov i A.M. Miklyayev, 'Paleogeografiya i absolyutnaya khronologiya pamyatnikov neolita i bronzy v

basseinye Zapadnoi Dviny,' in M.I. Neistadt (ed.), *Golocen*, Moscow, 1969, pp. 120-8.

[39] D. Ya. Telegin, 'Pozdniy mezolit Ukrainy: opyt kul'turnoterritoriyalnogo členeniya pamyatnikov', in S.K. Kozlowski (ed.), *The Mesolithic in Europe*, Warsaw, 1973, pp. 536-43.

[40] V.F. Isaenko, 'Mezolit', in V.F. Isaenko (ed.), *Očerki po arkheologii Belorussii*, Minsk, 1970, pp. 49-66; Isaenko, 'Geologičeskiye usloviya zalyeganiya mezoliticheskikh i neoliticheskikh poselenii Polesya', *Doklady AN SSSR*, XVI, 3, 1972, pp. 263-6.

[41] A. Rust, *Die Funde von Pinnberg*, Offa-Bücher, 16, Neumünster, 1958.

[42] J. Bröndsted, *Nordische Vorzeiit*, I, Neumünster, 1960; E. Brinch Petersen, 'Klosterlund-Sönder Handsunt-Böllund', *Acta Archaeologica Copenhagen*, 37, 1966, pp. 77-185.

[43] C.J. Becker, 'Die Maglemosekultur in Dänemark, Neue Funde und Ergebnisse', *Union Internationale des Sciences Pré- et Protohistoriques, Actes de la IIIe session*, Zürich, 1950, pp. 180-3; Bröndsted, op. cit. (Note 42), 1960; E. Brinch-Petersen, 'A survey of the late palaeolithic and the mesolithic of Denmark', *in* S.K. Kozlowski (ed.), *The Mesolithic in Europe*, Warsaw, 1973, pp. 77-127.

[44] B. Gramsch, 'Die Vegatationsgebiete des nördlichen Mitteleuropa und die Besiedlung dieses Raumes im älteren und mittleren Holozän, *in* M.I. Neištadt (ed.), *Palynology of Holocene and Marine Palynology*, Moscow, 1973, pp. 83-7.

[45] H. Schwabedissen, *Die mittlere Steinzeit im westlichen Nord-deutschland*, Offa-Bücher, 7, Neumünster, 1944.

[46] B. Gramsch, 'Das Mesolithikum im Flachland zwischen Elbe und Oder', Part I, *Veröffentlichungen des Museums für Ur- und Frühgeschichte Potsdam*, 7, Berlin, 1973, pp. 59-63.

[47] S.K. Kozlowski, 'Les civilisations mésolithiques en Pologne', *Archaeologia Polona*, 17, 1969, pp. 415-28; Kozlowski, 'Introduction to the history of Europe in Early Holocene', *in* Kozlowski (ed.), *The Mesolithic in Europe*, Warsaw, 1973, pp. 331-66.

[48] R.K. Rimantiene, op. cit. (Note 37), 1971, pp. 95-173.

[49] R. Indreko, *Die mittlere Steinzeit in Estland*, Uppsala, 1948; K. Orviku, 'Uber die Geologie des Kunda-Sees', *in* Indreko, op.cit., 1948, pp. 17-39. The faunal determinations are from K.L. Paaver, *Formirovaniye teriofauny i izmenčivost' mliekopitayuščikh Pribaltiky v golocenye*, Tallin, 1965; Radiocarbon dates from A. Liiva, E. Ilves, J.-M. Punning, 'Tartu radiocarbon dates I', *Radiocarbon*, 8, 1966.

[50] L. Jaanits, 'Mezolitičeskoye poselyeniye v Pulli', in B.A. Rybakov (ed.), *Arkheologiceskiye otkrytiya 1969 goda*, Moscow, 1970, p.33; L. Jaanits, K. Jaanits, 'Frühmesolithische Siedlung in Pulli', *Izvestiya AN Estonskoy SSR*, 24, 1975, pp. 64-70.

[51] F. Zagorskis, *Rannii i rezvitoi neolit vostočnoi Latvii*, Riga, 1967.

[52] Dolukhanov and Levkovskaya, op. cit. (Note 19), 1971, pp. 53-62; Dolukhanov op. cit. (Note 4), 1973, pp. 173-6.

[53] D. Ya. Telegin, *Dnipro-Doneckaya kul'tura*, Kiev, 1968; D. Ya. Telegin, 'O kul'turno-territorial'nom členenii i periodizacii neolita Vkrainy i Belorussii', *S.A.*, 2, 1970, pp. 3-31; D. Ya. Telegin, 'Neolitičeskiye pamyatniki Severnoi Ukrainy i Yužnoi Belorussii'. In N.N. Gurina (ed.), *Etnokul'turnye obščnosti lesnoi i lesostepnoi zon yevropeiskoi časti SSSR. Materialy i issledovaniya po arkheologii SSSR*, 172, Leningrad, 1973, pp. 173-83, Table 42.

[54] Geological and geomorphological investigations were carried out by the author in 1970; the pollen analysis was made by Mrs Agranova, Leningrad.

[55] Isaenko op. cit. (Note 40), 1972, pp. 263-6.

[56] V.I. Neprina, *Neolit yamočno-grebančatoi keramiki na Ukraine*, Kiev, 1976. Faunal determinations were made by Dr V.I. Bibikova, Kiev.

[57] Paaver, op. cit. (Note 49), 1965.

[58] Telegin, op. cit. (Note 53), 1968.

[59] V.I. Bibikova, 'Do istorii domesticakii konya na pivdennemu skhodi Evropi', *Arkheologiya*, XXII, 1969, pp. 55-67.

[60] V.I. Neprina, 'Pozdneneolitičeskoye poseleniye Les bliz sela Mněvo na

Černigoscine', *in* V.F. Isaenko (ed.), *Drevnosti Belorussii*, Minsk, 1966, pp. 67-78.

[61] Telegin, op. cit. (Note 53), 1968; V.N. Danilenko, *Neolit Ukrainy*, Kiev, 1969.

[62] Telegin, op. cit. (Note 53), 1968.

[63] Isaenko V.F., 'Neolit', *Očerki po arkheologii Belorussii*, Minsk, 1970, pp. 67-109.

[64] M.M. Čiernyavsky, 'Neolit severo-zapadnoy Belorussii', Minsk, 1971.

[65] R.K. Rimantiene, 'Stoyanki rannego neolita v yugo-vostochnoi Litve', *in* V.F. Isaenko (ed.), *Drevnosti Belorussii*, Minsk, 1966, pp. 54-62.

[66] B. Gramsch, 'Zum Problem des üergangs vom Mesolithikum zum Neolithikum im Flachland zwischen Elbe und Oder', *in* F. Schlette (ed.), *Evolution und Revolution im Alten Orient und in Europa*, Berlin, 1971, pp. 127-44; B. Balcer, 'Stanowisko Pieczyska (Zbrza Wielka) w Zawichoscie-Podgorzu, pow. Sandomièrz, w świete pierwszych wykopalisk', *Wiadomoście Archeolicznie*, 32, 1967, pp. 290-375.

[67] N.A. Peleščišin, *Drevneye naseleniye zapadnoi Volyny*, Kiev, 1967.

[68] J. Murray, *The first European agriculture: A study of the osteological and botanical evidence until 2,000 B.C.*, Edinburgh University Press, 1970.

[69] H. Behrens, 'Rössener Kultur, Trichterbecherkultur und Tiefstichkeramik', *in* J. Böhm and S. de Laet (eds.), *L'Europe à la fin de l'Age de la Pierre*, Prague, 1961, pp. 389-92; a special investigation of stroke ornamented ware by H. Knöll, *Die nordwestdeutsche Tiefstichkeramik und ihre Stellung im nord- und mitteleuropäischen Neolithikum*, Münster, 1959.

[70] A. Bagge, 'Favervik: Ein Rückgrat für Periodenanteilung der ostschwedischen Wohnplatz und Bootaxtkultureu aus dem Mittelneolithikum,' *Acta archaeologica Copenhagen*, XXII, 1951, pp. 57-118.

[71] Neprina, op. cit. (Note 56), 1973.

[72] D.A. Kraynov, N.A. Khotinsky, Yu. N. Urban, E.M. Molodcova, 'Drevnyeišaya rannyeneoliticeskaya kul'tura Verkhnyego Povolzya', *Vestnik AN SSSR*, 5, 1973, pp 80-4. The Yazykovo site has been recently dated to 6250-6260 B.P.; Kh. D. Sorina, Yu. N. Urban, *Iz istorii Verkhnevolzya*, Kalinin, 1976, p. 21.

[73] V.M. Raušenbakh, 'Plemyena layalovskoi kultury', *Okskiy basseyin v epokhu kamnya i bronzy*, Moscow, 1970, pp. 35-78.

[74] V.P. Levenok, 'Novye raskopki stoyanki Podzorovo', *Kratkiye soobščeniya instuta arkheologii*, 117, 1969, pp. 84-90.

[75] M.M. Čiernyavsky, op. cit. (Note 64), 1971.

[76] M.M. Čiernyavsky, op. cit. (Note 64), 1971.

[77] A.M. Miklyayev, op. cit. (Note 38), 1969, pp. 18-40.

[78] Zagorskis, op. cit. (Note 5), 1967; I.A. Loze, *Pozdniy neolit i ranyaya bronza Vostočnoi Latvii*, Riga, 1972; Dolukhanov and Levkovskaya, op. cit. (Note 19), 1971, pp. 53-62.

[79] Paaver, op. cit. (Note 49), 1965.

[80] L. Yu. Jaanits, *Poseleniya epokhi neolita i rannyego metalla v priust'ye reki Eimajögi (Estonskaya SSR)*, Tallin, 1959; L. Yu. Jaanits, 'Die frühneolithische Kultur in Estland', in *Congressus secundus internationalis fennougristarum*, 4, Helsinki, 1968, pp. 2-5; L. Yu. Jaanits, 'Neolitičeskiye pamyatniki Estonii i ikh khronologiya', *in* N.N. Gurina (ed.), *Etnokul'turnye obščnosti lesnoi i lesostepnoi zon yevropeiskoi casti SSSR v epokhu neolita. Materialy i issledovaniya po arkheologii SSSR*, 172, Leningrad, 1973, pp. 202-9, Table 57.

[81] Paaver, op. cit. (Note 49), 1965.

[82] Gramsch, op. cit. (Note 46), 1973; H. Kliewe, E. Lange, 'Ergebnisse geomorphologischer und vegetationsgeschichtlicher Untersuchungen zur Spät-und Postglazialzeit auf Rügen', *Petermanns Geographische Mitteilungen*, 112, 4, 1968, pp. 241-55. The author had an opportunity to visit the sites in 1971.

[83] Brinch Petersen, op. cit. (Note 43), 1973, pp. 77-128; J. Troels Smith, 'The Muldbjerg dwelling place: an early neolithic archaeological site in the Aamosen bog, West Zealand, Denmark', Smithsonian Report for 1959, Washington, 1960, pp. 577-601.

[84] J. Troels Smith, 'Ivy, mistletoe and elm. Climate indicators – fodder plants', *Danmarks Geoliske Undersögelser*, IV 4, 4, Copenhagen, 1960.

[85] J. Troels Smith, 'The Ertebølle culture and its background', *Palaeohistoria*, XII, 1966 (1967), pp. 505-28.

[86] H. Schwabedissen, 'Ein horizontierter "Breitkeil" aus Saturp und die manniglachen Kulturverbindungen des beginnenden Neolithikums im Norden und Nordwesten', *Palaeohistoria*, XII, 1966 (1967), pp. 409-68.

[87] Gramsch, op. cit. (Note 66), 1971, pp. 127-44; H. Kliewe, E. Lange, 'Ergebnisse geomorphologischer, stratigraphischer und vegetationsgeschichtlicher Untersuchungen zur Spät- und Postglazialzeit auf Rügen', *Petermanns Geographischen Mitteilungen*, 112, 1968, pp. 241-55.

[88] J. Troels Smith, 'Ertebøllekultur – Bondekultur. Resultater af de 10 Aars Undersögelser i Aamosen, Vestsjaelland', *Aarböger for Nordisk Oldkyndighed og historie*, Copenhagen, 1953, pp. 5-62.

[89] N.N. Gurina, *Iz istorii drevnikh plemyen zapadnykh oblastyei SSSR*, Materialy i issledovaniya po arkheologii SSSR, 114, Leningrad, 1970.

[90] L.V. Vankina, *Torfyanikovaya stoyanka Sarnate*, Riga, 1970.

[91] R.K. Rimantiene, 'Issledovanie stoyanok kamennogo vyeka v Sventoji, Kretingskogo raiona', in B.A. Rybakov (ed.), *Arkheologičeskiye otkrytiya 1969 goda*, Moscow, 1970, p.313.

[92] J. Machnik, 'The Corded Ware cultures and cultures from the turn of the Neolithic Age and the Bronze Age', in T. Wiślański (ed.), *The Neolithic in Poland*, Wroclaw-Warsaw-Cracow, 1970, pp. 384-420.

[93] T. Wiślański, op. cit. (Note 92), 1970, p.443.

[94] Z. Krzak, 'The Zlota culture', in T. Wiślański, op. cit. (Note 92), 1970, pp. 333-55.

[95] W. Tetzlaff, The Rzucewo culture, in T. Wiślański, op. cit. (Note 92), 1970, pp. 356-65.

[96] M.R. Jarman, C. Vita-Finzi, E.S. Higgs, 'Site catchment analysis in archaeology', in P. Ucko, R. Tringham, G.W. Dimbleby (eds.), *Man, Settlement and Urbanism*, London, 1972, pp. 189-205.

[97] J.B. Birdsell, 'On population structure in generalized hunting and collecting population', *Evolution*, 12, 1958, pp. 189-205.

Chapter 6

CONCLUSIONS

Evolution of subsistence patterns

A model of prehistoric society must include the means of production of material goods, and hence the subsistence pattern. In our model of prehistoric society, the subsistence pattern is regarded as a feeding component or a transformer of natural resources, operating in accordance with the principle of optimizer and satisfizer strategies. The subsistence pattern can only be reconstructed on the basis of a synthesis of the complex evidence produced by the various analytical disciplines.

The formation of important subsistence patterns and their evolution in time and space was largely determined by a combination of social and environmental factors. In different natural zones, characterized by different ranges of natural resources, different economic structures were formed. In each zone these structures tended to produce adequate energy inflow at the minimum possible risk. Thus a network of natural economic zones was formed.

The evolution of the natural economic zones was due both to environmental factors (changes in natural resources) and to social factors. Among social factors population stress was of prime importance, and a major role was played by the cultural subsystem, which acted as an accumulator of knowledge, habits and traditions (memory component). The dynamics of the evolution of subsistence patterns were complex, involving a number of elementary processes. Among these elementary processes the most important, in all probability, were: (1) adaptation to environmental changes; (2) population displacement; (3) diffusion of technical knowledge.

The Late Palaeolithic subsistence patterns were more or less homogeneous. The existing subzones may be distinguished on the basis of differences in hunting patterns, which were mostly due to the differences in Late Pleistocene landscape features. The passage from the Upper Palaeolithic to the Mesolithic subsistence pattern was primarily an adaptation to radical changes in the environmental setting. It can be asserted that population displacement and the diffusion of knowledge played a subordinate role in this process.

The formation and development of Mesolithic subsistence patterns in Europe were largely dependent upon the environmental setting – the distribution of food resources. The combination of social factors (population stress) and environmental factors (the existence of domesticable plants and animals) led to the appearance of incipient food production in certain natural zones of the Near East.

The appearance and spread of a food-producing economy in the Near East and in Europe was a determining factor in the further evolution of subsistence patterns. The spread of a farming economy in its turn was largely dependent upon environmental and social factors. Under environmental factors one should classify landscape features which ensured that primitive agriculture and stock-breeding were successful; under social factors one should classify the displacement of part of the surplus population from overpopulated primary agricultural zones. That population displacement played a major if not a decisive role in the spread of a farming economy in Europe is proved by the following considerations: (1) in the area of Europe where agricultural settlements initially appeared Mesolithic settlements were practically absent; (2) in Europe there were no domesticable cereals; and (3) according to the opinion of palaeozoologists all important farm animals were first domesticated in the Near East.[1]

Adaptation to the environmental setting was of the utmost importance in the evolution of subsistence patterns during the Neolithic epoch. This factor manifested itself in the formation of different natural economic zones having regard to local natural resources. Thus during the Early and Middle Holocene a food-appropriating economy survived in a considerable area of north-eastern Europe, being the best adapted to local environmental conditions. A part of the surplus population from the agricultural zones of Europe migrated into this area, adopting a hunting and fishing economy as the optimal strategy under local conditions.

Evolution of demographic patterns

The reconstruction of demographic patterns is an important and difficult aspect of the reconstruction of past societies. In Chapter 1 I quoted different approaches to the quantitative evaluation of prehistoric populations and the difficulties in such evaluation. In my opinion the most promising approach consists of building demographic models, and specifically in calculating the carrying capacity of different natural zones with regard to natural resources (or biomass) and the evolution level of the productive forces. Demographic calculations based upon the number and size of contemporaneous sites within natural zones are of great importance. The detailed examination of cemeteries also has a certain importance. But the selective nature of this record makes it less appropriate for demographic calculations. Reliable quantitative demographic reconstructions have to take all these factors into consideration, and this, at least at the present level, is beset by many difficulties. But such models may be built in the not too distant future.

The problem of the dynamics of prehistoric populations is just as important, and here a preliminary model can be suggested as follows. At the level of a food-appropriating economy population density is completely regulated by natural resources (or biomass). Thus, in the absence of environmental changes, the population density of hunting and fishing communities remains at a more or less stable level. The existing demographic evidence regarding the peoples of Siberia seems to support this assumption. An important conclusion follows: at the level of a food-appropriating economy, in the absence of environmental changes, the displacement of population played a subordinate role in economic and cultural evolution.

Environmental changes, in particular those connected with a decrease in biomass, could lead to population stress. There are several ways to resolve this situation: (1) Technical improvement of hunting weaponry. But this solution was only a temporary palliative; due to feedback regulation, the perfection of weaponry led to the killing of more animals, thus increasing overpopulation. (2) Population decrease by the imposition of artificial birth-control and by budding-off of a part of the surplus population to less populated areas. (3) Development of productive forces and transition to a higher economic level. Incipient food production originated from the realization of all these possibilities in the specific environmental conditions of the Near East.

Population displacement gained in importance during the Holocene, as a result of the evolution of food-producing economies in certain natural zones. The evolution of food-producing subsistence patterns caused a marked increase in surplus products and consequently led to a more sedentary way of life. At the same time, population pressure rose considerably. The latter is connected with a rapid increase in population density (caused by the improvement in nutrition and by the prolongation of the mating period) and by the intensive character of agricultural production leading to the rapid exhaustion of arable lands and pastures. In this case an intrinsic rate of population increase assumes a logistic form. As the population is saturated to its relative carrying capacity (which may range from 30 to 97% of the absolute carrying capacity) demographic stress is created. The stress situation may be resolved by the budding-off of a part of the surplus population.

The proof (or disproof) of migrations and the evaluation of their significance as prehistoric processes is a focal point of explanatory archaeology. The proof of the reality of prehistoric migrations is based upon three kinds of evidence: (1) anthropological; (2) archaeological and (3) palaeogeographical. In human genetics in recent times doubts have been cast on the validity of anthropological evidence as proof of prehistoric migrations. The trouble is that, in words of Th.Dobzhanski,[2] 'the migrant will bring not the entire gene pool of the original population but only a small slice of it'. This implies that the migrant population is never genetically identical with the original one. A population spread over a vast area is necessarily split into a number of genetic isolates by virtue of geographical and social factors. Random genetic drift will always lead to the accumulation of different genetic mutations in different isolates. Thus, considerable deviations may occur both between different isolated populations and between the budded-off population and the original one.

Thus the two remaining types of evidence, the archaeological and the palaeogeographical, gain in importance. Palaeogeographical evidence has already been quoted as proof of the migrations of farming populations. The spread of a farming population in the area of Europe where domesticable plants and animals did not exist implies the migration of this population from an area where these plants and animals did exist. Palaeogeographical evidence should be used for the evaluation of natural resources in different natural zones. Without this, the pattern of migrations cannot be understood. The principle of migration may be formulated as follows: the displacement of population proceeds from an area with relative overpopulation, that is, deficient in food resources, into an area relatively rich in food resources.

The difficulties connected with the use of archaeological evidence as proof of prehistoric migration are akin to the limitations imposed on the use of anthropological evidence. The fact that only a small slice of the original population is involved in migration implies that the migrant is never culturally identical with the original group. An important factor is what the Soviet archaeologist Leo Klejn[3] has termed a migratory transformation. The scarcity and deficiency of archaeological evidence is also an important limiting factor.

The limitations of archaeological evidence make it impossible to use polythetic operational units, such as archaeological cultures, as proof of prehistoric migrations. In reconstructing such migrations, only monothetic operational units, such as subcultures may be used. Of particular importance in this respect are artifact-types treated as material manifestations of spiritual culture, forming the cultural subsystem. Among these, specific importance is attached to the decoration of pottery (the elements and patterns of decoration). In the present work cultural zones are distinguished on the basis of the similarity of such attributes. These cultural zones were formed by the displacement of prehistoric populations.

Two main types of human migration may be distinguished in prehistory: (1) The populating of an empty ecological niche, when the spreading population settles in an area practically unused by the local population which is at a different economic level (for example the spread of farming communities in the loess area of Europe). (2) Migration into an already occupied ecological niche. In this case interbreeding occurs and there is partial assimilation of the migrating population by the local one. The migrating population assumes the subsistence pattern and the tool-kit of the local population. Links with the original population are noticeable in pottery decoration only, that is, in the elements of the cultural subsystem, an example being the spread of comb-decorated and of stroke-decorated pottery in eastern Europe.

Evolution of eco-social systems

20,000-10,000 B.P.

During the Late Pleistocene, periglacial or hyperzonal landscapes were the dominant types of environment in the Near East and in Europe. Treeless steppe-like vegetation was spread over the Zagros piedmont, the Syrian plateau, the Anatolian plains, the intermontane depressions of Bulgaria and Greece, the Danube plains, and the southern part of the Russian plain. It is assumed that forest vegetation survived in the coastlands of the Mediterranean Sea, the rift valley of the Levant, the mountains of Greece and Bulgaria, the Dinaric Alps, the Carpathians, the Moldavian highlands and the valleys of rivers crossing the southern Russian plain. Open birch and fir forests were partially spread over the Dnieper valley and in the Polessye.

It is relevant that the periglacial landscapes were comparatively rich in water. A system of glacial-lacustrine basins existed beyond the ice-sheet. The water drained from these lakes in a southerly direction through a system of rivers. Some of these rivers turned into chains of lakes. Large lakes occurred in the intermontane depressions of Greece and Bulgaria, in the Anatolian plain and in the Levantine Rift valley. The periglacial landscapes supported a considerable Upper Palaeolithic population. The following main zones of concentration of the Upper Palaeolithic population may be singled out: (1) the medium-height mountains of Zagros and Levant; (2) the mountains of Greece and Bulgaria; (3) the Dinaric Alps; (4) the Carpathians and the Moldavian highlands; (5) the Dniester valley; (6) the Pontic steppe area; (7) the middle Dnieper valley and the Polessye.

The subsistence pattern of the Upper Palaeolithic population in all these areas was based upon the specialized hunting of large herd animals and upon food collecting. The relative homogeneity of the periglacial environment implies the relative homogeneity of the subsistence pattern. All the territory of Upper Palaeolithic settlement in the Near East and in Europe may be regarded as a single natural economic zone. Within this single zone several subzones may be distinguished. These are:

(1) Sites in the mountains of the Near East. Cave sites. Subsistence pattern: hunting of bezoar goats and wild oxen in the Zagros mountains, of wild horses in the Judean desert and of fallow deer and gazelles in the mountains flanking the coastal area; food gathering.

(2) Sites in the mountains of south-eastern Europe and in the valley of the Dniester. Sites both in caves and in the open air, the latter mostly in river valleys. Subsistence pattern: specialized hunting of wild horses and of reindeer; food gathering.

(3) Sites of the Pontic steppic area. Open-air seasonal camp-sites. Subsistence pattern: specialized hunting of bison and aurochs.

(4) Sites in the middle Dnieper area and in the Polessye. Open-air, round-the-year settlements. Subsistence pattern: specialized hunting of mammoths.

About 14,000-12,000 B.P. considerable changes in the structure of the eco-system took place: forest-like vegetation spread in the Russian plain, in the mountains and in the intermontane depressions of south-eastern Europe and of the Near East; the size of the lakes in all these areas diminished; the Late Pleistocene fauna became extinct or was redistributed. These environmental changes triggered off corresponding changes in social systems. Food gathering and the exploitation of aquatic resources gained in importance in the Near East. The settlement area was enlarged: sites appeared in the rift valley and in the coastal area. Geometric microliths, primarily used as sophisticated hunting weapons, appeared in the stone industry. Numerous sites appeared in the areas directly adjoining the ice-sheet; their tool-kit contained large numbers of projectile points, and their subsistence pattern was based on the specialized hunting of reindeer (Fig. 60).

10,000-8,000 B.P.

About 10,000 years ago an important change took place in the structure of the eco-system. The ice-sheet disintegrated; glacial lakes disappeared and rivers and lakes became shallower; periglacial hyperzonal landscapes disappeared and modern natural zones were formed; the Late Pleistocene mammoth faunal complex was finally replaced by Holocene faunal complexes, consisting of forest and steppic non-herd animals. These marked changes in the structure of the eco-system, involving the redistribution of natural food resources, triggered off adaptive changes in social systems. At that time in the settlements spread in the piedmont area and the rift valley of the Near East there appeared evidence of the systematic use of cereals and domesticated animals for food. The acquisition of a new stable source of food in certain areas of the Near East led to chain reactions in

Conclusions

|||||||| Upper Palaeolithic natural
|||||||| economic zone

Figure 60 The Near East and eastern Europe 20,000-10,000 B.P.

various elements of the social system. The resulting increase of population caused population stress in the initial agricultural zone and the spread of the food-producing population into surrounding areas suitable for farming activities: to the lower piedmont of the Zagros, to the coastal area and to the inner plains of Anatolia. All these areas are included in the natural economic zone of the food-producing economy. During the time-span under consideration, hunting, fishing and food collecting retained their role as an important supplementary source of food in this zone.

At the same time, hunting, fishing and food collecting were the only source of food for the population of Europe. The subsistence pattern of this population was based upon hunting steppe and forest non-herd animals, upon intensive fishing and food-collecting. Thus the settlement in Europe forms a single natural economic zone, the Mesolithic food-appropriating economy.

Within this zone at least two subzones may be distinguished. The first subzone includes the coastal area and mountains of south-eastern Europe, the Danubian plain, the Carpathians, the Moldavian highlands, the western part of the Pontic steppe zone and the flood-plains and low terraces of the Dniester, Dnieper, Pripyat and Niemen. This subzone is characterized by a subsistence pattern based upon the hunting of red deer, wild pig, wild horse, and aurochs and upon the intensive gathering of edible plants and molluscs. Geometric microliths are numerous in the tool-kits of sites within this subzone. The second subzone includes the sites in the inner province of the area affected by the Last Glaciation. These sites are situated on the low terraces and on the flood-plains of rivers and inside large lake depressions. The subsistence pattern of these sites was based on the hunting of elk, brown bear and wild pig, intensive fishing and food collecting. In the coastal area of the Baltic Sea the hunting of sea animals was important (Fig: 61).

8,000-7,000 B.P.

During this time interval there was a further spread of the natural economic zone formed by the food-producing economy. This zone now included a part of the plains and coastland of the Near East, the intermontane depressions of Greece and Bulgaria, the Danube plains and the loess-covered plains of central Europe. The natural economic zone formed by the food-appropriating economy included the coastal area of the Mediterranean Sea, the forested southern Carpathians, the valleys of major rivers in the southern part and the western part of the Russian plain. Inside the zone of the food-appropriating economy, the two subzones formed during the preceding stage remained. In the coastal area of the Baltic Sea the hunting of sea animals became even more important.

The new element in the cultural subsystem was represented by

Conclusions

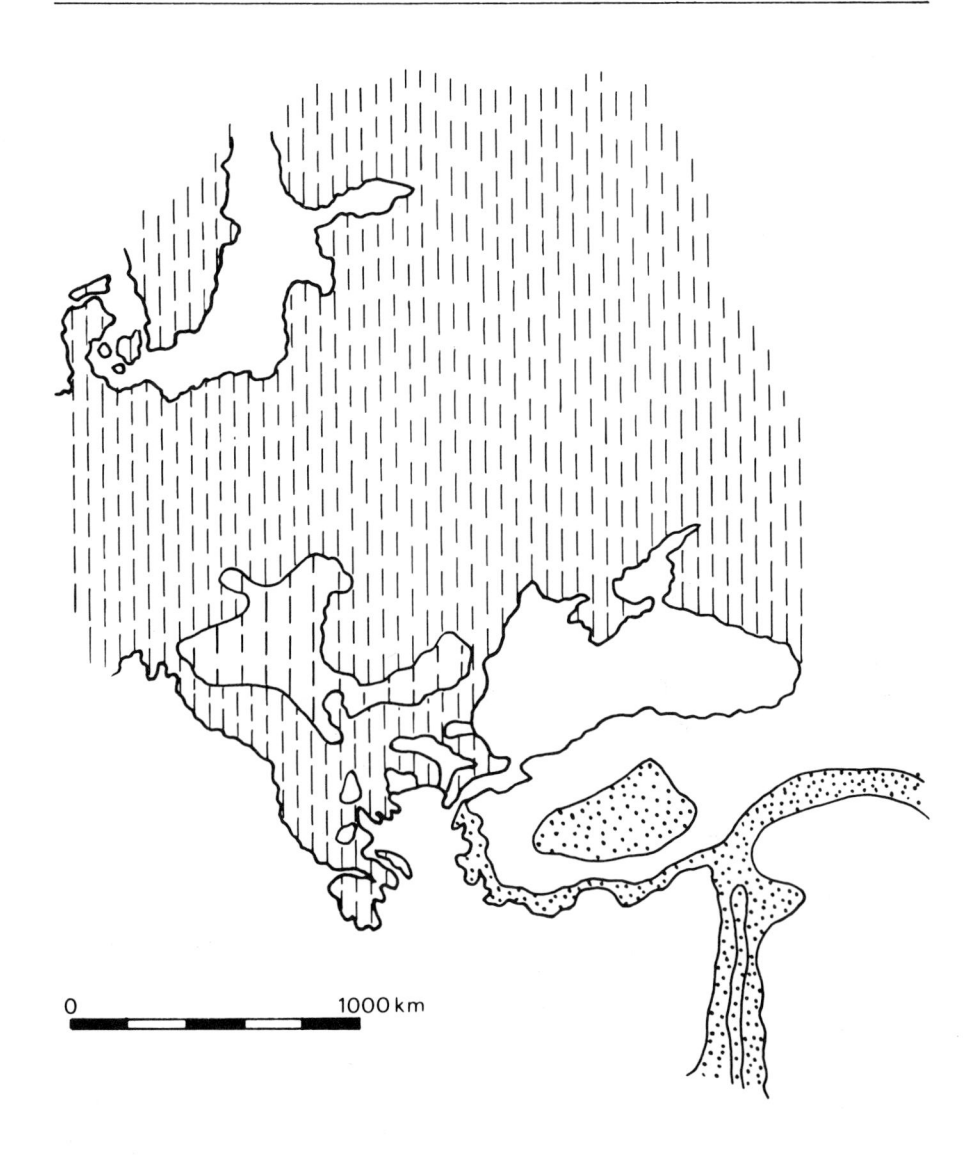

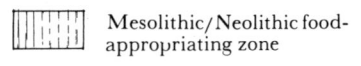

|||||| Mesolithic/Neolithic food-
appropriating zone

:::::: Neolithic food-producing zone

Figure 61 The Near East and eastern Europe 10,000-8,000 B.P.

pottery manufacture. Several cultural zones may be distinguished on the basis of similarities in the decoration of pottery. A huge cultural zone may be distinguished within which the vessels were decorated with rows of impressions of comb stamps or shell edges, or with incised lines forming simple patterns. This cultural zone includes Syria, Cilicia, northern Mesopotamia, the coastland of the Mediterranean Sea, the valleys of the Dniester and of the southern Bug and the area affected by the Last Glaciation. Other cultural zones correspond to the distribution areas of painted pottery in the Near East and in Europe.

7,000-6,000 B.P.

Population stress in the agricultural zones of south-eastern Europe necessitated a further outflow of surplus population. As before, the migrating population chose those economic strategies which guaranteed the optimal or most reliable energy inflow in the local environmental conditions. The population of the loess plains of central Europe chose agriculture and stock-breeding as the most effective means of food production; the population distributed in the river valleys and in the lake depressions of the Russian plain chose hunting, fishing and food gathering as the most effective strategies in their densely-forested environment.

In the first case the farming population spread into a practically empty ecological niche (although it is possible that a part of the local Mesolithic population in the surrounding areas was involved in food production). In the second case the new population spread into areas already occupied by local Mesolithic groups. In this case partial assimilation of the new population by the old one took place. At any rate, the migrating population acquired the subsistence pattern and the tool-kit of the Mesolithic groups (Fig. 62).

6,000-4,000 B.P.

Between 5,500 and 4,500 B.P. there took place a further extension to the north and to the east of the area occupied by farming communities. At that time over a vast territory of northern and central Europe there appeared the so-called funnel beaker culture. Roughly at the same time the Cucuteni-Tripolye culture made its appearance in the steppe and forest-steppe zones of the south-western part of the Russian plain. The subsistence pattern of the funnel beaker settlements was entirely based upon effective food production. The subsistence pattern of the early phase of the Cucuteni-Tripolye sites had a mixed food-producing/food-appropriating character. At later stages it acquired a stable food-producing character. The settlements of both the funnel beaker and Tripolye cultures attained considerable size.

Conclusions

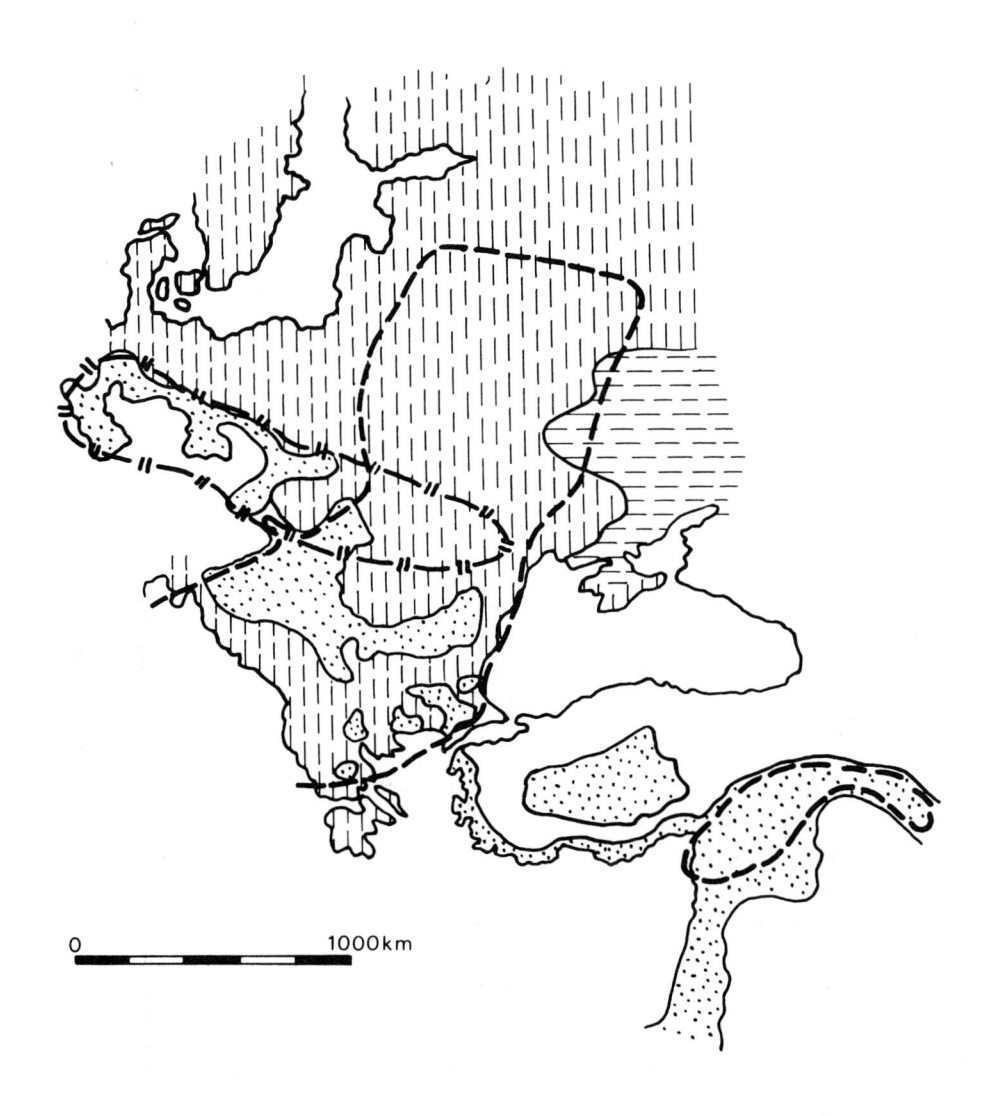

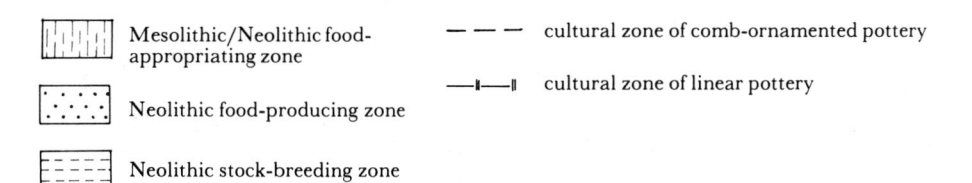

Mesolithic/Neolithic food-appropriating zone	– – – cultural zone of comb-ornamented pottery
Neolithic food-producing zone	—I—I cultural zone of linear pottery
Neolithic stock-breeding zone	

Figure 62 The Near East and eastern Europe 8,000-6,000 B.P.

Thus, in the time-span under consideration, two major natural-economic zones may be distinguished: (1) the zone of food-producing economies, covering the plains of the Near East, of south-eastern Europe, the south-western part of the Russian plain, the loess-covered plains of central Europe, north Germany and the north Polish plain; and (2) the zone of food-appropriating economies, including the central Dnieper area, the Polessye and the area covered by the Last Glaciation.

On the basis of similarities in pottery ornamentation, several cultural zones may be distinguished. The similarity in the use of two attributes, strokes and geometric patterns, enables us to distinguish a huge cultural zone in central and eastern Europe. This zone includes the distribution area of the funnel beaker culture in Europe; the Middle Neolithic sites in the middle Dnieper and in the western Polessye (Dnieper-Donetz culture); the sites in the area of the Last Glaciation (the first settlement of Usvyaty in the Pskov region and the Piestina-type sites in eastern Latvia); and the sites in the coastal area of the Baltic Sea (Narva-type sites, dwellings of the Sarnate type and the lower level of the Sventoji site). Another cultural zone is represented by the sites with pit-and-comb decorated pottery. The extension of the sites belonging to this cultural zone into the western part of the Russian plain occurred 4,700-4,500 years ago.

About 4,200-4,000 B.P. the influence of the corded ware culture becomes obvious in a number of Neolithic sites in the western part of the Russian plain. This phenomenon should be considered in relation to the infiltration of the population which had left the primary area of corded ware culture. This infiltration did not change the stable structure of the food-appropriating economy which already existed in this area. The very limited influence was reflected only in the cultural subsystem. In all probability the new population was rapidly absorbed by the local one. At that time population density rose considerably and the size of settlements increased (Fig. 63).

This suggested scheme of prehistoric development is only an approximation. It is a model in the sense usually ascribed to this notion. The model is selective; in building it not all the empirical data were used, but only those essential for the model-building. The model is structural; we were trying to follow up connections in the 'web of realities'. The model is suggestive; it explains the greater part of observed facts and allows suggestions to be made about the nature of the processes which occurred in prehistoric human society.

In any scientific investigation it is most important to evaluate the degree of reliability of the conclusions. This reliability is largely dependent upon the validity of the empirical data and upon the validity of the categorical analysis employed. Unfortunately, we have to admit that the analysis of empirical data is still the weakest point in

Conclusions 199

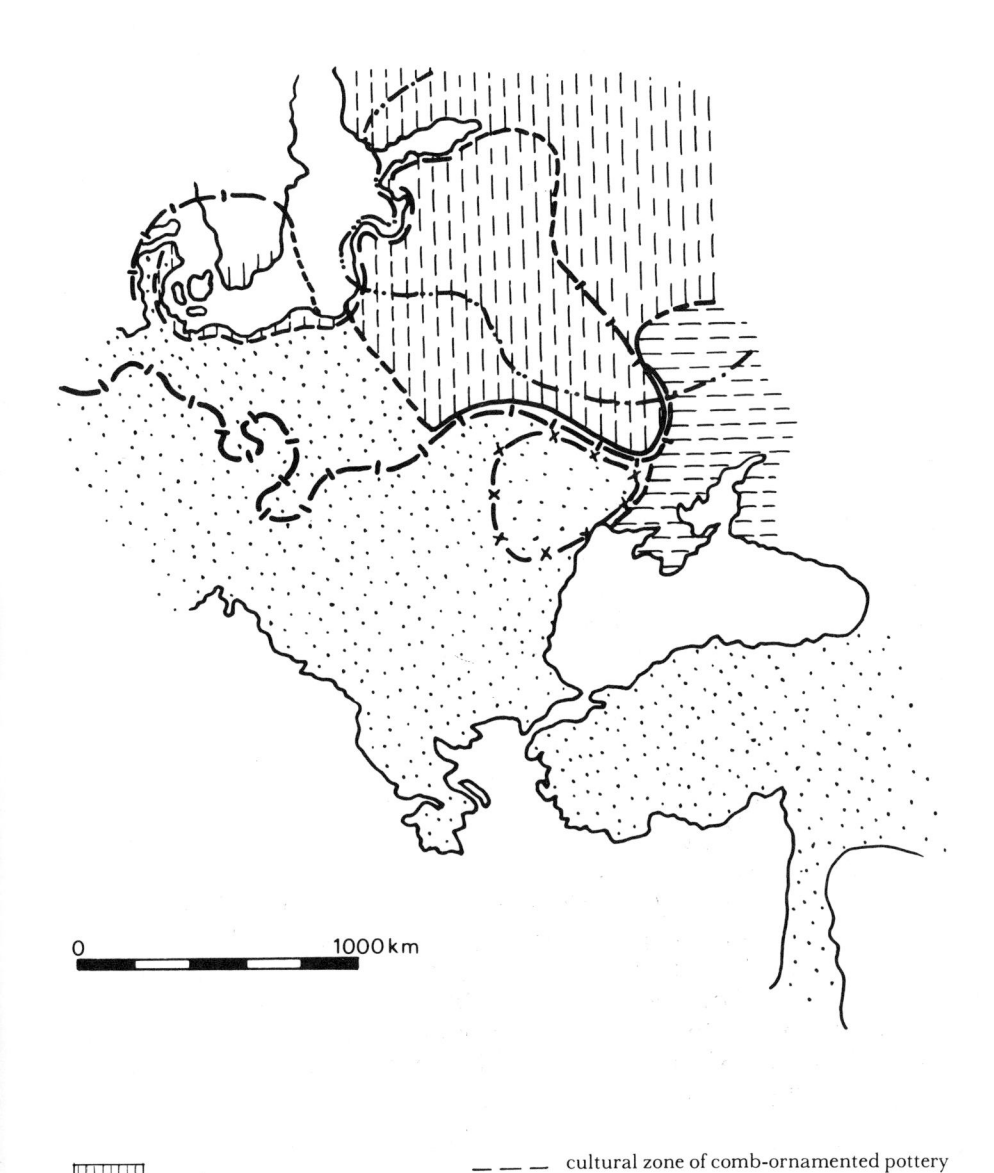

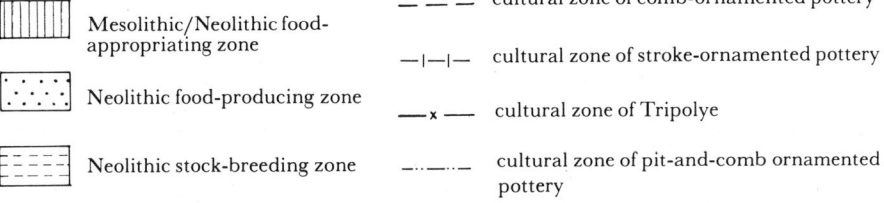

	Mesolithic/Neolithic food-appropriating zone
	Neolithic food-producing zone
	Neolithic stock-breeding zone

— — — cultural zone of comb-ornamented pottery

—|—|— cultural zone of stroke-ornamented pottery

—x— cultural zone of Tripolye

—··—··— cultural zone of pit-and-comb ornamented pottery

Figure 63 The Near East and eastern Europe 6,000-4,000 B.P.

archaeology. The accumulation of extensive empirical data in archaeology is not accompanied by full-scale analysis, even at an empirical level. In many respects this is due to the poor state of archaeological theory; to ambiguity in understanding such elementary empirical notions as attribute, type, assemblage, culture. The maturity of a science is often revealed in its ability to express its categories formally. The formal expression of basic archaeological empirical notions is still in its infancy. We have a very long way to go before the formal apparatus of archaeology acquires practical value. The need to possess formal apparatus is particularly acutely felt in dealing with such groups of archaeological evidence as stone tools and pottery. Reliable prehistoric models must be based upon stable methods of measuring resemblances and differences between groups of archaeological material, based upon a selected set of attributes.

In many respects palaeogeography faces the same set of problems. But formalization may be more easily achieved in this discipline, empirical palaeogeographical data necessarily having a formal character.

The handicaps listed above impose some limitations upon the reliability of the proposed model. This model is but one of the possible explanations of the observed empirical archaeological and palaeogeographical data. But we may assert that this model is one of the most probable at the present level of the analysis of empiric data.

These considerations make it possible to suggest the direction of future research. In my opinion this research must concentrate upon the elaboration of the formal analysis of archaeological and palaeogeographical data; upon the elaboration of attributes; and upon the quantitative measurement of resemblances and differences between groups of materials.

The next stage would be the quantitative modelling of prehistoric processes. Thus a complex history would be created, the history of mankind and the history of nature. For in the words of Marx and Engels 'History may be regarded as the history of mankind and the history of nature. But these two sides of history are inseparable. While the human race exists, the history of humans and the history of nature mutually influence one another'.[4]

NOTES

[1] V.I. Calkin, *Drevnyeišiye domašniye zivotnyye Vostočnoi Evropy*, Moscow, 1970.

[2] Th. Dobzhansky, 'Genetic drift and selection of gene systems', *in* Y.A. Cohen (ed.), *Man in Adaptation*, Chicago, 1968.

[3] L.S. Klejn, 'Arkheologičeskiye priznaki migracii', *IX International Congress of Anthropological and Ethnographical Sciences, Reports of Soviet scientists*, Moscow, 1973.

[4] K. Marx and F. Engels, *Die deutsche Ideologie* (Works, 3), Berlin, 1968, p. 18.

INDEX

Index

Abora pottery, 163
aborigines, Australian, 23
Adriatic coast, 64-5, 68, 70, 75-7
Aegean-Marmara coastlands, 48, 50, 52, 72
Africa, North, 70
agriculture, 12, 25-7, 188-9, 194, 196; the Levant, 44, 56; Asia Minor, 51-2, 56; Thrace, 67; south-eastern Europe, 74-5, 77; south Russian plain, 89, 92, 95, 101, 103, 108; west Russian plain, 141, 148, 150, 167, 172-3, 179
Ahlbeck group, 135
Ahrensburg site, 131-2
Aiviekste river, 156
Akali site, 163-4
Albanian slope, 65
Alleröd oscillation, 118, 124, 130-2
Alpine: meadows, 6; geosyncline, 37; folded zone, 48, 64; trough, 81
Ambrosyevka site, 126
America, 114
Amersfoort interstadial, 113; *see also* Upper Volga interstadial
'Amuq area, 47-8
Anatolia, 52-3, 191, 194; northern, 50; western, 51
Ancylus: lake, 116, 169; transgression, 138, 169
animal domestication, 15, 188, 192; recognition of, 26; Zagros mountains, 40-1; the Levant, 46-7; Asia Minor, 51; south Russian plain, 88, 90-2, 95, 101-3; west Russian plain, 141, 153, 156, 163, 166-7, 172; *see also* stockbreeding
animal ecology, 6-9, 14
Antalya region, 51
Antarctic, 18
Anti-Lebanon ranges, 43
Antioch, plain of, 42, 48
Anosovka site, 126

Anzabegovo sites, 69
Aqaba, gulf of, 42
Arabian plateau, 42, 52
Ararat, plain of, 50
Archaean age, 93; basement, 41
archaeology, 1-33 *passim*, 88, 190, 200; aim and definition of, 1-2; system of concepts, 2; theoretical objective, 3
architecture, 15, 27, 131, 151; city of Jerico, 44; Beidha village, 46-7; Ras Shamra settlement, 47; Hacilar, 51; Karanovo tell, 67; Lepenski Vir, 70; Soroki, 90-1; Bug, 96; Linear, 101; Gumelnita, 102; Kirillovskaya, Goncy and Dobraničevka, 127; Mezin, 128; Berdyž, 129; Pinnburg, 133; Mněvo site, 141; funnel beaker, 148; Krivna, 152; Lagaža, 163; Narva, 167-8; Sarnate, 169
Arctic, 6
Argissa Magula tell, 61-2
Arpachiyah, tell, 48
Armenian highlands, 48, 50-2
art, objects of, 15, 27
artifact, 15, 27; definition of, 2; types, 16-17; *see also* pottery, tools and architecture
Ashby, Ross, 9; quoted, 10
Asia, ix
Asia Minor, 48-52 *passim*
Asmak, tell, 67
Asprochaliko site, 60
assemblage, 27, 200; definition of, 2
Ataki VI site, 90
Atlantic: period, 84, 87-8, 124, 133, 136; ocean, 122, 125; zone, 135, 139-40, 153, 159
attribute, 28, 200; definition of, 2
Augustenhof site, 117, 164-5
Australia, 23
Axios (or Vardar) river, 63
Azov Sea, 86, 88

Balkans, 63-4, 68, 75, 77, 97-8, 108
Baltic: glacial lake, ix; Sea, 20-1, evolution of, 116-119, 122-3; region, 125-6, 136, 164, 167-8, 171-4, 176, 178, 194, 198
Baradostian industry, 40
Barbotine technique, 62-3, 68-9, 76, 92, 97, 108
Bass Strait Island, 25
Baz'kov Island site, 93, 95
Behrens, H., 148-9
Beidha village, 46
Begalnitsa valley, 69
Beldibi cave, 51
Belgium, 100, 130
Berdyž site, 129, 174
Berendeyevo site, 151
von Bertalanffy, L., 9; quoted, 10
Beqaa, 42
Bibikov, S.N., 23, 95, 103
Biblical records, 42
Binford, L., quoted, 22
biography, 4, 59
biomass, 7, 23, 31, 106, 126, 173-4, 179, 188-9
biome, definition of, 10
biosphere, 5-7, 18
Birdsell, J., 23
birth-control, 24, 189
Bistrita valley, 66
black boxes, definition of, 30
Black Sea, 50, 81-3, 106; coastland, 48, 52; new Black Sea transgression, 87-8; level of, 104
blubber lamps, 166, 170
Bohemia, 148
Bolgrad lake, 102
Boreal period, 124-5, 133, 135-6, 140, 153
Borinka site, 150
Bosphorus, 48
Braidwood, R.L., 23, 25; quoted, 47-8
Briansk soil, 83-4, 127
British Isles, 118
Bromley, Y.V., 15
Bronze Age, 153, 155
Brörup interstadial, 113-14
Brzesc-Kujawski group, 167
Buddelin site, 117, 164-5
Bug river sites, 82, 93-102 *passim*, 106, 108, 141, 144, 148-9, 176-9, 196
Bulgaria, 64-77 *passim*, 101, 191, 194
Buz'ki site, 141
Byblos settlement, 47-8
Bylany, 101
Byelorussia: field studies in, ix; 114; province, 121, 131-2, 144, 146-7, 149, 151-2, 171, 173

carbon 14 dating (C14, radio-carbon dating), 28-30; Zagros mountains, 41; the Levant, 44, 46-7; Asia Minor, 51; Greece, 60-1, 63-4; Yugoslavia, 66; Cris-Körö sites, 68; Serbia and Vojvodia, 70; Lepenski Vir, 70; south-eastern Europe, 75, 77; south Russian plain, Briansk soil, 83; Moldovia V, 85, 89; Soroki, 91, 93, 100; Bug, 100; Early Valdai, 113-14; Baltic marine basin and Sarnate site, 116; Baltic area, 117, 119; west Russian plain, 123-5, 129-31; Studenec, 132; Maglemosian, 134; Kunda, 138; Lubana, 139, 147-8; Klyazma, 151; Usvyaty, 153-4; Osa, 158; Piestina, 159; Eini, 161; Kääpa, 163; Buddelin, 164-5; Augustenhof, 165; Muldbjerg, 166; Sarnate, 170; corded ware, 172
Cardium impressed ware, 62-3
Carpathians, southern and eastern, 64-6, 72-3, 75, 77, 81, 191, 194
Çatal Hüyük, 25, 51-2
calibrations, tree-ring, 29-30
Carchemish, 48
carrying capacity, 8, 14
Caucasus, 48
Cenozoic age, 41, 64
cereals, cultivated, 27, 88, 192; identification of, 26; Iraq and Iran, 38-9, 41; origin of, 43-4, 46-7; Thrace, 67; south Russian plain, 92, 101-3; *see also* agriculture and farming communities
cereals, wild: identification of, 26; Iraq and Iran, 38-9, 41; the Levant, 43-4, 46, 53; Asia Minor, 51, 53
Chagir Bazar, tell, 48
Cheboksarov, N., 13
Chemchemal plain, 41
chemo-synthesis, 6
Chojnice-Pienki culture, 136
Chorley, R.J., quoted, 3
chronology, Egyptian written, 28
Chwalibojowice point, 131
Cilicia, 196
Clark, Grahame, 26
Clarke, David, quoted, 14, 16
climate, 5-6, 11; past characteristics, 17-21; Zagros mountains, 37-8; the Levant, 42; Asia Minor, 50; Balkan peninsula, 65; south Russian plain,

83; west Russian plain, 122-3, 148
climatic regions, 11
Cna river, 151
consumer level, 7
corded ware culture, 163, 172-3, 198; definition of, 171
continuity, law of, 5
Cretaceous age, 81-2
Crimea, 23, 81
Criş sites, 68, 101-2
Crvena Stena cave, 66-7, 70
Cucuteni culture, 196
Cuina Turului cave, 66
culture, 27-8; definitions of, 2, 14-17; systemic, 32-3
cultural change, explanations of, 3
cultural contact, 93, 149, 167
cultural zones, 17, 28, 76, 108, 150, 179, 181, 190, 196, 198
Czechoslovakia, 101

Dalmatian coastland, 65
Danilenko, V.N., 93, 95, 97, 142
Danish islands, 164
Danube river, 82, 148, 167, 191, 194; plain, 64-6; valley, 67-8; site, 70, 72-6; Delta, 87
dark-faced burnished ware, 48, 56, 63, 70, 77
Daugava (Zapadnaya Dvina), 156
Dead Sea, 52; fault, 42; fall in level of, 44
decoration, pottery, *see* pottery
demography, 14, 22-5, 101, 188-91; *see also* population
dendrochronology, 29
Denmark, 113-14, 131, 133, 135, 148
Desna: valley, 121; river, 127-8, 140, 150
detritus food chain, 6
Dinaric: folded system, 64; Alps, Karst and Maritime zone, 65-6, 72, 191
Diyala river, 37
Dnieper: river, 84; glaciation, 113; province, 121, 123, 127-8, 131-2, 139-42, 146-50, 173-4, 176, 179, 181, 191-2, 194, 198
Dniester river, 82-5, 90-2, 95, 98, 102, 104, 106, 108, 126-7, 144, 147, 149, 173, 176, 179, 191-2, 194, 196
Dobrugea: mountains of, 66; 72, 75-7
Dobraničevka site, 126-7
Dobzhanski, Th., 190
Donetz valley, 142, 146-50, 179, 198
Don river, 126
Drama, plain of, 60
Dryas, 131; younger, 119, 130-2, 153; middle, 124

Dubiča site, 147, 176
Duvensee sites, 134-5

East African rift system, 42
economic contact, 92-3, 141, 156
economic cultural type, 13-14
economic geography, 12-13
economic pattern, 31-3, 56, 89, 92, 177; *see also* economic zone, natural and subsistence pattern
economic zone, natural, 13, 14, 17, 28, 187, 191-2, 194, 198; the Near East, 52-3, 56; south-eastern Europe, 72, 75; south Russian plain, 86-7, 104, 106, 108; west Russian plain, 174
economies, prehistoric, 26-7; Zagros mountains, 39-44; the Levant, 43-4, 47; Asia Minor, 51; Greece, 60, 62; Serbia and Vojvodina, 69; Adriatic coast, 70; south-eastern Europe, 72-5; south Russian plain, 96, 101-2; reconstruction of, 95; west Russian plain, 119, 126-30, 134-5, 141-2, 148, 151, 163, 172
ecosystem, 10, 13; components of, 30-1
Eimajõgi river, 163
Eini site, 161
Elbe river, 135
Elinelund site, 117
empirical knowledge, 2-3
energy accumulator, 5
energy input, 5
Engels, Friedrich, quoted, x, 11, 12, 200
Epirus, 63
Ertebolle sites, 117, 158, 164-7
Estonia, 114, 125, 136-8, 163, 167, 169, 171, 179
ethnology, 13
ethnography, 14-15, 25
Eurasian continent, 48
Europe, ix, 100-2, 106, 123, 148-50, 167, 172, 181, 188, 191-2, 194, 196, 198; prehistoric, economy of, 26; south-eastern, 59-79 *passim*; temperate, 83; Atlantic period of, 84; glaciation of, 113-14, 118
Euphrates river, basin, 39
exponential curve, 8

Far'ah, tell, 47
farming communities: evolution of, 44, 46; south-eastern Europe, 74; south Russian plain, 102; 188, 190-1, 194, 196; *see also* food production
Fastov site, 127
faunal: complexes, 2; regions, 11; the

Levant, 43, 47; Asia Minor, 51; Greece, 60-3; the Balkans, 66, 68; Danube valley, 70; south Russian plain, 84-8, 90-3, 101-3; west Russian plain, 127-8, 134, 136, 138-41, 148, 153, 155-6, 158-9, 161, 163-5, 167, 170, 172

Federmesser, points and sites, 130-2

feedback (loop), 10, 30-1, 178

Finland, 116

fishing: 12, 189, 194, 196; community, 22-3, 27; Zagros mountains, 40-1, 53, 56; the Levant, 44, 47, 53, 56; Asia Minor, 53, 56; Adriatic coast, 70; Danube valley, 70; south-eastern Europe, 72-3, 77; south Russian plain, 87, 90, 92, 95, 100, 102-3, 106, 108; west Russian plain, 117, 119, 125, 134, 136, 140-1, 148, 150-1, 153, 156, 163, 165-7, 170, 172, 174, 179, 181; *see also* food gathering

Flandrian transgressions, 42, 118-19

Flannery, K.V., 41

Floreşti site, 102

food appropriation, 12, 27, 75, 106, 108, 176, 181, 188-9, 194, 196, 198

food chain, 6-7, 22

food-gathering (collecting), 12, 23, 27, 191-2, 194, 196; Zagros mountains, 41, 53, 56; Asia Minor, 52-3, 56; Yugoslavia, 67; Adriatic coast, 70; south-eastern Europe, 72, 77; south Russian plain, 86-7, 92, 95, 103-4, 106, 108; west Russian plain, 119, 129, 134, 136, 151, 153, 156, 163, 167, 170, 172, 174, 176, 179, 181

food-production, 12, 25, 27, 188-9, 194, 196, 198; Zagros mountains, 40-1; the Levant, 44, 46-7; Greece, 61, 63; Serbia and Vojvodina, 69; south-eastern Europe, 74-5; south Russian plain, 101-2, 106, 148-9; west Russian plain, 166, 181; *see also* agriculture, farming communities and stockbreeding

food-web, 7

Forth valley, 118

fossil: pollen, 4; spores, 4

France, 166

Franchthi Cave, 60, 75

Friesland, 119

funnel beaker culture, 148-50, 160, 167, 181, 196

Galilee, 43

Gdansky bay, 172

General Systems Theory, 9-11, 14

geneticists, plant, 26

geobotanical zones, 11

geocomplexes, 11

geographical belts, 11

geographical sphere, 4-5, 10, 12

geographical zones, 11, 192; the Near East, 37, 52; south-eastern Europe, 72; south Russian plain, 104, 106; west Russian plain, 121, 173; *see also* geobotanical zones, soil zones and natural zones

geomorphology, ix; units, 11; evidence, 27

geosystem, 9-11, 13

German plain, 130-1, 133

Germany, east, 119, 130, 135-6, 148-9, 164, 167

Germany, north, 198

Germany, west, 119, 130-1, 149, 164, 166

Gilead, slopes of eastern, 43

Girževo site, 87

Godwin, H., 29

Golan, basaltic plateau of, 43

Goncy site, 126-7, 174

Gramsch, B., 135, 164, 166-7

Gravettian industry, 66

grazing food chain, 6

Greece, 59-64 *passim*, 75-6, 191, 194; Neolithic sites in, 25; plains of, 68; mountains of, 72

Greek Macedonia, 60, 63

Greenland, 18

green plants, 5-7; *see also* photosynthesis

Grensk site, 131

Gricuk, V.P., 19, 123

Grigoriev, A.A., quoted, 4

Gumelniţa settlements, 102, 108

Gurina, N.N., 167

Hacilar, 51

Haggett, P., quoted, 3

Halaf, tell, 48

Haliakmon river, 63

Haltener sites, 135

Hamah, 48

Hamburg, 130-1, 133, 166

Hassuna, tell, 48

Hauran, basaltic plateau of, 43

heat balance, 5, 7

Hel bar, 172

Hintersee point, 131

Hohe Vicheln site, 135

Hole, F., 41

Holstein site, 138

Holland, 100, 113-14, 118-19, 130

Holocene age, 19, 188-9, 192; transgression, 20; Early, 41, 42-3; Asia Minor, 51, 53, 56; central Balkans, 67; south Russian plain, 82-4, 90, 93, 106; west Russian plain, 116, 119, 124, 137, 139-40, 151, 153, 157, 164, 169, 176
homeostasis, 30-1
Hungary, 101
hunting, 12, 187, 189, 191-2, 194, 196; community, 122-3; specialized and unspecialized, 27; Zagros mountains, 39-41, 52-3; Asia Minor, 51-3; Greece, 60; Romania, 66; Yugoslavia, 66-7; Thrace, 67; Adriatic coast, 70; Danube valley, 70; south-eastern Europe, 72-3, 75; south Russian plain, 84-8, 90, 93, 95, 98, 100, 102-4, 106, 108; west Russian plain, 117, 119, 125-31, 134-7, 140, 148-51, 153, 156, 163, 165-7, 172-4, 176, 179, 181
hydrosphere, 4
hyperzonality, 19

Ice Age, 50, 52, 65, 83, 124
Iceland, 122
Igren' 8 site, 141
Indonesian archipelago, 37
infanticide, 24
Institute of Archaeology in Leningrad, ix
Ionian: series rocks, 59; massif, 72
Iput' tributary, 131
Iran, 37-41 *passim*
Irano-Turanian province, 43
Iraq, 37-41 *passim*
Iron Gate: gorge, 64, 66; site, 70
Irpen river, 127
Isaenki, V.F., 146
Ismail, 87
isotope chemistry, 2; methods, 4
Italy, 70
Ivanovskoye site, 150

Jabail plain, 48
Jamina Sredi, 70
Janislawice culture, 136
Jarmo site, 41
Jericho settlement, 25, 44, 46-7
Jordan valley, 42-4, 46-7
Judaea: uplands of, 43; desert, 43, 53, 192
Jühnsdorf group, 135-6
Junus, 48
Jutland, 133, 138, 165-6

Kääpa site, 163-4

Kaistrova Balka site, 127
Kamennaya Mogila site, 88
Karanovo tell site, 67
Kattegat strait, 117
Kazatino, 93
Khuzistan plain, 41
Kiev, 127, 132, 141-2
Kiewe, H., 164
Kirillivka site, 126, 174
Kirillovskaya site, 127
Klejn, Leo, 190
Kliščev site, 103
Klosterlund site, 133
Klyazma valley, 151
Kolomiyščina site, 103
Komornica sites, 136
Kongemose group, 135-6, 166
Konya-Eregli, 51
Konya plain, 50
Körös sites, 68, 101-2
Kostenki, 126
Kreiči site, 161
Krjvina sites, 152
Ksar' Akil (Lebanon), 43
Kucurgan river, 87
Kunda site, 136-8
Kurdish mountain, 37
Kursh spit, 172

La Adam cave site, 66
Lacustrine terraces, 67
Lagaža site, 163
Lake Burdur, 51
Lake Echineis, 116
Lake Ioannina, 59
Lake Karla, 59
Lake Naroc, 132
Lake Sevan, 50
Lake Zeribar, 38
landscape sphere, 4
Last Glaciation: effect of, ix, 19; the Levant, 42-3; Asia Minor, 50; Greece, 59-60; Romania and Yugoslavia, 66; south Russian plain, 82-4, 90, 104; west Russian plain, 113-15, 121-5, 173-4, 176, 179, 194, 196, 198; *see also* Valdai Glaciation and Würm ice age
Latki site, 131
Latvia, 116-17, 119, 122, 125-6, 147, 156, 160-1, 167, 169, 179, 198
language, 15
Lebanon ranges, 43
Lęczya district, 131
Leimaniški site, 161
Leţ site, 68, 76
Lengyel culture, 148, 167

Leningrad, 114
Lepenski Vir site, 70
Levant, the: 41-8 *passim*; valley, 52; mountains, 53, 191
Levin, M., 13
Levkas, island of, 63
Libby, Willard F., 28-30
Linear pottery, 98, 100-2, 108, 167
Lisan stage, 42
Lithosphere, 4
Lithuania, 117, 119, 122, 125-6, 131-2, 136, 147, 167, 170-1, 174
Litovska site, 141
Littorina: Sea and transgressions, 117-19, 164-5, 167, 169-71
Litvin sites, 146
Litzow culture, 166
logistic model, 8
Louros river valley, 60
Loze, Ilze, 139, 163
Lubana lake depression, 119, 138-9, 156-63
Lyalovo culture, 150-1, 161
Lyngby point, 131-2, 138

Macedonia, 74-5; massif, 64
Machnic, J., 171
Maglemose sites, 133-5
mammoth complex, 19
mantle, 4
Maritsa river terraces, 67
Markevič, V.I., 92
Markov, K.K., 18
Marx, Karl, quoted, x, 11-12, 200
Masson, V.M., 26
materialism, historical: and population, 14; and mode of production, 21
Mediterranean Sea, 37, 59-60, 108, 191, 194, 196; rhythm, 42; coastland of, 43, 48, 50, 52; pottery, 70
Melitopol, 88
Mesolithic period, 23, 60, 188, 194, 196; sites, ix; Balkans, 66; Adriatic coastland, 70; south-eastern Europe, 72-3, 75; south Russian plain, 87-8, 90, 106; west Russian plain, 117, 124-5, 132-9, 142, 153, 157-8, 160, 166, 174, 179, 188, 194, 196
Mesopotamia, 37-8, 52, 56, 196
Mesozoic age, 41, 64
meteorology, 4
Mežerici site, 126, 174
Mezin: soil, 83; site, 127-8, 174
Michelsberg culture, 166-7
Mikolina Broyarka, 93, 95
Mikulino interglacial epoch, 113; *see also* Eemian interglacial and Riss-Würm interglacial
Milanovitch, M., 18
Milojčić, V., 60
minimax strategy, 13
Minsk region, 151
Mirnoye site, 87
Mit'kov Island site, 93, 95
Mněvo site, 141-2
models, 17, 30-3, 187-9, 198, 200; definition of, 3-4
Moldavia, 102, 191, 194; field studies in, ix; highlands, 64-6, 68, 72, 74-7, 100, 102, 104; plate, 81-2, 84-5, 89, 104; V, 85-6, 95
Moločnaya river, 88
Montenegro coast, 66
Moravia, 148
morphology, 41, 82, 86, 92, 139; *see also* geomorphology
Mörner, N.A., 117
Moscow: (Warth) glaciation, 113, 121; region, 151
Mostva, 140
Mount Billingen, 116
Mount Carmel, 43-4
Mount Hermon, 43
Mousterian Period, 23, 38, 66, 85
Muldbjerg site, 117, 167
Munhatta, tell, 47

Nainiekste site, 161
Narva-Riigiküla sites, 167-8, 179
Narva river site, 136-8, 167-8, 171, 198
Natufian sites, 43-5, 51, 95
natural economic zone, *see* economic zone
natural resources, 12, 106, 188-9; *see also* biomass
natural regions (areas), 13; Near East, 52; South-eastern Europe, 72, 104, 108; *see also* natural zones, structural units and geographical zones
natural zones, 6, 13, 42, 52, 72, 104, 106, 108
Nea Nikomedeia site, 63
Near East, ix, 26, 37-56 *passim*, 63, 70, 75, 77, 188-9, 191-2, 194, 196, 198
Neo-Euxine regression, 82
Neolithic age, 46-8, 51, 53, 188, 196-200; sites, ix; European, 25, 28; Near East, 25, 28; south-eastern Europe, 59-61, 63, 67-9, 70, 75-7; south Russian plain, 88-108 *passim*; west Russian plain, 117, 124-5, 139-73 *passim*
Nieman: basin, 132; sites, 136, 146-7,

171, 179, 194
Nineveh, 48
norms, legal, 15
North Sea, 116, 118
Novgorod Severski site, 127
Nymphaeum transgression, 82

Odessa, 86-7
Oldesloe-Kobrow group, 135
Old World, ix
open systems, 10
optimizer strategy, 12-13, 27, 77, 106, 108, 150, 172, 179, 187-8, 196
ornamentation, of pottery, *see* pottery
Osa sites, 147, 157-9, 176
Osovec site, 153
Ostelogy, 69, 103
Ovče Polje depression, 69
Oziornoye lake, 102

Paaver, K., 140
Pajuris peat bog, 170
palaeobotany, 2; evidence, 26-7; North Western Iran, 38, 41; Irano-Turanian province, 43; Anatolia, Northern, 50; Greece, 60, 63; southern Europe, 65, 69; Danube valley, 70; south Russian plain, 84, 100; west Russian plain, 123, 126, 135
palaeogeography, 2, 190, 200; theoretical objective, 3-4; the Levant, 42; Asia Minor, 51; west Russian plain, 156
Palaeolithic period, 22, 187, 191; Upper, 23; Zagros mountains, 39-40; the Levant, 43, 51-2; Greece, 60; Balkan, 65-6; population, 72-3; south Russian plain, 84-6, 89, 95, 104; west Russian plain, 126-32 *passim*, 137, 153, 173-4
Palaeozoic age, lower, 82
palaeozoology, 2, 188; evidence, 26-7
Palestine, 44, 95
palynology, 65
paradigms, 4
Pärnu river, 138
Pečera site, 93, 96-7
Pelagonian massif, 64
Peloponnese, the, 59-60, 72
pen-knives, 130; *see also Federmesser*
Perkins, D., 40
Phanagoraea regression, 82
photosynthesis, 4, 5
Pidopličko, I.G., 127
Piestiņa site, 159-61, 163, 170, 179, 198
Pinnberg site, 133
Pindhos Mountains, 59
Pindus series rocks, 59

Pitcairn Island, 25
plants, *see* green plants, vegetational cover
Pleistocene age, 191-2; flora, 18-19; climatic changes, 18-19; Greece, 58; south Russian plain, 82, 84-6, 89, 95; west Russian plain, 121, 123, 126, 132, 139-41, 151, 153, 173, 177
Podluz'ye site, 131
Podzorovo site, 151
Pogon site, 127
Pogorelovka site, 140
Poland, 131, 136, 149, 163, 167, 172, 198
Polessye province, 121-2, 126-7, 132, 139-40, 144, 148, 150, 173-4, 177, 179, 191-2, 198
pollen, 26; analysis, ix; analytical zones, 2; Lake Zeribar, 38; Jordan valley, 43; Anatolia, northern, 50; Greece, 60; south Russian plain, 88; west Russian plain, 114, 119, 122, 124-5, 130, 132-5, 139-40, 153-5, 161, 171
Pontic: depression, 81; steppes, 84; depression, 86-7, 191-2, 194
population, 22-5, 187-90, 194, 196, 198; density, 7; dynamics, 14; human component in social system, 32-3; Zagros mountains, 41, 52-3, 56; the Levant, 43, 52-3; Asia Minor, 52-3, 56; Greece, 60; the Balkans, 56, 65-6; south-eastern Europe, 72, 75, 77; south Russian plain, 84-5, 89-90, 95, 103-4, 106, 108; west Russian plain, 126, 132, 150, 167, 172-3, 179; *see also* demography
pottery, 26-7, 190, 196, 200; as spiritual creation, 15, 17; classification, 28; the Levant, 47-8, 56; Asia Minor, 51, 56; Greece, 60-4; Thrace, 67-8; Yugoslavia, 69-70; Adriatic coastland, 70; south-eastern Europe, 75-7; south Russian plain, 88, 90-2, 97-102, 106; west Russian plain, 118, 139, 142-51 *passim*, 156-63 *passim*, 166-71 *passim*, 177-81
Pre-Cambrian period, 64
Pripyat valley, 121, 123, 132, 140, 146-7, 150, 194
productive forces, 12
Proterozoic era, 81-2
Prut river, 81-2, 84, 102, 104, 106
Pskov district, 119, 132, 153, 171, 179, 198
Pulli site, 138
Puškari site, 127

Qal'at Jarmo site, 41

Quaternary age, 18; the Levant, 42; Asia Minor, 50; Greece, 59, 64, 67; south Russian plain, 81, 83; west Russian plain, 113-14

radiation, 5, 7
radiocarbon dating, *see* carbon 14 dating
Ras Shamra settlement, 47-8
Red Beds, 59-60
Red Sea trough, 42
Reed, C.A., 23, 25
regional units, distinguishing, 11
religious beliefs, 15
Renfrew, A.C., x, 15, 25
resources, natural, definition of, 12
Reut river, 85, 192
Rhodopian massif, 64-5, 72
Rhineline, 148
Rhine river, 135
Rift valley, 42, 44, 47, 52, 56
Rimantiene, R.K., 132, 136, 170-1
Riss-Wurm interglacial period (Eemian), 59, 83, 113; *see also* Mikulino interglacial period
Rodden, R.J., 63
Romanelli site, 66
Romania, 64-77 *passim*, 101-2
Rössen culture, 148-9, 167
Rouse, Irving, quoted, 1
Rudenko, S.I., ix
Rügen: island of, 117, 119, 164; sites, 166-7
Russian Plain, 191-2, 194, 196, 198; southern and western, ix; vegetational cover, 19; south, 81-111 *passim*; west, 113-85 *passim*
Rzucewo culture, 163, 172

Saale glaciation, 113
Sambia spit, 172
Samčincy site, 96-8, 100
Sarnate site, 116-17, 126, 169-71, 179, 198
satisficer strategies, 12-13, 27, 187
Saturper Moor site, 166
Savran site, 96, 98
Scania, 133
Scandinavia, 116, 133, 150
Schaeffer, C.F.Q., 47
Schleswig, 118
Schwabedissen, H., 166
Schwerin lake, 135
Sea of Galilee (lake), 42-3, 52
Semenov, S.A. 21, 26-7
Serbia sites, 69
Sesklo pottery (pre-Sesklo, proto-Sesklo), 62-3, 70, 76
settlement patterns, 22-7; Zagros mountains, 38-41, 53; the Levant, 43-7, 53; Asia Minor, 53; central Balkans, 67; south-eastern Europe, 72-3; south Russian plain, 87, 102-3, 106; west Russian plain, 135, 142, 177
Severski Donetz sites, 140, 150
Sheik Ali, tell, 47
Shanidar cave deposits, 38-41
Shovkoplyas, I.G., 127
Siberia, 25, 189
site-catchment analysis, 26
Skagerrak strait, 117
Skibency site, 96
Sobački site, 141
social systems (structures), 30, 101
soil: science, ix, 2; zones, 11
Sokol'cy site, 96-7
solar energy, 4-7; 30
solar radiation, 4-5, 119
Solecki, R., 38
Soroki sites, 90-3, 95, 147
Soudsky, B., 101
Sož river, 128-9, 131
Spain, 70
Sredni Stog site, 141
Stara Planina mountains, 64-5, 72
Starčevo sites, 68, 102
Starosel'ye site, 126
steppes, 6
stockbreeding, 12, 25, 27, 188, 196; Zagros mountains, 40-1, 53, 56; the Levant, 46-7, 53, 56; the Levant, 46-7, 53, 56; Asia Minor, 51-3, 56; Greece, 63; Thrace, 67; Serbia and Vojvodina, 69; south-eastern Europe, 75, 77; south Russian plain, 88-9, 101-3, 106, 108; west Russian plain, 141, 148-9, 156, 163, 166, 172-3, 177, 181
Stoddart, D.R., 10
Stone Age, 117
structural units (zone): 2-5; the Near East, 37, 41-2, 48, 52; south-eastern Europe, 59, 64, 72; Russian plain, 81
Strumel-Gastyatin sites, 142, 144, 177
Studenec site, 132
subsistence pattern, 191-2, 194, 196; central Balkans, 66-7; Adriatic coast, 70; south-eastern Europe, 72-3; south Russian plain, 85-6, 92-3, 98, 100, 104; west Russian plain, 128-9, 134, 136, 140, 149-50, 152, 155-6, 163-5, 167, 173-4, 179; evolution of, 187-9

Sub-Mediterranian region, 65
Sudost river, 128-9
Suez, gulf of, 42
Sulka site, 160-1
Supoi tributary, 127
Suess curve, 30
Šventoji site, 117-18, 170, 178, 198
Sweden, 116-17, 148, 164
Swiderian: site, 66; point, 131-2, 138
Switzerland, 166
Syria, 38-9, 42-3, 47, 52, 191, 196
systems: definitions of, 9-11; general properties of, 30; *see also* General Systems Theory

Tabaczyński, S., 101
Tambov region, 151
Tamula site, 164
Tansley, A.G., 10
Tardenoisian type site, 66
Taurus, western, 51
techno-complexes, 13-14
Telegin, I., 142
Tell al-Halaf, 48
Tell Arpachiyah, 48
Tell Asmak, 67
Tell Chaghir Bazar, 48
Tell Far'ah settlement, 47
Tell Hassuna, 48
Tell Munhatta settlement, 47
Tell Sheik Ali settlement, 47
Tenagi Philippon, 60
territorial productive complex, 13
Tertiary age, 90; Late, 18, 64, 69; mid, 81-2
textile pottery, 163
thermodynamics, second law of, 31
Thessaly: depression, 59; sites, 61-3, 70, 74-6
Thrace, 67, 72, 74
Tigris river, 37
tools, working (productive), 15, 26-7, 189, 191-2, 194, 196, 200; definition of, 21-2; component in social system, 32-3; Zagros mountains, 40, 53; the Levant, 43-4, 47, 53; Asia Minor, 51, 53; Greece, 60, 63; the Balkans, 66; Thrace, 67; Adriatic coast, 70; south-eastern Europe, 72-3; south Russian plain, 86-8, 90-1, 93, 95-6, 101, 104; west Russian plain, 127-39 *passim*, 142, 149, 153, 158, 161, 166, 168, 174, 177, 179
traditions, 15, 33
transport, means of, 15
Transylvania, 64, 66, 68, 72, 76-7;

highlands of, 65
Tripolye settlement, 93, 95, 100, 102-4, 108, 141, 148, 151, 196
Troels-Smith, J., 166-7
Trojan settlement, 102
trophic levels, 7, 22, 31
Turkey, 38-9, 47, 50-1
Turkish mountain, 37
type, definition of, 2

Udai tributary, 127
Ukraine: field studies in, ix; shield, 81-2; sites, 102-4, 141-2, 150-1, 180
United Nations Act, ix-x
Upper Tigris basin, 48
Upper Volga interstadial, 113
urban planning, 47
Usatovo sites, 103
USSR, 83
Usvyaty lake depression, 119, 132, 153-7, 198

Valdai glaciation, 113, 121, 173; *see also* Würm ice age, Last Glaciation and Weichselian glaciation
Vankina, L., 170
Vardar: axis, 64; zone, 68
Vavilov, N.I., 26, 38
vegetational cover, 191-2; process occuring in, 5; evolution of, 18; components in ecosystem, 30-3; Zagros mountains, 38-9, 52-3; the Levant, 42-3, 52-3; Asia Minor, 50, 52-3; Balkan peninsula, 65-7; Danube slopes, 70, 72; south-eastern Europe, 72; south Russian plain, 83-5, 88, 104, 106; west Russian plain, 122-6, 130-1, 133-5, 139-40, 153, 161, 174; *see also* green plants
Veličko, A.A., 18-19, 128
Ventspils, 169
Volga basin, 151.
Villa site, 164
Vilnius, 170
Vinnica, 103
Vinnitsa, 93
Vistule (group) valley, 171-2
Vojvodina sites, 69
Volyno-Podolia plate (plateau), 81-2, 89, 104, 149
Voznyačuk, L.N., 129
Vrsnik site, 69
Vulkanești river valley, 102

Wadi Shu'aib settlement, 47
Warth glaciation, 113-14; *see also*

Moscow glaciation
weapons, *see* tools
White, Leslie, 15
Wjorek phase, 149
wine-making, 52
Witòw site, 131
Würm ice age, 59, 83, 113, 173; interstadial, 85; *see also* Last Glaciation, Valdai glaciation, Weichselian glaciation
Weichselian glaciation, 113, 121, 173; *see also* Valdai glaciation, Würm ice age, Last Glaciation

Yaroslavl region, 151
Yazykovo site, 150
Yeliseyeviči site, 129
Yoldia Sea, 116, 138
Yudinovo site, 129
Yugoslavia, 64-77 *passim*

Zaᴅ river, Greater and Little, 37
Zacenye site, 147, 151, 177
Zaharia, E., 69
Zagorskis, F., 159
Zagros mountains, 191-2, 194; Iranian, 37-41, 53, 56
Zarharuk, Y.N., quoted, 1
Zawi Chemi Shanidar site, 40-1
Zapadnaya Dvina valley, 156
Zarečye site, 151
Zarzian industry, 40
Zarzi cave, 40
Zeeland, 117, 133, 166
van Zeist, W., 38, 50
Žitomir, 140
Zizica lake depression, 119
Zlota cultures, 163, 172
zonal divisions, hierarchical, 11
zonality, law of, 5, 13
zoology, 40